BIOCULTURAL EVOLUTION

BIOCULTURAL EVOLUTION

THE ANTHROPOLOGY OF HUMAN PREHSITORY

CLARE L. BOULANGER

Colorado Mesa University

WAVELAND

PRESS, INC.

Long Grove, Illinois

For information about this book, contact:
  Waveland Press, Inc.
  4180 IL Route 83, Suite 101
  Long Grove, IL 60047-9580
  (847) 634-0081
  info@waveland.com
  www.waveland.com

10-digit ISBN 1-57766-743-3
13-digit ISBN 978-1-57766-743-8

Printed in the United States of America

7 6 5 4 3 2 1

CONTENTS

About This Book

I thank you for having chosen this textbook, *Biocultural Evolution: The Anthropology of Human Prehistory,* for your class. Any textbook is a work in progress, and if you think you can help to improve the book, I would be happy to hear from you, at bioculturalevolution@gmail.com.

The reason I have written *Biocultural Evolution* is because I believe there is a need for a book on this topic that is relatively short, reasonably priced, and accessible to those who have doubts about the theory of biological evolution, though there are certain belief systems that cannot be accommodated here. Because the book is short, there are subtopics related to the broader topic of the book that are barely explored, for example, the evolution of nonhuman primates. Because the book is reasonably priced, the photos included are black-and-white, and I have done most of the drawings and cartoons (if you find them artful, they're drawings; if you find them funny and/or funny-looking, they're cartoons!). Because the book is meant to be accessible to people who have had or may still have difficulties approaching this topic, I may be accused of selling out science. I encourage instructors to present complementary and even contradictory material in their classrooms so that students receive a well-rounded exposure to the issues raised within these pages.

The textbook is not modular—each chapter is designed to lead into the next. Nonetheless, you may decide to skip some chapters or make only minimal use of their content. Chapter 1 is introductory, intended to give students exposure to the wide conceptual world of American anthropology before proceeding into sections on science, faith, and evolution. Chapter 2 deals with the history of evolutionary theory, concentrating on developments in Europe during the 18th and 19th centuries. The biology of genetics is treated in chapter 3; chapter 4 defines "primate" and locates human beings within the category. Chapters 5, 6, and 7 delve into the heart of the matter—human evolution, from the earliest potential hominins through the first evidence of culture in the way we currently understand it. Chapter 8 looks into domestication and agriculture, chapter 9 the rise of states, and chapter 10 connects the past and the present through an exploration of human variation.

There are exercises embedded within chapter text as well as discussion questions and key word lists that close each chapter. Key words are generally listed in the order in which they appear in the chapter, unless it makes sense to group certain terms together. The word lists draw on **boldfaced** names and terms that appear in the chapter. Words in boldface, whether or not they are in the key word lists—and they will probably turn up in one of the lists at some time—are words to which students should pay attention. Boldfaced words are in the glossary, but they are often defined within the chapter text as well, so there is generally no need to flip to the back of the book. The main point is that these names and terms are important and a student should take the time to know them well, especially given that they are likely to recur. A name or term will not be boldfaced every time it recurs, but if it surfaces in a new context or has simply not been seen in a while, it may be boldfaced again, as much for emphasis as to remind students the glossary can help.

Readers should be apprised that I do not use third-person-plural pronouns (e.g., "they") to represent singular entities. As you know, in English third-person-singular pronouns are gendered, and traditionally the default pronoun for generic entities is masculine. I will vary this standard by alternating "he" with "she," to make the point that when I refer to, for example, "a scientist" or "an archaeologist," such a person could as easily be female as male.

Finally, acknowledgments are in order. While this textbook includes an extensive reference list, some essential sources are missing. I have taught a "World Prehistory" course since 1993, and have used many textbooks that others have written. Though I do not cite these textbooks directly, I have learned a great deal from them over the years, and such authors as Brian Fagan, Kenneth Feder, William Haviland (along with those who have written under his aegis), Norah Moloney, Michael A. Park, Patricia Rice, and William Turnbaugh (along with coauthors) must receive due credit for what I now consider (erroneously) to be general knowledge on my part.

Additionally, I must tip my hat to Wikipedia. Many professors (I among them) discourage students from treating Wikipedia entries as the be-all and end-all of information on a subject, but there is no question Wikipedia is helpful for quick fact-checking and bibliographies that can provide leads for one's own work. I express my deep gratitude to all of the scholars who have contributed to this extraordinary corpus of knowledge in ways relevant to the topic of prehistory.

I thank Tom Curtin and Jeni Ogilvie at Waveland Press for their hard work on my behalf. Errors that appear in this book are most likely the result of my being stubbornly resistant to their wise counsel.

Finally, this book is dedicated to the World Prehistory students I have taught at Colorado Mesa University (formerly Mesa State College) over the years, especially the classes of 2010 and 2011 that "road tested" earlier manuscript drafts. I cannot say that within these pages I have done everything students have requested, but I hope I have given them enough "ownership" of the writing process for them to recognize their input was valuable and much appreciated.

1

ANTHROPOLOGY AND WHAT IT CAN DO

The difference between us
is not so much.
Tell me your story,
your piece of what is Humanity.

—Dai Cooper,
"The Anthropology Song: A Little Bit Anthropologist"

www.youtube.com/watch?v=LHv6rw6wxJY

Anthropology and Culture

Anthropology is the study of all things human: our bodies; our minds; our history; our ancestry; our past, present, and future. This is impossibly ambitious, and it is actually made no less so when I note that anthropology, for all its breadth, does have one guiding concept: culture. **Culture**—which we can take, for our current purposes, to stem from the ability to encode reality entirely in symbols (more on this in chapter 7)—is a uniquely human project, though this is not to say that other animals show no capacity for it. But other animals tend to entrust essential functions—eating, sleeping, mating—to biological programming, while for human beings even these fundamental activities are filtered through cultural systems that affect when they are accomplished, how they are accomplished, and even, in some instances, whether they are accomplished at all.

EXERCISE

Discuss how eating, sleeping, and mating differ between humans and other animals, and differ between human cultures.

Anthropology is a **social science,** but in some respects that seems to be only a halfway house between the **natural sciences** and the **humanities.** The product of an anthropological study can be a penetrating, poignant account of a remote people that reads nearly as well as a novel, or it can be a data set, readily subject to statistical analysis, derived from months spent observing the behavior of wild chimpanzees. Such a range of interests may strike the uninitiated reader as something close to random, but perhaps the point is humans themselves span this gamut. We are both biological beings whose cultural proclivities are supported by a complex brain and cultural beings whose power to alter our environments can, not incidentally, rework human biology.

The Four Fields of Anthropology

In the United States, it is customary to subdivide anthropology into four **fields,** each of which has subfields and sub-subfields. The most humanistic of these fields is **cultural anthropology,** the study of present-day societies and cultures, though "present-day" must be qualified by saying the term is relative to the time of the anthropologist. The larger point is that the cultural anthropologist generally works with and among people who are alive, living their lives to the extent possible, understanding their sense of themselves. The function of the culture concept is obvious with respect to such studies—it is a means to express how it is societies can be so different when they are clearly made up of beings united through their humanity. This common humanity is something the cultural anthropologist often inspires an audience not only to know but to *feel,* a task in which artists of all types also engage. Hence the **ethnographies** cultural anthropologists write about their study populations are generally more than mere collections of cultural facts.

The concept of culture obviously underlines, as well, the anthropologically informed study of linguistics (or **linguistic anthropology**), which entails more than the study of language structure. The anthropological linguist usually wants to observe and experience language in action, as it shapes human perceptions in a particular way. Language is the epitome of symbol-making. The fact that all human groups with which we are familiar construct and delimit their sense of reality through the ongoing and intertwined processes of creating, speaking, and understanding language gives us great insight into the nature of culture.

Since anthropology is a **holistic** discipline—meaning its fields and subfields do not stand alone but draw on each other to view human life through the widest possible lens—this textbook will certainly be influenced by insights derived from cultural and linguistic anthropology. Even so, our main focus here is on the other two fields—archaeology and biological anthropology.

With respect to **archaeology,** culture is still readily apparent as a guiding concept. For the most part, archaeologists are dedicated to the same mission that occupies cultural anthropologists—they want to comprehend and appreciate humanity in its myriad cultural forms. The difference is, of course, that while the cultural anthropologist usually works with people who are alive, the archaeologist is generally working with people who are dead, often long dead. As a cultural anthropologist myself, I can tell you that the "advantage" of having living people as research subjects does not mean that the intricacies of their culture unfold steadily before you—in fact, the interaction between the cultural anthropologist and her research population resembles a long, drawn-out process of negotiation—hence the archaeologist is confronted with that much more daunting of a task. Archaeologists must literally "flesh out" the bare bones of fossils and the cultures wherein the scant material evidence that can be recovered took on meaning.

The **archaeological record** begins about 2.6 million years ago (**mya**), with the first stone tools that, crude as they are to our modern eyes, seem to have been fashioned by a being with something approaching the mental capacity and manual dexterity we recognize as "human" today. Whether a stone tool actually constitutes physical evidence of a cultural mind at work is debatable. There are other animals that make tools, and whether they are behaving "culturally" has a good deal to do with how we define that term. Certainly there are many archaeologists who see the stone tool as their starting point, and there is no doubt that eventually the capacity to fashion natural material in accord with our own designs leads to the grand accomplishments often prized as the ultimate measure of the human being.

In this book we will join the archaeologists at the point of the human timeline at which the first stone tools appear and walk with them through more and more elaborate toolkits, through cave paintings and figurines, through domestication and cultivation, up to the point when human beings have formed, in various places and at various times, complex social structures we call **state** societies. Even though archaeologists proceed onward from this point (or these points, to state the matter more accurately), we will not follow them further, since that would entail a book in itself.

We *will* backtrack, however, from the first stone tools by more millions of years than tools themselves have existed, possibly to six or even seven million years out, depending on what one accepts as part of the human lineage. This is the realm of **paleoanthropology,** which is a subfield of **biological anthropology** (also known as **physical anthropology**). There are many subfields under the rubric of biological anthropology, the most well-known of which is **forensic anthropology,** always practical and currently even fashionable given its popularization in such television programs as *Bones* and the many *CSI* series. For our purposes, however, we will focus on those subfields that can best enlighten us with respect to what I call the **ape–human divide.**

In the present day, anthropological **primatologists** devote themselves to learning about our fellow **primates**, with an eye toward what they can teach us about being human. If we presume (as we will) that all modern primates grew out of a common ancestral root, then in studying them we can gain insight into what capacities that ancestor species may have had, and how these capacities became elaborated into the many variations (including those in the human line) we see today. The paleoanthropologist, on the other hand, studies the ape–human divide in the past—at what point did the lines leading to modern-day chimpanzees and bonobos and to modern-day humans diverge? And what happens to our line after that? Because the material hints of this progression are so scarce and will likely remain so despite our best efforts, the paleoanthropologist has to make the most of whatever information is available. Thus, it is good to know something about **geology, paleontology,** and even **cell biology,** among many other fields. Since the paleoanthropologist, no matter how clever he is, is unlikely to have sufficient mastery of all of these fields, paleoanthropological investigations are most often conducted by interdisciplinary teams.

You may well ask how the culture concept applies here. We witness what appear to be cultural capacities, at least, if not culture itself, on the part of nonhuman primates, and we have seen these capacities enhanced by intensive involvement with human beings (see, for instance, the video at http://www.ted.com/talks/ susan_savage_rumbaugh_on_apes_that_write.html). Both of these observations suggest culture, or the rudiments of it, reaches far back into primate heritage. Certainly the cultural mind is also a biological brain, and it is worth exploring how our brains developed to support such a mental aptitude. In treating culture, biological anthropologists are apt to stress its **adaptive** qualities—it is clear that culture can help us to handle environmental challenges much more quickly and far less ruthlessly than biological change, though it is also the case that cultural convictions can steer us away from optimal solutions. Over and above this low-level contrast, however, is the application of culture toward actually *transforming* environmental circumstances so that they are more easily managed. The ability to alter the environment is not unique to humans or their ancestors—think of how a beaver dam is the central piece in an entirely new ecosystem the dam creates—but culture is arguably a far more powerful and versatile terraforming tool. Thus, culture is not only adaptive (and maladaptive) but also constructive (and destructive). The study of the intricate and mutually constitutive relationship between humans and their environment, back to its beginnings, is a productive pursuit both intellectually and practically.

To summarize, then: this is an anthropological textbook which will draw most especially on the anthropological fields of biological anthropology and archaeology to illuminate, to the extent possible, the journey our ancestors took from the moment our line separated from that of the chimpanzee to the establishment of the first state societies. This is, in other words, the story of being human.

> **THE FOUR FIELDS (and some related subfields)**
> **OF AMERICAN ANTHROPOLOGY**
>
> 1. Cultural anthropology
> 2. Linguistic anthropology
> 3. Archaeology
> 4. Biological anthropology
>   a. Primatology
>   b. Paleoanthropology

The E-Word

I have come all this way and failed to mention the word—and the idea—that will guide us as we retrace the steps of our ancestral journey: evolution. Very simply, the concept refers to change through time, but we are all aware that the word carries much more baggage than that. There is no use pretending that stripping it down to its essential meaning allows us to bypass the controversy that continues to roil below the surface of American life, occasionally erupting into superheated bursts of antagonism that involve scientists, preachers, politicians, and school boards. We cannot ourselves go on without striding boldly onto the lava bed, but I will do what I can to cool its fires in advance.

Evolution, when applied to **biology,** is the word we use to describe the process of change that both takes place within **species** and results in the establishment of new species. If we observe a population of rabbits over 50 years' time, for instance, and note that coat color has become darker, this is evolution, even though no new species has resulted and the rabbits interbreed as freely as always. The same forces at work in introducing and causing the proliferation of a new coat color are those that, under the right circumstances and with more than a little serendipity, may bring about a new species, although this is a development we are unlikely to witness over a mere half-century. But we have learned enough about the rudiments of the evolutionary process to say with some confidence that a change in coat color and an increase in the number of species are kindred events. This conclusion has been reached via **science.**

Science and Faith

Science is, simply put, a *way of knowing*—a good college-level word for this is **epistemology.** Science is at once a philosophy, a methodology, and a set of outcomes that help us to understand and even manipulate our surroundings. The philosophy behind modern, European-born science is one of **logical positivism**—the notion that any phenomenon can be understood through rational (i.e., logical) consideration of factual (i.e., positivist) data. This is a powerful philosophy—it compels the scientist never to abandon the quest for truth, because she believes that somehow, through some means, it will be attained, even if it has eluded us to this point.

This sounds unspeakably arrogant, but this arrogance is tempered—ideally—by recognized limitations on methodology. Science begins with skeptical observation of natural phenomena—what we see before us seems to work, but why? Scientists gather as much information on these natural processes as possible, eventually separating them into their most basic component processes and developing facsimiles of these components that can be tested within the controlled confines of a laboratory. Here we can already become a bit nervous, because both the act of separating a process into component "parts" and devising versions of these "parts" that will submit to laboratory testing removes science even further from "the real thing." Nonetheless, goaded by the philosophy of logical positivism, scientists forge onward, with one experiment, and another, and another, designed, through increments, to determine what does seem to work and what definitely does not (yes, "untruth" is more knowable than "truth"). Eventually the scientist hopes to discover "truth," but honest scientists should be ever ready to admit that they never, actually, get there. They need always to keep in mind that in Sciencespeak, the verb, "to know," *should* be rendered, "to take our best guess for the moment, based on the evidence made available so far through many and varied experiments." Since this is too cumbersome to substitute every time for a simple, easy-to-use, four-letter word, scientists regularly fall back on "we know . . ." and, more often than they should, come to believe it.

None of this prevents scientists from using the information gained through experimentation, and it hardly need be pointed out to the reader that this has resulted in, among other things, a plethora of marvelous inventions that in their everyday functionality add more and more support to the soundness of the principles explaining why they function. Even so, no scientist should believe that he has stumbled upon anything more than an *operational* truth, something that appears to work in practice. Obviously if we have computers and space shuttles in the meantime, we are more than amply compensated for our failure to pin down truth to the extent it need never again be revisited.

Some boldfaced terminology is called for at this point. The question that a scientist distills from observation is a **hypothesis**, a good guess as to how what he is observing actually works. The portion of the process he seeks to understand is excised from context and re-created, to the extent possible, in the lab, where it is tested. Every test devised should attack the problem of understanding from different angles; it should also always provide for the possibility of **falsification**; that is, each component of a hypothesis must be subjected to scrutiny that might prove it *un*true, which the reader will recall is far more readily ascertained than truth (Popper 1965). If all experiments undertaken support the hypothesis, and no aspect is falsified that meaningfully affects that support, the hypothesis becomes a theory. A **theory** withstands all testing; it becomes our best guess for the moment and will remain so unless or until it is falsified by a test in the future. A theory is "true" insofar as we can build on it and from it, but it is not, and never will be, *absolutely* true if we keep in mind the fundamental, dynamic contradiction between the philosophy of science and its methodology.

Thus, when scientists refer to biological evolution as a theory, they are not saying they are unsure about it—they are in fact as sure about it as any scientist can be about any hypothesis that has held up to a barrage of testing. It is our best guess at the moment as to how life came into being on this planet, proliferated into a multiplicity of forms, and, eventually, how human life came into being.

Science, however, is not the only way of knowing. Despite its power and productivity, science does not now and likely will never totally slake human curiosity. Science *can* provide answers to such questions as "Who are we?" "Why are we here?" "Is there something about me that will go on after my death?" but the answers will probably be unsatisfactory in terms of our tremendous need for security and comfort in these areas of inquiry. For answers that are more emotionally fulfilling, many of us—including scientists—turn to **faith**, a very different way of knowing that underlies religion and other types of spirituality. Unlike science, faith is often founded on absolute truth, and unlike the scientist, for the person

Laboratory experiments on fruit flies have taught us a great deal about evolution.

of faith to declare he knows something is not arrogance but the conviction that comes from the real sense of a power outside oneself. One believes in God, or Allah, or the potential for Nirvana, or ancestral spirits not because hypotheses regarding their existence were mooted, tested, and passed the tests, but because a person of faith *must* believe. In fact, in many spiritual traditions the doubter is chided. The disciple Thomas (John 20:24–29) declares he will not believe Jesus has been resurrected until he examines his Lord's mortal wounds. Jesus provides Thomas with proof but praises those who believe without it.

Clearly this position is diametrically at odds with that of the scientist, who is equally compelled to have proof before she believes. "Believe," of course, is not quite the right word in this context, because science is simply not faith, and a scientist, *when it comes to science*, is not a person of faith. She accepts a set of outcomes indicated by the evidence gathered through experimentation; she acts on those outcomes; and she abandons those outcomes if they fall short of testing, either in the lab or in everyday practice. It is certainly true that some scientists stubbornly adhere to theories against which evidence has begun to accrue. But unless the case can be made that the new evidence was generated by flawed methodology, a scientist who cannot move on from a failing theory is not acting as a scientist.

To this point the theory of biological evolution has not failed, although it is constantly being reconsidered and qualified—it is, after all, a BIG theory, covering many aspects of life on the planet. So we are left with a problem—how do we reconcile the scientific theory of evolution with, for example, the religious conviction that life on the planet, and indeed, the planet itself, was created by a Supreme Being who worked this miracle in six days a mere 6,000 years ago? The blunt answer in this extreme instance is that we cannot.

If you adhere to a faith that enjoins you to take the Old Testament at its literal word on the matter of how the Earth and its life forms came about, you will never accept the theory of evolution. The fact that science cannot offer you one iota of support for your belief will make no difference, because, presumably, the benefits you derive from your faith—and these include an unshakable confidence in the rightness of your position—far outweigh the advantage a scientific understanding of the world may (or may not) confer. When it comes to the issue of life on the planet, the methodology of science cannot be applied to this research problem because you take, as a given, the absolute nature of God and the relatively recent weeklong process of Creation. Science, however, cannot take anything as a given until it is proved (at least as firmly as it will ever be), and nothing is proved until it has been subjected to *dis*proof, i.e., potentially falsified, and of course articles of faith cannot receive such dismissive treatment. Even as science generates a massive amount of data, from any number of experiments, that indicate the Earth is far older than 6,000 years and that the diversity of life on the planet looks far likelier to have resulted from a series of haphazard events than a brief and concerted flurry of divine Creation, the person of faith, or at least of the version of faith described above, can claim that such apparent outcomes are merely a test of that faith. For this contention science has no answer, because clearly it has already produced an answer, and will continue to produce an answer, that the person of faith cannot help but regard as illegitimate.

So, if the religious beliefs discussed in the preceding paragraph accurately represent the ones you hold, you are welcome to continue reading this book, but I suspect it will not interest you much. You subscribe to such a different way of knowing than the one this book will feature that the assumptions made here as a matter of course will strike you at best as fanciful, at worst as hostile. Yours is a viable alternative view, but it cannot be presented alongside biological evolution as though they were two sides of the same coin. We might say they are two different coins, save there is not even that degree of compatibility. One is a coin, perhaps, while the other is an apple, or light, or something similarly non sequitur.

It is likely, however, that if you are still reading this book you do not subscribe to religious beliefs that of necessity must exempt so much from the rigors of the scientific method. Those readers who see the theory of biological evolution as running afoul of faith may not reject the theory entirely—you may be open to the idea of a longer timeline for Creation, a longer timeline for the history of the earth, or even that evolution may have yielded most of the earth's life forms but could not have resulted in human beings. Or you may simply be uncomfortable with the notion of evolution because it is controversial, and your impression of the controversy, to the extent you have absorbed it, is that to accept the idea of biological evolution is in some fundamental way to reject God.

This does not necessarily follow, although much depends on your image of God and how She (or He) put His (or Her) divine prerogative into practice. While we can understand how biological evolution might work without supernatural intervention, no one, scientist or otherwise, can tell you that there absolutely was not a spiritual force involved. Remember, there is no scientific test for this. God may have created *through* the process of evolution, and while there is undoubtedly great majesty in conjuring the stuff of life and the universe out of nothing, there is also something miraculous about evolution, in that perfectly ordinary elements can be strung together in elaborate molecular chains and over time can yield such diverse products as amoebae and trees and elephants.

The preceding paragraph might seem to "out" me as a supporter of **intelligent design (ID)**, the idea that life on the earth is so complex that it must have been brought about by some sort of sentient entity that supporters of this proposition do not feel compelled to identify as God, though many of them are people

SIDEBAR

2010 Gallup Poll: Number of Americans Who Believe in Creationism Declining

At the Gallup.com website, the results of the 2010 poll on views regarding human origins are posted (Newport 2010). Such polls, which have been conducted regularly for a number of years, generally test for adherence to the "creationist" view (i.e., God created human beings within the last 10,000 years), the "theistic" view (i.e., evolution took place over millions of years under God's guiding hand), and the "secular evolution" view, in which God is not thought to have played a role in evolution. The creationist view remains the majority view, at 40%, but not by much, as 38% of respondents supported the theistic perspective. Sixteen percent of respondents supported the idea of secular evolution, up from 9% in 1999.

Unfortunately, the statements expressing these views, with which respondents agree or disagree, perpetuate the notion that evolution is a matter of "less advanced forms of life" progressing toward humanity, an idea I take pains in this Introduction, and in fact throughout this book, to refute. Were I to be polled by Gallup on this issue, therefore, I would feel compelled to answer, "None of the above."

of faith. But I am not a proponent of intelligent design. ID proponents insist that science affirm their belief in a Designer, and once again science cannot do such a thing. To reiterate what was said previously: through scientific methodology we may be able to discern ways through which the universe was assembled and continues to function without direct action being taken by a divine force, but once we are told a divine force *must* be accounted for in our explanation, scientific investigation is fatally compromised. Again, science cannot work around spiritual elements; everything must be grist for the mill of testability.

So, finally, we come to *you,* the reader whose faith, or lack of faith, can fully accommodate the theory of evolution. Perhaps you have become even a bit impatient with this discussion of religious beliefs; you are ready to move on. However, I have to warn you that what lies ahead may disturb *your* beliefs as well, because it is likely you harbor misconceptions regarding evolution. This might not be your fault—there is a good deal of misinformation in the popular sphere, some of which has been spread even by people who should know better. You, like the

Judge Jones Rules against the Dover School Board

In 2004, the Dover, PA, School Board voted to mandate that a statement promoting intelligent design be read to ninth-grade biology classes. The policy was challenged in court by a group of parents in the Dover Area School District. In December 2005, the presiding judge, John E. Jones III, appointed to the US District Court by President George W. Bush, ruled against the School Board. Appearing below are excerpts from the 139-page decision (*Kitzmiller v. Dover Area School District,* 2005).

4. Whether ID is Science

After a searching review of the record and applicable case law, we find that while ID arguments may be true, a proposition on which the Court takes no position, ID is not science. . . . ID violates the centuries-old ground rules of science by invoking and permitting supernatural causation. . . . [I]t is additionally important to note that ID has failed to gain acceptance in the scientific community, it has not generated peer-reviewed publications, nor has it been the subject of testing and research. (p. 39)

H. Conclusion

Both Defendants and many of the leading proponents of ID make a bedrock assumption which is utterly false. Their presupposition is that evolutionary theory is antithetical to a belief in the existence of a supreme being and to religion in general. Repeatedly in this trial, Plaintiffs' scientific experts testified that the theory of evolution represents good science, is overwhelmingly accepted by the scientific community, and that it in no way conflicts with, nor does it deny, the existence of a divine creator. (p. 136)

[W]e do not question that many of the leading advocates of ID have bona fide and deeply held beliefs which drive their scholarly endeavors. Nor do we controvert that ID should continue to be studied, debated, and discussed. As stated, our conclusion today is that it is unconstitutional to teach ID as an alternative to evolution in a public school science classroom. Those who disagree with our holding will likely mark it as the product of an activist judge. If so, they will have erred as this is manifestly not an activist Court. (p. 137) good student you are, have taken all of this in and may even have defended the concept of evolution, or at least your impression of it, to your parents and grand-parents, to your friends, or in front of a school board. I suspect you got your point across even if what you said bore little resemblance to what I have told you so far, let alone what I am about to tell you. We have a whole book ahead of us, but we need to start on a firm footing regarding what we are all talking about.

What Evolution Is; What It Is Not

The fish-with-legs stuck to the trunk of the car in front of you exhorts you to "Evolve," a not-so-subtle message to people who have a different sort of fish on their car trunks. A creationist in your biology class asks, "If evolution is true, why are there still monkeys? Why didn't they all evolve into human beings?" (You roll your eyes, but truthfully you don't quite know how to answer that.) Your little brother or your little boy tells his misbehaving friend, "Stop being a Neandertal." If evolution simply refers to change, why is there this persistent sense that we are talking about a particular *type* of change? A change for the better, whose potential is somehow built into whatever is evolving?

It hardly helps that we talk about the evolution of species in the same breath as the evolution of life, the evolution of the universe, and even cultural evolution, as if they were all governed by the same influences. We can certainly note

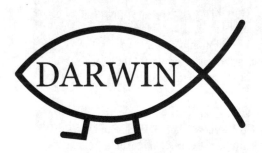

some similarities between some of these processes—in both biological and cultural evolution, for example, we are likely to weed out those attempts at adaptation that do not work from the outset, or that eventually fail—but there is nothing particularly helpful we can say about all of these processes across the board. To some extent they have been lumped together because they all must be defended against those who believe in instantaneous Creation of all things 6,000 years ago, but this is hardly a scientific basis for classification. We are not scientists when we allow nonscience to affect our judgment on such matters.

There is a prevailing notion that evolution entails movement from lesser to greater complexity, but this is problematic. What do we mean by "complex"? Astrophysicists tell us that the universe exploded from a point no bigger than a period on this page, and while its matter was thus expanding, galaxies, stars, and planets eventually coalesced out of the debris. Has the universe become more "complex" since it existed as a point with this extraordinary potential? Are stars and planets more "complex" now than they were a million years ago? This would seem to be an inadequate way of describing how the universe has changed and is changing. In fact, aside from the contention that the universe as we know it came about as a result of a developmental process for which there is no *scientific* evidence of a guiding hand, there would seem to be little comparability between the physics of the universe and the biology of life. So in this book I will say no more about the origins of the universe—that is a story for a different book to tell.

Surely, however, the idea that evolution moves from lesser to greater complexity applies quite well to the origins of life on the planet, and the subsequent proliferation of species, right? The answer here is yes . . . and no. I have to say at the outset that in this book I am also giving short shrift to the question of the origins of life—this remains a matter of debate among scientists, and I am not sufficiently well-versed in all of the disciplines that have a bearing on it to participate in the debate. So I will concede the point that the chains of molecules emerging from the primordial stew of life's chemicals were more complex than their component parts, primarily *because* they were made up of components parts. And, of course, they were animated in a way we still do not fully understand. All of this is fascinating, and science will continue to work on this eminently worthy and intriguing research problem, but again, this would be the subject of yet another book, since this book is long enough as it is.

Let us *really* start, then, with life on the planet after it has somehow gotten established. Following one of our best guesses of the moment, the first life form may have been nothing more than a strand of what we now call **RNA—ribonucleic acid**—though we can say with considerable authority that eventually single-celled **organisms** arose, and, thereafter, multi-celled organisms. This certainly can be described as a move from lesser to greater complexity, although it should be noted that we were not then and are not now lacking in viruses—many of them little more than RNA strands—and single-celled organisms, so it was hardly required that all organisms become "complex." Once multicellular organisms come about, they take on a number of forms, but this does not necessarily lead to greater complexity outside of the fact that more forms are spun off from common roots, and over time the number of species is bound to increase, even if some fall by the wayside due to extinction. If you have an orange tree that produces fruit over a 20-year period, you are not necessarily getting better oranges in 20 years' time, just more of them, taken altogether, over the period. I suspect this is not what most of us think we mean when we talk about evolution proceeding toward greater complexity.

There is an extraordinary variety of life forms on the planet today, but we sometimes forget that variety had to build up again after prehistoric moments of mass extinction. The dinosaur extinction is the one with which most of us are familiar, but there was a far more dramatic extinction event that occurred during the Permian-Triassic transition preceding the Age of Dinosaurs. The greatly reduced numbers of species after such events relatively quickly spawned new lines leading to new species, but it is not as though this alleged march from lesser to greater complexity did not suffer serious interruption.

At this point I imagine that some of you are champing at the bit—what about human beings? you ask. Aren't we the most complex life form that has appeared on the planet? We certainly seem to have the most complex brains on the planet, but with regard to other bodily systems we are really quite run-of-the-mill. The human digestive system hardly has the complexity of that of a cow; human arms do not enable us to fly or even to move readily through trees, something we believe our ancestors could do. Under natural circumstances our reproductive systems ordinarily generate only one offspring at a time, over a plodding nine months, and the birthing process is rendered shockingly difficult by the big heads that house our complex brains. Even so, our young are born with open skull sutures and very limited survival skills. We do not have the extraordinary capacities of cockroaches to survive just about everything we do to try and exterminate them. We have 46 chromosomes; chimpanzees have 48 while dogs have 78. Does the brain "count" for more than the extraordinary complexities of our fellow creatures in other respects? Leave it to a big-brained organism, I suppose, to say it is so.

And that statement betrays one of the primary activities of our complex brain: we make value judgments. Traditionally we have put ourselves at the center of the universe, seeing other organisms as somehow lesser. But a complex brain is one adaptation among many that have been successful. There is no reason a monkey would "aspire" to it even if it could acquire one, and certainly no reason a cockroach would swap out its tremendous evolutionary success to obtain the thinking equipment of a species that, truth be told, has not existed on the planet all that long.

Biological evolution makes no value judgments. In fact, evolution "does" nothing at all. We cannot replace the word God in the sentence, "God created all life on the planet," with the word, "evolution." Evolution has no agency; it is simply how we refer to directional patterns taking place in a population over time. Within any population, over, say, a thousand-year span, there will be individuals that live long and individuals whose lives are cut tragically short; individuals that produce many offspring, most of which survive and breed, and individuals that produce fewer offspring, and/or fewer of which survive and breed. It may become evident over time that the individuals that survive and have many healthy descendants have traits in common, and individuals that do not live long and fail to reproduce successfully also have traits in common. Furthermore, the traits that lend themselves to success in one environment may be disadvantageous in the face of environmental change, and in that event different individuals, with a different suite of traits, may gain the advantage. All of this is evolution, guided by what we call **natural selection,** and there is nothing mystical about it, at least from a scientific standpoint.

Notice that in the preceding paragraph I have made reference to "pattern." One word that has become associated with evolution is "random," and it is a word that evolutionists fling with abandon at creationists, since "random" events are by definition not guided by design. But we actually have to apply "random" here with some caution. It is true that environmental change, which sets the stage for evolution, is notoriously capricious. It is also true that **DNA—deoxyribonucleic acid,** the substance of genes—mutates chronically, and no one can predict absolutely when and how it will mutate, though we may be able to estimate the likelihood of that mutation having an impact on the survival of the individual or even the next generation. But there are other aspects of evolution about which we can reasonably have expectations. Once a pattern has been established, it is likely to be renewed and even intensified until the circumstances that brought it about in the first place have been altered.

When dogs interbreed, they will produce dogs and not rabbits. A mutation may cause a puppy to look rabbitlike, perhaps, but it is not and will never be a rabbit. Relative to dogs, monkeys are more closely related to human beings, but even so, monkeys that interbreed will produce monkeys. Monkeys may, over time, produce offspring that are better adapted to particular environmental conditions, but these offspring are better (relative to an environment) monkeys; they are not and will not become human beings.

It is equally true that, despite any number of legends in the world that support other possibilities, hu-

" WHADDAYA MEAN I'M NOT A RABBIT? "

man beings will only produce human beings. Again, even if a human being bears a baby that looks somewhat monkeylike, it will not be a monkey. Further, it is not a "throwback" to a prior evolutionary state—human beings are not descended from monkeys. Millions of years ago the evolutionary line leading to modern-day monkeys and the evolutionary line that eventually yields modern-day human beings (along with other strange and wondrous creatures) split in two, and have never reunited. Whatever genetic material our ancestors took with them from this divergence has undergone alteration since, and so has that of monkeys. There could certainly be a portion of human genetic material that, if not inhibited in its action by another gene or genes, may produce monkeylike effects in a child—increased bodily hairiness, for example, or a bit of an external tail—but this does not mean there is a monkey **genome** buried in your DNA, lying in wait for its chance at expression. Since all DNA is made up of the same building blocks, we *could*, in theory, manipulate your genetic material and produce a monkey genome, but it would be quite a feat of genetic engineering, and natural processes certainly do not operate with such intentionality.

So in a very important sense, biological evolution is not random—change is constrained by what is already on hand—and while over a great deal of time we might be amazed at the tremendous variety of species, within one line, from generation to generation, there is unlikely to be much drama. Evolution is also not random if certain traits intensify under the impetus of **sexual selection.** A peacock's luxuriant plumage may have had some other adaptive advantage to start, but once the association was made between a lavish tail display and a healthier bird—and any bird that could support such a tail successfully had to be healthy—females seeking the best mates would respond amorously. More indi-

" IT'S WHAT BIOLOGISTS CALL A 'COSTLY SIGNAL.'"

rectly, the healthier males would triumph in contests with rivals and would in this way win greater access to mates. In the area of sexual stimuli, bigger, louder, more odiferous, more colorful attributes generally win the day, and thus we see a vast potential for escalation to the level of the baroque. Nonetheless, once this degree of hyperelaboration begins to endanger the survival chances of the bird, the healthier males will be those that are less highly elaborated. This may have very little impact, at first, on the mate preferences of peahens biologically programmed to respond to overstimulation, but clearly the peahen that does not curb her taste for excess will compromise her chances for breeding, and the mate she selects may not produce healthy offspring in any event.

Thus, biological evolution does not necessarily lead to greater complexity or in fact to anything at all—it is, rather, *led*, by environmental changes that may favor one type of individual over another, and by a mate selection process that may favor one type of individual over another. Selection pressures may steer evolution in what appears to be a direction, but it would be unwise then to presume that this direction would continue to be followed if these pressures were altered or relaxed.

There are many examples of what I call "bad-science fiction" (that is, based on an erroneous understanding of science) that feature a species moving to its next "level" of evolution, as though evolutionary direction were built into its genes. The descendants of today's human beings are often depicted with huge brains and oversized eyes; sometimes they are even imagined as disembodied clusters of electrical energy. "Evolution" is often represented as the force behind such changes as super strength or the ability to teleport. I cannot say that these things will never come to pass, but it is hard to imagine the mundane conditions of environment and sexual selection, as we currently know them, that could bring forth such marvels from the basic stuff of human DNA. We may in the future be able to arrange, through our own artifice, dramatic change in the human genome, but this would not be evolution in the classic sense, though it is likely that, given the misconceptions described above, we would extend the term to cover it.

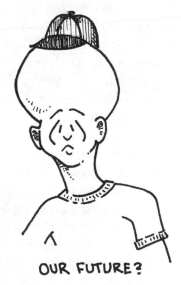

OUR FUTURE?

But surely, you might say at this point, the principle about lesser to greater complexity pertains to **cultural evolution,** right? After all, our ancestors were dressed in skins (if they were dressed at all) and made a meager living through hunting wild game and collecting plantstuffs, but today we have mass-produced, machine-stitched clothing and mass-produced, mechanically manufactured food, not to mention all the other alleged benefits of modernity. Chapter 9 will have much more to say on the issue of cultural evolution, but for the moment I can mention that biological evolution is best seen as a metaphor for cultural evolution, and while metaphor has both practical application and aesthetic appeal, its limitations should be recognized. Further, some of the misconceptions that have hampered a popular understanding of biological evolution have been transferred to cultural evolution to even more egregious effect. We are accustomed to using the words "primitive" and "advanced" to refer to hunter-gatherers and industrialists, respectively, but once again these are value judgments, generally leveled by the people who consider themselves to be "advanced."

There is no question that greater complexity in lifestyle and material technology came about as low-density hunter-gatherers changed over time to become high-density urbanites, but again, what is happening here may be better understood in terms of "more." As human beings produced more human beings, in increasingly compromised environmental spaces, we developed more ways to accommodate the new mouths to feed, the new bodies to house. We developed more knowledge and built on that knowledge to produce still more, but our heads have not gotten larger nor have our brains become any more complex than they were 50,000 years ago. We simply, in the aggregate, know more, due to the additive effects of accruing knowledge over time and recognizing and acting on the patterns that emerge within that knowledge.

To state that biological and cultural evolution are not the same thing does not mean that the two processes are not mutually involved—what we do culturally affects us biologically, and biology of necessity shapes and constrains culture—but even in these instances we must take care that our own cultural prejudices do not tempt us to misinterpret evidence. The renowned American anthropologist Franz **Boas** noted that the children of immigrants to the United States underwent bodily change, including a tendency to grow larger than their parents (Boas 1970[1911]; see also Shapiro 1939). We might interpret this change as evolutionary, and might credit it to what we see as our superior culture and means of child tending, but no genomic change has actually taken place. If children are fed a certain diet at certain key points in their childhood, they will grow into larger adults. This is testimony to human **plasticity**—the fact that the genome may, to a great extent, establish a baseline of potential, but the degree to which the potential is realized will depend on environmental factors and to no small extent on chance.

It should be added that a fuller realization of potential in this instance should not be taken as an unqualified endorsement of the end product. Americans may be larger than other peoples, but we are not necessarily healthier. Our bulk may certainly work against us, if not in childhood (and rates of obesity during this period in our lives have become alarming), then in later life, when our bodies can no longer process constructively the amount of calories we have become used to consuming. A smaller body, so long as sufficient nutrients are received in childhood, may actually be more adaptable in the long run, but Americans often value larger bodies, especially in men, and immigrants may easily see the growth of their children as a welcome sign of their success in a new country.

So, to summarize the points I have made in this section of the chapter:

1. **EVOLUTION IS NOT A FORCE;** the word is descriptive of a process.

2. **EVOLUTION HAS NO INTRINSIC DIRECTION;** rather, it is *directed* by selective pressures. While we may read trends in these pressures, e.g., a period of climatic warming, and thus read trends in evolution, these trends in selective pressures can be modified or even reversed, with consequent changes in the evolutionary process.

3. **EVOLUTION IS NOT RANDOM** in the sense that it is constrained by what has already taken place.

4. It is far **TOO SIMPLISTIC TO TALK ABOUT BIOLOGICAL EVOLUTION IN TERMS OF A MOVEMENT FROM LESSER TO GREATER COMPLEXITY,** although point 3 indicates that, for instance, a multicellular organism is highly unlikely to break down into single-celled organisms no matter how adaptive such a development might be. To apply "lesser to greater complexity" to all evolutionary processes, however, is to compromise scientific methodology by prejudging its results. Further, the tendency to read "greater complexity" as "improvement" is a cultural bias that also influences how experiments are designed and how their results are interpreted. We need to interrogate thoroughly what we mean by "complexity" and explain this meaning in discussions of research.

5. It is also far **TOO SIMPLISTIC TO TALK ABOUT CULTURAL EVOLUTION IN TERMS OF A MOVEMENT FROM LESSER TO GREATER COMPLEXITY,** for much the same reasons given in point 4, although it should be noted that cultural complexity often cannot be meaningfully subjected to the rigors of the scientific method, insofar as cultural processes cannot be broken down and examined in the controlled environment of the laboratory. We must therefore be even more careful about our inclination to apply value judgments to culture change.

With this introductory background, we forge onward into the rest of the book.

What This Textbook Is; What It Is Not

Alright, I lied. There are a few more cautionary notes I need to add before we continue. First, you should be forewarned that this book is wildly outdated. Now, don't take that to mean you should stomp off to your bookstore demanding your money back. All textbooks of this sort are outdated. With respect to evolution, and all the fields of study that impinge upon it, our best guesses change frequently. New information comes in nearly daily, and while some of this information may simply reinforce what we already "know," some triggers a drastic rethinking of heretofore-accepted conclusions. Of course, in scientific terms this is a healthy process, but it may not result in a revolution. We may decide that the new evidence can be sufficiently accommodated by the old explanation, or perhaps we tweak the old explanation just enough to encompass all the available data. So even though it may happen that while you are reading this textbook a news website will herald the discovery of a gene or a fossil or an artifact that appears to stand what we have known on its ear, you may find that in five years or so evolutionary science is still on its feet, though it may have shifted its weight from one foot to the other.

It should always be kept in mind that news portals and other popular sources of information are also businesses, and headlines like "the extraordinary find that changes everything" sell far more advertisements than more cautious pronouncements. Admittedly even paleoanthropologists may generate this sort of hype or will at least allow it to be spread, because they need money, too, for what have become exorbitantly expensive enterprises—exploration of the human past can no longer be done on the cheap (I'll say more about this in chapter 5). So, while it is true that certain finds *have* changed everything, most will not have such a radical impact, and reading a book like this will still be worth your while even as you keep an eye out for news items announcing discoveries that appear to challenge what is said here. What's good about this situation is that it encourages you to take an active approach to learning in this course. At the same time you are gaining a background in what *has* been our understanding of the human evolutionary saga, you will have acquired at least some of the conceptual tools you need to assess new data. A good rule of thumb is to be wary of anything written more than 30 years ago, and of anything written yesterday!

I will do my best to provide you with the most current and most influential interpretations of the data we have on hand. Note the word "interpretation*s*," plural. Yes, data often lend themselves to several different interpretations, and though each one may have merit given what we know for the moment, that does not prevent scholars from engaging in grand battles defending one hypothesis over another. I intend to be as fair as possible to all "sides" of a debate, which will simply guarantee that everyone will be angry at me. But the reader should be aware in advance that with respect to some of these debates, I am an "interested" arbiter, meaning I *do* have an opinion as to what view (and that includes my own) should prevail, and what I pledge to do for you is to be honest about these intrusions of my (hopefully informed) opinions into the book. Consider that an invitation to form your own opinions—there are few things more exciting in this world than being able to participate competently in an ongoing intellectual debate (okay, you have probably already guessed that I'm a bit of a nerd)—but gather your supporting material carefully before you do so. It is my sincerest hope that this textbook will help you to do that, but it is certainly not the be-all and end-all of what you can learn about human prehistory.

    Now we proceed.

QUESTIONS FOR DISCUSSION AND REVIEW

- What are the four fields of anthropology? What unites them? How?
- Why is it that the scientific method cannot be applied to matters of faith?
- Knowing what you know now, how might you respond to someone who asks, "If evolution is true, why are there still monkeys?"
- Discuss the problems with the notion of complexity.
- In what way is biological evolution random? In what way is it not?

KEY WORDS

anthropology	archaeology	(biological) evolution
culture	mya	cultural evolution
social science	biological anthropology	science
natural science	paleoanthropology	hypothesis
humanities	primatology	falsification
field	ape–human divide	theory
holistic	primate	faith
cultural anthropology	adaptive	intelligent design
linguistic anthropology		

2

A Brief, Incomplete History of Evolutionary Thought

> If you assume that an apple falls to the ground because that's its natural place . . . you have no science. If you begin to ask yourself why does the apple fall to the ground and not rise to the sky, if you allow yourself to be puzzled by that simple fact, well, then you find you have a rather serious question before you, and . . . science begins.
>
> —Noam Chomsky,
> Interview for *The Human Language Series*

If I were to say, "What name do you associate with the theory of evolution?" chances are you'd immediately respond, "Darwin." And that's fine—Charles Darwin, who published his *On the Origin of Species by Means of Natural Selection* in 1859, certainly deserves a good deal of credit for his work on the theory—but he was hardly the first to propose it. In fact, the idea that present-day life forms evolved from prior life forms has been around for millennia. In Europe just before Darwin's time, there were several influential scholars who considered themselves to be evolutionists; count among these Darwin's paternal grandfather, Erasmus. However, there were also influential scholars who rejected the theory wholeheartedly, and even those who found it a reasonable explanation for the great variety of life on the planet could not figure out how it worked. What caused a life form to change so drastically? Explanations were mooted, but none garnered sufficient supporting evidence—the scientific method itself was in the process of evolution. There was at once a great lack of knowledge, of such things as cell biology and the mechanics of heredity, and too much knowledge, derived not from experimentation but through faith, that informed popular European convictions regarding the nature of life and its interrelationships. So to grant Darwin his rightful place in the development of Western thought, we need to go back quite far in time to understand why such a simple concept—the origin of species by means of natural selection—was so elusive for so long.

The Shape of God

From the time of the Christianization of Europe, the Bible—cobbled together from Judaic and early Christian sacred writings more than three centuries after the birth of Christ—was widely accepted as a historically accurate text. It is well-known, for instance, that in the 1600s Archbishop Ussher of Ireland used the account of generations from Genesis (supplemented by details from other Old Testament events) to arrive at the date and time of the start of Creation—the evening of October 22, 4004 BC. That the Bible was considered history, however, did not keep theologians from debating its meaning. Even writings deemed divinely inspired were subject to interpretation. What, for instance, was the nature of God? How could we ever hope to understand Him? He is perfect, and we human beings are imperfect. But what does it mean to be perfect? To answer this question, European religious scholars looked not to ancient Palestine but to ancient Greece. Such pre-Christian philosophers as Plato and Aristotle, whose thinking was frequently resurrected in the intellectual phases through which Europe proceeded, equated perfection with completeness (Tatarkiewicz 1979). Perfect things were seamless, complete in and of themselves. In keeping with this idea, the circle was held to be the most complete geometric figure, having no beginning and no end. So Europeans came to believe that God was manifest in circles, both literally, in that the planets were thought to have perfectly circular orbits, and in the aspect of centrality—the Earth was seen as the center of the planetary system (that is, the system was **geocentric**), with the other planets, and even the Sun, arranged in concentric circles around it.

Of course, this arrangement was not confirmed by science, and in fact, alternative schemes, again dating back to the ancient Greeks, existed. But eventually, in Europe, debate with respect to the appearance of what we now call the solar system became greatly constrained, because to suggest that planetary orbits were not perfectly circular and/or that the Earth did not occupy the center of the universe was to deny that God was perfect, and this, understandably, was heresy. Those who did not want to risk being branded as heretics had to explain the erratic movement of planets—evident through simple observation—within the confines of a geocentric model. Fortunately, the Greeks had devised a solution European scholars could adopt—the **epicycle.** Planets did not actually travel in perfectly circular orbits; rather, they traced smaller circles within larger circles as they moved. This could be seen as even more profound testimony to God's perfection—circles within circles; how (divinely) inspired!—but it was difficult not to notice that the consequent orbital path, viewed in its entirety, was hardly circular.

It has not been unusual for flawed explanations to be given, in their death throes, embellishments verging on the baroque. What is extraordinary is that such embellishments often involve some violence to the principle that was allegedly to be defended at all costs, the equivalent of removing a patient's vital or-

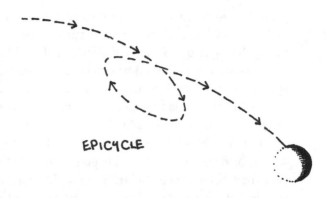

EPICYCLE

gans in order to save him from a dread disease. The good news is that when scholars resort to such desperate measures to resuscitate a failing theory, there is often a scientific breakthrough on the horizon, one that occurs in large measure because one scholar learns to look at the same problem in a very different way. With respect to reframing the issue of what lay at the center of the universe, the man generally given credit within modern times is Nicolaus **Copernicus.**

In the early 1500s, Copernicus—like most scientists of the period, his name, initially a German one, was Latinized—mooted his theory among friends that the universe was not Earth-centered (see, e.g., Kesten 1945; Rosen 1984; Stachiewicz 1973). In the immediate vicinity of the Earth, if one had to speak of a center, that had to be the Sun, a body around which all the planets of the solar system revolved (that is, the system was **heliocentric**). Copernicus arrived at this conclusion without a telescope, which had yet to be invented—he used mathematics and the naked eye. Everything that had been observed about planetary orbits could be explained by the fact that the Earth is a body in motion just as other planets are bodies in motion; only the Sun is stable. Copernicus spent his life

Nicolaus Copernicus, 1473–1543.

perfecting his theory—his math never did come out quite right, since he continued to believe that orbits were circular—but demurred about publishing it. It was finally brought out as a book shortly before his death in 1543. Death conveniently spared him the ordeal that Galileo, a staunch defender of the heliocentric system, went through nearly a century later when he was prosecuted for heresy by the Roman Inquisition, and condemned to house arrest for the last nine years of his life (Shea and Artigas 2003).

To open this chapter, I have ventured into what might appear to be a diversion to bring out two instructive points. The first is the operation of what in science has been called **Occam's** (or Ockham's) **Razor,** the principle that the simplest answer to a problem may well be correct. Copernicus had sliced through the theoretical buildup that had gathered around geocentrism and gotten to the heart of the matter: situating the Sun as the anchor of the planetary system, and releasing the Earth from its moorings to circle the Sun as did any other planet, explained far more, far more concisely, than had any geocentric proposition. While Occam's Razor is not by any means a law, it has proved useful in adjusting scientific thinking on more than one occasion. The history of science is strewn with "aha" moments, when a scientist slaps his palm to his head and exclaims, "Why didn't I think of this before?" But as obvious as the simplest explanation may eventually seem, the fog that prevents us from recognizing it may not arise merely from ignorance, but, in this instance, from deeply held convictions regarding divine order. To question these is to imperil the relationship human beings have with their God(s), and that cannot be taken lightly. And indeed, Galileo was hardly the only proponent of heliocentrism to suffer for his convictions; in the centuries following the publication of the work of Copernicus, other "heretics" lost their freedom, and even their lives.

Eventually, however, Christianity adjusted to what became undeniable, and as far as I know, there is no Christian sect today that rejects the idea of the Earth revolving around the Sun, even though the Biblical story of Joshua, who holds the sun in place so that the battle for Gibeon could continue (Joshua 10:12, 13), does not support this. So the second point is that even when scientific evidence mounts against a view expressed in the Bible, believers may find ways to accept the conclusions of science without losing their faith. Now perhaps that involves an insulting comparison—one passage about stopping the "movement" of the sun hardly measures up to the account of God's greatness in creating the universe. But if Christians could maintain their faith even as they abandoned geocentrism, a similar happy fate may lie in store for the proposition that life on Earth evolved over time rather than coming into being all at once.

Returning now, however, to Copernicus and his impact on European thought: evicting the Earth from the center of the universe of stars and galaxies presaged a parallel movement in the biological sciences to evict human beings from the center of the universe of living things. This event was no less messy and contentious than in astronomy, and in biology, the dust has yet to settle.

The Circle of Life

Clearly God did not create many circular organisms. But in Europe prior to the nineteenth century, the idea of the perfect circle was embedded in the life sciences as a hierarchy of life forms culminating in God's most spectacular earthly creation, Man (with Woman beneath him). This hierarchy, which came to be known as the *scala naturae* or the **Great Chain of Being** (see the following page), again harks back to the thinking of Plato and Aristotle (Lovejoy 1936). You can picture the Great Chain of Being as a series of concentric circles, like a target, with the bull's-eye containing Man, the immediately surrounding circles containing animals considered noble and intelligent, and the farthest circles containing such seemingly lowly life forms as worms. But then we must notice that we are actually looking down on a three-dimensional figure that is less a target than a wedding cake, with Man constituting the crowning layer (the part you would put in your freezer!) and all other animals arrayed on the layers beneath him, in descending order.

Importantly, the Great Chain of Being in its original form denoted a stable hierarchy, not one where "lesser" beings might aspire to be greater someday. God had set each species into its place at the time of Creation. Species could not give rise to other species, nor could any species go extinct—either development would mean that God had erred when He first organized the hierarchy of life forms, and God could not err. Everything He had made was right at the time He created it, and remained right for all time. This idea became known as the **fixity of species.** It is this concept, in fact, that gave rise to the "chain" metaphor. Life on the planet was not a chain because organisms were related in any way (outside of the commonality that God had created them all), but because if one link is missing one no longer has a chain, just as no "link" in God's Creation could go missing.

One believer in the fixity of species was a Swedish scholar who inherited his Latinized surname, **Linnaeus,** from his father. Though Linnaeus believed the species were divinely fixed in place, he also believed the Great Chain of Being could be subjected to scientific scrutiny. Christianity, like Islam, has passed through phases when scientific research was condemned as blasphemous, a questioning of God's Plan to which human beings were not entitled, but in the Europe of the 1600s and 1700s, many scholars regarded the quest for scientific knowledge as one of which God would approve. What better way to glorify Him than to develop

a fuller understanding of His works? This "natural theology" is yet another legacy from ancient Greece; in Linnaeus' day it was popularized by such scientists as John Ray (e.g., Ray 1977[1717]). Ray was not only a man of science but a man of the cloth, and in fact a number of European scientists during this period were clergyman, the clergy being a profession where one might have a good deal of time to dedicate to research. Linnaeus did not become a clergyman, much to the disappointment of his parents (Koerner 1999), but he saw his intellectual activities as entirely in keeping with a devout life (Lindroth 1994).

Carolus Linnaeus, 1707–1778.

God may have created life forms in tremendous diversity, but Linnaeus recognized patterns in this diversity. There were similarities in **morphology** that indicated God worked from a somewhat more limited set of basic blueprints. Linnaeus devised a five-tiered **taxonomic** system, where broad **classes** were subdivided into **orders,** which were subdivided into **genera** (singular: **genus**), which were subdivided into **species** (singular: species!), which were subdivided into **varieties** (Koerner 1999). As it would have been cumbersome to refer to species by regularly identifying all of the ways they were classified, Linnaeus eventually adopted a system of **binomial nomenclature,** wherein species names were rendered in the following format: [*Genus*] [*species*]; a third, varietal name was tacked on as warranted (note that the genus is capitalized but the species is not; the designation should be italicized or otherwise set off from normal text). Both names were in Latin, of course, or at least Latinized. For instance, Linnaeus called modern human beings *Homo sapiens, homo* being the Latin word for "man" (compare with Spanish *hombre*, French *homme*), plus *sapiens,* meaning "wise." It became allowable to pronounce such names not in proper Latin but in local vernaculars; hence, as English speakers (which most of you are in some measure, I presume), you can say "HOE-moe SAY-pee-enz" even though back in the days of the Roman Empire this would be unintelligible.

It should be clear by this time that Linnaean taxonomy, despite having been devised in the 1700s, is still with us today, though it has certainly been modified (not to mention greatly expanded), and there have been calls, as we will soon see, to scrap it altogether. Linnaeus believed his taxonomic work reflected divine order—God, with His supreme intellect, did not create willy-nilly. However, toward the end of his career Linnaeus came to question the idea that species were fixed—he was aware that human beings themselves had produced hybrid plants—and who knows what he might have done had he had more time to digest the implications of this fact? Nevertheless, we should be grateful that he espoused the fixity of species during his most productive years as a scientist, since he might not have undertaken such a monumental task as devising a system of classification for all organisms on the planet had he any idea that the stable hierarchy he thought he was cataloguing was really more of a moving target. This bears out something I have long observed about science—a good deal has been achieved by men and women who, at the start of their research, were just ignorant enough not to recognize that what they actually meant to accomplish couldn't be done.

As stated, Linnaeus was a God-fearing man who did not consider his research to be a threat to that status. He was, however, meticulously observant, and he could hardly help but notice that human beings bore a striking resemblance to other creatures on the planet, notably apes and monkeys. This he duly acknowledged taxonomically, by placing human beings among the primates (see, e.g., Broberg 1994). Lutheran authorities were incensed (Aczel 2007); the Catholic Church went so far as to place the works of Linnaeus on its list of prohibited books (noted in Soulsby 1833). The theological objection was that humans constituted a higher order of being, qualitatively removed from animals. While Linnaeus did not mean to invite religious opprobrium, he knew that according to the principles he himself had devised, humans, at least biologically speaking, were animals, and he defended this view (cited in Broberg 1994:172). The idea that Man stood at the center of the circle of life had been challenged, and this opened doors to further research into the relatedness of life forms even as Christian scions chafed at this line of thinking.

Throughout the time of Linnaeus, another key dogmatic tenet was suffering challenge. Europeans had long been aware of fossils; Linnaeus himself collected and catalogued them. A growing body of scholars, observing that some of these fossils seemed vastly different from anything else that was then alive, began to speak in terms of extinction—perhaps links had been removed from the Great Chain of Being after all. Linnaeus himself, while admitting to the possibility of extinction, preferred to believe that since there were many places on Earth, especially the depths of the oceans, that had yet to be explored, potential legions of obscure organisms remained to be discovered (Stilwell 2006). This was in fact true—it is still true—but other fossil hunters were given to wonder if the explanation could be applied to all of their finds.

In the late 1600s, humankind actually witnessed an extinction—the dodo bird on the island of Mauritius was quickly dispatched by the nonindigenous species introduced through human colonization. If the dodo could vacate its link in the chain so quickly, in this instance under the watchful eye (and sometimes club) of human

" IF I'M SO DEAD, WHY DO YOU KNOW WHAT I AM? "

beings, had other species done so in the past? And if it had happened in the past, how long ago was that, given those instances when there would seem to be no record of the fossil creature save its own remains? As people dug more deeply into the Earth, both literally and in terms of understanding its secrets, Archbishop Ussher's careful calculations with respect to the age of the universe did not impress everyone, even pious men like Linnaeus, as necessarily correct.

Deepening the Circle of Life

Fossils—proof of life, so to speak, projected far into ancient times—link **biology,** the study of life, to **geology,** the study of the Earth. When we think of fossils we may imagine a large dinosaur bone, and of course a bone of any sort is a fossil, though minerals may gradually displace the original bone material. But there are many different kinds of fossils; for example, pollen; the imprint of a leaf into river sediments that later harden; the shell of a mollusk; footprints a human being, or something very much like it, laid down in mud. All of these things interact with the stuff of the Earth in some way, and hence have as much bearing on the study of geology as they do on the study of life.

Fossil of an ammonite, an ancient mollusk.

Those fossils uncovered through excavation are more than just proof of life; they also constitute a timeline. If the layers, or **strata,** of earth have not somehow been disturbed—and this is frequently something we can detect—it is very likely that fossils found close to the Earth's surface are from relatively recently deceased organisms, while those buried more deeply are older, sometimes much older. Fossils are certainly found in the same layers as **artifacts,** material traces of human cultural behavior. Eventually the human component drops out of the mix, but there are still fossils. There may be strata where there are no fossils, and then suddenly, digging deeper, there are fossils again, though these may bear no resemblance to what was found in higher strata, or to anything alive today. So what was the developing science of eighteenth-century Europe to make of this, especially when science was still in large part governed by articles of faith that pegged the creation of the Earth to 6,000 years ago, and could not allow for the possibility of extinction?

According to the Bible there was, of course, a great flood in ancient times, and such an event might explain at least one of the blank strata. The Bible claimed that Noah saved all the animals of the Earth, but it may have been that a few species failed to reach the Ark and perished in the roiling waters. While God pledged never again to visit the world with such a flood (Genesis 8:21), perhaps there were similar disasters that brought about the end of species. In addition to explaining the presence of fossils in the deepest layers of the earth, a succession of disasters could collapse the age of the earth into the requisite 6,000 period.

This type of thinking became known as **catastrophism,** the idea that the Earth, and its life forms, had undergone substantial change only through the intervention of catastrophic events. It should be noted that though most catastrophists believed God delivered such events, not all of them were insistent on a 6,000-year overall timeline. Further, catastrophists were clearly open to the possibility of extinction. God, in His wisdom, had for some reason allowed a number of His creations to go by way of the dodo.

Catastrophism had its fierce proponents throughout the eighteenth century and into the nineteenth, but an opposing version of the history of the Earth was gaining ground and eventually rode to triumph. **Uniformitarians** held that no extraordinary interventions were needed to shape the Earth—such common, observed processes as volcanic eruptions, earthquakes and faulting, the action of wind and water, and other ordinary events were more than adequate to the task. While the earliest uniformitarians believed such processes could work their magic within a short period of time, as the theory matured, later advocates, like the Scotsman James **Hutton,** recognized that a considerable amount of time would be needed (Hutton 1959[1795]). This argument was famously taken up by Charles **Lyell** in the nineteenth century (Lyell 1990[1830–1833]).

Lyell's eminence within geology was secured not so much through original contributions to the growing body of geologic thought but through his eloquence in oral and written defense of uniformitarianism, and this eloquence largely won the day, or at least Lyell's day. Uniformitarianism did not compel supporters to abandon their faith, but they did not necessarily see the account of generations in Genesis as an accurate measure of the age of the Earth. Even as uniformitarians remained God-fearing, however, there was an ominous implication embedded in uniformitarianism: while one certainly *could* believe the hand of God was present in these everyday

Charles Lyell, 1797–1875.

earth-shaping processes, it was also possible to conceive of these processes as natural rather than supernatural, operating entirely on their own.

The triumph of uniformitarianism in nineteenth-century geology brings up Occam's Razor once again. Science became skeptical of catastrophism because it relied on the action of extraordinary events that had never been witnessed and for which there was no scientific evidence. As the famous Harris cartoon implies, if a scientist has to presume a miracle occurred for his theory to work, he is probably on the wrong track. Ironically, however, we now believe uniformitarianism went too far in positing that no extraordinary processes were involved in shaping the Earth and its inhabitants; for instance, it would seem as though meteor strikes have had significant effects. But the modern version of catastrophism is evidence-based and advocates neither for a short timeline nor the necessary action of a divine hand. It is as though geology had to go through a phase of doctrinaire uniformitarianism before catastrophism, now stripped of its tendency to involve supernatural elements, could be revisited and given some credence.

The naturalism of geology began to have an impact on the biological sciences as well. The concept of biological evolution could be far better accommodated by a longer timeline and the proposition that everyday processes, taking place slowly, could be transformative. First, however, the concept had to undergo growing pains as the shackle of the Great Chain of Being was thrown off.

"I THINK YOU SHOULD BE MORE EXPLICIT HERE IN STEP TWO."

The Unfixity of Species

Jean-Baptiste Pierre Antoine de Monet, Chevalier de Lamarck (mercifully known to history as, merely, **Lamarck**) had an answer for those during his era (1744–1829, to be precise) who were bandying about the possibility of ancient extinctions: no species had gone extinct. Instead, they simply evolved into new forms.

As mentioned at the start of this chapter, Darwin was by no stretch of the imagination the first evolutionist. He was preceded by many thinkers along these lines, reaching back, yet again, to classical Greece. But in terms of immediate predecessors, Lamarck must be given due credit (or blame, if the theory of evolution does not sit right with you). As the lengthy name implies, Lamarck was a nobleman, though this did not mean that he was wealthy, as his family line had no fortune and Lamarck himself died penniless. But during his academically productive years, Lamarck gained inspiration from another nobleman, the Comte (Count) de **Buffon** (Fellows and Milliken 1972). Throughout his career, Buffon toyed with several risky lines of thought, evolution and uniformitarianism among them, but often retracted, at least officially, his more daring propositions. One in particular, however, was to resurface in the work of Lamarck—the idea that organisms were changed in form in accord with the demands of their physical environments. While Buffon did not commit himself to the view that such changes could bring about the development of separate species, Lamarck was not so reticent. From the hypothetical shreds and patches of his day, brought together with his own astute zoological observations, he developed a theory of evolution.

According to Lamarck, evolution was driven by two complementary processes: the quest for perfection and the sculpting power of the environment (Burkhardt 1977; see also Packard 1901). Living things strove for perfection; that is, improvement over what had gone before. Such improvement was generally achieved through greater complexity, elabora-

Statue of Lamarck (1744–1829), Paris.

tions that better suited an organism to its environment. The organism would direct a mysterious inner substance to the part of the body requiring improvement, and this part would undergo the desired modification. The environment would put its stamp of approval, so to speak, on the organism's efforts by locking appropriate changes into place and removing what was no longer necessary. Hence, a species would take on its characteristic appearance, and beneficial features, developed in concert with the environment, would be passed on to offspring.

As if dying in poverty were not sufficient punishment for having espoused controversial views during his lifetime, Lamarck was even reviled posthumously (Cuvier 1836), and this has undoubtedly contributed to an ongoing tendency to heap disrespect on his achievements. Nowadays, Lamarck is ridiculed in biology textbooks for his suggestion that a giraffe could grow its neck long in response to food sources moving out of reach (cited in Packard 1901:351). An organism can respond behaviorally to new stimuli, and its fellow organisms, including offspring, may imitate this behavior, but organisms cannot bring about changes in their fundamental genetic endowment no matter how great the need.

Lamarck, however, knew nothing about genetics, and his thinking about how organisms evolve is preserved even today in the concept of **adaptation,** which is frequently used carelessly. When we say an organism *adapts* to environmental change—the example of England's peppered moths comes to mind, coping with the decline in effectiveness of its speckled camouflage when local trees became sooty—we imply that the organism has made some sort of conscious assessment of its situation and has reinvented itself in line with that assessment. But individual moths cannot change color. Even on the species level speckled moths cannot suddenly reproduce legions of dark-colored moths just because the trees have become dark in color. No development of this sort is supported by the Darwinian concept of evolutionary change, and yet Darwin, who also knew nothing about genetics, made Lamarckist pronouncements on occasion, as modern scientists, not to mention science writers, continue to do. I must add here that in a peculiar way, Lamarck's basic proposition—that the life experience of an organism can have a direct, biological effect on subsequent generations—may in fact be vindicated in light of new data, but this is a subject for chapter 3.

So, while the part of Lamarck's theory that is today known as the **Inheritance of Acquired Characteristics** rightly deserves criticism even as we still, perhaps innocently, make use of it, it is the idea that organisms proceed from states of lesser to greater complexity that has actually caused far more damage, and the astute reader will recognize, I hope, that I dedicated a significant portion of chapter 1 to repudiating it. I would hardly have had to do that were this impression no longer prevalent. The upshot is that Lamarck never actually set aside the Great Chain of Being even as he rejected fixity of species. In essence, what he did

The Fall and Rise of the Peppered Moth Example

Peppered moth camouflaged on pristine bark.

For years it was standard fare in biology textbooks—for a snapshot of natural selection in action, cite the case of the peppered moth. As the story went, the peppered moth, an otherwise unremarkable species found in the English countryside, came in two colors—the speckled variety, and a rarer black variant. The speckled form blended in with natural tree bark and was thus less vulnerable to flying predators than the black form, which could be easily spotted from the air. When trees became sooty due to industrial pollution, blackness became an advantage. Over time the speckled variety declined in numbers, while there was a significant uptick in the number of black moths (see Kettlewell 1973). Cleaning the air, hence the tree bark, reversed this trend, thus conveniently demonstrating natural selection twice over (Clarke et al. 1985).

Then questions arose. In the 1990s, a scientist named Michael Majerus challenged the methodology that E. B. Ford and Bernard Kettlewell used to conduct the original experiment. Creationist websites were abuzz—had the peppered moth research been jury-rigged in order to produce the desired result? And if the experiment had been hokum, perhaps natural selection was also hokum. Without actually checking into the facts, some evolutionists quietly abandoned the peppered moth example, and textbook writers scrambled to find another story that illustrated natural selection in a similarly straightforward way.

(continued)

Majerus (1998), among others, had in fact questioned the experimental methodology of Ford and Kettlewell, but he hardly jettisoned the concept of natural selection on that account. He concluded that despite the flawed methodology, the conclusion Ford and Kettlewell had reached was essentially correct. The real problem lay, he claimed, in reading too much into this one example—the situation was not as simple as it appeared. Were the black moths more often plucked from pristine bark? Observations of the peppered moth continued to bear this out, but the results of experiments conducted on similar species of moth were not so clear-cut (Cook 2003). It seemed *likely* that predation was a factor in the differential mortality of the two colors of moth, but definitive support was elusive (Cook et al. 2005).

The moral of this episode is that a good deal of what students might read in textbooks is oversimplified with the intent of highlighting a worthy point. Most students are probably happy that they are not subjected to the long form of any particular example, but they might keep in mind that these streamlined versions of events can become increasingly removed from the facts as they are told over and over again.

was transform a hierarchy in which places were fixed into one that defined levels of progress, with all organisms seeking to reach the next level of perfection. The Great Chain of Being was anti-evolutionary in its original concept, but was no less so after Lamarck grounded his theory in the allegedly progressive nature of life. The American essayist and poet Emerson encapsulated this view in a famous couplet: "And, striving to be man, the worm / Mounts through all the spires of form" (1948[1836]:xv). Up to the present day, people who are open to the concept of evolution nonetheless often harbor the misconception that evolution proceeds toward intrinsically more "advanced" states, with the definition of "advanced" derived from the values of those who consider themselves to be so. Thirty years after Lamarck's death, however, there was one man who tried to argue differently.

Natural Selection

Actually, two men: Alfred Russel **Wallace** and Charles **Darwin.** Though they became well acquainted with each other, they did not work together—each inde-

Charles Darwin, 1809–1882.

A. R. Wallace, 1823–1913.

pendently arrived at the concept of natural selection. Each, in his world travels, had marveled at the abundance of species on the planet, but each was also given to wonder why, *within* these species, there was such a high degree of variation. No two organisms were alike. Why did such variation persist in species? Could it serve some sort of function?

Wallace was influenced in his thinking on such matters by the work of Thomas Robert **Malthus,** a clergyman who wrote a treatise on overpopulation (see Himmelfarb 1960). Malthus opened his essay with the premise (unsupported by scientific evidence) that human populations grow exponentially, while their food supply grows at a much slower rate. Thus ensues a brutal "struggle for existence" (Himmelfarb 1960:21) as desperate people compete for the basic stuff of life. This level of competition could be alleviated by what Malthus called "positive checks"—famines, wars, epidemics, and similar scourges. Malthus saw positive checks as necessary means to trim off excess population. Until they occurred, however, life was like a grand game of musical chairs—when the music stopped, so to speak, some people had enough food, and some did not.

Malthus had painted an ugly picture, but Wallace had experienced enough of nature to know that it could be cruel. As he traveled through the islands of what he called the Malay Archipelago (modern-day Malaysia and Indonesia), he pondered what quality individual organisms that emerged victorious from the

Thomas Robert Malthus, 1766–1834.

struggle for existence might have—were they stronger? smarter? The answer, Wallace himself claimed, came to him in a febrile dream (cited in Slotten 2004:144). *Contra* Lamarck, individual organisms had no real control over their destinies. An organism that survived did so because it happened to be born with traits that were especially suited to its environment; an organism that died young likely did not have these traits. The "winners" of the struggle for existence weren't necessarily stronger or smarter, just luckier.

While Wallace was putting this theory together, he was in correspondence with Darwin, who received the younger man's letters in amazement and some apprehension (Raby 2001; Slotten 2004). The thinking was so much like his own, right down to the influence of Malthus. But when Wallace finally produced a full-blown paper on the subject, Darwin realized he had to do the same—quickly.

As a young man, Charles Darwin did not seem to be marked for greatness. He was well-born, and this meant that he could fritter away his youth to some extent, but his father, a respected doctor, eventually insisted Charles apply himself to his studies so that he also could enter the medical profession. When Charles turned out to be squeamish, his father recommended study for the clergy, but Charles was little inclined to pursue this line of work. What young Charles liked most to do was hunt, and collect specimens from nature (Gribbin and White 1995). He had a curiosity about nature that conventional schooling did not satisfy. Today's student—the one who prefers hands-on projects to sitting and reading—will relate to Darwin on this point (I must quickly add, however, that with respect to topics in which he was interested, he was hardly ill-read).

When he was 23 years of age, Charles Darwin was offered a shipboard position on the *Beagle*, which was about to undertake a 'round-the-world voyage. The position was advertised as "naturalist," but the duties entailed went well beyond scientific endeavor. Ship captains were well-born, while the crew was composed of men from the lowest social class. Darwin was hired in part so that the captain, a man named FitzRoy, could have a suitable companion with whom to converse (Browne 1995a). FitzRoy was volatile and held many rigid opinions about the way of the world, most of them derived from a fundamentalist reading of the Bible. Although Darwin adhered to a faith in God, his views on Biblical truth were not nearly so doctrinaire, and he and FitzRoy frequently argued. Hence, as an intellectual sparring partner, Darwin fulfilled his duties admirably. He also functioned as a naturalist, however, and was in fact expected to collect natural specimens from all of the venues the *Beagle* would visit. Darwin's observations during the voyage of the *Beagle* contributed to the broadening of his thinking regarding variation both between and within species.

Nonetheless, when he returned to England in 1836, he did not develop this thinking into a publishable work. Instead, he carried out extensive research that enhanced his reputation as a scientist. For instance, Darwin became Europe's foremost authority on barnacles, having conducted an exhaustive—and exhausting—study of the creatures, becoming thoroughly sick of them in the process. Nothing he learned about barnacles, or any other object of study, contradicted his ideas on evolution, and hints of these began appearing in his writing. Why was Darwin reluctant to say more? While we cannot ask him, one interpretation of his dawdling was that he knew full revelation of his theory would upset his wife, to whom he was devoted (see Browne 1995a and b). Emma Wedgwood Darwin was an intelligent woman who realized her husband had conceived of a mechanism through which life may have evolved without the necessary intervention of a divine Being. Emma was also a devout Christian who

DARWIN WAS NEVER A VERY GOOD SAILOR...

greatly feared for Charles' immortal soul should he continue to develop his views on evolution (Browne 1995a). So long as these views were confined within the household, Emma could entertain the notion Charles might come to his senses and reverse himself. Unfortunately for Emma (and perhaps her husband's immortal soul), the Wallace essay convinced Charles Darwin that he had to present his theory without delay.

In the gentlemanly times of mid-nineteenth century Europe, it was agreed that papers from both Wallace and Darwin would be read at the Linnean Society conference of 1858. The papers had surprisingly little impact; Thomas Bell, in his presidential report, wrote: "The year which has passed has not, indeed, been marked by any of those striking discoveries which at once revolutionize, so to speak, the department of science on which they bear" (cited in Browne 1995b:42). But in the following year, Darwin published the first edition of what turned out to be his masterwork, *On the Origin of Species by Means of Natural Selection* (2006[1859]), and on the strength of this effort Darwin's name has thoroughly eclipsed that of Wallace in both scholarly renown (as well as infamy) and popular thought.

Natural selection was what Darwin called the mechanism through which evolution was accomplished. As his wife had feared, it was thoroughly unremarkable, with the hand of God nowhere evident, save, perhaps, in the utter simplicity of the process. The natural environment was ever-changing, across space and through time. Of course it greatly varied from latitude to latitude, and even within latitudes there were mountains and deserts, oceans and lakes, year-round coastal temperateness versus the seasonal extremes of the inner continent. Each zone contained certain types of abundance, in terms of potential foodstuffs, and also certain types of threats, in terms of disease, predation, and competition. Add to this the fact that the environment could change through time, sometimes gradually and predictably, and sometimes drastically, as a consequence of an unforeseen event.

No species could follow such changes; its only advantage lay in maintaining within its boundaries a stock of variations, some proportion of which might enable certain individuals to handle the next environmental shift. This did not proceed gently—many individuals would die young, others would merely survive, still others might thrive—but so long as a sufficient number of individuals lived, they would reproduce the very traits that had contributed to their success, and these traits would thus become so prevalent within the population that what had been one variation among many would come to typify the entire population. Over time so many of these helpful traits would accumulate, in response to further environmental shifts, that a new species, significantly different from its ancestors, would emerge.

What Darwin had proposed was in many ways continuous with the ascendant theories of both predecessors and contemporaries. Darwin was something of a "biological uniformitarian" in that he believed everyday occurrences could produce dramatic change given enough time. And the potentially determining power of the physical environment was, of course, a vital component of Lamarck's thinking, as well as that of Lamarck's patron Buffon. Both Darwin and Lamarck promoted approaches that could be seen as naturalistic—no supernatural agent was needed to cause erosion or to bring about a drought that would favor the development of water-retention properties in organisms. But in Darwin's view of the world, nature did not have agency either. The environment did not decide how it would change, and organisms could not decide what traits they would have. The phrase "natural selection" was actually intended to show that selection could take place without there being a conscious selector of any sort. That there are oak trees, and trout, and pigeons, and yes, human beings (though Darwin was less than explicit about this to start), was simply a matter of that which lived and that which died under particular environmental circumstances.

For scholars who had championed Darwin, like Lyell and even Wallace, this was going too far. It was difficult for them to abandon the comforting notion that there was some sort of plan behind it all, and some sort of scale on which Man could be placed in a higher situation above the animals. Darwin had no such qualms. His faith in a kindly God was shaken by the death of his young daughter Annie (Keynes 2001), and from then on he did not feel as though he owed God any more consideration than He had shown. But Darwin did not espouse the concept of natural selection out of spite. He saw it as the best way to explain how different forms of life had developed on the planet, and he wanted others to agree; whether they became agnostic in the process was immaterial to him.

Darwin, of course, continued to tinker with the concept; he put out *On the Origin of Species* in several editions, and wrote another book, *The Descent of Man*, in which he finally and firmly committed himself to the proposition that humans had evolved as other life forms had. Despite this ongoing work, Darwin was dissatisfied. He was aware there were problems. Variation within species was the raw material for natural selection, but he did not understand how this raw material was produced, and, more importantly, reproduced. Europeans had long held to the "common sense" notion that heredity was a matter of blending parental characteristics, in the same way that yellow and blue, mixed together, make green. If this were entirely the case, however, variation should be gradually eliminated by the breeding process—green, so to speak, cannot be re-separated into yellow and blue. But variation was not eliminated. This was, from Darwin's perspective, a very good thing, but it would be a better thing if he had an inkling as to why. He sketched out a convoluted hypothesis on the matter, but it garnered no scientific support. In fact, in Darwin's day, there was only one man in Europe (of whom we know) who had an insight into how inheritance actually worked.

Mendel and the Foundation of Genetics

Johann **Mendel** was born in 1822 in what is now the Czech Republic (it was the Austrian Empire at the time). A studious young man, he joined a monastic order in 1843, adopting the name of Gregor and relocating to the city of Brno. To be a monk at that time was not necessarily to commit oneself to a lifetime of quiet service to God. Abbeys also housed scholars, who through becoming monks had support and leisure enough to pursue scientific investigations. After two years of university study, Mendel became a teacher as well (Orel 1984).

Mendel had an interest in plant hybridization and ultimately wanted to produce higher-yield crops for the betterment of humankind. First, however, he realized he needed to know much more about how desirable plant traits were passed on to offspring and what type of offspring plants with contrasting traits would yield. He chose to experiment with garden peas, which have many contrasting, and seemingly mutually exclusive, traits. Pea plants can either be tall or short; peas can be yellow or green, wrinkled or smooth. When Mendel interbred tall plants with short plants, the result was a generation of tall plants. Immediately, then, it was shown that height in pea plants did not involve blending—there were no medium plants in the lot. But what *had* happened? Had tallness exterminated shortness? Mendel intrabred the first generation (i.e., the plants within the generation were bred with each other—

Gregor Mendel, 1822–1884.

yes, I'm afraid there's pea in-breeding going on here), and came out with a second generation in which short plants reappeared, though they were outnumbered by the tall plants three to one.

Garden pea plants.

From these simple experiments, carried out with an extraordinary number of plants over time, Mendel was able to infer a good deal about heredity. The first revelation was perhaps the most far-reaching—inheritance was not a matter of blending. This was readily demonstrated in the case of the traits tested in garden peas, but Mendel believed the principle held true in more complicated circumstances. Inheritance, he deduced, is actually reliant on some sort of constant particle. Mendel dubbed this particle a "factor." Today, of course, we know it as a **gene.**

Not only is inheritance **particulate,** but the particles are also **segregated.** With respect to the example of height in garden peas, each parent contributes one factor for height, and these factors are discrete—that is, they remain as separate entities—throughout the breeding process. To continue with the color metaphor, yellow and blue remain yellow and blue, whether or not offspring are green. The height of garden peas makes this obvious, in that offspring are always either tall or short, but Mendel suggested that even if there is an intermediate result, the factors themselves are not altered. Any "greenness" in the offspring results not from any sort of blending and consequent destruction of factors, but from the way factors *interact.* If a garden pea inherits one factor for tallness and one for shortness, it will be tall, because the tallness factor is **dominant** over the shortness factor, said to be **recessive.** These are perhaps unfortunate terms, in that they imply that the shortness factor is somehow "weak" and might actually disappear altogether from a population over time. But keep in mind the 3:1 ratio in the second generation: what this indicates is that in a reasonably large population undergoing steady reproduction, the shortness factor will be paired with another shortness factor in one out of four matings. Hence there will continue to be short offspring, although they will be in a minority relative to tall.

Mendel also checked to see whether two different traits involved in his research design were fundamentally linked; that is, would tall plants always bear yellow peas? would short plants always bear green peas? Mendel interbred tall plants bearing yellow peas to short plants bearing green peas and discovered that in the first generation, all the plants were tall and produced yellow peas. From his earlier experiments, Mendel knew that all this might indicate is dominance, not linkage. And in fact, intrabreeding the plants from this generation yielded a subsequent generation of tall plants with yellow peas, tall plants with green peas, short plants with yellow peas, and short plants with green peas in a 9:3:3:1 ratio, respectively, exactly what one would expect if the traits, and the factors, were not linked. There was nothing preventing a tall plant from bearing green peas, or a short plant from bearing yellow peas, although the fact that one trait was dominant and the other recessive would determine how often such offspring would occur. But the two traits assorted independently of each other within the breeding process.

Mendel's inferences regarding inheritance are often codified in the following manner, although Mendel himself did not summarize his results thus:

1. Inheritance is particulate.
2. Inheritance conforms to the **Law of Segregation.**
3. The appearance of offspring is determined by the **Law of Dominance and Recessiveness.**
4. The **Law of Independent Assortment** indicates that traits, and the factors that determine them, are not linked.

These principles are elegant, but entirely too simplistic. The interaction between **alleles**—the various forms one gene might take—is not limited to dominance and recessiveness, and not necessarily limited even to the two alleles (from each parent) that pertain to the trait being studied. Further, the term "trait" is notoriously subjective—the form of what we see as one trait may actually be determined by the action of several genes, or one gene may produce what we see as several different traits. None of this even approaches the complexity of genes themselves—what are they? how and why do they interact?—but even for us, this is a subject that will take up yet another chapter. In the meantime, let us be grateful that for his experiments Mendel chose garden peas, and chose to focus on such properties as height and seed color, since in peas these are in fact determined by the action of one gene; i.e., they are **monogenic.** In studying garden peas Mendel did not lead us down the garden path, so to speak, even though he did not otherwise lead us very far. But one has to start somewhere. What Mendel inferred about heredity was correct within a very limited set of circumstances, and his research proved to be a working foundation on which to build the modern science of genetics. If subsequent discoveries in the field have involved rip-ping out the foundation to some extent, this did not happen until the overall structure of the science was reasonably sound.

It is often stated that Mendel did not receive the credit he was due for his re-search. Given how important genetic science has become to our lives today, he could hardly have received enough credit even if he had become the most cele-brated scientist of his time. But Mendel's report on his work was not immedi-ately consigned to obscurity. The report was read at a conference in 1865 and published the following year in its proceedings, which were circulated to a num-ber of European libraries. Mendel himself sent his paper to scholars he believed might have an interest. Subsequently Mendel's research was cited in a small number of sources, but not in a way that indicated an awareness of its far-reach-ing implications. Gribbin and White (1995: 288) hazard that the problem could have been one of timing. Mendel's paper came out just before scientists discov-ered the existence of chromosomes, and had this order been reversed, the lead-ing connection between the two bodies of research may have been more readily discerned. As it happened, however, scientists newly equipped with the knowl-edge of chromosomes proceeded swiftly to replicate Mendel's principles of he-redity. Before these new efforts could be advertised as pathbreaking, however, Mendel's work was recovered from the dusty annals of sci-ence—the fact that it had been carried out not so very long be-fore must have been shocking— and Mendel is now presented to us as the Father of Genetics.

There was perhaps another reason why Mendel was not duly honored for his achieve-ments during his lifetime. The nineteenth century was a period of development for all manner of sciences in Europe, and what began to emerge was specializa-tion. Rather than students of an eclectic "natural history," scien-tists became astronomers, geolo-gists, biologists, and so forth. Even within, for instance, biol-ogy, one might take up the

MENDEL PLANS HIS NEXT EXPERIMENT...

study of plants *as opposed to* the study of animals. As information accrued on natural phenomena, it was understandable that no one scholar could apprehend all of it, and certainly worthwhile discoveries have issued from the intense focus encouraged by increased specialization. But occasionally a scientist needs to see the forest for the trees, and this becomes more difficult when the trees are enclosed by disciplinary "walls." While in Mendel's day these walls were not built nearly so high, there still may have been a tendency to view his work as relevant only to a very narrow area of science.

Charles Darwin was by no means confined by discipline walls, and he actually owned a book in which Mendel's research was cited. But it appears that he never read the section of the book where this occurred (Sclater 2000). Of course, even if a cursory mention of Mendel's work had inspired Darwin to track down the original paper—unlikely in and of itself—he still may have failed to realize how much garden peas could contribute to his own observations regarding the origin and continuation of intraspecies variation (Howard 2009). The fact that Darwin had no

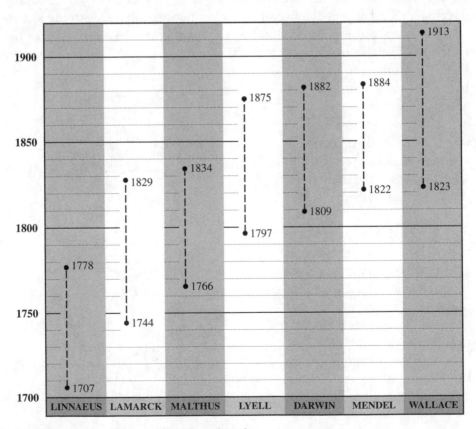

Key figures in European evolutionary thought.

understanding of genetics drove him into error regarding the nature of heredity, and it took science quite some time to redirect and synthesize the intellectual legacies of both Darwin and Mendel. For all that, it has to be said that even today we do not know all we hope to know in the future about heredity, and that many ideas that seemed well supported only a few years ago are now subject to serious question. These questions, to the extent this textbook will address them (they are ultimately the focus of at least one other course), will be featured in the next chapter.

A Closing Note on Interdisciplinary Work

In the preceding section I mentioned the nineteenth-century tendency toward specialization in the sciences. This trend was no less true in the social sciences; hence, we witnessed the emergence of economics, political science, and sociology from a parent area of inquiry known as political economy (Wolf 1982). Anthropology, too, emerged at this time, but while in Europe it gravitated toward specialization, sacrificing portions of its initial purview to the humanities and to the other social and natural sciences, in the United States it became, in and of itself, a massive interdisciplinary behemoth along the lines described in chapter 1. Over the years, centrifugal pressures have threatened anthropology's four-field approach, and in fact, at some American universities and colleges students may find that the stuff of the different fields has been broken out and redistributed to the biology, history, sociology, and language/literature departments.

While today's American student is not necessarily rewarded for generalization (try selling "Renaissance Man" on the job market), I believe that in a world suffering from huge financial upheavals and ecological devastation, we need far more people who can see the "big picture," who have the intellectual equipment and drive to cinch together insights from various disciplines and apply them to improving the human—and planetary—condition. I gently suggest (yes, this is what's known as a "plug") that four-field anthropology, as difficult as it is to pursue, is one of the best ways to turn out such well-rounded observers and actors, and of course I encourage any student, especially one interested in far too many things to be considered reasonable by the narrower thinkers of the present moment, to continue on with anthropology courses and possibly to major in the discipline if the spirit (of inquiry) so moves you. Who knows, you may go on to save the world, but in the meantime, you can really cause some worry to your parents regarding your career ambitions. This, however, is good, since in more ways than one, your college education is their college education. Unless, by some happy chance, your parents are anthropologists, you will have something to teach them about the usefulness of anthropology even as you yourself begin to appreciate the myriad of career and life paths you might successfully follow.

EXERCISE

Have a classroom debate on which man discussed in the chapter had the most influence on modern science.

QUESTIONS FOR DISCUSSION AND REVIEW

- How did the principle of Occam's Razor figure in the eventual refection of the geocentric universe?
- Compare the Linnaean and Lamarckian versions of the Great Chain of Being.
- Describe the geological and biological realizations that led most scientists to abandon the 6,000-year timeline.
- Describe how natural selection operates.
- What aspects of his garden pea experiments led Mendel to the conclusions we now know as Mendelian Law?

KEY WORDS

epicycle	variety	adaptation
Copernicus	binomial nomenclature	Malthus
heliocentric	fossil	Wallace
geocentric	biology	Darwin
Occam's Razor	geology	natural selection
Great Chain of Being	catastrophism	Mendel
fixity of species	uniformitarianism	particulate
Linnaeus	Hutton	Law of Segregation
morphology	Lyell	Law of Dominance and
taxonomy	Lamarck	Recessiveness
class	Inheritance of Acquired	Law of Independent
order	Characteristics	Assortment
genus	Buffon	monogenic
species		

3

BEYOND DARWIN
AND MENDEL

Each step of survival does not start from a blank
and random slate but from a previous parental
blueprint already evolved over millions
of generations. . . . Each change is a minor
tweaking of a previous body plan.

—Alison Jolly, *Lucy's Legacy*

The Mathematics of Mendel

As noted in the previous chapter, what Mendel called "factors" we now call genes. There are other ways we should update the language of Mendel's experiments before we update what we currently "know" about the biological substance of things whose existence Mendel could only infer.

First, I must introduce a helpful device, known as a **Punnett square,** used to illustrate the likelihood of any one result from the breeding process. Remember that breeding is a crapshoot—you probably already know that under ordinary circumstances you have an equal chance of producing a baby boy as a baby girl (there *are* circumstances that skew this chance one way or the other, and sex itself is not so cut-and-dried as being *either* male or female in all instances, but we will leave these complexities aside here). You also know mothers who had nothing but boys, or nothing but girls, and what has most probably happened in these instances is that these mothers simply beat the odds—they flipped a coin, so to speak, and it just happened to come up "heads" every time. Punnett squares do not record what the breeding process *will* produce; they illustrate what it *can* produce, and the odds for each result.

Mendel, you may recall, tested for no more than two traits at a time, and each trait came down to the action of one gene. So through the Punnett square we can represent this one-gene focus, while keeping in mind that the overall breeding process actually involves the interaction of thousands of genes.

To draw a Punnett square, the genes the parents can potentially contribute to the breeding process are arrayed on the outside. Continuing with the example of height in garden peas: each pea parent has two genes for height. The parent may carry two of the *same* genes for height—it is **homozygous** for the trait ("homo-" here referring to similarity)—or it may have two *different* genes for height; that is, it is **heterozygous** ("hetero-" referring to difference). Recall that variations on one gene—in this case the gene for height in garden peas—are called **alleles;** in this example we have an allele for tallness (represented as a capital "T" in the Punnett squares below) and an allele for shortness (represented as a small "t"). Both alleles pertain to height, but they affect it in opposite ways. Genes do not have to come in more than one allele; for those that do, generally there are only two alleles, though there are well-known exceptions. In human beings, for instance, there are three alleles that determine whether your blood type is A, B, AB, or O, but we will pursue this a little later.

When he began his experiment, Mendel interbred tall plants, which must have issued from generations of tall plants, with short plants, whose ancestry had to be similarly pure. The resulting generation—the first **filial** generation, represented as F_1, consisted entirely of tall plants. The Punnett square that illustrates the potential results of this mating appears thus:

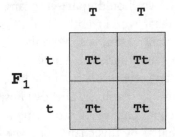

Note that the parent organisms are both homozygous for this trait; that is, the tall parent can contribute only tallness alleles ("T") to the breeding process, the short parent can contribute only shortness alleles ("t"). As you can see, there is 100% probability that the offspring will be tall, because tallness is dominant over shortness and barring a genetic accident, there is no wiggle room in this result. A tallness allele *will* be paired with a shortness allele. On the surface this is unexciting, but clearly there has been no blending. Something else important has happened as well—while all of the plants are tall, they are not tall in the same way as their tall parent. They are heterozygotes (Tt) rather than homozygotes. In other words, their **phenotype,** or outward appearance, remains the same as their tall parent, but the **genotype,** or genetic combination, that determines this is different. Hence the heterozygotes bring different possibilities to the breeding process, something for which Mendel tested by interbreeding the offspring from the first filial generation to produce the second filial generation (F_2):

	T	t
T	TT	Tt
t	Tt	tt

F_2

So here is where things get really interesting. There is a 3 out of 4 chance that offspring in the second generation will be tall, but only a 1 out of 4 chance that offspring will be homozygous for tallness (TT). There is a 50% chance (i.e., 2 out of 4) that offspring will feature the tall phenotype, but their genotype for the trait will be heterozygous (Tt). This should not be taken to mean that the heterozygote is somehow only "weakly" tall, or that its tallness can potentially collapse into shortness; in this instance "dominance" has effectively masked the phenotypic expression of shortness. But with respect to the entire breeding process, there *is* a 25% (1 out of 4) chance that offspring will be short; such offspring must be homozygous for shortness (tt).

Breeding for two different contrasting traits, e.g., tallness or shortness and yellow or green pea color ("Y" standing for the dominant allele, "y" for the recessive), Mendel interbred tall pea plants bearing yellow peas (TTYY) and short pea plants bearing green peas (ttyy). The offspring of this mating all shared the phenotype tall with yellow peas, but in terms of genotype, they were heterozygous for both traits (TtYy). These offspring were bred to each other, producing the second filial generation. To represent this generation in Punnett terms, we need to expand the table to 16 squares, as there are 16 possible results (i.e., 4 x 4) when testing for two traits.

	TY	Ty	tY	ty
TY	TTYY	TTYy	TtYY	TtYy
Ty	TTYy	TTyy	TtYy	Ttyy
tY	TtYY	TtYy	ttYY	ttYy
ty	TtYy	Ttyy	ttYy	ttyy

F_2

Note that, as indicated in the previous chapter, there is a 9 out of 16 chance offspring will exhibit both dominant traits, a 6 out of 16 chance offspring will exhibit one dominant and one recessive trait (either tall but bearing green peas [3/16], or short but bearing yellow peas [3/16]), and a 1 out of 16 chance offspring will exhibit both recessive traits. These are, of course, the odds for the phenotypes; the genotypes are more varied and hence the odds must cover more possibilities. Note also, as did Mendel, that there is independent assortment—nothing inhibits the production of the various phenotypic combinations that can be had here save the regulating effect the Law of Dominance and Recessiveness has on proportions. In other words, these traits in garden peas do not **co-vary.**

Since these are odds laid on the breeding process, it is by no means assured that if you begin with two plants that were heterozygous for a single contrasting trait and interbred them, the subsequent generation would feature plants in a 3:1 ratio, phenotypically speaking. With every four offspring there would be four chances to beat the odds. Testing for two contrasting traits, with every 16 offspring there would be 16 chances to beat the odds. In fact, it is highly unlikely these ratios would be realized if you began your experiment with only a limited number of plants. Mendel's experiments involved nearly 28,000 pea plants all told, and his ratios, in the end, were not perfect (Orel 1984). This has led some to suggest that Mendel must have manipulated his data, but if this were the case, he moved them toward a sound conclusion that was likely emerging in any event. To resolve 315:101:108:32 to 9:3:3:1 would not seem to be too much of an abuse of the facts, though it helps, of course, that Mendel's underlying thinking as to why this might be the ultimate outcome turned out to be correct.

There are certainly traits in human beings that operate in the one-thing-or-the-other manner as the traits Mendel investigated in pea plants, but many of these are pathologies and are thus likely unfamiliar to you (thankfully). As mentioned above, however, the A-B-O blood system is governed by a single gene occurring in three different alleles, A, B, and O. Both the A and B alleles are dominant over the O allele, but the A and B alleles are **codominant** with respect to each other; that is, they will both be expressed in offspring. Hence, you will have Type AB blood if you inherited an A allele from one parent and a B allele from the other. If you have Type A blood (your phenotype), your genotype is either AA or AO, and if you have Type B blood, your genotype is either BB or BO. If your phenotype is Type O, your genotype has to be OO.

Note that the term "phenotype" is not in this instance referring to physical appearance, since blood looks the same no matter what type it is (it will *react* differently to other blood types, however, which is why we have had to be mindful of this property of blood when we give or receive it). It is better to think of phenotype more generally as the end result of the interaction between alleles. Again in this instance the result is fixed in place by the breeding process—just as a pea plant that is heterozygous for tallness is no less tall than a homozygote, your blood type is A whether your genotype is AA or AO. However, if your genotype is AO, it is possible for you to have a Type O child if in the breeding process your O allele is matched with an O allele from your partner.

EXERCiSE

Track down as many blood types as possible in your family and see if you can put together an allele map.

Height in human beings is certainly not dependent on the action of a single gene (i.e., monogenic), however, and this is true of most traits that matter to us. Human stature results from the action of several genes; that is, it is **polygenic.** Polygenic traits will not take on a one-thing-or-the-other appearance but will occur over a range, as does height in humans. What's more, genetic action only establishes a potential for height, and the extent to which a person realizes that potential is also affected by the environment; for instance, the amount and type of food she receives during her growth years.

So, monogenic, polygenic, the influence of the environment on genetic potential—they all beg a question: what is a gene? And to answer that, even to the extent needed in what is likely not a biology course, is by no means an easy task. This is partly because the very definition of gene is changing, in response to new discoveries and new ways of thinking about the old discoveries. As always, readers are encouraged to update their information as it becomes available, but be forewarned that in the area of genetics especially, the terms and even the concepts have not been consistent, given the (hopefully productive) degree of flux in the field.

What's in a Gene?

Before I begin this section, I must qualify what is presented here by stating at the outset that it is grossly oversimplified—you should thank me for this unless you were counting on this part of the book to help you pass your biology test. I also have to mention that throughout what appear to be "rules," below, there are exceptions, even where, for the sake of sparing you too many asides, I resign myself to using such words as "only."

Mendel held that inheritance was particulate, and he had good reason, because in his experiments, "factors" behaved like particles. But a gene is not really a particle, if by that one thinks of something like a hard-shell sphere with a "T" marked on it. A gene is more accurately described as a segment of **deoxyribonucleic acid (DNA),** a stringlike molecule composed of repeating components. In most cells that make up a multicellular organism, DNA exists in two places: the **nucleus** and the **mitochondria.** For our current purposes, we will focus on nuclear DNA, though mitochondrial DNA becomes very important to our story later on.

The "snap-together" components of DNA, called **nucleotides,** consist of a sugar, a phosphate group, and one of four possible **nitrogenous bases: adenine (A), thymine (T), cytosine (C),** or **guanine (G).** The sugar-and-phosphate-group portions of one set of nucleotides are attached to each other in a line, forming a "vertical" support, oriented upward, for the DNA molecule, while the exposed nitrogenous bases join "horizontally" (in **base pairs**) with their inverted counterparts that are in turn attached to their own sugar-and-phosphate-group "vertical" support, oriented downward (of course, since DNA is a free-floating molecule in a liquid matrix, there is no actual "up-down" orientation, but it may help you to think in these terms for the moment). The entire structure resembles a ladder, but in nuclear DNA, a twisted one (the more technical term for "twisted ladder" is **double helix**). The coiling of the ladder is functional, and its degree actually varies relative to the different tasks in which DNA is engaged. One remarkable task that DNA must accomplish periodically is its own **replication.** Enzymes divide the length of the molecule at the sites where the base pairs are joined, the exposed nitrogenous bases attract an additional complement of nucleotides, and the opposite side of each ladder is rebuilt. The result is—hopefully—two identical molecules of DNA.

SIDEBAR

The Abuse of Rosalind Franklin

> There was not a trace of warmth or frivolity in her words. And yet I could not regard her as totally uninteresting. Momentarily I wondered how she would look if she took off her glasses and did something novel with her hair. (Watson 1969:68–69)

The passage above is taken from James Watson's account of the race to determine the actual structure of the DNA molecule. Watson, along with

Francis Crick and Maurice Wilkins, won the race, and the chronicle of this exciting development in science, *The Double Helix*, became popular perhaps on the strength of such nontechnical enhancements. The reader can picture Franklin, frumpy and shrewish, concealing her more feminine features under a veneer of overplayed professionalism. The problem is that this image was more stereotype than reality; one we continue to apply to "women scientists." It would seem as though Watson took advantage of the stereotype to sell his book.

WHAT WATSON SAW

Rosalind Franklin was most certainly a woman in a man's world. The academy in post–World War II Britain was an old boys' club, and merely the provision of a women's restroom in the august buildings of King's College, London, was seen as an imposition. Wilkins, evidently expecting a more deferential attitude from his female colleague, clashed with Franklin repeatedly. She feared she was suffering discrimination not only because of her sex but because she was Jewish (Maddox 2002). And yet, with a single-minded sense of purpose, Franklin produced the X-ray photograph that finally led Watson and Crick to propose that the DNA molecule was in the shape of a double helix. Eventually in his book, Watson gives her the credit she was due, admitting, in a somewhat left-handed way, that he was wrong about her ("her past uncompromising statements . . . reflected first-rate science, not the outpourings of a misguided feminist" [1969:212]). He is downright gracious toward her in his Epilogue, but by this time the damage has been done, and the rest of the book was not rewritten in light of Watson's newfound appreciation for his colleague.

Doubtless the DNA puzzle would have been solved by another scientific team in short order, but Rosalind Franklin's work was key to its having been solved, when it was, by Watson, Crick, and Wilkins. Would she have received, along with them, the Nobel Prize for the Physiology of Medicine awarded in 1962? We will never know, because by that time Franklin was dead, her life cut short by ovarian cancer, and the Nobel Prize is seldom awarded posthumously.

Anne Sayre, who also knew Franklin, paints a very different portrait of her—funny, attractive, lively. And, recalled Sayre in her 1975 biography, Franklin did not even *wear* glasses.

Base pairs form the "rungs" of the DNA ladder, but in very limited combinations. Adenine is joined only to thymine, via two hydrogen bonds; cytosine is joined to guanine via three hydrogen bonds. However, down the side of the ladder the nitrogenous bases can occur in any order, and it is these bases that constitute genes. In other words, a gene consists of a sequence (not necessarily contiguous) of nitrogenous bases on a **strand** (i.e., one side of the ladder) of DNA (the entire helix is often referred to as **double-stranded**). The strand supporting the gene is called the **antisense strand**, while its "mirror image," so to speak, across the ladder is the **sense strand** (be forewarned there are other terms for the strands, some of them downright contradictory). However, the entire length of the strand is not necessarily antisense, because one gene can be situated on one strand of the DNA while the next is on the other.

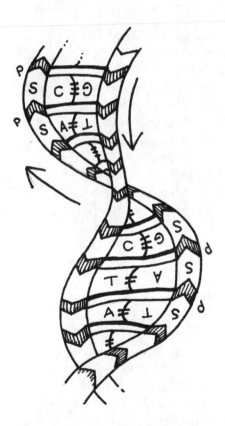

PORTION OF DNA MOLECULE
(S = SUGAR [deoxyribose];
    P = PHOSPHATE GROUP)

We can tell where genes begin and end not by how they appear but by what they do. **Coding genes** call for the manufacture of a protein or a portion of a protein. Like DNA, **proteins** are lengthy molecules made up of repeating components, in this case, **amino acids.** Coding genes are subdivided into **codons,** nitrogenous bases organized in sets of three. Each codon either corresponds to an amino acid, or stops protein synthesis. For example, ACC (adenine-cytosine-cytosine) is DNA code for the amino acid tryptophan. Since there are only 20 amino acids that can be involved in protein manufacture, but 64 possible combinations of the four bases in groups of three, there is redundancy in the DNA code; that is, one amino acid may have several corresponding codons (tryptophan is an exception; it has only the one).

Coding genes can be seen as blueprints for protein synthesis, and like blueprints, they are far too valuable to circulate. Just as an architect keeps the master plan for a project safely in her office and takes a copy to the work site, coding genes are copied and their instructions are sent outside the nucleus of the cell to the **ribosomes,** where proteins are assembled. How this happens is through the intervention of **ribonu-cleic acid,** or **RNA.** RNA is similar to DNA, except that it is single-stranded, with the "vertical" part of the strand involving a slightly different sugar; and another nitrogenous base, **uracil,** is used in place of thymine. These alterations enable RNA to be mobile. There are several different forms of RNA, one of them being **messenger RNA,** or **mRNA.** In order for mRNA to copy the DNA code, the hydrogen bonds that join the base pairs must be separated. Recall that the two DNA strands are similarly separated for the process of replication, but in this case only the relevant gene is exposed. The mRNA forms itself against the antisense strand, lifting off what is known as a **transcription** of the actual code. That is, mRNA duplicates the sense strand, not the antisense strand, except, of course, that in the mRNA uracil substitutes for thymine. The mRNA then migrates to the ribosomes, where the transcribed code is **translated** back into the original code (save, again, with uracil in place of thymine) by a type of RNA known as **transfer RNA (tRNA).** The nitrogenous bases of the tRNA bond with those of the mRNA, and the tRNA, which has the needed amino acid in tow, places this in the appropriate position within the developing protein, whose components are then linked together.

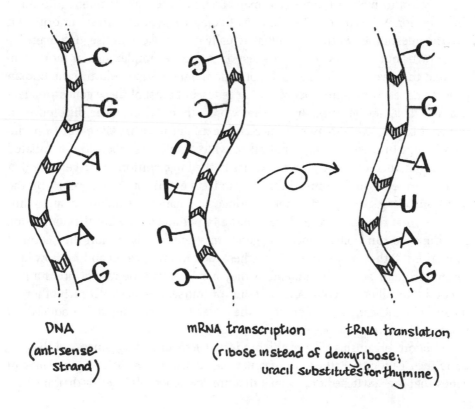

DNA
(antisense strand)

mRNA transcription
(ribose instead of deoxyribose; uracil substitutes for thymine)

tRNA translation

✴ The total genetic endowment of an organism or a species is referred to as its **genome.** A genome comprises coding genes, but there is also an extraordinary amount of noncoding material. Initially it was thought that this noncoding material was largely "junk" that had accrued in DNA over time, and that only the coding genes were relevant to understanding a species; in fact, the term "gene" was applied only to what we now specifically identify as a coding gene. Throughout the 1990s there was an extraordinary competition that took place between government-sponsored research institutions and a private company to decode the "entire" human genome (what was actually mapped was half the genome, since the other half featured the same genes, only in potentially different alleles). The naïve presumption behind such efforts was that the genome functioned in a straightforward fashion: one gene, one protein, one organism. But what emerged was shocking. Initial results indicated that in human beings there were only about 30,000 to 40,000 coding genes, roughly the same number as a mouse has (Lander et al. 2001. And in fact, the human number has been steadily revised downward ever since [see, e.g., Clamp et al. 2007], but let's continue to believe, for the moment, that human beings are as complex as mice). This was baffling to the scientific community, let alone the general public—how could it take as many genes to make a mouse as a man? Some of the astonishment informing this question issues from a Great-Chain-of-Being sense of human superiority, but still the question is worthwhile. What actually does make a mouse, or a man?

It turns out the answer to that question is at once simpler and far more complicated than we had suspected. Not only do the mouse genome and the human genome have a similar number of coding genes, but most of these genes are identical in what they accomplish. In other words, there is very little difference, in terms of coding genes, between mice and men. But mice *are* different from human beings in so many ways, not all of which can be ascribed to our inflated ideas about ourselves. The secret here lies in the huge portion of the genome that we used to see as junk. Some of this may in fact be junk, but there are within the mix **noncoding genes** that, despite the negative name (we should change this, because what they do is considerably more important than what they don't do), perform vital functions. Noncoding genes may completely inhibit the action of coding genes; they may serve as "switches," determining when and for how long certain proteins are produced; and/or they may regulate the rate of protein production (Carroll et al. 2008). And proteins, of course, interact with each other, so it can be significant with respect to the order in which they are produced, or whether they are manufactured simultaneously.

In short, organisms are not the product strictly of coding genes and the proteins they generate. Rather, an organism results from an intricate interplay of genes that are "switched on," genes that are "switched off," genes that are held back in their productive capacities, genes that are accelerated, and gene products (proteins) that have their own interplay. This is why mapping the human genome has not yet yielded the medical miracles promised, although certainly it may do so in the future (Wade 2010a). The point is, we know now what most of the genome looks like, but we are still hazy on what it does and how it does it.

These revelations about genetics ramify on evolutionary studies in two significant, and related, ways. Darwin was fascinated with the study of embryos, noting that in embryonic form vastly different species bear a resemblance to each other. He ascribed this resemblance to the common ancestry of all life forms on the planet (Darwin 2006[1859]). This sort of thinking came to be expressed in a pithy aphorism, "Ontogeny recapitulates phylogeny" (well, maybe it's only pithy to an evolutionary biologist), which, more simply put, suggests that the stages an embryo goes through in its development parallel the evolutionary stages its ancestors went through. But this is not quite what is going on. While it is true, for instance, that a human embryo has both gills and a tail, the gills are soon reworked into inner ear bones, and the tail is absorbed into the growing body. The reason these features appear is not because the embryo is reliving its evolutionary history (though indeed evolutionists agree with Darwin that if one goes back far enough, there is something fishlike in our ancestry, and for that matter in the ancestry of all land animals), but because there is DNA that is common to the genomes of all multicellular creatures. This baseline DNA lays the groundwork for living things, but then the sorts of interactions described in the preceding paragraph, which vary relative to the genome in operation, determine whether gills develop further as gills or become ear bones, or whether an organism *in utero* grows fins (true of most fish), limbs (true of most land animals), or does *not* grow limbs (true of snakes and, tragically, of human babies exposed to certain chemicals during gestation).

What has recently emerged to prominence from these observations is a branch of biology called **evo-devo,** or evolutionary development (see, e.g., Amundson 2005; Carroll 2005). The upshot of evo-devo thinking is that there is actually comparatively little *direct* genetic action that translates into differences between life forms, but a great deal of action of genes *on* genes, and gene products (i.e., proteins) on gene products, that through seemingly minor alterations in the timing and/or amount of protein manufacture can yield spectacular effects. It is as though the baseline DNA provides a lump of clay that is then pinched and pulled into a grand variety of shapes. There is evidently more "clay" in this process than anyone previously suspected. This is why a human being can share over 98% of her DNA with a chimpanzee and still be, indisputably, a different organism. The two genomes vary in small ways, but it is precisely *how* they vary, and the knock-on effect one genetic action can have, especially in the malleable stages of embryonic development, that distinguish the species. This further implies that the amount of time needed to bring about new species may be much less than we have thought. In the first place, the species, despite outward appearances, are not so different from one another; in the second place, what strikes us as radical change can be accomplished through a minimum of genetic alteration.

The second recent shift in evolutionary studies concerns the **epigenome,** a term that refers to the ways in which organisms are shaped by *nongenetic* factors. Some forms of RNA can produce the same genetic "switching-on" and "switching-off" effects described above, as can (as already mentioned) exposure to chemicals. This exposure can be direct—if your mother used particular types of drugs during her pregnancy, for example—or indirect, in that some environmental conditions, like drought or a dearth of nutrients, may induce the body's own production of chemicals that have a similar effect on gene action. There is even evidence now that experiences girl babies have in the womb, when their eggs (**ova**) are forming, and experiences boys have at puberty, when they are beginning to produce **sperm,** can turn genes on and off in these cells, thus affecting subsequent generations (e.g., Pembrey et al. 2006). These types of switches can become embedded in the genome and may be passed on through the inheritance process even though they are nongenetic. So after all this time, we may be able to give Lamarck credit for his oft-ridiculed idea—some acquired characteristics may possibly be heritable after all.

Investigation into evo-devo and the epigenome will doubtless continue to generate hypotheses that may survive the testing process to become theories. The point here is to acquaint you with genetic discoveries that will likely have a great impact on evolutionary studies. Stay alert! But for now, we can return to information that is better established regarding the comparatively straightforward mechanics of maintaining variation within species.

Making New Cells; Making New Organisms

Most of your cells divide to produce new cells—when you need to grow, when you need to heal, when cells themselves age. But this sort of simple cell division is actually a tricky process, since everything in the cell, including its DNA load, must be duplicated. The type of cell division producing the ova and sperm that of course potentially lead to entirely new organisms is trickier still. Before we discuss cell division, however, we need to understand more about how DNA is organized in the nucleus of a cell.

DNA does not exist as one long string in your cells—it is subdivided into **chromatids.** A chromatid is a stand-alone length of DNA, relatively loosely coiled, save for a highly compact midsection (roughly)—the **centromere**—and compact ends (the genetic material is in fact so tightly wound in these areas that it cannot be decoded using current methods). Ordinarily, human cell nuclei contain 46 chromatids, or more accurately, a set of 23 chromatids from each parent. Each chromatid in the set contains different genes, and geneticists have numbered the chromatids so that we can say, for instance, that the gene for A-B-O blood type is on Chromatid 9. The portion of the chromatid taken up by the gene is the gene's **locus** (pl. **loci**) within the genome. A gene's locus is consistent; that is, in the human genome the gene that determines your blood type is always, in everyone, in its designated place on Chromatid 9. While the 23 chromatids in one parental set are unique relative to each other, they have their counterparts, or **homologues,** in the other set. Homologous chromatids contain the same *genes*, but, of course, not necessarily the same *alleles*.

When a cell is preparing to divide (and much of a cell's life is taken up either by preparing to divide, or actually dividing), the chromatids undergo replication. The two identical chromatids thus produced are bound together at the centromeres with a little dab of protein glue, and just prior to cell division, both coil so tightly that the resulting structure—the X-shaped (generally) figure you know as a **chromosome**—is visible through a light microscope. In **mitosis,** or simple cell division, the 46 chromosomes line up in single file at the axis where one cell is separating into two. As

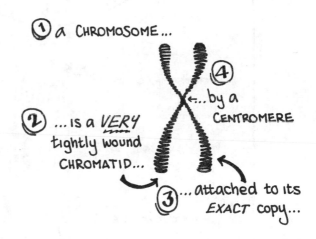

the cells begin to pull apart, the chromosomes are pulled apart as well, and each new cell receives a full complement of 46 chromatids, that is, 23 homologous pairs (see the YouTube video at http://www.youtube.com/watch?v=VlN7K1-9QB0).

Meiosis is a more complicated form of cell division that yields potential **gametes,** that is, ova and sperm. Only a very few specialized cells, located in the ovaries and testes of a sexually reproducing species—let's stick with the human example for the moment—undergo meiosis. Meiosis yields not two but eventually four daughter cells, each with 23 nonhomologous chromatids, that is, one set. In other words, the number of chromatids is *reduced* through meiosis, and hence the specialized cells must undertake two divisions. In advance of the first division, the chromatids replicate, and the resulting chromosomes line up at the axis of the split. In meiosis it is important, however, for the homologous chromosomes to form a *double line*, so that when the cell divides each resulting cell receives only one member of each homologous pair (an attraction between homologous chromosomes is facilitated by an enzyme).

Note that it is not that all the chromosomes received from one's mother migrate to one cell and all the chromosomes received from one's father migrate to the other; it only matters that each new cell has just one of each pair. This is the first randomizing element of meiosis, ensuring that gametes will have a mix of

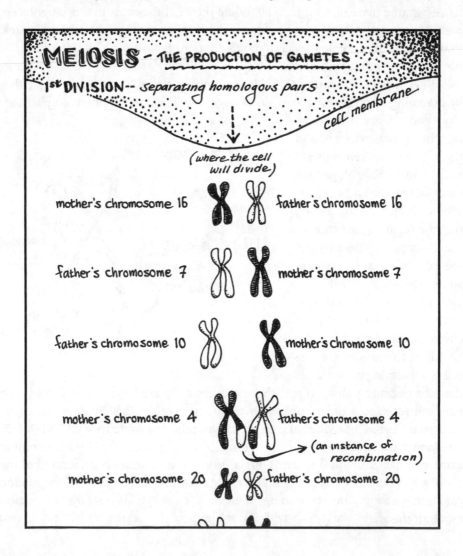

chromosomes from two parental sources. The second randomizing element is introduced when the homologues are arranged in their double line at the site of the impending cell split. The homologous chromosomes may swap genes, in a process called **recombination** or **crossing over.** The genes being traded are the *same* genes—that is, each chromosome comes apart at the same locus—but the alleles, of course, may be different. Hence while most of a chromosome may come from one parent, there may be a little bit of the other parent's chromosome incorporated as well—hanky-panky right down to the molecular level! (See the YouTube video at http://www.youtube.com/watch?v=D1_-mQS_FZ0.)

This first division produces two cells with 23 nonhomologous chromosomes apiece, but remember chromosomes are replicated chromatids. Since this genetic overload is the signal for mitosis to begin, the cells oblige—they divide again, salting the duplicated genetic material into two separate cells. So the four cells that result have 23 nonhomologous chromatids. This is, of course, only half the number of chromatids needed to make a human being, but the 23 chromatids will meet their homologues when a spermatozoon has fertilized an ovum, and a **zygote**—the earliest form of what may become an entirely new organism—comes into being.

There is a much-needed aside I must make at this point. In popular parlance, we usually use the word "chromosome" to identify both chromosomes and chromatids. This likely stems from the fact that it is as tightly wound chromosomes that science first became acquainted with the actual form of genetic material, since under ordinary circumstances (that is, when the cell is not about to divide), chromatids could not be seen using the equipment available at the time. Thus far, I have felt compelled to distinguish chromosomes from chromatids because it is important to realize that chromosomes actually contain double the genetic material of one cell. However, even scientists do not say, "The human genome consists of 46 chromatids"; rather, they refer to 46 chromosomes. So from here on I will do the same, unless there is some need to revisit the fact that chromosomes, as we generally envision them, are actually made up of two identical chromatids that do not, ultimately, end up in the same cell.

The description of meiosis shows how variation is maintained within a species. Genes may not have the form of particles, but they behave like particles, distributed among gametes so that offspring result that are in some ways like one parent, in some ways like the other, and in some ways like neither. In your case, genes make you human; alleles make you *you.* But there is one other important question to be answered here: we know that natural selection acts on variation that is maintained, through sexual reproduction, in a species, but where does the variation come from? We will address that question in the context of population genetics, because ultimately evolution is not a matter of *your* alleles; it is a matter of all the alleles available within your species.

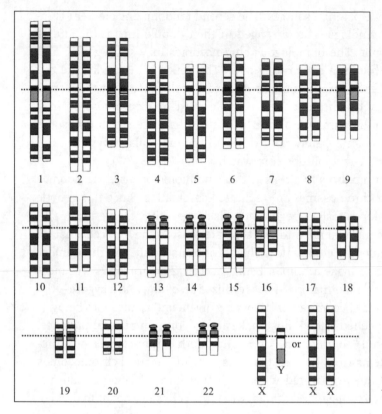

Schematic of human karyotype (chromatids arranged by number).

Population Genetics

A **species**, ideally, is a group of organisms that can breed successfully only within the group (in the next section we will discuss how this ideal is not necessarily met). Thus, genetic material is effectively enclosed within the group, and the species could, in theory, be taken as the most appropriate unit of study for the understanding of evolutionary dynamics. But the fact is that under natural circumstances, *all* alleles are unlikely to be available for mixing and matching within the breeding process. Species range over a territory and sometimes that territory can be very large, even involving different environments. Portions of the species may become somewhat isolated, given geographical and climatic impediments. The subterritories that are thus formed contain **populations,** groups within which individuals are likeliest to find mates. The word "likeliest" indicates that populations in nature are rarely absolute—their "boundaries" are fluid and permeable. Nonetheless, we can reasonably apply the term population to a cluster of organisms that breed within the cluster far more often than they breed outside.

In his experiments, Mendel established a bounded population of pea plants and controlled breeding within that population. Like any good scientist, he was eliminating variables that could skew results away from the purest conclusion. But, even given the number of plants involved and the cut-and-dried traits selected for investigation, Mendel's experiments did not yield perfect ratios. In fact, for the ratios to be perfect, the following conditions would have to pertain:

1. The population is infinitely large.

2. No new alleles can be introduced.

3. Mating is entirely random.

4. All individuals have equal reproductive success.

If these conditions are met, a population reproduces itself exactly, generation after generation, and the only thing you would have to know about genetics would be Mendelian laws—there would be no evolution. But clearly the conditions are impossible to meet, so why bother to propose them? There is a point to imagining ideal states in science—we establish a baseline from which reality noticeably deviates, and we can then zoom in on the deviations to try and understand how and why they occur. In this instance, there are four key processes—gene flow, mutation, genetic drift, and natural selection—that disrupt a population's tendency toward equilibrium. Before I discuss them, more basic concepts and jargon should be introduced.

SIDEBAR

Peas, Not Again!

The Hardy-Weinberg equilibrium is an algebraic statement meant to represent evolutionary stasis; that is, an ideal state in which no evolution occurs. The statement is represented thus:

$$p^2 + 2pq + q^2 = 1$$

Let's say we're investigating whether evolution is taking place at a locus where the gene comes in only two possible allele forms; p represent the frequency of the first allele ("frequency" referring to how frequently the allele occurs in a given population) and q represents the frequency of the

(continued)

second allele. If no evolution is taking place, p and q, whatever their proportions within a gene pool, will reproduce those proportions generation after generation.

We can demonstrate this by plugging Mendel's data into the equation. Recall that for each garden pea trait (height and seed color having been discussed in this book) Mendel selected, there were only two possible outcomes (hence two possible alleles). For our purposes here, let's stick with height—tallness (allele T) and shortness (allele t). After two interbred generations, Mendel achieves evolutionary stasis, with phenotypes occurring in a 3:1 ratio. The Punnett diagram of the second generation, you'll recall, looks like this:

	T	t
T	TT	Tt
t	Tt	tt

F_2

Note the parent organisms' alleles arrayed outside the square. Each parent has a T and a t that can be contributed to the daughter organism. If you have a gene pool with two Ts and two ts, your chance of drawing a T from the pool is one out of two, or 50% (decimally represented as 0.5). Your chance of drawing a *second* T is 25%; that is, 50% x 50%, or p^2. These are also the odds you play with respect to t; the probability that the daughter organism will have two t alleles is one out of four, or 25% (q^2). The Punnett square verifies this in that only one of the four offspring depicted is homozygous for T, and only one homozygous for t. Your chance of drawing a T and a t out of the pool is 50% each time; that is, $2pq$. So if we fill in these variables in the Hardy-Weinberg equilibrium, we proceed thus:

$$(0.5 \times 0.5) + (2 \times 0.5 \times 0.5) + (0.5 \times 0.5) = 1$$
$$0.25 + 0.5 + 0.25 = 1$$

There is thus no evolution at this locus, and from this point forward, so long as no change is introduced into this closed breeding system, the four Mendelian laws discussed in chapter 2 accurately represent what has happened to these garden peas and will accurately represent what will happen in the future. But of course this book is about evolution, so there is no rest for the weary student, who is likely still reeling from the complexity of stasis.

First, it must be stressed that the population, not the individual, is the primary unit of study for evolutionists. Populations are thus not thought of in terms of their individuals but in what those individuals can contribute to the aggregate of genetic possibilities, generally referred to as a **gene pool,** although it might be better to call it an allele pool. "Pool" in this instance is best thought of in terms of "pooling one's resources"; the gene pool is *not* a large body of liquid in which alleles are dissolved. Having said that, particular alleles can "pool," or concentrate, in population "basins," called **demes.** Demes, in other words, feature allele frequencies different from the population at large. If these differences are amplified, and begin to compromise the possibility of interbreeding between one deme and another, a new species may come about. In population genetics, however, **speciation** is not the be-all and end-all of evolution. Evolution is quite simply defined as a significant shift in allele frequencies over time, and a mere shift in frequencies may not result in a new species.

Gene Flow

So, returning to the task of understanding the key processes that disrupt a population's equilibrium, we can start with proposition #2: "No new alleles can be introduced." But in the real world, new alleles are introduced into populations all the time. One way to do this is simply through **gene flow,** or the movement of alleles from one population to another (again, this should probably be rendered "allele flow"). Recall that populations are unlikely to be completely isolated, and if there is proximity between populations, there is likely to be some mating. Alleles that enter via the perimeter of a population can slowly travel, through subsequent matings, to the center of the "basin," where they may proliferate. Alternatively, two populations may merge given the migration of one into the subterritory of the other, hence setting up the conditions for a great deal of gene flow. However, keep in mind that there does not have to be actual population movement for alleles themselves to "migrate" across population "boundaries."

Mutation

A far more dramatic way for new alleles to be introduced into a population is via **mutation,** brought about through change within genes, or disarrangements of chromosomes. Mutation gets a bad rap in the media, and the word "mutant" calls to mind people with arms growing out of their heads. However, as lock-and-key as the genetic processes I have described in this chapter seem, mutations happen all the time, and you—yes, the current reader of this book, YOU—are a mutant. Even as you read, some of your bodily, or **somatic,** cells are undergoing mitosis, and there has been an error—for example, a nitrogenous base has been knocked out of place, or a chromosome has failed to separate at the centromere and thus both chromatids have been drawn into the same cell. The cells thus affected will likely die, but this is of no account to you—you lose cells all the time. Some errors, like those that induce out-of-control production of your somatic cells (i.e., cancer), *are* of consequence to you as a whole organism but have minimal effect on the gene pool, save that you may not be able to contribute to it in the event of your early death. However, when mutations take place in the specialized cells that produce potential gametes, or when mutations take place in the gametes themselves, such events may certainly have an evolutionary impact.

EXERCiSE

Look into possible sources for kicking up the rate of mutation.

Most of the time they will not. If a **point mutation,** a change that swaps out or eliminates one nitrogenous base, takes place, it may have no effect whatsoever—recall that several different codons may call for the same amino acid, so one codon might seamlessly substitute for another. Or it could be that the displacement of one nitrogenous base does alter protein manufacture, but not to the extent that anything vital is affected. More serious changes in DNA, like **frame shift mutations,** which happen when a nitrogenous base goes missing from one strand and the bases from the opposite strand find whatever counterpart is available further down the line, rather like a zipper skipping teeth, may easily result in a gamete or zygote that is not viable. On the level of the chromosome, meiotic accidents may salt genetic material unevenly—one gamete may receive three copies of a chromosome, the other only one. These mutations too may never be in evidence; even if the gamete is able to participate in fertilization, the resulting zygote may not live.

On the other hand, we are well familiar with chromosomal imbalances that do produce viable offspring—Down syndrome, for instance, results from a "triple dose" of Chromosome 21—but mental, physical, and/or social disabilities, fairly or not, may prevent such individuals from surviving to maturity and/or having offspring of their own. It should be mentioned here that mutations are not entirely random. There are specific weaknesses in the processes of DNA replication and chromosomal distribution that increase the likelihood of certain mutations; physiological and/or environmental factors can exacerbate such weaknesses.

So there are viable offspring that bear mutations, and if these offspring grow to adulthood and reproduce successfully, the mutation may become fixed in a population. All variations within a population began as mutations at some point. A mutated trait caused by a dominant allele may not have any adaptive value (for the moment—things could change), but so long as it does not inhibit survival and/or reproduction it will not be bred out of a population save by chance.

Before we move on from the issue of the creation of new alleles, it should be noted that there are means to do this that are even more remarkable than mutation. Genetic sequences introduced by retroviruses (Belshaw et al. 2004) or parasites (Gilbert et al. 2010) can at the very least add useless clutter to a gene, but in some cases this clutter takes on active genetic properties. There are even naturally occurring instances when genetic material from one species is spliced into the genome of another (Moran and Jarvik 2010). Generally, none of these possible sources of new alleles is accounted for when evolutionary processes are discussed. It is true that such events are likely rare relative to the occurrence of mutations, but as more findings of this sort are made, our understanding of the genome—how it is constructed and how it might change—may have to undergo considerable adjustment.

Genetic Drift

Proposition #4, above, states that in a population that is absolutely stable, "all individuals will have equal reproductive success." That success should include the realization of all genetic possibilities from the breeding process—for example, if two heterozygous garden peas are bred, the offspring, which will number four or a multiple of four, will always conform precisely to the probabilities predicted by the Punnett square. Of course this will not happen, but in a large population any possibilities left unrealized (or too abundantly realized) by one breeding pair may be compensated for by another—one woman may bear four daughters, for instance, but another may bear four sons. The problem is that populations are certainly not infinitely large, to hark back to Proposition #1. They are seldom even large enough to compensate fully for all the ways genetic odds might be beaten. Hence allele frequencies in the gene pools of real-life populations can be greatly affected by an evolutionary process known as **genetic drift.**

The word "drift" calls to mind a slow, uncontrolled movement off-course, and this is exactly what happens to the frequencies of alleles in a gene pool. In a small population, such movement can bring about noticeable change in a relatively short time. Populations may begin as small units, or they may lose members through a natural disaster, or through fission—the hiving-off of small subpopulations from larger ones. In these subpopulations, not only is the gene pool smaller overall, but merely by chance it may contain a higher proportion of certain alleles than would have been present in the large population. This slight skew may be widened by the breeding process, as alleles that might seldom find expression in a large population have more chances to be paired with a counterpart that allows for their expression in a small population.

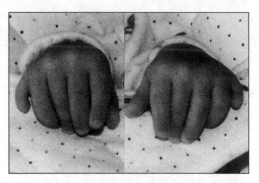

People with Ellis-van Creveld syndrome are often polydactyl; that is, they have extra fingers.

Human beings, of course, have been no less prone than other animals to spin off subpopulations, and we have witnessed several examples of **founder effect.** For instance, the Pennsylvania Amish established their colony with the help of one couple that perpetuated an allele for Ellis-van Creveld syndrome, a form of dwarfism (McKusick 2000). Thereafter, more dwarves were born within this population than would otherwise be expected (it should be noted that this was still not a terribly large number). Founder effect, in short, is an extreme and noticeable form of genetic drift, but drift can also work more slowly and subtly to equally well-marked end effects. It should be noted that by definition, genetic drift makes no judgments as to what survives: undesirable as well as desirable alleles can be brought out by the process. It is also the case that an allele present in a large population may be totally eliminated, through drift, in a small population, either because its founders just happened not to carry the allele or because so few of them had it that it was not able to find its mate via breeding.

EXERCiSE

Discuss biological and cultural human behaviors that set up conditions for drift.

NATURAL SELECTION

Genetic drift may make no judgments, but it does yield results that must run the gantlet of **natural selection.** The same, in fact, is true of mutation and gene flow. How do new alleles, and new allele frequencies, fare within the environmental conditions at hand? Do organisms that have new alleles survive and reproduce more successfully than their fellows, thus spreading those alleles into subsequent generations? Does a population whose allele frequencies have been altered by drift thrive and proliferate? Whether selection is actually taking place may not be obvious for some time, since in any generation there will be those individuals that survive and breed successfully simply (or at least as simply as anything can get when considering evolution) as a matter of luck; survival is a matter of statistical probability, and there are always those that beat the odds against them. For all that, the odds may be fairly beatable—just because one organism has a genetic "edge" does not mean that several others, put together in genetically different ways, will not survive. It is also the case that organisms are composites of alleles, and a new allele may "piggyback" on the success of other alleles without conferring any real advantage in and of itself. Even so, if over time, a particular allele, embedded in a variety of genetic combinations, increases significantly within a gene pool, we have to consider the possibility that the reason comes down to natural selection.

These reasons can be convoluted. Scientists have long suspected that dangerous mutations may be retained within a gene pool because the population as a whole faces a greater threat—disease, for instance—that the mutation parries in some way. The example usually cited in textbooks like this is the **sickle-cell allele,** which in homozygotes causes a frequently lethal deformation (sickling) of human red blood cells. Such cells die quickly and cannot carry the requisite load of oxygen the body needs. This problem increases the likelihood that afflicted individuals will not live long enough to reproduce; thus, their ability to transmit the allele into the next generation is compromised. So who is doing so? It has been thought that heterozygotes, individuals with one allele for sickling and one for normal blood cells, have a greater resistance to malaria than homozygotes for normal blood. The two alleles interact in a manner described as **incomplete**

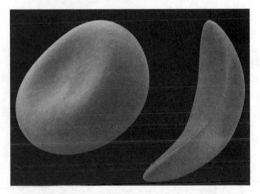

Comparison of normal red blood cell and sickled cell.

dominance; in response to infection by the malarial parasite, the heterozygote's blood supply, functionally adequate under most circumstances, develops just enough sickling to set up inhospitable conditions for the parasite. Ironically, then, heterozygotes may be healthier in a malarial environment than individuals who are homozygous for normal blood, and healthier individuals are likely to have greater reproductive success. Hence the sickle-cell allele would be maintained at a certain level within the gene pool because of the advantage that accrues to the heterozygote.

I must add here that malaria has been a severe enough threat to humankind to have favored the retention of all sorts of makeshift genetic equipment to counteract it, and the extent to which this one mechanism conveys resistance would seem, at the very least, to be limited (see McCombie 2009). The basic principle, however, remains: that natural selection is taking place may not be clear at first glance. To understand why allele frequencies change, the entire environmental context must be taken into account.

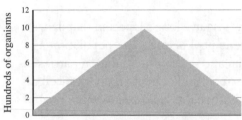

Stabilizing Natural Selection: Selection for Norm

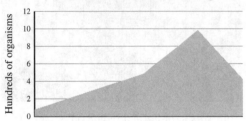

Directional Natural Selection: Selection for One End of Range

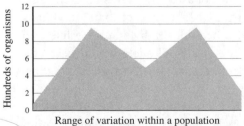

Disruptive Natural Selection: Selection for Both Ends of Range

The three types of natural selection.

In all species there is a range of variations, and even when this range remains relatively constant, it can be said that natural selection is still at work, reinforcing the species norms. This is referred to as **stabilizing natural selection.** Natural selection can be seen as **directional** when an allele, made evident by its associated trait, steadily increases in frequency, indicating that it provides some sort of benefit within a changing environment. Thus, the range of variation with respect to that trait is tugged toward one extreme or the other, and eventually the norm would be reset. **Disruptive natural selection** results when the environment is altered in such a way as to favor *both* extremes of the normal range. With *two* new norms being established, conditions would be ripe for rapid speciation.

So all of these evolutionary processes work in collusion to prevent populations from achieving equilibrium. Mutation contributes entirely new alleles and chromosomal patterns; gene flow transfers alleles from one population to another; genetic drift, entirely by chance, brings some alleles to the fore while eliminating others; and all of this activity is sorted through the guiding principle of natural selection: "That which survives."

At one time there was a lively debate among scientists as to which of these processes had had the most impact on evolution, but today it seems clear they all play a role, though in particular circumstances one may be especially key. Certainly the introduction of new alleles into a gene pool provides that much more raw material on which natural selection can operate. If a large population, because of environmental change that closes down old **niches** and/or opens new ones, fragments into several small populations, each small population is like a laboratory where unique allele frequencies are tried out against a fresh environmental backdrop. Speciation might take place very rapidly in these situations. The occurrence of such bursts of evolutionary activity, known as **punctuated equilibrium** (Eldredge and Gould 1972), is difficult to support directly; rather, it is the *absence* of evidence, that is, an unbroken line of fossils within which speciation has occurred, which initially suggested evolution may occasionally proceed at this accelerated rate. However, Darwin's impression that speciation could be a matter of gradual change within a line remains valid, sparse fossil evidence notwithstanding. As the peppered moth example illustrates, we have in fact witnessed in modern times alteration to the environment driving significant shifts in allele frequencies, and such instances give us a model to understand how directional frequency shift could yield a different species over time.

SUMMARY OF KEY EVOLUTIONARY PROCESSES

- **Gene flow:** Transfers alleles from one gene pool to another
- **Mutation:** May introduce entirely new alleles into a gene pool
- **Genetic drift:** Occurs when chance events alter allele frequencies
- **Natural selection:** Subjects all of the above to the test of fitness—
  do these changes detract from or enhance survival and reproductive success?

Updating Terms and Concepts

Alan Swedlund once referred to the Human Genome Diversity Project as "21st-century technology applied to 19th-century biology" (cited in Armelagos and Van Gerven 2003:60). While much credit is due the pioneers whose research led to modern science, there is no question that the conceptual equipment they developed may no longer be helpful in light of more recent discoveries. We have already seen how the term "chromosome" substitutes for "chromatid," even in scientific writing, and paints a somewhat inaccurate picture of the makeup of genetic material. We are only now modifying our understanding of the term "gene" to include noncoding DNA. Nonetheless, "chromosome" and "gene" have become conventional ways of referring to reality, and to some extent this is not merely linguistic convenience—we actually *see* reality through these forms. The claim has been made that European languages are exceptionally thing-oriented (Whorf 1941), converting continuous phenomena (like DNA) into seemingly concrete, regularized objects (like genes). Since we cannot rework the English language, we should at least bear in mind that its "thing" orientation is imperfect and sometimes downright misleading. Nonetheless, we often lapse into the comforting sense that our language accurately reflects reality; we may even engage in debate on the level of terminology, and not what it purports to represent.

Take the concept of "species." As previously indicated, a species is a group of organisms that can only breed successfully within the group. Species are thus seen as neatly bounded units, stackable into genera. But is reality nearly so neat? Taxonomists have named several species of savanna baboon, based on their appearance and range, but these alleged species can and do interbreed (Jolly 1993). Dogs are all one species, yet to mate a male St. Bernard with a female teacup Chihuahua would be quite a feat for both animals, not to mention ominous for the poor Chihuahua were she actually to conceive. Then there is that word, "successfully." You are likely aware that the offspring of a female horse and a male donkey is a mule, whose sterility bears out the fact that its parents come from separate species. But female mules are not always sterile. So how do these animals manage to overcome their alleged genetic deficiencies? Truthfully, we do not yet know.

Traditionally, taxonomic systems have been organized via the principle of **homology,** similarities between groups of organisms that testify to a common ancestry. The idea was to avoid being fooled by **analogies,** which are similarities that come about in two descent lines well *after* they have split from a common ancestor (this is also known as **convergent evolution**). But given the contention held by evolutionists that all life on the planet harks back to one origin, homology is a matter of *degree;* that is, there is always a common ancestor to be found if we go back in time far enough. We can chop up this continuum of life into species, and sort these species into generic boxes, which are then sorted into higher-level classifications, but we are treating something that developed organically as a mechanical entity with clear dividing lines between components. It is not as though there is no value to doing so, but we should always keep in mind that taxonomic systems are artificial, and the Linnaean system especially so, given that it was initially organized by a man who believed in the fixity of species. That legacy continues to haunt us, in more than one way.

Science is a quest for universal laws, which lend themselves to reliably pre-
dictive models. It is understandable that the scientist wants things clear-cut,
even to the point of fudging experimental ratios, or conceptually hacking DNA
into genes and descent lines into species, genera, orders, and classes. I have
abided by these traditions and will continue to do so—they simplify many tasks,
including teaching—but as we move on, it may be worthwhile for the wise
reader to keep a thought in the back of her mind: what appear to be well-defined
boundaries between genes, organisms, and species may actually be, at the very
least, a little fuzzy.

QUESTIONS FOR DISCUSSION AND REVIEW

- Answer the question, "What is a gene?" in terms of both structure and function.
- Describe how DNA is transcribed into mRNA and then translated into tRNA.
- How have evo-devo and knowledge of the epigenome altered our thinking
  about evolution?
- Describe how meiosis in humans reduces the number of chromatids in a
  daughter cell to 23.
- Discuss how each evolutionary process interferes with a population's tendency
  toward equilibrium.

KEY WORDS

(Sure, there are a lot of them, but this is literally the meaning of life!)

Punnett square	adenine	codon
homozygous	thymine	RNA
heterozygous	cytosine	uracil
gene	guanine	mRNA
allele	base pair	transcription
genotype	double helix	translation
phenotype	replication	tRNA
codominant	strand	genome
polygenic	double-stranded	noncoding gene
DNA	antisense strand	evo-devo
nucleus	sense strand	epigenome
nucleotide	coding gene	chromatid
nitrogenous base	amino acid	chromosome

centromere   gene pool   directional natural selection
locus   deme   disruptive natural selection
homologue   speciation   sickle-cell allele
mitosis   gene flow   incomplete dominance
meiosis   mutation   punctuated equilibrium
gamete   genetic drift   homology
recombination   founder effect   analogy
zygote   stabilizing natural convergent evolution
population   selection

4

MAMMALS, PRIMATES, US

There is grandeur in this view of life . . .
whilst this planet has gone cycling on according to
the fixed law of gravity, from so simple a beginning
endless forms most beautiful and most wonderful
have been, and are being, evolved.

—Charles Darwin, *On the Origin of Species*

Mammals, Primates . . .

You likely already know that human beings are **mammals**—in Linnaean terms, humans are members of the class *Mammalia*. The class was named after the fact that its members have mammary glands, sweat glands adapted to exude milk. Mammals are also characterized by their body covering—generally fur, or hair, although in some mammalian lines this substance has become further modified into, for example, the porcupine's quills or the armadillo's shell. Hair, and sweat glands proper, help mammals maintain a constant body temperature regardless of environmental conditions, a property known as **endothermy.** Biologically, this property can be achieved by other means; birds have it, for instance, even though they followed a different evolutionary path from mammals. This is, of course, one more cautionary tale against taking what are actually superficial similari-

GELADAS

87

ties as an indication of recent common ancestry, and/or as a measure of a similar level of "advancement." (**Ectotherms,** creatures, like modern reptiles, whose body temperature is determined by external conditions, continue to survive in this world and actually have advantages in food-poor environments.)

Mammals have other traits in common. There are aspects of dental and skeletal morphology that serve to distinguish mammals from other classes of four-limbed **vertebrates;** these can also help us to identify ancient mammals so long as the right features were fossilized. Another oft-mentioned characteristic of mammals is that they bear live young, as opposed to laying eggs, but here we run into trouble—the duck-billed platypus, for instance, is a mammal that lays eggs. Clearly it helps to know something about evolutionary relationships to determine why a platypus is thought to be a mammal even though it has reptilian and seemingly bird-like attributes.

Evolutionary relationships are, of course, located in time as well as space, and obviously it would be good to learn, for instance, just when one species line diverged from another. It is possible nowadays, by measuring genetic divergence between two lines, to estimate the temporal point of divergence, but these estimates generally go back quite a bit further than the fossil evidence. This is not unexpected, given that the initial population of a new species would likely be small and fossils therefore rare; nonetheless, it certainly could be that the means we currently use to measure genetic divergence (a subject I will treat in greater depth in chapter 7) produce estimates that are too generous. To err on the side of caution, then, I tend in the section below to rely on fossil evidence where available, but if you consult other sources, you will likely encounter far older dates for at least some of the events I identify below.

I should also mention, before we embark on a very long trip back through time, that I will be making reference to the **Geologic Time Scale,** or at least one version of it. Just as Linnaeus tried to classify life, the Geologic Time Scale is an attempt to classify time, dividing Earth's history into eons that are further subdivided and subdivided again. A momentous geological event, like an environmental transformation or a shift in climate, marks where one interval ends and the next begins. For our purposes, it is not necessary to know that much about the Geologic Time Scale—I will bring in the divisions and subdivisions as needed—but you should be forewarned that with respect to how time is classified and when events occurred, this, too, is an area where scientists are not necessarily in agreement. Thus, again, you may find that what you read below varies somewhat from what you may see in other sources.

According to our best guess of the moment, it was during the late Paleozoic **era,** Carboniferous **period**—specifically the Pennsylvanian subperiod, extending from 320 to 295 **mya**—when the evolutionary line (*Synapsida*) eventually yielding mammals split from the line (*Sauropsida*) that would eventually produce such creatures as crocodiles, dinosaurs, and birds (Kemp 2005). The common ancestor to all of these animals might strike us today as somewhat reptilian, but keep in mind that reptiles as we know them today also did not yet exist. Subsequent synapsid lines were greatly reduced by the late **Permian** extinction; however, one surviving line eventually led to the morphological modifications we now associate with mammalian status. Most sources place the emergence of mammals proper (as opposed to mammal-like reptiles) in the late **Triassic** pe-

ERA	PERIOD	SUBPERIOD
CENOZOIC 65 mya to present	Quaternary 2 mya–present	
	Neogene 23.5–2 mya	
	Paleogene 65–23.5 mya	
MESOZOIC 250–65 mya	Cretaceous 135–65 mya	
	Jurassic 203–135 mya	
	Triassic 205–203 mya	
PALEOZOIC 540–250 mya	Permian 295–250 mya	
	Carboniferous 355–295 mya	Pennsylvanian 320–295 mya

Excerpt from the geologic time scale.
(Divisions do not reflect actual duration.)

riod of the **Mesozoic** era, the so-called Age of Dinosaurs. Today, there are three main groups of mammals: **monotremes,** or egg-laying mammals; **marsupials,** mammals that bear live young at a very early stage of development, and **placental mammals,** which bear live young at a more advanced stage. It was once presumed that these three groups must have evolved in the order listed, since both the monotreme and marsupial methods of reproduction seemed "primitive" to us, but this is a value judgment that could be leading us astray. For the moment, although alternatives have been mooted, the possibility that the ancestors of these modern groups went their separate ways at roughly the same time, from a single stem line in existence during the early **Cretaceous** period, cannot be dismissed.

The three methods of mammalian reproduction represent three different solutions to an intractable problem for sexually reproducing species, though, as is so often the case, each solution creates further problems. An embryo, as the synthesis of two distinct genomes, is essentially a foreign object to which the mother's immune system quite correctly reacts defensively. A creature that lays eggs (hard- or soft-shelled) literally walls itself off from its young, but then the egg has to be a self-contained unit, with everything offspring need to develop until hatching. Once laid, eggs must also be tended, introducing the risk that they might be lost to predators or simply to accidents. Marsupials expel their young early, relocating them from uterus to external pouch, but this can be an arduous transition, laced with peril. Placental mammals are named after the **placenta,** a mass of tissue that regulates traffic between mother and developing offspring (Lillegraven 1975). The placenta in placental mammals is present throughout the relatively long gestation period. It is selectively rather than generally permeable, allowing for nutrients to reach offspring while waste passes in the other direction. Since offspring are thus shielded from the mother's immune system, they can be sheltered inside the mother for a significant portion of their development and are born at a point when they are more ready to handle life on the outside (as noted in the first chapter, humans sacrifice some of this advantage for big heads). This system, as well, is not perfect—there *are* occasions when mother attacks offspring, and the immune systems of *in utero* offspring can threaten the mother— but there is evidently sufficient advantage to bearing more mature offspring to have given placental mammals the survival edge over other mammals in most environments. The vast majority of mammals today are placental mammals.

Scientists who study ancient life forms are known as **paleontologists.** Because life has occurred in a great variety of forms, paleontologists often specialize in the study of particular plants or animals. For instance, paleontologists with a specific interest in primate origins and development would be **paleoprimatologists.** Human beings are primates, but we can apply the term **paleoanthropologist** to those scientists who study our ancestors no further back than the split between the human and chimpanzee lines. Insofar as we do not yet know precisely when that was, however, there is bound to be some overlap between the two specialties.

Just when the first primates appeared is also a matter of some debate. Of four **superorders** of mammals, primates are grouped with rodents (this explains why you really *are* very like a mouse) but the two lines are thought to have diverged shortly after the appearance of mammals generally, with molecular changes building up well before fossils show evidence of the split. If one accepts **plesiadapiforms** as primates, then primates emerge early on relative to other mammal groups, at the cusp of the changeover from the Mesozoic to the **Cenozoic** era (around 65 mya). However, plesiadapiforms have recently fallen out of favor as **stem** primates, and though they continue to have supporters who may be able to have them reinstated in years to come, it is perhaps safer to identify somewhat later fossils as more securely primate.

Common Primate Characteristics

But what *are* primates? Taxonomically speaking, primates constitute an **order** of the class *Mammalia* (the Linnaean name for the order is also *Primates,* but it is pronounced "pry-MAY-teez," in Anglicized Latin). Before I list modern primate traits, I must stress that the order *Primates* is vast, and over millions of years primates have established themselves in different types of environments. Hence, with respect to much of what I write below, there are exceptions, sometimes a good many of them. When we run through the finer points of primate taxonomy in the next section, I will identify some of the exceptions, but for now, simply keep in mind that by definition, generalizations, for all their usefulness, mislead us into imagining absolute uniformity.

The basic primate form is **primitive,** which in this case means that primates retain a number of traits, little modified, from their pre-primate ancestors. In evolutionary terms, primitivity is not at all a bad thing—basic forms are obviously successful forms, having withstood the test of time, and evolution reinforces success through the stabilizing kind of natural selection. Ironically, primitivity also lends itself to ease of specialization should this be adaptive in a particular environmental context. To return to the metaphor cited in the previous chapter, primitivity is like an unworked lump of clay. If a body form has not already changed much in any one direction, it can potentially change in all of them. However, primates *have* undertaken a number of changes in common, or nearly so, and thus we can helpfully draw together a list of primate **derived** traits, ways in which primates do in fact differ from their ancestors, and from other orders of mammals. These **shared derived** characteristics help us to classify primates in general, and classify the different relationships between primates within the order.

Relative to most other mammals, primates have a higher proportion of brain to body, and primate brains are also more complex in their organization. This brain matter likely evolved in concert with visual equipment—the primate eye–brain interface is quite intricate. Primates have forward-facing eyes, unlike the eyes of, for instance, a horse; hence the primate brain always has two visual images, each set off slightly from the other, to interpret. The images are woven together across the hemispheric midline of the brain, an arrangement known as **stereoscopy.** In this way the primate sees what appears to be one image through both of its eyes, but importantly, given the two converging lines of sight, the image is three-dimensional, allowing the primate to gauge distance accurately. Primates also have a small pit at the back of the eye, the *fovea centralis,* which helps them to focus on faraway objects. If you have ever snapped a picture of something you thought was eminently noticeable, only to find that in the resulting photo you could barely see what it was that had interested you, blame the *fovea centralis.* It fools you into assigning more prominence to a point within a landscape than it actually has, but, of course, this illusion can be very useful if you need to spot a predator or the next tree branch. One last point to make about sight is that many primates have color vision, though this may not approach the spectral range of the human eye. Color vision is a quality primates share with other classes of animals, like insects and birds, but not with fellow mammals, whose ability to see color is exceedingly limited. This is yet another example of convergent evolution.

Primate brain matter is also directed toward connecting what the eyes see with what the hand does. Primate appendages are primitive in that they end in **digits,** a feature held in common with many rodents and even some reptiles and amphibians. In contrast, a number of mammals have appendages that are significantly derived relative to the original plan, ending in paws and even in hooves. But the primate grip is certainly derived. Primate hands (and often feet) are **prehensile,** meaning that they can grasp objects firmly. In most primates, this grip is enhanced by the presence of a thumb that has some degree of **opposability** against the other fingers. One frequently hears of the opposable thumb as the measure of the human place above the animals, but once again we need to get over ourselves—we are hardly the only primates with opposable thumbs. That having been said, there is something further derived about the human grip. The fact that we can oppose each finger in turn to the thumb imparts a precision that even a close relative like the chimpanzee cannot hope to match. A final note about primate appendages: many primates also receive a good deal of tactile information through the tips of their digits; hence what is a claw in other mammals is often modified in primates to fingernails and toenails.

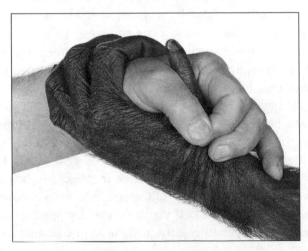

Comparison of primate hands.

Since so much of the primate brain is dedicated to vision and the dexterous operation of appendages, it stands to reason that less of it supports the senses of hearing and smell, which tend to be far more developed in other mammals. But it is not as though these senses were simply crowded out; the primate line, by and large, was not negatively affected by the weakening of hearing and smell. Today's primate sprang from **arboreal** stock, and even though there are several primate species nowadays that do not live in trees, our bodies remain marked by this ancestry. Vision and grip are regularly applied within the primate order to swift, sure movement in the trees, although the type of **locomotion** is hardly uniform. A number of primates species maintain something like the classic mammalian **quadrupedal** posture while moving from branch to branch, using all four limbs, roughly equally, to negotiate a path. A much smaller number has the ability to **brachiate**, that is, swing from branch to branch using only the arms. Human beings do not regularly move in this way—we rely primarily on our capacity to walk **bipedally**— but the fact that as a child you likely dangled from a jungle gym indicates that your ancestors were, at least to some extent, brachiators. You have a great range of movement in your arms that is facilitated by ball-and-socket shoulder joints and steadied by a collarbone. A human being can throw her arms open wide, but if you were to try and force your dog or cat to adopt the same position, you would quite rightly be arrested for cruelty to animals; that is, if the pet didn't teach you a lesson first.

Many primates have a food preference, but few are so attached to a particular food that they will not vary their diets. The generalized dentition recurrent within the primate line testifies to this capacity to be **omnivorous.** Primate gut arrangements are equally flexible. Clearly humans are champion omnivores, able to survive on vegetarian diets; on diets, like that of Arctic peoples, consisting mainly of meat; and even on diets that involve little more than ramen noodles and Red Bull. But as ill-advised as that last example might be, a good many of our primate cousins could manage on those foods as well.

To conclude this less-than-exhaustive list of primate traits, it is worth mentioning that primates seldom bear many offspring at a time—one is the norm— and over a lifetime they are not especially fecund when compared to their very distant cousins, the rodents. Rather than producing a number of offspring that get comparatively little parental care, primates produce few offspring to which they dedicate abundant parental care, over a considerable period of time. These are alternative means to the same end—enough surviving offspring to produce yet another generation—but there are certainly environmental circumstances that place species with low reproductive and maturation rates at something of a disadvantage. The large primate brain, with its enhanced potential for problem solving, may provide a counterweight to this disadvantage; even so, the brain requires a great deal of nurturing, both within and outside of the womb, to reach its full capacity.

The Human Place in the Primate Order

At this point we will situate human beings, and their ancestors, among the primates by wending our way through the intricacies of the Linnaean taxonomic system, modified again and again by our increasing knowledge of genetics. As previously noted, to some extent this knowledge is revising Linnaean taxonomy, but it is also the case that our continued adherence to the Linnaean system, even highly modified, interferes with our ability to allow new discoveries to work the conceptual revolution of which they might be capable. For the moment, however, it remains helpful within the science of biology to identify taxa, and to organize them using familiar Linnaean designations. **Taxa** (*sing.* **taxon**) are groups (e.g., species, genera, etc.) of related organisms; such groups taken altogether, along with all of their antecedents going back to the common ancestor of their kind, constitute **clades.** In theory, members of taxa and clades are more related to each other than they are to members of other taxa and clades. Of course, "more" is a slippery word, and even if it is quantified, in terms of, say, number of genetic changes, what we are now learning about the epigenome cautions us against presuming that mere amounts of change translate absolutely into taxonomic barriers. Keep in mind as well that the scheme of classification I follow below may not conform to other schemes you may see. There is certainly ongoing disagreement regarding primate taxonomy, resulting in several schemes existing at any one time; furthermore, opinion changes so rapidly that even on the ever-changing World Wide Web, with its capacity for instantaneous revision, outmoded and/or minority versions of taxonomy linger.

The taxonomic order *Primates* is divided into two **suborders,** but what these are called is a matter of conflicting views. On some taxonomic charts the suborders are listed as *Prosimii* and *Anthropoidea*, while other charts identify the suborders as *Strepsirhini* and *Haplorhini*. The sticking point is the **tarsier,** a small primate that looks to have been the model for the alien life forms you might see in the movies. Tarsiers were initially classified with

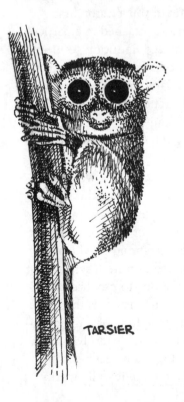

TARSIER

ORDER	SUBORDER	INFRAORDER	PARVORDER	SUPERFAMILY	FAMILY	SUBFAMILY	TRIBE	GENUS	SPECIES
Primates	Haplorhini	Simiiformes [monkeys]	Catarrhini [Old World monkeys]	Hominoidea [apes]	Hominidae [humans and African apes]	Homininae [humans, bonobos, and chimps]	Hominini [humans]	Homo	sapiens
							Panini [bonobos and chimps]		
						Gorillinae [gorillas]			
					Pongidae [orangutans]				
					Hylobatidae [e.g., gibbon]				
				Cercopithecoidea [e.g., baboon]					
			Platyrrhini [New World monkeys]						
		Tarsiiformes [tarsiers]							
	Strepsirhini [e.g., lemur]								

Human beings in Linnaean terms.

the prosimians, but this has been reconsidered. Today, many taxonomists see them as more closely allied with monkeys (e.g., Kay et al. 1997; Martin 1993). The suborders change relative to where the tarsier is placed. I will support the view that the tarsier is more like a monkey, and hence included, along with the monkeys, in the suborder *Haplorhini*. According to this view, then, the strepsirhines—creatures like **lemurs** and **lorises**—occupy the other suborder.

RING-TAILED LEMUR

Lemurs, which occur in several distinct species, live only on the island of Madagascar and some of the islands nearby. Because they are thought to have split away from their fellow primates early on, lemurs do not share some of the typical primate traits listed above. For instance, the lemur nose tends to be doglike, not only in appearance but also in its ability to pick up scents; in addition, lemurs are thought to have very limited color vision. Lemurs today are very much threatened by human encroachment on their habitat, but until relatively recently they enjoyed great success in their isolated land. We can only guess why they failed to thrive on the continents. Perhaps it was because, unlike their cousins the lorises, lemurs tended to be **diurnal;** that is, primarily active during the day. Lorises are **nocturnal,** and their range extends through South and Southeast Asia; there are also numerous close relatives of the loris in a large swath of central Africa. Time transforms what is spatially the same environment; during the day, an organism can access foods and face predators and competitors that are different from those present in the nighttime environment. Lemurs evidently were outcompeted on the mainland, but fortunately Madagascar became their stronghold. Today, while a few species of lemur are nocturnal, and some diurnal, quite a number confound their enemies and rivals through pursuing a **cathemeral** existence, with activity and quiescence alternating throughout a 24-hour period.

There are many fascinating aspects to the strepsirhines—for example, females are dominant over males in several species of lemur (e.g., A. Jolly 1999), and one type of loris exudes a toxin that it can use to venomize its bite (Wilde 1972)—but because, as primates go, strepsirhines are only distantly related to humans, we will not have much more to say about them in this textbook.

The suborder *Haplorhini* is divided into two **infraorders,** one for tarsiers and the other for monkeys. The monkey infraorder (*Simiiformes*) is further divided into two **parvorders.** Parvorder *Platyrrhini* comprises all of the monkeys of the **New World** (the Americas). It would make sense to align the split between **Old World** (Africa, Eurasia, and Oceania) and New World monkeys with the moment the continent of Africa separated from the continent of Latin America, but the current best guess on the timing of the split is 35 mya, which postdates continental separation. Many scientists support the idea that the ancestors of platyrrhines "rafted" to the New World on huge "islands" of tangled vegetation (e.g., Ciochon and Chiarelli 1980). This is not quite as far-fetched as it sounds—lemurs are believed by some to have arrived in Madagascar in much the same way (e.g., Kappeler 2000), and while that trip was very short in comparison, the distance between the continents was not as great as it is today. Even so, it is something of an awkward explanation, but for the time being there is no viable alternative.

Platyrrhines with which you may be familiar include the capuchin monkey, the companion of choice for organ grinders, and the spider monkey, which can hang from a branch using its prehensile tail. Popularly this feature is ascribed to monkeys in general, but actually very few species have it, and none at all outside the New World. New World monkeys have been the subject of much careful and illuminating primatological research, but once again, they are too distantly related to hu-

NORTHERN WOOLLY SPIDER MONKEY

mans to teach us much about ourselves. In terms of shared derived primate characteristics, both opposability and color vision are limited in platyrrhines.

Old World monkeys belong to the parvorder *Catarrhini*. This parvorder is further divided into the **superfamilies** *Cercopithecoidea* and *Hominoidea*. Among the cercopithecoids are such successful monkey genera as baboons and macaques, with the former ranging throughout much of the African continent and a small corner of Asia, while the latter have a range spanning North Africa (with a colony on Gibraltar, technically Europe), and across Asia, even into the icy climate of the Japanese mountains. Although baboons are, genetically speaking, still at quite a remove from the human line, they have often figured prominently in classic books on human evolution. Baboons are **terrestrial** more than arboreal, and it was once thought they could tell us a good deal about human behavior, since our ancestors, too, at a key moment in their evolution, became ground-dwellers.

It can certainly be the case that similar environments can bring about behavioral analogies in two different species, and the idea that human ancestors behaved in at least some baboonish ways is a reasonable hypothesis. However, we must be mindful of two important caveats, the first applicable generally while the second addresses the baboon in particular: (1) there is more than one way to survive and thrive within the same environment, and (2) for years our impres-

BABOONS

sion of the baboon was colored by the belief that males were aggressive and nearly tyrannical in defense of their places within a rigid status hierarchy (e.g., DeVore 1965; see also the popularizing works of Ardrey, e.g. 1961, 1966), and this was the sort of behavior many of us could well imagine our ancestors adopting, given that we are none too peaceful ourselves nowadays. Mind you, our ancestors *could* have lived thus, but according to more recent studies, the baboon is perhaps the wrong creature to lend support to this view. Shirley Strum, for example, has asserted that the fierceness seen in male savanna baboons is largely a function of insecurity. Baboon troops are centered on female descent lines, with males roving from troop to troop. Males that must establish themselves in a new troop sometimes behave aggressively but will generally become more placid once their position is secure (Strum 2001[1987]). Hence, our impression of the baboon as an exceptionally combative animal would seem to be an exaggeration.

Superfamily *Hominoidea* comprises **apes** and humans. The ancestors of modern-day apes—perhaps something like *Proconsul,* a fossil often touted as the first ape (see Walker and Shipman 2005)—diverged from the monkey line about 24 mya. Apes are distinct from most monkeys in that apes have no external tail, although there are some monkey species that are tailless as well. Apes are further differentiated by their relatively broad torsos, which accommodate the locomotive form of brachiation, although today very few types of apes are habitual brachiators. On the ground, apes may move about quadrupedally, but they are not always terribly proficient at this type of locomotion, given that in most species, hindlimbs are a different length from forelimbs. Some species of ape hardly ever leave the trees, and as they move about in the branches, they often adopt an upright posture, one that can serve them on the ground as well—most apes have at least some ability to walk bipedally. Overall, apes tend to be larger than monkeys, although there are some large monkey species and some small ape species.

In Linnaean terms, I will adhere to the scheme that subdivides *Hominoidea* into three **families:** *Hylobatidae, Pongidae,* and *Hominidae* (again, bear in mind you may encounter alternative schemes). The hylobatids comprise several genera of **gibbons.** Residents of South and Southeast Asia, these are the true brachiators among the apes. Compared to other apes, gibbons are smaller, though hardly tiny. They also exhibit behaviors that are rare not only in apes but among primates generally. For example, in stark contrast to the image of the primate as the quintessential social animal, gibbons are so territorial that they will barely suffer the presence of a mate, let alone a group of fellow gibbons (e.g., Mitani 1987). While it was once thought that the gibbon was as resolutely committed to one lifelong mate as geese are (and as we humans like to believe we are), we now know that clandestine trysts outside the "marriage" take place at the edges of a gibbon couple's territory (Fuentes 2000). Nonetheless, male and female gib-

WHITE-HANDED GIBBON

bons generally cleave to each other, though less out of mutual affection, it would seem, than of an animosity toward outsiders. But this may be merely a human gloss on the situation.

Of the apes, gibbons are least closely related to humans, so once again we can set them aside for our purposes here. It is the larger apes—orangutans, gorillas, chimpanzees, and bonobos—that are our closest cousins from the animal kingdom. Studies of genetic change indicate that the line leading to modern orangutans split off first (around 13 mya), then the gorillas went their way (around 10 mya), then the ancestors of humans and the ancestors of chimpanzees and bonobos diverged (around 7 mya), with the latter line yielding the two species possibly as recently as 1 mya. There has been some question as to whether scientists interpret these genetic data correctly, as we shall see, but for the moment, some semblance of this version of events is widely accepted. In terms of understanding human behavior, and the physiological and behavioral changes that make us uniquely human, we have tended to look at the chimpanzee first and foremost for obvious (and solid) reasons, but a broader overview is essential to setting human beings into the "big picture." So we will consider all of these apes, below, for what they can tell us about being human, but first, a brief interlude is warranted to explore some ways animal behavior is rendered scientifically comprehensible.

Notes on Ethology

Ethology is the study of naturally occurring animal behavior. While there is a great diversity of animal species, and a consequent diversity of behaviors, there are certain problems that all animal species must resolve in some way; for example, the need to eat, the need to drink, the need to rest, the need to mate (for organisms that engage in sexual reproduction), the need to ensure an adequate survival rate for offspring, and so forth. Hence, as scientists, we can construct frames through which animal behavior can be compared across species and understood in broad terms, while always being watchful for exceptions and what they can teach us. There is no one frame through which all ethologists have operated over time and even within the present moment; further, there is leeway to mix and match frames. However, two frames have been especially influential in the past few decades and have left their mark on many a study. The difference between the frames is instructive, as will become clear.

Sociobiology, first promoted by E. O. Wilson (1975) but subsequently adopted and adapted by other scholars, sees the gene as the unit around which behavior is organized; it is the gene, after all, that endures into subsequent generations, not the individual. This is not to suggest that genes have agency—the ability to act—but the individual that carries them does. An organism, then, can be defined in sociobiological terms as a gene-delivery system, driven to pass on as much of its genome as possible. Everything an organism does can be reduced to this motivation. While organisms act as individuals, social groups are perpetuated through these common strivings, though clearly some individuals triumph over others in terms of their reproductive success. Even **altruistic** behaviors—those that seem to be selfless—can be reframed through sociobiology. It has been noted, for example, that social animals intercede far more readily on behalf of known or likely kin than unrelated, or more distantly related, organisms, presumably on the understanding that kin share at least some genes; hence to help kin survive is to add to one's own genetic legacy.

Sociobiology would seem to offer the most logical explanation for such mysterious animal behaviors as infanticide, observed in many social species, including an Old World monkey known as a langur. Langurs live in multifemale groups dominated by one male; at any one time, there will be several females that are caring for offspring sired by him. If a rival male succeeds in taking over the group, he may kill all of these offspring. The females, no longer suckling an infant or engaging in other nurturing activities that suppress the reproductive cycle, will quickly resume it. The victorious male, then, does not have to share his females with his dispatched rival's offspring but can apply his efforts to the creation and survival of his own (Hrdy 1977). Hence what appears to be an irrational behavior—surely a species is better served if as many offspring as possible survive—is rational when seen through the lens of sociobiology. Since the infanticidal male has greater reproductive success, this behavior will recur in subsequent generations; that is, so long as it has a genetic trigger, something that Alison Jolly claims is "clear in mice" (1999:115; see also Jakubowski and Terkel 1982; Perrigo et al. 1993), though Hrdy (1984) admits that evidence for heritability is indirect. (I wonder if the behavior might be epigenetically triggered, insofar as a murderous rampage just prior to mass impregnation might have an effect on the makeup of sperm.)

Sociobiology has had its critics—there are those who point out, for instance, how this interpretation of animal behavior is consonant with the values of free-market capitalism (Sahlins 1976). According to the sociobiological model, organisms are self-contained, self-interested entities that work constantly toward the maximization of their genetic legacy, even through ruthless methods, at minimal cost. This image is so much in line with that of the rugged entrepreneur that it certainly is worth considering whether sociobiology is too **culture-bound** to recognize alternative explanations. On the other hand, perhaps, as its defenders might insist, capitalism has become dominant as a world economic system precisely because it is predicated on the natural impulses of life on the planet. Having brought up this issue, I will now bow out, since this book is not meant to resolve such deep-rooted philosophical debates. For our purposes, however, it is worth keeping in mind that science, despite its better efforts, can be influenced by *zeitgeist* and by the views of particular scientists who, for one reason or another, may control discourse at certain moments in history.

The second frame through which to understand animal behavior, **socioecology,** does not stand opposed to sociobiology, but it does offer interesting points of contrast. For example, the definition of "organism" is markedly different. If in sociobiological terms the organism can be seen as a being with boundaries, so to speak, that enclose its own genetic material, the "boundaries" of the organism as conceived within socioecology are much less solid, subject to shaping and reshaping by the shifting constraints of its environment. In other words, the organism is in a very real way a part of its surroundings and cannot be thought of as an agent independent of those surroundings. The environment presents a scenario—what kind of food is available, how much of it is available, what types of predators are present, what types of competitors are present, etc.—within which a species develops adaptive behaviors. Group size, group interrelationships, and group dynamics are mutually involved with feeding strategies, parenting techniques, the time of day a species is active, and so on. That species can, reasonably quickly, develop behavioral solutions to environmental problems indicates that while behavior may not be entirely free of the action of genes, they do not determine it to the extent it is unchangeable in the face of changing circumstances. The implication is that we might see the same species behave wholly differently in different habitats, and this is in fact what we often do see.

The socioecological approach to ethology has been especially prevalent in primate studies over the past few decades (see Janson 2000 for an overview and critique). In its focus on material conditions and the extent to which they structure the habits of a species, it may seem to avoid the accusations of politicking that have dogged sociobiology, but it is precisely what socioecology does *not* assert that makes a statement. For the socioecologist, there is no central actor—not the gene, not the organism—pursuing its own interests without regard to its environment. Rather, the gene, the organism, the species, all species taken together, are integrated with the environment, and any change in the system produces a ripple effect that redefines these phenomena and their relationship to each other. The image is holistic rather than individualistic.

If sociobiology may seem to err on the side of individual agency, and socioecology on the side of blurring arguably real boundaries between entities, there is potentially a productive bridge concept known as **niche construction** (see Odling-Smee et al. 2003). In ecological terms, a niche is a "place" within an environment that a species "occupies," in the sense of becoming very well adapted over time. The quotation marks intimate that we are not merely talking about physical space here, but rather an intersection of the many environmental factors that engage the attention of the socioecologist. Species are said to "fit into" niches, but a more proactive verb phrase may be more appropriate. While certainly species are transformed relative to their niches, they may in turn transform their niches simply by living the lives laid out for them. The beaver is an obvious example—through its activities, as noted in chapter 1, it creates its own ecology. But other

Beaver dam.

species, perhaps more subtly, can have this same effect. And if the ecology a species creates sets up conditions within which some alleles—those that influence behavior, physiology, or both—are favored over others, the species can be said to have some impact on its own evolution, once again redeeming Lamarck, though via a succession of discoveries and interpretations he could never have imagined. The idea of niche construction preserves some of the agency assigned to organisms by sociobiologists while acknowledging the socioecological premise that an organism is the product of an ongoing interaction with its environment.

As the beaver example illustrates, niche construction does not require braininess. And in fact, as we explore the lives of the "great apes," whose brains work like ours in so many ways, we do not see niche construction on anywhere near the level of the beaver dam. There is a certain knack, however, in managing environment and species life so that they exist, through time, roughly in equilibrium. In the wild, we have witnessed the great apes readily adapting to circumstances through behavioral innovations, some subtle, some drastic. They are certainly capable of applying their considerable mental capacities to exert some control over their own evolution. Hence, the fact that human beings have engaged in niche construction at its most ambitious has to be understood in the context of a biological and behavioral legacy in which the potential for such a development has long been evident.

The Great Apes

As previously mentioned, the great apes are great because they are larger than hylobatids, and not because they are "more advanced," though the lingering influence of the Great Chain of Being feeds this impression. In recent years, the Linnaean taxonomic system has been reworked with respect to classifying the great apes. It used to be fairly simple—orangutans, gorillas, chimpanzees, and bonobos were consigned to the family *Pongidae*, while the family *Hominidae* was reserved for human beings. Colloquially, we could refer to the great apes as pongids, and to humans as hominids; **hominid** could also be applied to human ancestors back to the point when they diverged from the line that led to chimpanzees and bonobos. But when genetic studies seemed to indicate that humans and the African pongids were more closely related than previously thought, many taxonomists extended the family designation of *Hominidae* to include all of these creatures. The designation of *Gorillinae* was inserted to set off the more distantly related gorilla at the **subfamily** level, while subfamily *Homininae* covered humans, chimpanzees, and bonobos. Yet another level was inserted—**tribe**—to separate chimpanzees and bonobos (*Panini*—yes, the word doubles as an Italian sandwich) from humans and their ancestors (*Hominini*).

Some radical taxonomists (e.g., Groves 2008) have suggested that even this degree of differentiation is unwarranted, given the similarities between the human and chimpanzee genomes, and propose that the two species occupy the same genus, *Homo;* Jared Diamond, who has made a habit (and a living) out of challenging our most cherished assumptions, has sought to popularize this view (1992). On the other hand, there are far more scientists who refuse to apply the term "hominid" to any beings aside from humans and their ancestors, genetic similarities to chimps notwithstanding. It is certainly the case that a tremendous amount of research carried out on human ancestry uses "hominid" in this way, and thus to make any sort of change creates confusion. Nonetheless, in this book I will follow the middle path—human beings along with African apes are hominids; but only human beings and their ancestors, none of whom shares a generic or even a tribal designation with chimpanzees, are **hominins.** But we will leave that term aside for the moment, while we meet our closest ape cousins, many times removed.

According to the scheme I am using, the only extant member of family *Pongidae* is the orangutan, *Pongo pygmaeus* in Linnaean terms, but popularly known as the orang. Like gibbons, orangutans are Asian apes, although their range is far more restricted to the islands of Sumatra and Borneo. Some taxonomists assert that Sumatran and Bornean orangs constitute two separate species, although this would not seem to be warranted according to conventional standards, since the groups are interfertile if given the opportunity. A larger point is that even within their respective territories orangs are having difficulty replenishing their populations, because their numbers have been decimated by the overall habitat loss entailed by logging and other forms of "development" and, less broadly but perhaps more horribly, by the outright murder of females in order to seize their offspring for the pet trade (for the record, orangs do not make good pets). The upshot is that orangs today, like great apes generally, are endangered, and despite efforts on the part of some organizations to rectify the damage already caused by human activity, habitat loss continues apace, and the Sumatran orang, in particular, is very much at risk. This of course is a pity, not least because though there is much we have learned from the orang, there is a good deal more that we need to learn.

The name "orangutan" comes from the Malay expression *orang hutan*, literally "man of the forest" (please note that there is no "g" at the end of *hutan*, and hence no "g" at the end of "orangutan," although alternative spellings used to exist). An orang indeed does bear a resemblance to a man—a red-haired one at that—when it shambles bipedally across the forest floor. This is seldom how it

ORANGUTAN

gets about, however, since orangutans, despite their bulk, are virtually always in the trees. Remarkably, the orang's size helps it to navigate the treetops. On a visit to a wildlife rehabilitation center in Borneo, I saw orangs transfer from tree to tree by bending one toward the next. The creaking of the trees as they swayed added a spooky sound track to the extraordinary sight of these huge primates moving overhead. Orangs are in general large, but they are also **sexually dimorphic** in the sense that males are much larger than females. Also in contrast to females, the faces of mature males develop a bony rim that makes them look rather like a dinner plate.

Again like gibbons, orangutans are not terribly social apes, though environment can have a remarkable influence on this quality—Carel van Schaik (2004) writes of a swamp in Sumatra where the orangs interact far more frequently—which reminds us of the potential impact environment, behavior, *and* genes can have on an organism's alleged "nature." Popularly, orangs are thought to be a bit slow, but in fact, with respect to mental capacity, they are on a par with chimpanzees if toolmaking and problem solving are a measure of this. In captivity, orangutans, like the other great apes, have shown an aptitude for using symbols, though in all of these cases, whether "using" is equivalent to "understanding" is a matter for debate. The orang, in short, despite its Asian habitat and its comparatively early departure from the line that would evolve into humans and the other great apes, has all of the characteristics we see as humanlike in African ape species.

In some ways the orang is even more like us than the African apes, insofar as it has a very soulful face and tooth enamel that is of the same thickness found in humans. Jeffrey Schwartz (1987, 2005), in fact, has long promoted the audacious view that orangs may be more closely related to humans than chimpanzees. The orang only seems to be distantly related because it has undergone a good deal of genetic change over the past few millions of years, while humans and chimps have changed relatively little. Needless to say, the majority of scientists reject this hypothesis, but it does raise the possibility that our interpretation of mere genetic change as a steady measure of time and lineage divergence may be in error.

However, we will join the majority in turning our attention away from orangs to the African great apes—gorillas, chimpanzees, and bonobos—believed to be even our closer cousins. Although according to most interpretations of the data, gorillas are set somewhat apart, genetically speaking, from chimps and bonobos (and from humans), it is worthwhile to lay sketches of the three apes side by side, to illustrate what each can and cannot teach us about each other and about human beings.

For some time it was thought that there was only one species of gorilla, *Gorilla gorilla*, but recently the Eastern Gorilla populations (residing in, e.g., the Democratic Republic of the Congo [DRC] and Rwanda) have been set off by the species designation *Gorilla beringei*, thus complicating what was formerly an easy exam question for students to answer. While Western Gorillas, whose range includes such countries as Gabon, Cameroon, and the Republic of the Congo (a separate country from the DRC), are more numerous than their Eastern relatives (total numbers were given a boost by a large population only recently discovered;

MOUNTAIN GORILLA

see Bosveld 2009), it is one population of Eastern Gorillas, the Mountain Gorilla, that has most frequently made headlines, given that it has been in the thick of some of the most vicious of the region's (human) conflicts. Gorillas have been far more endangered by less spectacular events, however; for example, Western Gorillas have succumbed in large numbers to the Ebola virus (Vogel 2007). And all gorillas have been subject to the activities of poachers, who can market gorilla meat and body parts—head trophies for the wanna-be hunter and gorilla hands that can serve as ashtrays. Though it was never conclusively proved, it is possible that gorilla specialist Dian Fossey, who publicized the atrocities carried out against Mountain Gorillas, was herself slain by poachers; alternatively, others have speculated that poachers might have been convenient as scapegoats for far more powerful figures in Rwandan society (e.g., Mowat 1987).

As previously mentioned, chimpanzees (*Pan troglodytes*, known as the common chimpanzee) and bonobos (*Pan paniscus*) are very closely related, genetically speaking, having diverged from the same line only recently. We can refer to both species together, along with their ancestors, as **panins,** after *Panini.* The bonobo was originally thought to be merely a pygmy form of the chimpanzee, although it is not, as it turns out, appreciably smaller, but rather, somewhat more **gracile,** with longer legs and a less chunky body. Bonobos live only in the Democratic Republic of the Congo, while chimpanzees, existing in several **subspecies,** have a much wider range, spanning western and central Africa. The ranges of the two species do not overlap. Like gorillas, chimpanzee and bonobo populations have suffered mightily from habitat loss and hunting.

While gorilla populations vary as to whether they prefer highland or lowland habitats, all are forest dwellers. Bonobos are also creatures of the forest. In Senegal, in far West Africa, there are **savanna chimpanzees,** whose terrestrial lifestyle may be more instructive than that of the baboon in terms of suggesting how our ancestors may have adapted to the same environment, but the success of this subspecies notwithstanding, most chimps, like gorillas and bonobos, inhabit the forests.

Contrary to popular thinking, tropical forests are not especially rich in edible resources. The thick tree canopy prevents sunlight from reaching the forest floor, which has significant bare patches. It is also the case that multiple species vie for what is available. To thrive in a forest environment, a species might evolve to exploit a relatively small amount of high-quality food, like fruit (developing, at the same time, the means to defend it against competitors); or it might exploit a variety of far more abundant but lower-quality foods, for which there is less competition. The gorilla lives by the latter strategy—it can sustain its great bulk primarily through consuming shoots and leaves, that is, a folivorous diet—but there is a cost. Gorillas must dedicate much time and effort to eating (see Schaller 1963).

In the wild, gorillas are placid animals, expending little energy on such frivolities as boisterous play or dominance struggles. Generally an **alpha male** presides over several females, monopolizing their breeding services. Clearly this means that there are many unattached males roving the forest, looking to cull away a female for some clandestine amorous activity, but surprisingly this is accomplished fairly readily, without too much fuss; the alpha male either allows it or is unaware of it. On occasion, however, a lone male may challenge an alpha male for control of all of the females, and then gorillas swing into action. Even so, their fights are seldom bloody, let alone lethal—as we well know from popular culture, gorillas are masters of what is known as **display**, generally involving the *threat* of force. Chest pounding, teeth baring, and fierce vocalizations serve the purpose of telling an adversary, "You'd better not mess with me, bub," and if the adversary agrees and backs down, everyone can return that much sooner to the calm, steady task of eating. Gorillas are perfectly capable of inflicting real damage and do so when it is warranted, but if they can maintain their dominance with a minimum of time and effort expended, so much the better.

The lifestyle of the forest chimpanzee presents a study in contrasts. Although gorillas, especially lowland gorillas, hardly turn their noses up at fruit, chimpanzees live for it, being largely **frugivorous**, though they will supplement this main course with insects and meat. Fruit is a precious resource in the forest, existing in limited supply while many species hanker for it. Chimpanzees enter the interspecies competition with distinct advantages; for example, their intestinal tract has evolved in such a way that they can pack in a good deal of fruit, digesting it at leisure once it is safely "stored" (Milton 1999). But fierce competition takes place among chimpanzees as well, both within **troops** and between them, and once fruit is obtained it is not shared. Even when not competing overtly for food, chimpanzees keep their competitive tendencies honed through all manner of Machiavellian intrigue (e.g., de Waal 2007). Males vie for dominance with other males, females scrap for dominance among females. When males hunt—a not-infrequent pastime—the proceeds, unlike fruit, *are* shared, but there would seem to be strategy behind this apparent generosity. Meat is doled out to build favor among potential mates, but also—and perhaps more importantly—to create alliances among males, through which they may plot to overthrow higher-ranking males. While dominance struggles within the troop are often resolved through display, encounters between troops can be exceptionally gory.

Given that chimpanzees are so closely related to humans—the genetic differences, while obviously profound in their effects, are statistically negligible—it has been hard even for scientists to resist using them as a "mirror for man," as Clyde Kluckhohn's venerable anthropology textbook was titled (1949). We look into the chimp's eyes and see ourselves. But the image does not come back to us unfiltered. When Jane Goodall first began to report on her pioneering studies of the Gombe Stream chimpanzees (1971), she portrayed the animals as lively but genial creatures, and the general public in the United States, awash in media products that further simplified this basic image, became captivated by this amiable relative. Did the chimp taunt us with the possibility of paradise forever lost? Or could it be that even after the Vietnam War the chimp showed us that the better angels

The Eastern Hemisphere.

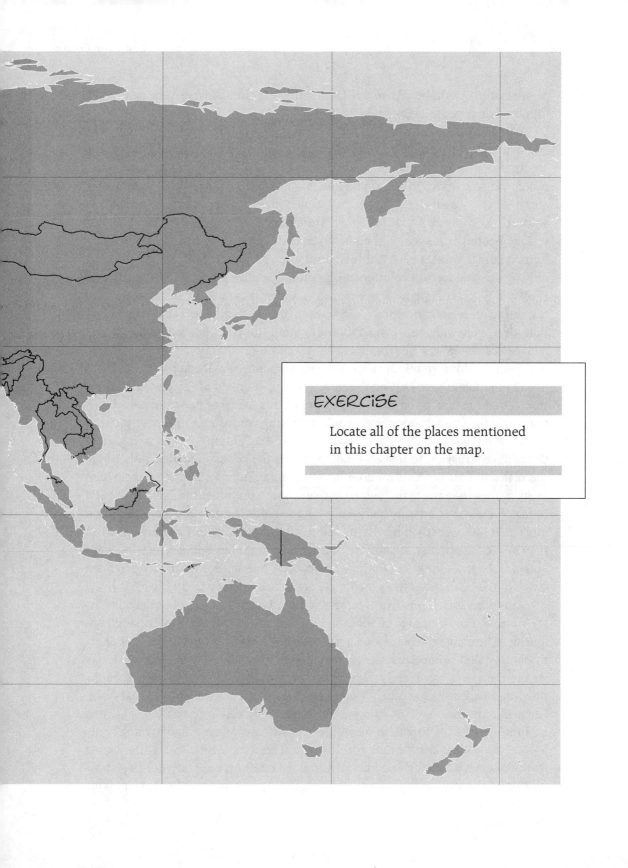

EXERCISE

Locate all of the places mentioned in this chapter on the map.

of our nature might be recovered? During this era chimps were very nearly like hippies: hairy, peace-loving, and laid-back.

When news of chimpanzee turf wars came out, however, and the attacks could no longer be explained away as aberrations, we certainly had to look at the chimp in a new light. On the one hand we could admire it for its cunning; on the other, the fact that a group of marauding chimpanzees, seemingly with malice aforethought, could seek out and destroy a neighboring group could not be squared with the idyll that had previously been entertained. But the reworked image of chimpanzees could then be taken up by people motivated to prove that human beings were at base ruthless murderers, prevented from killing (usually) only by the pale force of countervailing cultural institutions (e.g., Wrangham and Peterson 1996). It is perhaps needless to say at this point that both portraits of the chimpanzee are caricatures, colored more by what we believe about ourselves than by a well-rounded consideration of chimp life (see Haraway 1989). Chimpanzees *can* be killers, but for most chimps, most of the time, life is free of serious conflict, although minor skirmishes are endemic (see Goodall 1986).

One problem with casting the violent chimp as the stuff of raw human nature is that the bonobo, equally related to humans, behaves in a markedly different way. Like chimps, bonobos are primarily frugivorous and thus motivated to protect a high-quality but scarce food resource. Like chimps, bonobos engage in dominance struggles. In this area, however, it is the bonobo females, rather than the males, whose contests for dominance are more intense, and the female hierarchy, rather than the male hierarchy, that is more prominent in bonobo society. In fact, females can actually bully males. But females will also engage males in far more pleasurable activities. When chimpanzee females go into **estrus,** or heat, they take on a number of partners during the period, but bonobo females, even outside of estrus, have been known to choose one male consort for extended trysts in the bush, away from the hustle and bustle of daily troop life.

American social conservatives who got wind of this aspect of bonobo behavior praised the seeming "monogamous" foundation of bonobo sociality but quickly abandoned the bonobo as a role model for humans once it was popularly recognized that bonobos use sexual stimulation to address just about every situation in their lives, not merely the problem of finding good mates. Sexual stimulation not only resolves conflict, it prevents conflict from arising in the first place. Females stimulate females through a practice delicately referred to as "genital rubbing"; males participate in playful bouts of "penis fencing"; and young bonobos are by no means off-limits for this sort of contact, which in fact they must learn to survive as bonobo adults. If you have ever marveled at your dog strapping itself obsessively to your neighbor's leg, imagine that sort of behavior taking place almost constantly, with eminently willing partners, and you have some idea of the feel of everyday bonobo life (see, e.g., de Waal 1997).

While it is tempting to summarize bonobo behavior by citing the old chestnut, "Make love, not war," and inverting the saying to describe chimpanzees, it is important, once again, to avoid exaggeration. Bonobos are hardly free of the impulse to take violent action on occasion, and chimpanzees deploy various affiliative (if nonsexual) strategies, like **grooming,** that maintain harmony within the group. Nonetheless, the overall difference in behavior between bonobos and forest chimpanzees is striking, especially when we consider that, genetically speaking, chimps and bonobos are nearly identical.

One area of ape life in which we have had a keen interest is technology—do apes use tools? Humans tend to see this ability as a sure sign of the intelligence

BONOBOS

we believe is concentrated in the primate line, and residual Great Chain of Being thinking encourages us to expect more tool use among our nearest relatives, but this keeps us from noticing how much tool use goes on across the entire spectrum of the animal kingdom, among other mammals (e.g., sea otters), birds (e.g., crows), and even, according to a recent report, a type of octopus (Finn et al. 2009). Nonetheless, the great apes are in fact **tool users** as well, in that they can direct objects from nature toward a particular, thought-out purpose, and sometimes also **toolmakers,** able to *modify* these objects to fulfill a purpose even more effectively. It was once thought that gorillas did not use tools in the wild, but not long ago a female was observed dipping a log into a body of water to measure its depth (Breuer et al. 2005). So far as we know, bonobos are not much prone to deploying tools in the wild, but in captivity they have shown a remarkable aptitude for tool using and making, so further observation of wild bonobos may yet yield examples of such endeavors among them.

Chimpanzees are extraordinary tool users and makers. Just about everyone is familiar with the chimp termiting stick, but chimps have also been known to crack open nuts on stone anvils (there is archaeological evidence of this activity going back 4,300 years [Mercader et al. 2007]), draw liquid out of tree trunks with leaf "sponges" (Sugiyama 1995), and treat their ills by consuming medicinal plants (Grisanzio 1993). Savanna chimpanzees have been reported to whittle spears to hunt bushbabies (a type of strepsirhine), which can be stabbed and then extracted from the tree hollows in which they sleep (Pruetz and Bertolani 2007).

As the last example intimates, not all chimp subspecies engage in the same technologies, and even within subspecies, there may be a troop that regularly deploys a tool while a neighboring troop would seem to have no knowledge of it. Such behaviors are likely transmitted from generation to generation not through genes but via learning, and this has prompted some primatologists (e.g., Whiten et al.

CHIMPANZEE

1999) to apply the word "cultures" to the different traditions that are maintained within different chimpanzee troops; the idea is that these troops vary in the same way that, for instance, Americans and Chinese do. For many experts the fact that there is "cultural variation" among chimpanzee troops speaks to a level of mental development not previously suspected. While I readily acknowledge that chimpanzees are very intelligent by our standards, I do not go so far as to extend the word "culture" to cover them. It will take up a good deal of chapter 7 to explain why, but for the moment, let me assure you that I mean no slight to our chimp cousins.

With the African great apes, especially the panins, exhibiting so much near-human behavior, it is tempting to see them as prehuman, the perfect models for understanding our own development. This sort of thinking can certainly generate worthwhile hypotheses for which supporting data can be supplied. However, in this area of theory, we must take great care. Keep in mind that according to our best guesses of the moment, hominins and panins split around 7 mya, and only 1 million years produced the extreme behavioral contrast we see between modern chimpanzees and modern bonobos. The answer to the question, "Are today's human beings more chimplike, or more like bonobos?" can easily be, "We are like both," or "We are like neither." And the Last Common Ancestor (**LCA**) to chimps, bonobos, and humans, millions of years ago, could have been different from all of us.

QUESTIONS FOR DISCUSSION AND REVIEW

- How do we know human beings are mammals?
- What characteristics do human beings share with their fellow primates? What shared derived characteristics do humans alone have?
- How does niche construction bridge the two ethological schools?
- How does the changing image of the chimp over time bear out the influence zeitgeist might have on science?
- Compare and contrast gorilla, chimp, bonobo, and human behavior.

KEY WORDS

vertebrate	arboreal	culture-bound
Geologic Time Scale	locomotion	socioecology
era	quadrupedal	niche construction
period	bipedal	hominid
monotreme	brachiate	hominin
marsupial	omnivorous	sexual dimorphism
placental mammal	taxon (*pl.* taxa)	panin
paleoprimatologist	clade	subspecies
paleoanthropologist	diurnal	alpha male
plesiadapiformes	nocturnal	display
Cenozoic	cathemeral	frugivorous
primitive	New World monkey	folivorous
derived	Old World monkey	troop
shared derived	terrestrial	estrus
stereoscopy	ape	grooming
digit	ethology	tool user
prehensile	sociobiology	toolmaker
opposability	altruism	LCA

5

THE FIRST HOMININS
. . . MAYBE

We have to admit to being baffled about the origins
of upright walking. Probably our thinking is being
constrained by preconceived notions. . . .
[Ancient primates] are not just primitive versions
of today's apes or of us. They had developed their
own special adaptation, and this is something
we really must keep in mind when we're peering
into that fossil void trying to pick out some images
of our ancestors' way of life.

—Richard E. Leakey and Roger Lewin, *People of the Lake*

Proceed with Caution

In October 2009, an issue of *Science* magazine was dedicated to *Ardipithecus ramidus*, a putative early hominin species. Although the first remains of *Ardipithecus* (abbreviated *Ar.*) *ramidus* were actually recovered in the early 1990s, what had happened prior to the special issue of *Science* was that a reasonably complete skeleton had been painstakingly assembled, and its features challenged previously held notions about human evolution. Several of the allegedly new ideas, for example, that full bipedalism may have developed in a woodland environment and that human ancestors may not have been particularly chimplike, had been mooted before, by the *Ar. ramidus* team and/or by others. Nonetheless, when news of "Ardi," as the fossil became known, hit the popular press, the headlines announced that a revolution had taken place. Ardi had displaced the famous "Lucy" as *the* first hominin; some subheadings even speculated that apes had descended from humans. People who took the time actually to read the articles, or to watch the Discovery Channel program on the subject, were generally exposed to a far less sensationalized presentation of the material, but first impressions stick. So it was understandable, if disconcerting, when my students came into my World Prehistory class asking, "Have you heard they found a new human ancestor?" especially when they had just read (or were supposed to have read) the textbook chapter in which *Ardipithecus ramidus* was discussed.

This is only one of the many tales I can tell about how research on human evolution is distorted once it reaches the popular media. One reason the media print such stories is to support (presumably) scientifically derived explanations

119

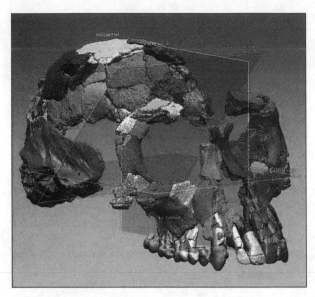

Ardipithecus ramidus.

for phenomena over those derived from faith, but ironically, the very distortions the media create through the "sound byte" approach to reporting provide ample fodder from which to craft counterarguments. Even the mention of disagreement among evolutionists as to the significance of this fossil or that trait, which from the point of view of science should be regarded as healthy debate, can inspire creationists to crow, "Scientists unsure about evolution!" But the main and not unrelated reason stories are run on evolutionary discoveries is that such stories sell, and they sell better when advertised via hyperbole, or overstatement, the source of the media buzzword, "hype." Over the years, publicity hooks, designed to reel in readers with a concise expression meant to encapsulate the discovery at hand, abound: "missing link," "mitochondrial Eve," "Millennium Man," "Lucy's Baby," "hobbit." All of this catchphrase invention is entirely appropriate from the standpoint of media professionals, but it can wreak havoc on the public's understanding of evolution, and it can sometimes even rebound into the world of evolutionary science to ill effect.

The problem is that scientists are to some extent complicit in stoking the hype. In the first place, research teams can hardly be faulted for coining popular names for their finds; it is, after all, part of the thrill of discovery, not to mention a convenience (try saying "TM 266-01-060-1" over and over). But beyond this rather innocent practice, there is a good deal of campaigning going on, and much money at stake. Professional science writers bridge the gap between dry scientific data and the public's desire to know, and while most of these writers take their responsibilities seriously, they must, of course, earn their keep through colorful turns of phrase that make science "interesting," that is, simple and salable. Research teams may themselves try to shape this discourse to their financial advantage; at the very least they may tacitly allow a publicity campaign to begin and to escalate. The point is that research into human evolution is expensive—it is hardly a matter of a lone scientist scratching fossils out of the dirt—and one does not win grants by underplaying the significance of one's findings. If researchers can approach foundations riding a wave of publicity, so much the better. On the other hand, no research team wants to get caught in the undertow of bad press when rivals manage to discredit new work fairly quickly and effectively, so this can serve as a check on ill-considered announcements. Thus, when and how to release information to the public is something of a dangerous game. The game has not always been played skillfully, and it is often science that suffers.

None of this is intended to turn interested students into indifferent cynics. The point is to advise caution. As much as we would like to believe science is beyond economics and politics, research is of necessity carried out in as much as on the real world. Skepticism should not discourage you from learning; it should, rather, compel you to learn more. Having said that, when it comes to the very first hominins, there is not so much, yet, to learn *from.*

Paleoanthropology

As noted previously, the study of ancient hominins is known as **paleoanthropology,** literally "ancient anthropology" ("paleo-," you will find, is a very important prefix for us). In this case, "ancient" is applied to hominins from the **LCA** onward to what we can recognize as the beginnings of human **culture.** The **paleoanthropological window,** then, is open from about 7 mya to about 2.5 mya, give or take a few hundred thousand years in any direction. That should be plenty of time for enough fossils to accrue so that an accurate history of the precultural hominin line comes readily into view. Alas, this is not the case.

One problem is that fossilization is not as easily accomplished as people assume. Even bone disintegrates relatively quickly under most circumstances. Of all the bones of the skeleton, teeth have the highest density and thus are most likely to last over time, but even so, teeth are small and liable to scatter once loosened from a more fragile jaw. Cold may preserve soft tissues, aridity may discourage the growth of microorganisms that break down organic materials, and the anaerobic conditions found in bogs or river bottoms can seal off entire organisms from decay, but the fossilizing properties of all three matrices are readily disrupted by earth movement and/or changes in climate. Further, while these environments have shifted over time, they have never covered the entire earth equally, leading to bias in the fossil record as to what has been preserved, when, and where.

Mineralization—when organic materials are infiltrated and, potentially, completely replaced by minerals dissolved in liquid—is a mixed blessing. On the one hand, DNA is destroyed, and in other aspects the composition of the original organic matter can only be inferred; on the other hand, mineralization lends itself to more effective preservation, and stone casts even of soft body parts, like brains, can be remarkably revealing. Finally (for the moment), fossils are displaced by any number of processes, and we cannot assume that where they are found today was the actual "deathbed" of the organism. Fossilization is so complex, and subject to so many variables, that an entire scientific specialization—**taphonomy**—is dedicated to its study. No paleoanthropological team today can be without access to a good taphonomist, and taphonomic review of fossil finds can help us "dial back" the initially rash conclusions that might be reached.

Nevertheless, a number of hominin fossils, from potentially a number of different genera and species, *have* been located. To this point, the paleoanthropological window opens only on the continent of Africa. This does not absolutely rule out hominins in other parts of the world during this period, but nothing whatsoever has been located yet. However, it should be noted that efforts so far have been concentrated in Africa, in large part because nothing succeeds like success, and to interest a grant agency into bankrolling an excavation elsewhere would be a hard sell.

African investigations into human origins began in the southern part of the continent (primarily in the country of South Africa) but migrated northward to the tectonically active **Great Rift Valley,** a treasure trove of **fossil localities** that cuts through the countries of Tanzania, Kenya, and Ethiopia, among others. The

Great Rift Valley in Kenya.

Rift Valley is replete not only with eroding cliffsides out of which fabulously ancient fossils may simply emerge—the problem lies not so much in excavating
them as in finding and recognizing them—but also with such geologically useful
features as dry river beds, in which fossils may be especially well preserved, and
volcanic rock, that, as we will see, provides us with a means of determining dates
in the millions-of-years range. That statement should suggest to you that **geologists,** as well as taphonomists, are an invaluable part of any paleoanthropological
team, and no geologist who loves her work could fail to find the Rift Valley
greatly conducive to research. But unfortunately, the tendency has been to assume that just because research is extraordinarily productive in the Rift Valley, it
must therefore be the cradle of hominin evolution. Of course, the South African
research contingent has long objected to this claim, and the relatively recent excavations in the central African nation of Chad, well to the west of the Rift Valley,
further serve to warn us against the comforting thought that just because eastern
Africa has yielded such a prodigious amount of fossil evidence, it is the *only*
place where this evidence is to be found.

Another expert essential to paleoanthropological research is a **paleontologist;** more than one may in fact be necessary, since, as the socioecologists advise,
an organism is productively thought of as integrated with its environment, and
that environment includes animal life, plant life, and microorganisms, all of
these requiring paleontological specialists. From plant life we can learn a great
deal—whether a habitat was woodland or savanna, what the climate was like,
what foods were available. Of all plant parts, pollen is likeliest preserved within
the fossil record (my apologies to allergy sufferers, but I'll bet you are hardly sur-
prised), and an expert known as a **palynologist** can match pollen grain to plant
type. Of course, animal fossils may also be recovered, but then the problem is to
sort them into separate organisms and species. This requires the practiced eye of
the **comparative osteologist,** who can distinguish the skeletons of a great many
genera and species. It may be possible, through an excavation that cuts through
several strata of earth, to build an evolutionary sequence—say, a line of pig species—that can be used as a **temporal** measuring stick for determining the age of
other finds in the vicinity.

Of course, the ultimate point of paleoanthropological study is to build a line
of hominin species, but this line did not exist in a vacuum. One area where more
paleontological research is urgently needed is the reconstruction, using fossil evidence, of the evolutionary sequence of chimpanzees. If the LCA was neither particularly chimplike nor particularly humanlike, then it may be difficult to
distinguish the chimpanzee's distant ancestors from our own. What little that
has been found of ancient chimpanzees has already challenged our assumptions—in 2004, three teeth, thought to be those of a chimpanzee, were located in

Kenya (McBrearty and Jablonski 2005). While these teeth, dating back roughly 500,000 years, are not so old as to shed much light on chimpanzee descent, the fact they were found *east* of the Great Rift Valley throws into question the hypothesis that the genetic divide between hominins and panins was facilitated by the geographical (and climatic) divide between the lush jungles of the African interior and the drought-prone region between the Rift Valley and the coast (see, e.g., Coppens 1994; Kortlaandt 1972). Mind you, a mere three teeth should not invalidate a hypothesis, and much more evidence needs to be recovered, as much for the old hypothesis as for the new. What we must keep in mind, however, is that just because something would seem to be a commonsense explanation for a phenomenon does not mean it is true. In other words, for as often as Occam's Razor seems to work, sometimes the answer to a problem is in fact complex.

The upshot here is that paleontologists in a variety of specialties, along with geologists in a variety of specialties, are required within the paleoanthropological enterprise to establish **context,** because again, a species cannot be adequately understood when it is amputated from its environment. Species exist in both space and time, and further, these two dimensions of context are interrelated, so it is important to assemble a team of thinkers who can accomplish the everyday gathering of data while simultaneously organizing those data through complex theoretical frameworks, some of which may have more, some less, explanatory power as data are applied. Factor in a support staff of local guides, land surveyors, cooks, and security guards (some of the most fruitful hominin fossil localities have been situated in dangerous country) and you can see why budgetary matters must also be of concern. It is hardly any wonder that paleoanthropologists may occasionally "oversell" their finds.

But is there actually someone called a paleoanthropologist who emerges from this interdisciplinary mishmash? That is, is there someone on the paleoanthropological team who has the four-field education generally advised for American anthropologists? The answer is, not necessarily. The four-field model is not accepted even in many American anthropology programs, and in Europe, the subfields of anthropology are often broken up and salted among several other disciplines—the archaeologist may have schooled in history, for example, while the biological anthropologist considers herself to be more firmly aligned with the natural sciences than is true for many Americans in the subfield. So someone identified as a "paleoanthropologist" may actually be a geologist or a paleontologist with a special interest in the study of hominins.

Nevertheless, a solid background in four-field anthropology, American-style, is invaluable to such a study. The worth of biological anthropology is obvious, as is a thoroughgoing familiarity with archaeological recovery techniques. And while, within the paleoanthropological window, we are not dealing with linguistic or cultural beings (so far as we can tell right now), we are always on the look-out for the stirrings of these properties in the hominin line; it is also the case that knowledge of present-day language and culture can certainly help settle a paleo-anthropological team into the field. So there are and have been broadly trained (in the American sense) anthropologists who have become paleoanthropologists.

Paleoanthropologists are often so well-versed in so many ways that it is not surprising they may come off as somewhat "larger than life," especially if the media seek them out as team spokespeople. It is also not surprising if the paleoan-thropologist learns to milk his more telegenic qualities for the purposes of capturing all-important media exposure. Not only the finds but also the discov-erer may be "oversold"—ultimately, it is to be hoped, for a good cause.

Big Heads or Two Feet?

I opened this chapter with an account of the (re)discovery of Ardi, but it is not the usual cautionary tale recounted when the topic of the most ancient hominins is introduced. The story of **Piltdown Man** is perhaps the most leading, in terms of what *not* to think, at this point in our exploration of human biocultural evolu-tion. In the early 1900s, an allegedly early human was recovered from a gravel pit in England. Dubbed Piltdown Man, it seemed to have both human and ape fea-tures. The find was greeted with skepticism, but it should be said that most hom-inin fossils were treated skeptically at the time. Unsurprisingly, however, there were those who accepted the fossil as legitimate, and some did so even up until 1953, when its status as a human ancestor was definitively debunked. Piltdown Man stood exposed as a hoax, a deliberately organized assemblage of an old (though not prehistoric) human skull and a relatively recent ape jawbone.

Why do we still tell the story of a find that from the start was fishy? As is generally the case, the point lies more in what the story tells us. Some authors have noted that Piltdown was perhaps more readily accepted than it should have been insofar as it satisfied British national pride in some measure—that ancient hominins were being located in the rest of Europe was a situation British patriots may have been strongly motivated to rectify (e.g., Blinderman 1986). But it was also true that Piltdown fulfilled then-current notions as to what a "proper" hu-man ancestor should look like—a big-headed being with residual apelike traits that would soon fade away. In other words, Piltdown was a lesson in the pitfalls of **teleological** thinking.

In applying teleological thinking to human evolution, one would observe what exists today and presume that its developmental course was entirely geared

Who Was the Piltdown Perp?

It's a bit curious why the Piltdown hoax has inspired so many "history detectives" to take up the case. A number of suspects have been considered, including none other than Sir Arthur Conan Doyle, who penned the Sherlock Holmes mysteries. Time and time again, however, the finger of accusation has come to rest on the man who benefitted most from the find: Charles Dawson (e.g., Russell 2003). Dawson discovered Piltdown Man, which was given the Linnaean name of *Eoanthropus* ("dawn man") *dawsonii*. In fact, Dawson discovered several other fossils in the same vicinity, as well as a variety of artifacts. It is possible that someone else could have seeded the Piltdown gravel pit with these "finds," but somehow Dawson always knew where to look.

So, I apologize for taking the fun out of the question at hand, which actually has two answers: (1) we'll likely never know for sure, but (2) it was probably Dawson. In fact, there is a third answer: what does it matter anymore? The Piltdown find led a few paleoanthropologists down the garden path, but even these few readily abandoned their belief in the fossil's authenticity once evidence was produced showing that the skull was far older than the jaw (and of course, the bones were subsequently shown to have come from two different species). The Piltdown case is well and truly closed . . . *or is it?* [cue creepy organ music . . .]

toward producing this result. Imagine that the LCA resembled a modern chimpanzee—this may be entirely wrong, as I have already intimated, but it has been a prevalent image in science and remains lodged in popular thought. Imagine, as well, the gradual "morphing" process a chimp would have to undergo to become human—the chimp would lift its knuckles from the ground to stand upright, its legs would elongate, while at the same time its skull would enlarge and its body hair would become thinner. All of these processes would take place smoothly and simultaneously over a period of millions of years. In theory, then, we should be able to recover "missing links" from this unbroken chain of transformations, and we could even estimate at what link in the chain a parent species was likeliest to have, for example, a certain-sized head relative to a certain degree of bipedalism. Piltdown fit right into this preconceived timeline. It had the large head—

surely, evolutionists of the time largely agreed, **encephalization** was the vanguard of the human "rise" from the apes—but retained some "regressive" features, still in the process of transition.

Not long after the discovery of Piltdown, however, scientists began to have an inkling that human evolution may not have proceeded so "logically." Fossils were recovered from Africa that exhibited chimpanzee-sized heads but a suite of additional features associated with bipedal locomotion. What was more, the chimpanzee-sized head remained relatively constant over a span of time during which bipedal equipment became more and more refined. The conclusion was inevitable—our ancestors had not developed big heads first, with all other human changes following on that one development. Rather, it would seem to be the case that full bipedalism greatly predated encephalization. Hence, paleoanthropologists had to focus on how bipedalism came about in the hominin line, and how its inception might be detected in fossil bits and pieces that did not necessarily offer direct evidence for it.

Obviously this revolution in the thinking of paleoanthropologists was essential and overdue—Sir Kenneth Oakley, of the British Museum, famously chastised himself and his colleagues for their prejudices: "Of course we believed that the big brain came first! We assumed that the first man was an Englishman!" (cited in Ardrey 1961:27). Nonetheless, there is always the possibility that a corrective measure might become an *over*correction, and it could be that we have to consider that possibility now. Today paleoanthropologists rush to prove, through a variety of ever more sophisticated means, that their latest find was fully bipedal or at least well "on the way" there; the organism is then dubbed "hominin," and speculation immediately ensues as to how and where it fits into the line of our direct ancestors. But if in fact the LCA, like modern apes, was reasonably capable of bipedal locomotion, and the **knuckle-walking** of today's chimpanzee was a later rather than prior development, there could have been a number of bipedal species existing within the paleoanthropological window; for all that, the ancestors of gorillas could have been reasonably bipedal as well. Hence, it is possible that at least some of the ancient apelike bipeds we find in Africa are ancestral to modern chimpanzees and modern gorillas, and not to humans. It is also possible they are not ancestral to anything that exists today.

Modern primates generally, even if they are routinely quadrupedal, are accustomed to assuming upright postures; they do not need to have four limbs planted on a surface at all times. As noted in the previous chapter, this degree of comfort with verticality is even more obvious among pongids and hominids. An orangutan is remarkably adept at negotiating a branch-to-branch path through the expansive use of its entire body, and at times the animal, when in the trees, can resemble the famous da Vinci sketch of a man with outstretched arms and legs, though much differently proportioned, of course. On the ground, orangs are most often "knuckle"-walkers (they actually walk on their fists, palm-side down) but can manage a bipedal gait, though as previously mentioned they are not so facile with any form of terrestrial locomotion. Gorillas, chimpanzees, and bonobos, primarily knuckle-walkers on the ground, are nonetheless eminently capable of standing and moving about on two feet; the bonobo is especially prone to doing so. In short, the array of locomotor choices available to the modern great apes suggests

BONOBO

that the common ancestor to all may have been a highly generalized creature in this respect, and such adaptations as pongid fist-walking and hominid (excluding humans) knuckle-walking could be derived developments that came about as recently as, or even perhaps even more recently than, human bipedalism.

The upshot is that the grand hurrah that went up when paleo-anthropologists shifted their attention from big-headedness to two-footedness may have to be scaled back to a cautious "aha! hmm. . . ." Bipedalism may not be as diagnostic as we thought in terms of distinguishing the hominin line from the panin line, or even the LCA from other hominin-like species around at the time. This is not to say we should cast bipedalism aside as well, since one bipedal strain clearly led to us, and we may never have a better means of tracing our line. As always, however, the watchword is caution, and an openness to alternative conclusions the available evidence may support.

Bipedalism

All of this having been said, the modern human being is tremendously well adapted to bipedalism, and in fact the physiological entailments of this form of locomotion in humans have effectively precluded other forms. Human beings *can* crawl on all fours, and they *can* swing from branches, but not well in either case, precisely because our bodies are built for an entirely different way of getting around. The really good news for paleoanthropologists is that hominin skeletal morphology was eventually completely reworked by habitual bipedalism, and so even if we have found only a skull, or a vertebra, or a piece of pelvis, or a piece of femur, or a piece of foot, we may be able to say with some security that the organism from which it came was bipedal.

Cranial remains indicate bipedalism primarily through the location of the **foramen magnum,** the hole in the base of the skull through which the spinal cord passes. If this hole is positioned toward the rear of the skull, the head of the organism was suspended from a horizontal spine; a hole more toward the center of the skull base indicates the organism's head was routinely held erect, like a lollipop on a stick. There are, of course, abundant clues to be found in **postcranial** remains as well. As bipedalism was becoming fixed in the hominin line, the spine took on an S-curve to absorb the shock of verticality, the pelvis became shorter and wider while the legs became longer, constant pressure on the underside of the hip joint encouraged greater bone density there, the femurs angled inward to balance on knees that locked in place to facilitate standing as well as walking, and the foot sacri-

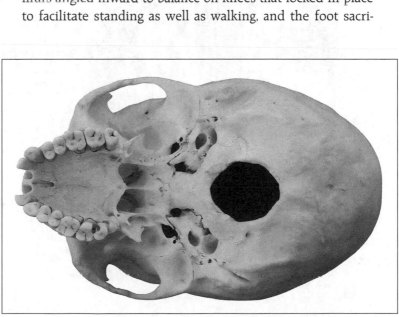

Above, human spine. *Right,* foramen magnum of *H. sapiens.*

ficed a good deal of its primate flexibility and dexterity for a tensile arch (there really *is* a spring in your step) and a big toe in line with the other toes. There *are* ways the design could be improved—see, for example, the vision of S. Jay Olshansky and colleagues (2001), below, regarding changes that might ease the aging process—but altogether it is an extraordinary package of traits that in its full-blown form is unlike that of any other primate.

In picking apart this package, however, we have a problem reminiscent of the big-heads-or-two-feet conundrum—what came first? Did all of these traits evolve together, slowly and evenly; or did one lead and the others follow? It would help, of course, if we had an inkling as to *why* our ancestors became committed bipeds. How did a merely serviceable means of getting about, which in other ancient hominids was likely used in combination with alternative means to which they were better suited overall, become a hominin imperative? Perhaps needless to

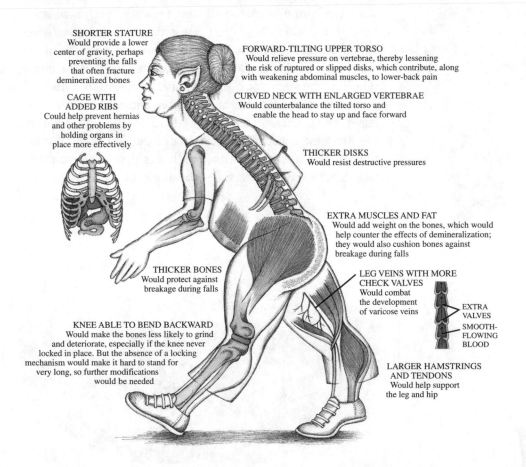

SHORTER STATURE
Would provide a lower
center of gravity, perhaps
preventing the falls
that often fracture
demineralized bones

FORWARD-TILTING UPPER TORSO
Would relieve pressure on vertebrae, thereby lessening
the risk of ruptured or slipped disks, which contribute, along
with weakening abdominal muscles, to lower-back pain

CAGE WITH
ADDED RIBS
Could help prevent hernias
and other problems by
holding organs in
place more effectively

CURVED NECK WITH ENLARGED VERTEBRAE
Would counterbalance the tilted torso and
enable the head to stay up and face forward

THICKER DISKS
Would resist destructive pressures

EXTRA MUSCLES AND FAT
Would add weight on the bones, which would
help counter the effects of demineralization;
they would also cushion bones against
breakage during falls

THICKER BONES
Would protect against
breakage during falls

LEG VEINS WITH MORE
CHECK VALVES
Would combat
the development
of varicose veins

EXTRA
VALVES
SMOOTH-
FLOWING
BLOOD

KNEE ABLE TO BEND BACKWARD
Would make the bones less likely to grind
and deteriorate, especially if the knee never
locked in place. But the absence of a locking
mechanism would make it hard to stand for
very long, so further modifications
would be needed

LARGER HAMSTRINGS
AND TENDONS
Would help support
the leg and hip

say, a number of scholars have tried to answer this question, and while many of the answers have been sound, most have been supported by reasoning more than evidence. To be honest, the evidence might never be found, so it may be all we can do to sort through the reasons, deeming them sensible or implausible.

One problem with reasons mooted to date is that many of them stem from what has been called the **Savanna Hypothesis**—the notion, harking back to Darwin's *Descent of Man*, that all formative changes in the human line can be traced to the move from the trees to the wide-open spaces of the African plains. Clearly our ancestors did become more terrestrial over time, eventually abandoning an arboreal habitat nearly completely (climbing trees remains a fairly prevalent exercise for some groups of people even today), but if the latest assessment of the bipedal proclivities of *Ar. ramidus* proves to be correct, we have to direct our attention away from the savanna and back into the forest.

This, however, would weaken most of the ideas regarding bipedalism that are predicated on a terrestrial existence. There is, for instance, the observation that a vertical being would suffer less from the heat of the sun than a horizontal one (Wheeler 1991a), but why would verticality benefit the hominin living in the sun-dappled coolness of the forest? Similarly, the observation that a two-footed means of locomotion is more efficient than quadrupedalism when covering long distances (Rodman and McHenry 1980; Wheeler 1991b) could justify bipedalism as the locomotor method of "choice" on the savanna (given that the hominin *had* a choice, unlike most other savanna-dwelling animals), but this does not explain why a forest-dweller might get about in this manner as well. The notion of "efficiency" has been extended to cover the issue of encephalization, in that whatever energy saved from simplifying the locomotor process became available for mental processes, but recall that brain growth of any significance is not observed for millions of years following what we currently take as the earliest evidence for bipedalism. As Karin Isler and Carel van Schaik (2006) have noted, it is likelier that brain growth was actually held up while the energetics of bipedalism were being hashed out. I can close this litany with the idea, suggested by the research of Elaine Videan and William McGrew (2000), that our ancestors may have stood erect in order to spot predators (or prey) above the long grass of the plains. But once again, this has no explanatory value in a woodland environment.

It is not as though these explanations must be discarded out of hand. They may well have some bearing on why bipedalism continued to develop on the savanna but cannot contribute much regarding the *origins* of this locomotor preference. The same critique might be leveled against what is perhaps the most attractive, and in many ways the simplest, proposition regarding bipedal origins—our ancestors stood up and walked because this freed the hands for carrying things. Not only does this make eminent sense, especially in light of the extent to which we rely on the ability to do this today, but we can note that other present-day primates—bonobos, for instance—stand up and walk for much the same reason. When not carrying things, however, the bonobo is back down on all fours, most of the time. While we know that eventually our ancestors had a good deal to carry, at the time bipedalism seems to have become routine we have no evidence that they were living all that differently from today's bonobos, at least in terms of what they had to carry, and how far they had to carry it. Hence we cannot say with certainty that carrying things was the prime mover behind hominin two-footed walking, although down the road, so to speak, it likely provided a good deal of secondary reinforcement.

All of this casting-about regarding hominin bipedalism speaks to a larger problem than the leftover effects of the now-questionable Savanna Hypothesis. Paleoanthropologists remain vulnerable to the teleological trap—we observe the marvelous ways in which routine bipedalism figures in human lives today and presume that this "result" was destined to have beaten out the competition. The fact is, however, bipedalism was far from a foregone conclusion. Bipedal capabilities in nature are not exactly rare; however, few species rely solely on two feet as a means of getting around. Birds are bipedal, but of course for most birds flight is their primary form of locomotion, and in such species forelimbs are so well adapted for flying that they cannot serve as feet; hence, the hindlimbs, by default more than design, assume the entire burden when the bird is earthbound. Penguins swapped out flight for swimming, but their forelimbs became flippers, not legs. Ostriches and their ilk settled on bipedalism as their preferred form of locomotion, but only after flight was no longer an option. Like ostriches, many species of dinosaur had forelimbs that were useless for locomotion; hence such dinosaurs had to rely on their hindlimbs. A tail, in these instances, helped the animal attain balance without the complication of an S-shaped spine; the same can be said of the bipedal kangaroo. Human forelimbs are not so modified that their use in locomotion is absolutely precluded, and external tails were sacrificed back when the ape line diverged from the monkey line. Hence, in nature, there was really no precedent for the human form of bipedalism, which, of course, makes it all the more remarkable.

It could be that bipedalism, as one of several locomotor capacities available to the earliest hominins, was favored for no particularly compelling reason, though once it became more prevalent, there were advantages, like the ability to carry things, that encouraged its further development. Yet another lesson to be learned from the course of evolution is that there is more than one way to skin a cat (my apologies for a distasteful, if accurate, proverb). Importantly, however, we must recognize that bipedalism evolved in a complex environment with any number of factors influencing hominin locomotor "choice." I will sketch out one possible ecological scenario toward the end of this chapter, but first we will consider some of the fossils that have been put forth at the very least as hominins, and possibly as directly ancestral to humans.

Hominins Step Away from Panins

Molecular evidence, which I will discuss in chapter 7, suggests the LCA existed prior to 5 mya, likely not well prior. At the time of this writing, there is only one find for which its discoverers (a team led by French paleoanthropologist Michel Brunet) claim LCA status, or something very close to it (Brunet et al. 2002). Cranial remains, unearthed in the central African nation of Chad (formerly spelled "Tchad") within a period from 2001–2002, were assigned to a new genus and species dubbed *Sahelanthropus tchadensis,* though a popular name, "Toumaï," was coined for the full cranium that appeared in press reports. "Toumaï"

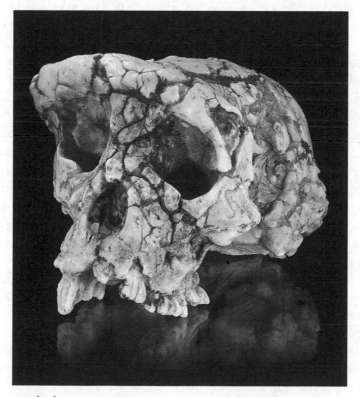

S. tchadensis.

means "hope of life" in a local Chadian language and is often the name bestowed on a child born just before the rains come to this arid land, part of the long, sub-Saharan band of desiccation called the Sahel.

Sahelanthropus is a problematic discovery in a number of ways, not least, as indicated earlier, in that it was found in Chad. But its date of approximately 7 million years goes back further than many scientists can accept; additionally, the evidence for routine bipedalism is not unequivocal and continues to generate debate (Gibbons 2005). It has been posited that Toumaï may actually fall within the gorilla line (Wolpoff et al. 2002), but while this would be a welcome addition to our knowledge of ancient hominids, there is no agreement in this area either. Clearly more evidence is needed to come to any sort of consensus as to what Toumaï was, but for the moment there is little to draw scientists toward a single conclusion.

One of the paleoanthropologists who has suggested Toumaï might be ancestral to gorillas has a particular reason for doing so, given that she herself has a very early potential hominin to tout—*Orrorin tugenensis*, popularly known as "Millennium Man" for the fact it was found in the year 2000 (*not* the millennium, as any mathematician can tell you [2001 actually starts the next thousand years], but the title is catchy, which is the point). The paleoanthropologist, a Frenchwoman named Brigitte Senut, worked with a British-born, Kenyan-raised geologist, Martin Pickford, at a site in the Tugen Hills of Kenya. The *Orrorin* fossils, which comprise bits and pieces of cranial and postcranial remains from different individuals, date back to approximately 6 mya (Sawada et al. 2002). Unsurprisingly, Senut and Pickford claim that *Orrorin* was fully bipedal, despite meager and not wholly convincing evidence (there is greater bone density on the underside of the femur's neck [Pickford et al. 2002]); they also have some indication, from the other fossil fauna present, that *Orrorin's* bipedalism developed in a forested environment. More surprisingly, the duo believes that *Orrorin* (the name means "original man" in a local language) may be directly ancestral to humans, bypassing the species I will discuss below. While the paleoanthropological community has been willing to admit *Orrorin* into the elite club of potential early hominins, there are lingering negative effects from the circumstances surrounding the find. In his career Pickford had run afoul of the Leakeys, the "first family" of paleoanthropology, and charges and countercharges have been flung as to whether Senut and Pickford had legitimate clearance to hunt for fossils in the Tugen Hills region (Butler 2001).

Of course the story of *Ardipithecus ramidus* heads this chapter, but there is more to say. The fossils of *Ar. ramidus*, and those of a sister species, *Ar. kadabba*, were recovered in the Afar region of Ethiopia, part of the Rift Valley System. The oldest *ramidus* finds date back to approximately 4.4 mya, while the scant *kadabba* remains are somewhat older, between 5.2 and 5.6 mya (there is more on how these dates are obtained in the next chapter). But it is *ramidus*, and most specifically the reconstructed skeleton dubbed "Ardi," that has captured recent media attention. Some of the claims being made for the "new" *ramidus* are difficult to square with what has been accepted about human ancestry to this point, and if these conclusions survive further testing, yet another revision of conventional wisdom is in order. That *ramidus*, like *O. tugenensis*, may have been a woodland biped, and the revolutionary implications of that status, have already been discussed, but the assertions that the species was bipedal on the ground and quadrupedal in the trees (more like a monkey than an ape) and that *ramidus* was a relatively large creature with, moreover, little difference in size between males and females, are startling (White et al. 2009). Now, it could be that *ramidus* was not directly ancestral to modern humans, as its discoverers admit, but that subsequent candidates for admission into the human line seem to reverse at least some of these ardipithecine traits (as they do the alleged traits of *Orrorin*) may set *either* Ardi *or* the later species on a separate evolutionary path.

Before I move on to a discussion of later hominins, it is worth mentioning that though the name most often associated with *Ar. ramidus*, as well as other finds in the region, is that of American paleoanthropologist Tim White, there are Ethiopians, among them Berhane Asfaw and Yohannes Haile-Selassie, who have become prominent paleoanthropologists in their own right, and in fact it is Haile-Selassie who is credited with the discovery of *Ar. kadabba* (Bower 2001). Additionally, there have been Africans involved in all the excavations listed thus far, in positions of team leadership as well as crew, and they will also figure in the discovery of most of the finds described below. That these Africans have not always received the media attention that is their just due—they are either left out entirely from news reports or depicted as answering to foreign experts—speaks, unfortunately, to the lasting effects of anti-African racism on global society.

Australopithecines, Anti-Australopithecines, Ex-Australopithecines

Although southern Africa sounds like it is distant from eastern Africa, the swath of land that has been so productive with respect to fossil finds in countries like Ethiopia and Kenya continues down into the far southern part of the continent. As previously indicated, it is the country of South Africa, which occupies the southernmost tip of Africa, where most fossil hunting has taken place, largely under the direction of paleoanthropologists from the University of the Witwatersrand. Like eastern Africa, southern Africa has proved to be a good place to locate fossil hominins, but its advantages are different. Southern Africa has none of the volcanic rock that helps us determine dates in the millions-of-years range, nor does it have dry river beds where fossils can be preserved. In fact, its landscape is largely **karst**; that is, limestone, deposited when the area was ocean floor, eroded to the point that it resembles Swiss cheese. Karst is brittle—sinkholes are common phenomena—and shot through with caves. In these numerous depressions fossils, over millions of years, have collected, and it is possible to locate them simply by stumbling across them. It is also the case that South Africa has long been host to quarrying and mining enterprises, and a good deal of fossil-bearing earth has been moved. Locating fossils in quarry waste is undesirable, since they are loosed from a potentially datable context, and yet, had quarry waste been passed up as a source of fossils, it may have been many more years before paleoanthropologists recognized that South Africa could contribute a good deal to our understanding of the hominin line.

As it happened, however, we had some inkling of this as far back as 1924, when Raymond Dart, an Australian paleoanthropologist, happily accepted a crate of quarry waste through which he could sift. One item contained therein looked like a rock, about the size of a softball, but Dart realized it had a face, albeit a very small one. Very careful removal of the matrix in which the fossil was embedded—it took Dart four years to tap the tiny jaws apart—yielded an **endocast** of a brain, which was nowhere near the size of that of a modern human, and enough

Australopithecus africanus.

of a skull to show that the foramen magnum was centrally located. Colloquially the fossil became known as the "Taung Child" (or "Taung Baby"), after Taung, the quarry where it was found; its youth was betrayed by the fact its adult teeth were only beginning to emerge. For its scientific name, Dart chose *Australopithecus africanus; Australo-* for his native land (it also means "southern"). The terminological component *-pithecus,* meaning "monkey" or "ape," indicated that Dart was hedging his bets at a time when big-headedness was expected to be *the* leading trait of our ancestors (Dart 1925). Given the lack of context, we still do not know how old the Taung fossil is—the estimated range is from 2 to 3 mya—but it was certainly the oldest hominin discovered at that time.

SIDEBAR

South Africa in the Spotlight

Eastern Africa may attract more attention nowadays as a treasure trove of early hominin fossils, but it is worth keeping in mind that it was the Taung child, found in 1924, that gave rise to the productive generic designation *Australopithecus*. Once *A. africanus* became widely accepted as a hominin, it was frequently placed at the base of the human family tree. After the discovery of *A. afarensis* in Ethiopia, however, many paleoanthropologists set *africanus* on a side branch. On

Lee Berger.

occasion someone comes forward to argue the case for restoring the species to its former pride of place; not surprisingly, these arguments generally emanate from South Africa. A recent *africanus* supporter is Lee Berger of the University of the Witwatersrand, Johannesburg.

When it comes to paleoanthropology, Berger, an American who has taken up residence in South Africa, does not sit still. His work, though situated mainly in southern Africa, has taken him all the way to the South Pacific island of Palau, and his discoveries range widely in time as well. A telegenic man, he is a featured paleoanthropologist on the *National Geographic* website (see http://www.nationalgeographic.com/features/outpost/), and has made numerous television appearances, most recently in connection with the discovery of the new species *Australopithecus sediba*, which will be discussed briefly in the next chapter. All of this media exposure—some might say overexposure—is a blessing and a curse not only for Berger but for paleoanthropology, because if it turns out a discovery is revealed prematurely or attracts a level of attention that far exceeds its importance, the subfield is trivialized. Over the years Berger has drawn a good deal of criticism for his seemingly cavalier attitude toward the scientific vetting process (see, e.g., Thomas 2010). Notwithstanding the criticism, Berger continues to seek out new fossils, and new opportunities to promote them.

Unquestionably, however well Berger's body of work stands up in years to come, southern Africa will continue to have a good deal to tell us about human origins and development, and the University of the Witwatersrand, which houses the Institute for Human Evolution, is well placed to continue exploration of the region.

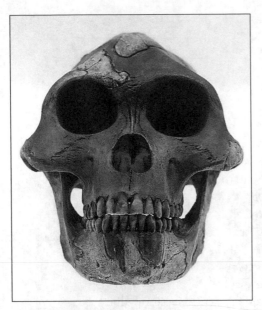

Australopithecus afarensis.

We must credit Dart, then, with coining what would prove to be a popular generic name. Other South African fossils, some older (and dated more reliably), were to be identified as *Australopithecus* (or *Au.*) *africanus*, and once the idea that our distant ancestors may have been small-brained became widely accepted, *africanus* was touted as directly ancestral to the genus *Homo*. There are those who support this view even today, but for many paleoanthropologists *africanus* was knocked out of the human line by a roughly contemporaneous eastern African find—*Au. afarensis*, typified by the famous "Lucy." Lucy was recovered in 1974 by Don Johanson's team, working in a region of Ethiopia known as the Afar Triangle. Initially her remains were dated to 3.6 mya, but redating brought her age down to 3.2 mya. What she lacked in antiquity, however, she made up for in completeness—a remarkable number of her bones were preserved, and she served as a prototype for other *afarensis* finds. Most eastern African fossils found between 4 and 3 mya are attributed to *afarensis*, even when evidence is indirect. For instance, the footprints at Laetoli, Tanzania, discovered by Mary Leakey's team, are taken as *afarensis* primarily because they date to around 3.75 mya. The prints were fortuitously laid down in a freshly laid bed of volcanic ash—this being a datable material—and constitute the tracks of two, possibly three, bipedal individuals (one track may have been placed within another—the scenario of a child trying to match its parents' steps springs to mind—although of course we may never know whether this was actually the case). After a good deal of study, these famous footprints have been reburied, as exposure to the elements was putting them at risk (Agnew and Demas 1995).

Don Johanson is not only an expert paleoanthropologist but a fine publicist, and he found many ways to place Lucy in the spotlight and keep her there. He has appeared in many documentaries and has cowritten books on prehistory meant for the popular market (e.g., Johanson and Edey 1981; Johanson and O'Farrell 1990). It is unsurprising, therefore, that for years most paleoanthropologists put Lucy's kind at the root of the human family tree. Even after a slightly older australopithecine appeared—*Au. anamensis*, whose remains, dating back prior to 4 mya, were first identified thus by the Meave Leakey team excavating in the Lake

SIDEBAR

The Leakeys: The "First Family" of Paleoanthropology

In any account of paleoanthropology, a name that recurs is Leakey. While Louis Leakey was hardly the first paleoanthropologist, the work he and his wife Mary carried out in Olduvai Gorge, Tanzania, became popularized in a globalizing mass media whose appetite for sensational stories was growing. It helped that Louis enjoyed the limelight; luckily for all of us, Mary, a descendant of the British antiquarian John Frere, was a workhorse who preferred making discoveries to promoting them (she outlived her husband by 24 years). Louis held strong, often controversial opinions on a great many matters and was not afraid to speak his mind.

Louis Leakey, 1903–1972.

But this did not detract from his considerable abilities as a fund-raiser, and he managed to bankroll not only his paleoanthropological work but other projects that had a bearing on biological anthropology: for instance, the primatology studies of Jane Goodall and Dian Fossey.

Louis and Mary had a son, Richard, who is much like his father, colorful and strong-willed. Richard's base in paleoanthropology was the Lake Turkana region of Kenya, where he made such discoveries as "the black skull," eventually designated *Paranthropus aethiopicus*. Though Richard curtailed his paleoanthropological work in the 1980s, his wife Meave and daughter Louise have continued on in the same region, unearthing both *Australopithecus anamensis* and *Kenyanthropus platyops*.

The Leakeys have been territorial with respect to their paleoanthropological "turf," and have openly clashed with colleagues over views regarding the place of particular fossils in the human family tree. Nonetheless, the name of Leakey has been indelibly imprinted on the subfield of paleoanthropology, and Louis and Richard have embodied the iconic image of the paleoanthropological adventurer, tirelessly scouring the landscape of eastern Africa for clues that will lead to a greater understanding of the human past (Barras 2009; Johanson 1999).

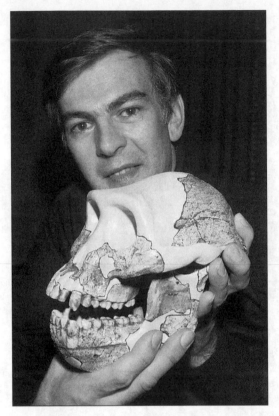

Donald Johanson, 1981.

Turkana region of Kenya (Leakey et al. 1995)—*Au. afarensis*, and especially Lucy, still captured headlines (for example, a nearly complete *afarensis* skeleton recovered in 2006, thought to be that of an immature individual, became known as "Lucy's Baby," even though it dates back earlier than Lucy [Alemseged et al. 2006]). *Au. anamensis*, for all that, did not upset then-prevailing thinking about Lucy and her kind; the species shares several traits with *afarensis* and seems, like *afarensis*, to have inhabited only a semiwooded environment, suggesting we had finally located that formative moment when our ancestors left the trees. Publicity on both species tended to confirm what we thought we already "knew," although dissenters—paleoanthropologists who questioned Lucy's bipedal capacities, for instance, or even her sex (see

Shreeve 1995)—continued to garner at least professional attention on occasion.

As previously mentioned, however, Senut and Pickford believe that *Orrorin tugenensis*, which differs from *Au. afarensis* in significant respects, is a better candidate for inclusion in the direct human line. Recent statements about *Ar. ramidus* also throw Lucy's ancestral status in question; for example, as mentioned earlier, Tim White asserts that *ramidus* males and females were roughly the same size, while our current interpretation of the *afarensis* data speaks to a marked degree of **sexual dimorphism** in the species, with males larger than females. *Homo* populations, in various times and various places, have exhibited size differences between males and females, but not to the extent, purportedly, of *afarensis*, which approached an orangutan-like contrast. Meave and Louise Leakey have joined the campaign against *afarensis*-as-human-ancestor by touting their own find, *Kenyanthropus platyops*, as a more likely candidate (Leakey et al. 2001). The *K. platyops* fossils, dating back to approximately 3.5 mya, were placed in a separate genus in order to set them apart from australopithecines; *platyops* describes the key feature of the species: a flatter face more typical of humans than of earlier hominins. However, whether a new generic name or species name is warranted, let alone speculation as to whether *Australopithecus* denotes cousins, not grandfathers, to genus *Homo*, remain in dispute. White, for instance, suspects that *platyops* is likelier a representative of species *Au. afarensis* whose flat face was merely flat*tened*—that is, crushed during the process of fossilization, while mineralization replaced both the original bone and filled in its cracks to create what seemed to be a very different visage (White 2003).

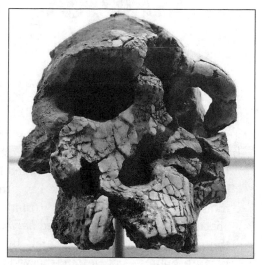

Kenyanthropus platyops.

There are other fossils that have been relegated to genus *Australopithecus*; e.g., a Chadian specimen named *Au. bahrelghazalia* (Brunet et al. 1995) and the australopithecines *garhi* and *sediba*, both of whom will figure briefly in the next chapter. But before we leave the subject for the moment, it is worth mentioning a **clade** of hominins described by some paleoanthropologists as "robust australopithecines," though this designation has been largely displaced by the generic name *Paranthropus*. We have known about *Paranthropus* nearly as long as australopithecines, since the remains of a South African species, identified today as *Paranthropus robustus*, were picked out of the same sort of quarry waste that yielded *Au. africanus*. A second paranthropine species, *P. boisei*, lived in eastern Africa, and while some paleoanthropologists identify an unusually robust skull from the Lake Turkana region as *boisei*, others see it as representative of a third species, *P. aethiopicus*. Paranthropines are referred to as **robust** (as opposed to **gracile**, the term applied to australopithecines), not because they are overall larger than their australopithecine cousins, but because they have especially heavy facial features, with jaw muscles attached to a prominent **sagittal crest.** Perhaps this exaggerated arrangement helped paranthropines reduce tough roots to an edible pulp and access foods like nut meats within shells.

While we have very little additional information about paranthropines, outside of the fact they were still around as recently as 1.75 mya, from appearance alone no paleoanthropologist considers them to be directly ancestral to humans. Hence, they would no longer concern us here but for two related reasons: first, Mary Leakey's 1959 discovery of *Zinjanthropus boisei* (*P. boisei* today), at Oldu-

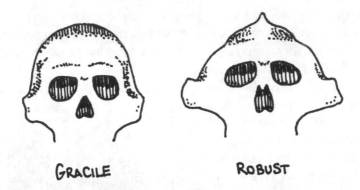

GRACILE   ROBUST

vai Gorge in Tanzania, put both the gorge and the Leakeys' paleoanthropological efforts "on the map," so to speak. Second, *Zinjanthropus* was found in **association** with stone tools. Mary's husband Louis came to reject the idea that such a brutish-looking creature could have the mental wherewithal to manufacture tools, and conveniently, fossils attributed to early *Homo* were found nearby. The species was promptly designated *habilis* by Louis—the word refers to ability, in the sense that *Homo* would surely be the toolmakers and not the heavy-faced paranthropines—but despite the wide acceptance of this seemingly common-sense notion, no one today can say with certainty that paranthropines, or for that matter australopithecines, were unable to make stone tools. This, however, is again a subject to be pursued further in the next chapter.

Plaque at Olduvai Gorge commemorating the *Zinjan-thropus* find.

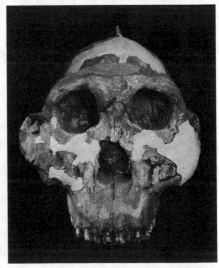

Paranthropus boisei, formerly *"Zinjan-thropus."*

SIDEBAR

What's in a (Linnaean) Name?

By this time I imagine a number of students have broken out in a cold sweat, wondering, "Will my professor really expect me to remember all these Latin names?" Your professor may well spare you, because so many designations that have been assigned are questionable (indeed, some have already been set aside) and she may not be so good at remembering them herself. But just in case she's a stickler, take heart—you *can* remember these names. I'll go even further— you *want* to remember these names, because they give off clues as to where fossils were found, and what their discoverers thought regarding their place in the human line.

Note some repeating elements: *-anthropus* (a Greek root with a Latin ending; this drives classicists crazy!) refers to "human being," and, of course, the same root yielded *anthropology*. When *-anthropus* appears in an Linnaean name, the namer is often making a statement—he's suggesting the hominin was directly ancestral to humans. The ending *-pithecus*, or ape, means the namer was somewhat more cautious—the organism may be directly ancestral, but it is also possible it is not.

The site at which a fossil was found is frequently commemorated in its Linnaean designation. *Sahelanthropus tchadensis* contains a double dose. The genus name refers to the Sahel, that band of semidesert just below the Sahara (of course *-anthropus* indicates its discoverers aspire to have their find admitted into the human line). When it comes to hominin fossils, it is more often the species name that reflects place of origin, and in this case *tchadensis* refers to the country of Chad, which was once spelled "Tchad." Other place names contained in hominin designations include the Tugen Hills of Kenya (*Orrorin tugenensis*) and the Afar Triangle of Ethiopia (*Australopithecus afarensis*). So knowing the Linnaean names for hominins is a kind of crash course in geography.

Recently it has also been a crash course in African languages, which have been mined especially for their words pertaining to origins. *Orrorin* is the Tugen word for "original man"; the *ardi-* of *Ardipithecus* is an Afar word meaning "floor," in the sense of "forest floor" (hence the base of the human family tree); *ramidus*, from *ramid*, or "root," reiterates the point. *Kadabba* means "oldest ancestor." The *anam* of *Australopithecus anamensis* is the

(continued)

Turkana word for "lake"; that is, Lake Turkana (dubbed Lake Rudolf during the colonial period).

We often think that scientists incorporate their own names, or the names of their spouses or friends, into Linnaean designations (Linnaeus himself named an invasive plant pest after a man who criticized him), but the only surname appearing in hominin designations discussed so far is that of Charles Boise (*Paranthropus boisei*), who provided financial backing to the Leakeys' work.

The point is that Latin names have a rhyme and reason, and it may be easier to remember the names, and to remember information associated with them, if you know what they mean. So from here on in, when you encounter a Linnaean designation, don't just skip over it in frustration—investigate it!

Notes on Identifying the Genus/Species/Sex/Age of Fossils

So genus *Homo* has yet to appear in this account of the hominin line, but already I have mentioned six genera (not counting the discarded designation *Zinjanthropus*) subdivided into 13 species (not counting the questionable designation *aethiopicus*). How, you might ask, were genera and species teased out of the mix of fossils found within the paleoanthropological window? Recall that in chapter 3 I defined a species as a group of organisms that is fertile only within itself, but we can hardly determine whether two fossils, when they were living organisms, could have interbred. This criterion is difficult enough to apply in the present day, and it is impossible, given current methods, to project into the distant past. Some scientists have tried to devise a quantitative measure of speciation by focusing on change in **mitochondrial DNA (mtDNA).** Mutations take place in mtDNA at a calculable rate, so the buildup of mutations is like the ticking of a clock (see chapter 7). If the mtDNA of two otherwise-related organisms varies by 10% or more, we can reasonably assume that over the time it would have taken for this degree of change to occur, two species had likely developed from the same root (Groves 1997). There are problems with this assumption—it might be that while the mtDNA faithfully kept track of the passing time, nuclear DNA was kept constant through stabilizing natural selection; it could also be that while nuclear DNA change had in fact mounted up, it did not interfere with reproductive compatibility. Nonetheless, the 10% rule may be all we have to go on if we cannot observe organisms mating and bearing fertile offspring.

The problem with fossils that are millions of years old, however, is that there is no DNA to be had. What, then, can we go on to sort fossils into different species? Space and time are obvious starting points—if a collection of similar fossils is recovered only from a particular region and only within a particular time frame, it might reasonably be suggested that we are witnessing the lifespan of a species, at least until further evidence is found. Differences in dentition and jaw formation can also provide further clues—it is not coincidental that we have developed a veritable subscience of determining species from dental evidence, since teeth, as the most durable bone in the body, may be all there is to be found. Ultimately, however, carving new genera and species out of a fragmented fossil record is a matter of informed guesswork, further guided by theories that stake out opposing positions on such issues as, for instance, the pace of evolution.

Recall from chapter 2 that there is something of a scholarly difference of opinion between those who believe that speciation results from situations of punctuated equilibrium, in which rapid environmental change encourages equally rapid separation of populations into breeding isolates, and those who hold fast to the Darwinian idea that the slow, inexorable change taking place within populations is more productive, over time, with respect to producing new species. The adherent to the former theory would hence be more prone to seeing several species and genera within a mix of fossils—we call such people **"splitters,"** for their tendency to establish new taxonomic categories—while Darwinian **"lumpers"** would advise more caution. And so, for instance, we have paleoanthropologists today who see the clade of robust hominins as worthy of generic distinction—*Paranthropus*—while others are content to continue classifying the robusts as *Australopithecus* until more evidence of a generic "split" is available.

The upshot here is that one paleoanthropologist can see a mix of fossils and pick out several species within it, while another paleoanthropologist discerns only one or two, and such differences of expert opinion do not merely turn on the debate as to how much skeletal variation, and what types of variation, suggest that more than one species is represented, but on deep-seated professional convictions regarding the nature of evolution itself. Even so, for students on the introductory level, the effect of all this is simply to saddle you with more work come testing time—there are that many more generic and species names to commit to memory!

On something of a less grand level of argument, this chapter's account of the hominin line also includes facile pronouncements about age and sex—but how do we know the Taung fossil was a child? how do we know Lucy was female? In the case of Taung, the emergent adult teeth provided strong evidence that the individual was immature, but once such teeth have fully descended, where then do we look for clues? There are cartilaginous rings toward the ends of long bones that are eventually, at a known rate within adulthood, displaced by bone; there are also certain skull sutures that do not fully knit together until later in life, though exactly when is less predictable. To utilize either of these properties for the purposes of aging a skeleton, however, entails locating the appropriate skeletal parts, which may or may not provide conclusive information. Sexing a skeleton would seem to be easier—but recall that doubts have been raised even about the sex of the iconic Lucy. If we presume, as we have, that the size differential among *Au. afarensis* fossils sets off the larger males from the smaller females, then Lucy's diminutive size certainly would seem to relegate her to the female category; however, not all paleoanthropologists have interpreted the size differential in terms of sexual dimorphism. The shape of the pelvis can also help us to pin down sex, but we would need an assortment of pelves, from both male and female specimens, to understand fully how the pelvic girdle varied across sex within a species.

Modern **forensic anthropology** has certainly contributed in the area of aging and sexing skeletal remains, but we must be very careful not to assume that what is true of today's human being is true for ancient hominins. Lifespan, the rate of maturation, the diseases to which one might be exposed that have an effect on bone, the ways in which an infant might be birthed—all of these might vary greatly from hominin species to hominin species even within the same time period, and obviously can vary through time. Lifestyle, too, may have an impact on the aging process—we might think that if an individual's teeth show a good deal of wear, that individual must have lived into old age, but certain diets and activities might produce a significant degree of dental wear quite early in life.

If our first estimate of age or sex turns out to be dubious when further evidence is on hand, this would not seem to be tragic—after all, that science can suffer correction is one of the great strengths of this model of understanding—but if a fossil has come to be known as "female" in the media, the error is far less easily rectified. Even so, it may be worth taking the risk, since the public is understandably more captivated by a fossil that has such basic human characteristics as age and sex.

SIDEBAR

Human Phylogeny

So how do all of these genera and species figure in human **phylogeny**—that is, our family tree? Are they direct ancestors, cousins, only distantly related? Here again, we don't know. We can make educated guesses, and hopefully we will become even better educated as to our origins in time, but until we find more fossil material and/or new ways to assess it, we can only wrangle at conferences regarding possible sequences. Most paleoanthropologists are willing to set off the paranthropines on a side branch, but some would like to do the same to the australopithecines. A few believe a direct human ancestor within the paleoanthropological window has yet to be located. These few are not creationists; they are simply dissatisfied with the candidates available thus far.

Again, none of this back-and-forth indicates science is abandoning the theory of human evolution. There is plenty of evidence, but with respect to how it all fits together, there remains plenty of debate, and the dust is unlikely to settle any time soon, if ever. And I have to say that the reader who is unnerved by this level of disagreement will find no comfort in chapter 6, when we are on the allegedly firmer ground of genus *Homo*.

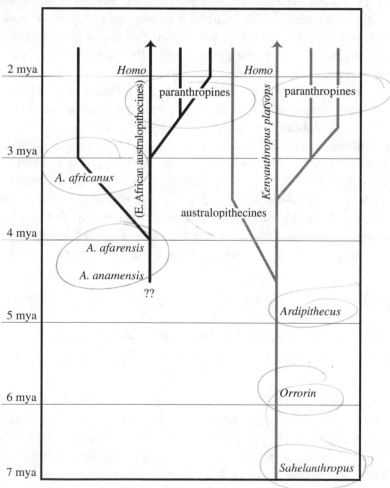

Two versions of human phylogeny.

Peering at Daily Life through the Paleoanthropological Window

This has already been a long chapter, and perhaps a more frustrating one than most for the student reader, because you have been asked to wade through a wealth of species names with no indication so far of an answer to the most interesting question: what were these early hominins like? What did they think? How did they live? Did they make sentences, make tools, make art, make love? And the bald fact is: we don't know. We can guess that they used tools—for example, breaking open a nut with a rock—and likely made such perishable implements as a termiting stick, but neither of these activities distinguishes early hominins from a modern chimpanzee. Holloway, who has studied how brain capacities are imprinted on skulls, maintains that australopithecine brains were, in terms of organization if not size, more human than panin (Holloway et al. 2004), but how that actually affected australopithecine behavior is unknown. Until there is definitive evidence to the contrary, it is prudent to presume that these earliest hominins behaved more like nonhuman animals than modern humans.

That presumption, however, does not limit our impressions of them much, since nonhuman animals behave in a number of fascinating ways. But this number is constrained by the demands of survival. Recall that animal behavior evolves in concert with an environment, shaping and being shaped by the larger project of building a working ecosystem. Further, ecosystems change, and the living things embedded within them must also change if they are to continue as living things. These two simple principles have suggested a course that many paleoanthropologists believe our ancestors may have followed.

EXERCISE

Add the places mentioned in this chapter to the map in chapter 4.

When the vast forests of sub-Saharan Africa were shrinking during the Pliocene **epoch** (5.3–2.6 mya), eventually giving way to grasslands occasionally dotted with trees, the habits of a number of species must have been disrupted. Prior to this development, hominins may have competed with panins for the fruits of the forest, but panins won out, forcing hominins to the edge of the wooded areas, where they were confronted not only by a dearth of their favorite foods but by a raft of strange and fearsome predators. If in fact the human line can be traced back to *Ardipithecus,* our ancestors may have had the defensive advantage of size, but this likely did not wholly eliminate the threat of predation. Brain's analysis of the fossils in South African caves indicates hominins frequently served as fodder for carnivores (Brain 1981).

With respect to their own food quest, however, hominins were not so helpless. Fruit may not have been as readily available to them, but hominins, like panins, are omnivorous, open to being carnivores themselves on those occasions when they could obtain meat. They were doubtless capable of hunting, but they may also have taken advantage of meat they did not directly obtain; for instance, leopard kills cached in the trees (Cavallo 1990). The addition of carrion to the hominin diet not only would have broadened the supply of available foods but also might have given hominins an incentive to venture further into the savanna, where more dead animals, baked relatively clean of harmful bacteria by the intense sun, might be found. If the human line were more australopithecine than ardipithecine in terms of sexual dimorphism, it could even have been the case that the smaller females continued to exploit arboreal foods, while males, grounded by their bulk, began to forage extensively on the ground.

So over time, hominins may have become **scavengers,** not simply on an opportunistic basis but as a full-time food-getting strategy (Binford 1981). Scavenging sustains many a species in the world today, but there is one drawback that would have hit our ancestors head-on. Scavengers, like hyenas, jackals, and vultures, are some of the most cunning beasts on the planet. To compete in this niche hominins had to be equally cunning. But they did not apply their brain power, at least at first, toward enhancing brawn or stealth, since in both cases hominins, despite their considerable potential, would have been soundly defeated by their rivals. Rather, the trick to survival may have been to make effective use of a carcass after it had seemingly been picked clean by a first wave of scavengers. Working over an already well-worn carcass had a distinct advantage in that the chances the other scavengers would revisit the site were minimized; the disadvantage, of course, lay in the problem of how to access any remaining food value.

Bones contain marrow, a substance rich in nutrients. Some predators and scavengers can obtain it by dint of their powerful teeth and crushing jaws, two attributes hominins did not share. But, as previously suggested, hominins probably did know how to crack nuts with stones, and it would make sense to apply this technology to the cracking of bones. If, while roaming the savanna, a hominin could nab an intact long bone from a carcass, it could scurry back to the relative safety of the forest and open the bone at its leisure. Perhaps there was already a flat "anvil" rock set up against which many a hard object had been bashed. It

THE WISE HOMININ WAITS HIS TURN...

would be a long time before hominins would shift from tool use to toolmaking in this area—selecting naturally occurring stones to serve these purposes, versus actually manufacturing the appropriate stone implements—but once our ancestors knew what features in a stone facilitated access to marrow, these features might be replicated through artificial means. And that subject leads us to our next chapter, after a closing note.

   None of us knows for sure if this is how human behavior evolved, although we do have some evidence in the form of cracked bone ends from prey animals and cut marks on bone suggesting that every scrap of meat, even after it had dried and hardened, was removed. But by this time readers should be painfully aware that when it comes to human evolution, what makes sense isn't always true. Even so, the Scavenger Hypothesis currently has great cachet, from a practical standpoint if not from an aesthetic one. Sensible though it may be, the idea that today's human beings sprang from carrion-eating forebears may seem ignoble, to say the least. For those of you who miss the image of our earliest ancestors as Mighty Hunters, striding, spear in hand, across the windswept plains, I can offer no solace outside of the demonstrably adept end product. According to the Scavenger Hypothesis, the extraordinary human capacities of the present day were honed in the cutthroat competition of hominin-against-hyena, and that the hominin was able, eventually, to hold its own (though surely it was touch-and-go at more than one juncture) testifies to the value of the experience.

From Central Africa:

SITE	COUNTRY	PALEO-ANTHROPOLOGIST	DISCOVERY	DATING BACK TO
Toros-Menalla	Chad	Ahounta Djimdoumalbaye (Brunet team)	*Sahelanthropus tchadensis* ("Toumai")	6–7 mya
Bahr el Ghazal	Chad	(Brunet team)	*Australopithecus bahrelghazalia*	3.5–3 mya

From the Great Rift Valley, eastern Africa:

SITE	COUNTRY	PALEO-ANTHROPOLOGIST	DISCOVERY	DATING BACK TO
Lukeino, Tugen Hills	Kenya	Brigitte Senut, Martin Pickford	*Orrorin tugenensis* ("Millennium Man")	6 mya
Aramis, Middle Awash	Ethiopia	Y. Haile Selassie	*Ardipithecus kadabba*	5.6–5.2 mya
Aramis, Middle Awash	Ethiopia	Tim White	*Ardipithecus ramidus*	4.4 mya
Kanapoi/Allia Bay, Lake Turkana	Kenya	Meave Leakey	*Australopithecus anamensis*	4.2–3.9 mya
Lomekwi, Lake Turkana	Kenya	Justus Erus (Meave Leakey team)	*Kenyanthropus platyops*	3.5 mya
Laetoli	Tanzania	Paul Abell (Mary Leakey team)	*Australopithecus afarensis* footprints	3.75 mya
Dikika, Afar Triangle	Ethiopia	Zeresenay Alemseged	*Au. afarensis* ("Lucy's Baby")	3.3 mya
Hadar, Afar Triangle	Ethiopia	Don Johanson	*Au. afarensis* ("Lucy")	3.2 mya; other finds at site date earlier
Bouri, Afar Triangle	Ethiopia	Berhane Asfaw	*Australopithecus garhi*	2.5 mya
West Turkana	Kenya	Richard Leakey	*Paranthropus aethiopicus* ("Black Skull")	2.5 mya
Olduvai Gorge	Tanzania	Louis/Mary Leakey	*Paranthropus boisei* ("Zinj")	1.75 mya

From southern Africa:

SITE	COUNTRY	PALEO-ANTHROPOLOGIST	DISCOVERY	DATING BACK TO
Taung	South Africa	Raymond Dart	*Australopithecus africanus* ("Taung Baby")	possibly 3 mya
Kromdraai, Swartkranz	South Africa	Robert Broom, John Robinson	*Paranthropus robustus*	2–1 mya
Malapa	South Africa	Lee Berger	*Australopithecus sediba*	1.9 mya

Paleoanthropological finds (hominin [maybe?] but not *Homo* [maybe!]).

QUESTIONS FOR DISCUSSION AND REVIEW

- Why might paleoanthropological discoveries be "oversold"?
- What does each of the following experts contribute to a paleoanthropological team?—taphonomist, geologist, paleontologist.
- What did the Piltdown hoax teach us?
- How and from what is bipedalism determined?
- Why are "splitters" likely to support the concept of punctuated equilibrium?
- How does scavenging explain some of the developments within the hominin line?

KEY WORDS

paleoanthropological window	temporal	gracile
mineralization	context	robust
taphonomy	Piltdown Man	sagittal crest
Great Rift Valley	teleology	splitter
fossil locality	cranial	lumper
geologist	postcranial	epoch
paleontologist	Savanna Hypothesis	scavenger
palynologist	endocast	phylogeny
comparative osteologist	karst	

HOMININ NAMES TO KNOW

Sahelanthropus tchadensis   *Australopithecus afarensis*
Orrorin tugenensis   *Australopithecus africanus*
Ardipithecus kadabba   *Kenyanthropus platyops*
Ardipithecus ramidus   *Paranthropus robustus*
Australopithecus anamensis   *Paranthropus boisei*

6

GENUS *HOMO*
A LONG, STRANGE TRIP

Homo habilis
you set us up for *erectus*
who would travel the world, but it was you not he
who was the first of the genus *Homo*
. . . that led to me.

—pRiYaAnNo, "The Song of *Homo habilis*"

www.youtube.com/watch?v=U0zrGzxjEAY

A Head for Toolmaking

The oldest stone tools of which we currently know, dating back to approximately 2.6 mya, were discovered in the Gona River region of Ethiopia (Semaw et al. 1997). As previously suggested, stones were likely used as tools far earlier than this, but these are the first implements that show signs of deliberate manufacture, presumably by hominins. While no hominin fossils have yet been found in association with these tools, at Bouri, a nearby site, the bones of game animals dating back nearly as far exhibit cut marks of the sort a sharpened stone would make (de Heinzelin et al. 1999). In this instance there are hominin fossils in the vicinity, attributed to an australopithecine species dubbed *garhi*, which in the local language means "surprise." And indeed, *Au. garhi* would be a great surprise if it could ever be proven to be responsible for making the stone tools. But downright startling, if it holds up, is a recent claim that at Dikika, Ethiopia, where "Lucy's Baby" was unearthed, bones with cut marks date back nearly 3.4

OLDOWAN TOOLS (Core and flake)

mya, clearly within the time span of genus *Australopithecus* and well before the emergence of genus *Homo* (McPherron et al. 2010). There has been resistance to such conclusions, despite the fact that similarly circumstantial evidence has been accepted as sufficient support for other allegedly firm contentions in paleoanthropology. But in this case the problem is that australopithecines have panin-sized brains.

Paranthropines have larger brains, but only because their heads are larger. Outside of this fact, the heavy facial features of paranthropines would seem to consign them to a more apelike level of intelligence (although this is a prejudice on our part that we would do well to discard). Recall that when stone tools were found in association with what first became known as *Zinjanthropus*, Louis Leakey scrambled to find another, more human-headed hominin that could have been responsible. It was all very well and good to admit these panin-brained bi-peds into the human line, but surely, when it came to the purposeful manufac-ture of stone tools, we could finally expect to find the Big Brain.

There are two points to be made here. The first is that the history of modern science is marred by the conviction that a big brain is necessarily a more intelli-gent brain. Allegedly "scientific" experiments, like Morton's infamous compari-son of human "races" (see chapter 10), were premised on this assumption, and of course, since it was accepted on a commonsense basis, it could not be "dis-proved"—everyone "knew" larger meant better, and this in itself was not investi-gated. Now, when comparing markedly different species, there is *some*thing to having a proportionately larger brain—it follows that a human being is more in-telligent than, say, a rat, although frankly, rats have extraordinary capacities and perhaps cannot be judged according to human standards (the difficulties with es-tablishing such standards in the first place will be addressed in the next chapter). But the extent to which one ancient organism may have been more intelligent than a related organism based on differential skull size (and alleged behaviors rooted in that difference) may never be known, or even knowable.

The second point inverts the first—just how much brain power might be needed to fashion a stone tool, in any case? If australopithecines and paranthro-pines had been using stone for millennia to break open nuts and bones, why would the crude chipping of a stone to suit its purpose better entail that much more brain matter? Do chimpanzees that know how to make and use termiting sticks—and not all do—have significantly bigger brains than their conspecifics? Was there an increase in brain size when this technology was developed? It could be that we make too much of the alleged connection between brain size and the ability to manufacture tools. Chipping stone may have been less a revolutionary breakthrough than a straightforward progression, a matter of degree as opposed to kind, requiring no additional brain development.

Those who have believed that non-*Homo* hominins did not have the mental wherewithal to make stone tools were bolstered in this claim by early assess-ments of the australopithecine/paranthropine grip, which was also deemed inad-equate to the task. Even this conclusion, however, has been re-evaluated (see, e.g., Panger et al. 2002). The fact is we simply cannot state with security that australopithecines and/or paranthropines were unable to work stone.

That having been said, it is undeniable that eventually species within the human line did undergo **encephalization** to a dramatic degree and that our ancestors developed capabilities that were distinct from those of any ape. In other words, there is ample justification for establishing a separate genus, _Homo,_ for those species of bipedal hominins that were also big-brained. But just when was this evolutionary course begun? And exactly why did it take place? If these seem like amazing questions to pose after more than a century of concerted paleoanthropological research, it is even more amazing to note that the existence of _Homo habilis,_ the species thought to have launched the genus, has never been pinned down.

Before I address this disconcerting situation—and there are others in the offing—I will dedicate a portion of this chapter to a discipline that will soon entirely displace paleoanthropology as the guiding field of study behind our inquiry into human evolution.

Archaeology

As you already know, **archaeology,** in the United States, does not stand alone as a field of study but is drawn under that outsized umbrella we call anthropology. You should also recall that what archaeology shares with its sister fields is a concern for culture, the extraordinary means through which human beings have organized their disparate lifeways. Within the paleoanthropological window, we have likely only laid the biological groundwork for culture, or at least there is no evidence that hominins were behaving in ways we would recognize as human in this aspect. Manufactured stone tools, however, change the game a bit—they suggest the creature that made them had the rudiments of a cultural mind. As I have hinted before, this may not, in fact, be the case—just because a nonhuman animal makes tools, we do not then say it is cultural—but when it comes to human ancestry, from the first simple stone tools we can reasonably look down the road to more complex stone tools, in a variety of styles; and tools designed for a greater variety of purposes; and such related developments as the making of fire, the making of art, and so on. Our evidence at the moment (or absence thereof, actually) suggests this is a much longer road than we have previously believed, and yet we know that eventually human beings do master all of these things. Stone tools may not be the right place in the timeline to stand and survey everything that followed, but for lack of a more secure starting point, they are as good a place as any.

While prior to the onset of culture we cannot really claim to be archaeologists, even experts tend not to split hairs—if an archaeologist has an interest in australopithecines, few will indict the avocation as inappropriate. For all that, paleoanthropologists are archaeologists in that they employ a range of archaeological recovery techniques. Archaeologists are well aware of the importance of **context**—*where* something is found, in **association** with *what*, can often tell us as much about an object as the object itself—and do whatever they can to preserve it. To the extent possible, paleoanthropologists follow this example. We have come far from the days when Raymond Dart became excited about quarry waste—for today's paleoanthropologist, a load of quarry waste would be something of a disappointment, though of course no one would throw the Taung Child back in the trash heap.

While conclusions about culture can certainly be drawn from fossils, archaeologists are generally more interested in **artifacts,** which, as was noted in chapter 2, are material items that exhibit the traces of human cultural behavior. Manufactured stone tools are the very first items on which the tag of "culture" might be hung; hence, rightly or wrongly, their appearance establishes the start of what we call the **archaeological record.** Thereafter, any further artifacts that are added to this "collection" can, through careful study, tell us what it has been to be human even before our immediate ancestors appear on the scene. Artifacts that are not readily portable, like hearths or buildings, are called **features.** Artifacts and features constitute what is known as **material culture,** the tangible residue of human thought. The task of the archaeologist is to re-create that thinking from the things—only the nonperishable ones, to boot—left behind. In other words (harking back to chapter 1), archaeologists literally have to "flesh out" the human story from an incomplete and distorted compilation of human physical and cultural remains. This is not at all easy, but fortunately, it is a task whose challenges many have been eager to tackle.

Until cultural thinking becomes more obvious in this account of the human line, the term "paleoanthropology" will continue to crop up from time to time, especially when we are discussing fossils more than artifacts. Nonetheless, archaeology will be with us in one form or another from now until the end of the book. Aspects of the field that cannot yet serve our purposes will be introduced in subsequent chapters. In this chapter, it might be best to return briefly to the issue of context, specifically in its **temporal** dimension, although of course the spatial dimension will not be neglected. I have already referred to fossils being so-many-millions of years old; it is certainly time I explain why.

Dating Techniques

Alas, the title of this section is not signaling that this book is taking a turn toward a subject in which young adults are *truly* interested. By "dating," of course, I mean that as archaeologists—and, for that matter, as paleoanthropologists, paleontologists, and geologists—we want to know how old things are.

Dating techniques are either **chronometric,** yielding a numeric range, or **relative,** referring to the ordering of finds on a timeline. The most well-known relative technique is called **stratigraphy,** which, literally translated, makes it seem as though a timeline is "written" onto layers of earth. This is not far wrong. If we dig straight down into a plot of land, the exposed earth may be composed of distinct horizontal bands. A thin, rocky **stratum** may have been laid down during a brief period of drought; while thicker, darker strata could indicate years of lush plant growth, with a good deal of organic matter being added to the soil. The need to preserve stratigraphy is why archaeological excavations are often con-

STRATIGRAPHY

ducted in a geometric pattern, governed by right angles—the verticality of the dig against the horizontality of strata provides the "cross" of "cross-section."

You may recall from chapter 2 that the simple principle guiding our interpretation of stratigraphy is "the deeper, the older." This principle, enshrined in such terms as Lower, Middle, and Upper when referring to ancient time periods, holds true unless stratigraphy has been disturbed, though we can often detect this disturbance and account for it. Note that the principle does not deal in numeric dates, but rather, sequences—we can tell that one thing is older or younger than another. This is why we call stratigraphy a relative dating technique, since "dates" are established only through comparison.

You might wonder how useful such a technique might be nowadays when chronometric dates are seemingly more obtainable, but sequencing fossils and artifacts remains worthwhile. It certainly may be that chronometric dating techniques cannot be applied reliably, or at all, to a particular context; it is also the case that sequencing identifies which specimens are best sent off to the laboratory for chronometric assessment, since all such techniques are expensive to carry out and the excavator must be selective. Finally, a series recorded at one site and assigned chronometric dates might reasonably serve as a gauge for dates at another site where the same sequence is observed. If, as suggested in chapter 5, a site yields a good many pig-like (suid) fossils over a period of years—and suids were likely more plentiful than hominins at any given time, making the piggy fossils easier to obtain—we could have the materials to reconstruct the evolutionary sequence of suids in the region; this exercise is known as **biostratigraphy.** If, further, we can have the suid fossils dated through chronometric techniques (for example, a species could be estimated to have existed between 3.5 and 3 mya), we can posit that nonsuid fossils found in association with suid fossils from that species are likely also between 3.5 and 3 million years old. This is how some of the South African hominin fossils have been dated—recall that such fossils have often been decontextualized, and in fact the South African landscape does not lend itself to the formation of stratigraphy. But layers of fossils have accrued for millennia in limestone caves, and if hominin fossils co-occur in a layer with a pig species believed to have lived 3 mya in eastern Africa, we have a logical figure to apply to the hominin.

So relative dating techniques cannot be set aside in these modern times; however, if we *can* obtain chronometric dates, we certainly want them. The term "chronometric" literally refers to the measurement of time, and what we ideally learn from a chronometric technique is a number, be it 100 years ago, 100 thousand years ago (which we abbreviate as 100 **kya**), or a million years ago. Within the paleoanthropological window, we have applied a number of chronometric techniques, but far and away the most common is **potassium-argon dating,** though recently a variant of this technique, called argon-argon dating, has largely displaced it. Even so, many of the dates that have already been introduced in this account were obtained through the original method.

Potassium is an **element** whose chemical symbol is K. Like other elements, it has more than one form, or **isotope,** existing in known proportions. Potassium-39, generally notated as ^{39}K, is the most common potassium isotope; it is stable, meaning that under ordinary circumstances it does not break down. The same cannot be said for ^{40}K, a **radioactive** isotope of potassium that undergoes a form of decay yielding Argon-40 (^{40}Ar), a gaseous element. The **half-life** of ^{40}K is 1.3 billion years old; that is, it would take 1.3 billion years for half of the ^{40}K in a given sample to decompose into ^{40}Ar—wait another 1.3 billion years and half of that remaining half will become argon, and so on. One billion years is, of course, an extraordinarily long time. Potassium-argon (or K/Ar) dating, therefore, is more suited toward measuring very old dates; in fact, it becomes progressively less useful as we move out of the millions-of-years range to the thousands-of-years range, and should not be used at all beyond 100 kya. As is true of most of the dating techniques I will discuss, there is a large margin of error for K/Ar dates, but a plus-or-minus factor of 200,000 years, say, is less significant when the item to be dated is millions of years old.

Only a very few substances can be subjected to K/Ar dating; by far the most common is the **igneous** rock produced by a lava flow. Not only does such rock tend to contain high amounts of potassium, but when it is molten, all gases are driven off. Hence, any argon that has accrued from the time the rock was liquid is presumed to be **radiogenic;** that is, the product of radioactive decay. This "new" argon is trapped in the hardened matrix and is thus available to be measured. The amount of argon is assayed against the amount of remaining ^{40}K to determine the date when the rock first solidified. In the argon-argon variant of this technique, all of the potassium in a sample is converted to argon via subatomic bombardment, and in this way only argon (though in two different isotopes, ^{39}Ar and ^{40}Ar) need be measured, eliminating the need for a separate process to measure potassium.

As indicated above, no one expects pinpoint accuracy from K/Ar dating in and of itself, but with respect to the dated materials we have discussed so far, accuracy can be further compromised by the fact that K/Ar dating cannot be carried out on fossils themselves, unless, like the Laetoli footprints, they were conveniently laid in a fresh bed of volcanic ash. Since such fortuitous placement is understandably a rare occurrence, the backup plan is to locate volcanic layers nearby and to make the case that one layer is contemporaneous with the fossil find, or that two layers sandwich its time period.

Although every effort is made to ensure that the K/Ar date is at least in the ballpark, of necessity it must be checked through numerous other techniques,

Argon gas is driven off while the rock is still
molten; when the rock hardens, radiogenic argon
begins to build up.

which are less accurate even than K/Ar but can often tell us when we are far off
the mark. Most of these alternative techniques are also **radiometric**—that is,
they rely on the radioactive properties of elements and/or isotopes of elements—but one that is not is **paleomagnetism.** Paleomagnetism is premised on
the fact that, due to processes going on in the Earth's core, the magnetic pole of
the planet has oscillated between north and south. These shifts have taken place
over thousands of years; we have for quite some time been in a phase in which
the magnetic pole is north, though geologists tell us that the next polar shift is
not far off, in geological terms. The upshot is that your compass needle does not
have to point north, and will not point north once the pole shifts; if human history (as opposed to prehistory) had taken place entirely within a period when the
pole was southerly, we would not think of "north" as "up," or depict the Earth
with the North Pole at the "top."

That, you might say, is cool, but how does it help us to date paleoanthropological and archaeological finds? Once again we need a liquefied rock matrix, but
for paleomagnetic assessment we can potentially use **sedimentary** as well as igneous rock. In a liquid matrix, magnetic particles are free to orient themselves toward the pole of the moment, but once the rock hardens, the particles are locked
in place, pointing south, for example, even after the pole has shifted north.

Hence there is a record of the pole's position that can be matched against the record geologists have drawn up from studying the sea floor spreading taking place at **tectonic** sutures. Since the magnetic pole has not shifted all that often, a paleomagnetic measurement can only delineate a broad range of time, so we cannot rely on this method to get us anywhere close to an exact date. However, we can sometimes discover, through a paleomagnetic cross-check of a K/Ar date, that the latter is not wrong or, alternatively, is very wrong.

It should be evident by this time that I could dedicate an entire chapter to dating techniques and how they work, but I will spare you for the moment. Fear not, however; we will revisit this issue in chapters to come (though before then you can consult Ludwig and Renne 2000). You may be wondering why I did not describe radiocarbon dating, since that is a technique with which most people are somewhat familiar. We will get to it, but there is a good reason for its having been deferred. The radiocarbon method comes nowhere near the paleoanthropological window; if we take this as having closed at 2.6 mya, with the appearance of stone tools, 2.5 million years have to go by before radiocarbon dates even begin to apply. In the meantime, we have more troublesome issues to which to return.

The Mysterious Rise of Genus *Homo*

If we cannot take stone tools as absolutely indicative of the appearance of genus *Homo*, then how old are the oldest *Homo* fossils? Most fossils attributed to *H. habilis,* all found in eastern/southern Africa, have been dated back nearly to the 2 million-year mark, although one of the oldest is identified by some to be representative of a different species, *H. rudolfensis.* Nonetheless, the rise of *H. habilis* (or *H. rudolfensis*) is generally set well prior to 2 mya, even though at this time the only fossil evidence supporting this contention is a 2.33 million-year-old jaw fragment recovered by the Johanson team in Ethiopia (Kimbel et al. 1996).

Setting aside the possible distinction between *habilis* and *rudolfensis,* why are fossils identified as genus *Homo* in the first place? Compared to australopithecines, the cranial capacity of early *Homo* fossils is greater, while the facial profile is flatter. Even so, these differences are not so pronounced that everyone has felt comfortable drawing a generic line—the fossils could conceivably represent yet another species of australopithecine. But of course more definitively *Homo* fossils, in terms of change in these same features, do begin to turn up in greater numbers as we approach 1.5 million years, so if we want to identify prior fossils as potential ancestors, those that exhibit even the slightest tendency toward a more *Homo*-like appearance are the best available candidates. Additionally, by placing relatively small-brained fossils in genus *Homo*, we are then able to classify other small-brained hominins, like those found at the Dmanisi site in Georgia (Europe), as *Homo* rather than *Australopithecus*. In other words, this version of the generic line delimits australopithecines to Africa and to a time span that is ending rather than beginning.

This is not to assert that the *Homo* and *Australopithecus* genera do not overlap in time. Indeed, if the origin of genus *Homo* goes back to a date in advance of 2 million years, then there are certainly australopithecine fossils that are younger, including Berger's latest South African find, *Au. sediba*, first brought to the world's attention in Berger et al. 2010. More recently, in a series of new reports published in *Science* (see especially Pickering et al. 2011), Berger and his team have seized on the doubt surrounding *Homo* origins to put forth the claim that *sediba* could have given rise to the genus. Since Berger's *sediba* fossils are now dated to nearly 1.98

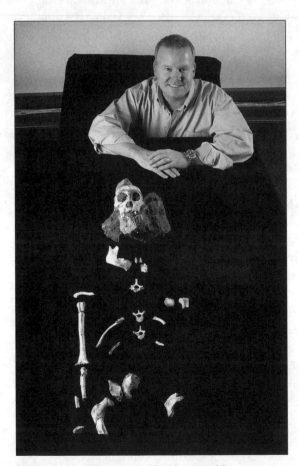

Lee Berger with *Australophithecus sediba*.

mya, acceptance of this claim throws into question the assignment of *Homo* status to any fossil prior to this date, including the Ethiopian jaw fragment mentioned above. Understandably, Johanson contends, as he has since news of the South African fossils was first released (see, e.g., Wong 2010), that *Australopithecus sediba* is simply another form of early *Homo*. Where this debate will go from here is anyone's guess—eminent paleoanthropologists have already lined up on both sides of the divide—but it is interesting to note that in the issue of *Science* that features the latest reports, two lead-in articles (Balter 2011; Gibbons 2011) treat the more controversial hypotheses concerning *sediba* somewhat coolly, mindful of Berger's history as a loose cannon (see the sidebar, "South Africa in the Spotlight," in chapter 5).

It may sound strange to suggest that genus *Homo* existed alongside australo-pithecines, given the common view that at least one of the *Australopithecus* spe-cies is in the direct human line. And this may in fact be true, but just because a parent species spawns a daughter species does not necessarily mean the parent species disappears (hence another possibility with respect to the debate just out-lined is that a population ancestral to Berger's *Au. sediba* fossils could *also* have given rise to genus *Homo* over two million years ago). Now, if both species are competing for the same resources, in the same ecological niche, then the chances for the **competitive exclusion** of one species are greater, but one reason the split may have occurred in the first place is that a population of the parent species moved into a new niche. Eventually, of course, australopithecines did become extinct, but that certain lines could have persisted after genus *Homo* took hold more firmly is not so startling. For all that, paranthropines, like *P. boisei*, also co-existed with genus *Homo*, though in this instance they would seem to be our far more distant cousins.

The possibility has also been raised that multiple species of early *Homo* coex-isted. There is a growing sense that *Homo erectus*, the species heretofore thought to follow *H. habilis* and indeed to be descended from it, might actually have co-evolved, from some common root (or a different one), with *habilis*. In Africa, *H. erectus* fossils, at least those found so far, are not as old as those attributed to *ha-bilis*, but the problem is that some of the *erectus* fossils found *outside* Africa are nearly as old. So if in fact *Homo erectus* arose in Africa, older fossils must exist on the continent, and we simply have yet to locate them.

The story of *Homo erectus* used to be unexciting. The species was thought to have emerged in eastern/southern Africa about 2 mya, and after a million or so years breakaway populations, beset by a strange wanderlust, migrated into other parts of Africa, then to Southwest Asia, nicking the easternmost reaches of Europe before heading to East and Southeast Asia. But this account is now vastly more complicated. A redating of fossils from Sangiran and Modjokerto, on the island of Java, yielded ranges whose upper limits reached 1.8 my (Swisher et al. 1994); the fossils from Georgia date back equally far. Further redating of all the fossils forced in a bit more time between African emergence and Asian migration; nonetheless, it still seemed as though no sooner had *H. erectus* evolved in Africa than it was making a beeline for the furthest reaches of the Indonesian archipelago, with pre-cious few stops along the way. Terrestrial animals certainly do migrate; herd ani-mals, especially, have been known to cover great distances very quickly. However, our ancestors were not herd animals, nor was it likely that they were imbued, at this point, with the same sort of enterprising spirit that sent Columbus halfway around the world. The extraordinary, seemingly spontaneous journey on the part of one of the earliest representatives of genus *Homo* remains baffling.

Perhaps we are going about this the wrong way—literally. Is it possible genus *Homo* actually emerged in Asia and spread to Africa? This once-popular idea introduces more problems than it solves. The reason it is dismissed by most paleoanthropologists today is because there is no indication whatsoever that hominins existed in Asia prior to *Homo erectus*, while in Africa we have nearly seven million years' worth of fossils from primate bipeds, not to mention modern cousins whose genomes are remarkably like our own. We cannot say what the future will bring in terms of grand discoveries, but if we were to unearth hominin fossils in Asia going back to well over two million years, we would have to reconsider the entire human story as we have told it to date.

So we return to Africa as a starting point for the journey of *H. erectus*, and it would seem the species left in such a hurry that it forgot its signature tool, the **bifacial handaxe,** or biface. The first example of this tool, dating to around 1.76 mya, was recently recovered in the West Turkana area (Lepre et al. 2011); early handaxes have also been found at sites in southern Africa as well as at other east-

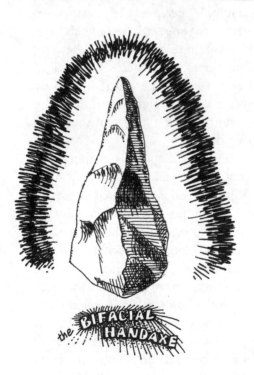

ern African sites. Prior to the development of the biface, hominins engaged in simple stone tool manufacture in a style that has become known as **Oldowan,** named after Olduvai Gorge. The Oldowan **tradition** (or **industry**) consists of little more than crudely flaked cobbles, though in terms of the marrow-harvesting demands of scavenging, they presumably did the trick. In contrast, however, the biface is a marvel of sophistication, struck on two sides (hence bifacial) to produce a highly versatile implement. In fact, there are those paleoanthropologists who believe the biface is such a revolution in stone tool technology that only a new species with greater mental abilities could have produced it. Accordingly, larger-headed specimens from the African finds are often referred to as *Homo ergaster* rather than *H. erectus*, though again we should be wary of equating brain size with tool-making ability, and certainly of designating a new species merely because one population is found in association with a particular tool, while the other is not.

If the biface is indicative of enhanced mental capacities, however, it would seem as though there were few further enhancements, at least in the area of stone toolmaking skills, for over a million years. The biface is seen as the centerpiece of an industry we call **Acheulean,** thought to be typical of *H. erectus* (*H. ergaster* if you believe the split is warranted). It is true, however, that while bifaces become common implements throughout Africa, western Asia, and eventually throughout Europe, they are rare east of what is called the Movius Line, drawn vertically through the midsection of Asia. *H. erectus* populations in northern China made do with a modification of the Oldowan industry. Otherwise, in Southeast Asia, "rare" means handaxes were nonexistent, so far as we know, on Java (in fact we find no tools with the older Javanese fossils), though possibly present on the more easterly island of Flores; a cache of handaxes in southern China near the border with Viet Nam; and a recent claim, not yet fully vetted by the archaeological community, to very old handaxes in Perak State, Malaysia. The earliest explanations of this phenomenon cast South-east Asian *H. erectus* as back-ward compared to more "advanced" populations else-where (Movius 1944), though more recently it has been proposed that perhaps the Southeast Asians tended to make their tools from perish-able substances, like bamboo (Pope 1989).

So what does it all mean? The *H. ergaster* designation recalls the idea of mental su-periority; *ergaster,* arising in Africa and later migrating to western Eurasia, is able to make the biface, while those African populations, dubbed *H. erectus,* that went on to people East Asia could not. Or, more simply, it could be

Homo erectus.

that *H. erectus* evolved in Africa and migrated to Asia before the African biface became widespread. However, I wonder if we may be barking up the wrong tree with respect to all of these species designations and their alleged associated mor-phologies and capabilities. I suspect that the earliest *Homo* population, likely emerging (from an australopithecine line?) prior to 2 mya, was one within which cranial capacity was a highly variable trait that, initially at least, had no bearing on whether an individual could make tools, and what type it could make. As this population dispersed into subpopulations, a larger head might predominate in some groups simply due to genetic drift, although at some point it might be favored via natural selection. Even so, small-brained groups continued to exist—this might explain the *habilis*-sized heads of the Dmanisi finds—though larger heads came to prevail in most populations both in Africa and in eastern Eurasia.

Whether these subpopulations actually became separate species will continue to be a matter for debate. I can accept species designations of *Homo habilis* for the earliest *Homo* populations both to evolve and to migrate, *Homo erectus* for the eventual eastern Asian populations, *Homo ergaster* for the eventual African and western Asian populations, and *Homo georgicus* for the group at Dmanisi. However, I also believe that none of these species designations must be imposed, and to the extent we reify separate species on the basis of scant clues, these namings may occasionally be less than helpful, and sometimes even counterproductive. Note that we can eliminate the problem of *H. erectus* suddenly appearing on two different continents by allowing for an earlier migration out of Africa of a species whose populations varied greatly in terms of exhibiting what would later be classic *erectus* traits.

Of course, the usual cautionary tale is attached to all of this speculation: just because it makes sense doesn't mean it's true. So again we can back off from controversy for a little while (there will be plenty more to come) to discuss something about which our information is more secure—how *Homo erectus* was brought to paleoanthropological attention.

Unearthing *Erectus*

Creationists tend to vilify Darwin as the man whose work led to a wide acceptance of the idea of human evolution, but they should likely save a little ire for Eugène **Dubois.** Darwin doubtless believed fossils of human ancestors would be found, but Dubois was the first person who set out, with a grim, near-fanatical determination, to find them.

In the early 1800s, Europeans, in their excavations of their home turf, began to uncover the fossils of strange beings—humanlike, but stout and with exaggerated facial features. Eventually such fossils were given a name—Neandertal—from one of the German sites that had yielded them. More and more of these remains began to turn up, but no one was quite sure what they might be. Was this some sort of deformed human population, one afflicted by a dread disease? With the publication of Darwin's treatise on natural selection, at least some scholars began to consider the possibility that Neandertals represented a prior stage of human evolution, but many remained unconvinced. You would think that at this point supporters of evolution would embark on an all-out search for more fossil evidence, but that did not immediately happen—instead, evidence for evolution was sought in anatomy laboratories and from studies of embryonic development. Hence when Eugène Dubois undertook a field expedition to dig for human ancestors, this was actually considered a novel approach to the problem.

Eugène Dubois was born in the Netherlands (his Francophone name notwithstanding) in 1858. He came to believe that the "missing link" between ape and man had to be a tropical creature, and he thought it might be found not in Africa but in Asia. He began his excavations on the island of Sumatra in the archipelago known as the time as the Dutch East Indies—today the country of Indonesia. To the extent the subject was even discussed, no one else at the time was proposing the cradle of humankind lay in the Dutch East Indies, but Dubois was not simply spinning the globe and sticking a finger down. As an anatomist, he had noted similarities between gibbons and humans, and thought these might be more than coincidental. Additionally, there were numerous caves, ideal dwelling places for what were thought (erroneously, as it turned out) to be "cavemen." But it has to be said that one reason Dubois chose to dig in the Dutch East Indies was merely because he had access—the Dutch were, at the time, the colonial masters of the archipelago.

On Sumatra, Dubois' investigations bore no fruit. Undaunted, he relocated to the island of Java, where, lo and behold, he found humanlike fossils, the most dramatic of which was a skullcap he recovered from Trinil in 1891. Dubois dubbed the specimen *Pithecanthropus erectus,* the term *Pithecanthropus* ("ape-man") reflecting his conviction that this was *the* missing link. While some colleagues accepted this to be true, many were critical—even evolutionists did not necessarily embrace the discovery as Dubois had represented it. Dubois was incensed. When more transitional fossils began to turn up, in northern China and later at other sites on Java, Dubois did not welcome these developments, feeling as though he had never been given proper credit for *his* work. He remained embittered until his death, and was capricious about granting fellow scientists access to his fossil collection (Shipman 2001).

The Chinese fossils were recovered from a site called Zhoukoudian, not far from modern-day Beijing (then known to the West as Peking). Canadian anatomist Davidson Black, on the strength of a few teeth granted him from previous excavators, began an active search for hominin fossils in the late-1920s and was rewarded for his efforts with the remains of a being he called *Sinanthropus pekinensis* (Hood 1964). The genus and species names were discarded when scholars acknowledged a marked similarity between the Chinese and Javanese fossils;

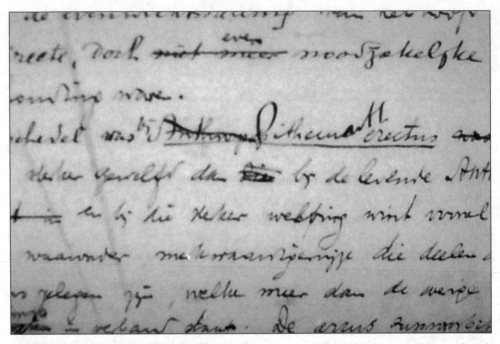

Dubois' manuscript describing "*Pithecanthropus erectus*" (notice that he initially considered the name "*Anthropus*").

all were eventually dubbed *Homo erectus*. Since most of the Chinese fossils are dated much later (under a million years) than the earliest fossils from Java, we can surmise that stabilizing natural selection was at work, despite the fact that over the millennia *H. erectus* was handling vastly different environments. The common species designation also indicates paleoanthropologists believe the various populations of *H. erectus* could and likely did interbreed, a large gene pool in and of itself tending to reinforce the normal range of variation within a species.

It should be mentioned that some of the Chinese fossils have been assigned dates similar to the early Javanese dates, but these very old dates have suffered serious challenge. At Longgupo, for instance, fossils believed to be that of *H. erectus* may actually belong to a species of ape (Etler et al. 2001), and at Yuanmou, stratigraphy containing hominin fossils would seem to have been inverted by some sort of upheaval of earth, thus also inverting the guiding principle of stratigraphy, "the deeper the older" (Liu and Ding 1984). For the moment, unless and until further evidence is uncovered, it seems best to treat the Chinese populations as the product of later migrations.

Of course very old fossils are found in Africa, but recall we have yet to sort out whether they are *H. erectus*, *H. ergaster*, or initially *H. erectus* evolving into

H. erectus Follies

Eugène Dubois was, by many accounts, not a likable man. He was possessive of his fossil finds and tended to reject any further discoveries assigned to the species he had named *Pithecanthropus erectus.* One paleoanthropologist whose work received this dismissive treatment was G. H. R. von Koenigswald. But von Koenigswald eventually gave as good as he got. He arose to great prominence as an expert on *Pithecanthropus* and took advantage of his position to disparage the work of Dubois. It was von Koenigswald's opinion that was to stick, not only because he was generally respected in his field but because he outlived Dubois by 40 years. So today we know Dubois as an unreasonable man who impeded, rather than furthered, the advancement of science (Shipman 2001). You may recall a similar situation from chapter 2, when Lamarck's reputation was greatly damaged by a derogatory eulogy written by Cuvier. One would think that gossip and back-biting should have no place in determining what we as scientists hold to be "true" (for the moment), but the stormy history of evolutionary studies testifies to the frequent—and unavoidable?—violation of this ideal (see Marcus 1991).

One scholar with whom von Koenigswald did have a productive relationship was Franz Weidenreich, who continued excavations at Zhoukoudian in China after the premature death of Davidson Black. When von Koenigswald compared his collection of *Pithecanthropus* material to the *Sinanthropus* ("China Man") fossils unearthed in China, he and Weidenreich agreed they came from the same human species—*Homo erectus.*

Weidenreich continued his studies of the Zhoukoudian material until the Japanese invasion of Manchuria in 1937 forced him to flee, leaving the fossils in the care of the medical college that had housed his work. As the war progressed, a staff member at the college decided to ship the fossils out of the country for safekeeping. The fossils disappeared and have not been found to this day, despite a well-publicized search conducted by financier and huckster Christopher Janus in the 1970s (see Miller 2009 [Janus' obituary]). The loss to science was not considered irreparable—there were casts made of each fossil, and more fossils have been discovered since from the same site. Nonetheless, like the question of who perpetrated the Piltdown hoax, the disappearance of the Zhoukoudian fossils adds to the mystery of paleoanthropology, as though the origins of the earliest humans were not mystery enough.

ergaster (or the other way around). One fossil often attributed to *H. ergaster* is that of the Turkana Boy (or Nariokotome Boy), a fairly complete skeleton, dating back to 1.6 mya, found in Kenya. It has been estimated that the Turkana Boy might have grown to a height of six feet—much taller than we would expect for genus *Homo* at this time—had he lived beyond his twelfth year (though see Graves et al. 2010 for a less generous estimate of the Boy's growth potential). Some have suggested that the Boy is illustrative of **Allen's Rule,** which states that body type is influenced by climate—in hot, dry areas, a long, lean body might be favored as a means to dissipate heat quickly from a maximal amount of exposed skin surface. In observing present-day humans we can certainly cite instances where particular body types proliferating in particular climates seem to bear out Allen's Rule, but with respect to *H. ergaster,* we would need many more fossils like the Turkana Boy to make the claim that its body type was shaped by climate.

If exposed skin surface had indeed become important in terms of dissipating the intense savanna heat, we might presume that *H. ergaster* was relatively hairless, much like modern humans. We might also presume that its skin was relatively dark from the production of the natural sunscreen **melanin,** because hairlessness might help to alleviate one problem (heat dissipation) while compounding another (protection from the burning effect of the sun's rays). Again, however, we must be aware that teleological thinking might tempt us to rush these developments within the human line—we know that they happened at some point, but can we really say, based on such sketchy evidence, that this is the point? It should also be noted that the majority of mammals on the African plains did not lose their hair; hairlessness, like bipedalism, is hardly a foregone adaptation to such conditions. The lesson may be to continue to treat all events within the human line as problematic rather than automatic, though we should not allow this approach to keep us from entertaining reasonable hypotheses and critically evaluating the support they garner.

Along these lines, the tenure of *Homo erectus* (and/or *ergaster*) on the planet has come to generate a great debate among paleoanthropologists and archaeologists, though mostly on the strength of the fact that this tenure was very long and seemingly so undifferentiated, save by the presence of a particular tools in the western part of its range and the comparative absence of the tool in the east. Just how human was *Homo erectus*? Outside of the toolmaking, did it have other leading human capacities? Did it control fire? Did it have the capacity to speak? Did it hunt in a more concerted way than its scavenging ancestors? Once again teleology may prompt us to rush these developments, but undue skepticism may induce us to delay them unduly. Unfortunately, the available evidence in all of these areas remains insufficiently convincing, one way or the other.

Hearths are a devilishly tricky feature to pick out of the most ancient archaeological record. Charcoal can occur naturally, and fires can certainly be set by agents other than human beings. Thus, with respect to any evidence of fire control prior to 400 kya, archaeologists tend to be skeptical (see, e.g., James 1989). We have a good idea, from studies of the modern human brain, just what changes have to take place to support language, and while we see some of these in the *erectus* brain, we cannot know to what extent they were applied to enhancing communication beyond the sorts of calls many animals issue to warn their conspecifics of danger. Data on the physiological adjustments needed to support modern speech are also inconclusive—there are those who believe that the vertebral canal of the Turkana Boy was too constricted to permit speech, and others who disagree (see, e.g., Walker and Shipman 1996). Regarding hunting, we have no firm support for the position that this activity had begun to displace scavenging; instead, we have more evidence that *H. erectus,* like its forebears, was hunt*ed*—the hominin remains in Chinese caves, for example, that had been assessed as proof *H. erectus* lived as "cavemen" in the vicinity, have been re-evaluated taphonomically as hyena kills (Boaz et al. 2000).

Again, this may not be the picture of our ancestors we hold dear. We have had a tendency to lionize "the weapon" as the be-all and end-all of human achievement, and as soon as we see stone tools, we think of the Mighty Hunter striding across the savanna with his stone-tipped spear. Stone tools, however, could have simply been tools—that is, implements to process scavenged meat. Doubtless many a stone tool was desperately flung in the direction of a charging predator, but until such a maneuver actually worked to take down the predator, this strategy would not necessarily inspire the hominin to make the connection between tools and killing, especially since aim would have been especially compromised under these circumstances.

So we continue to wonder just what *Homo erectus* could do, and when it could do it. What we *do* know is that, beyond some morphological variations that not all paleoanthropologists see as sufficient grounds for new species designations, *H. erectus* does not vary greatly for at least a million years, and, as will be considered in the next section, possibly much longer. From footprints, we know that these hominins were irreversibly bipedal; there is no indication the foot could double as a grasping instrument (Bennett et al. 2009). There are minor variations with respect to head shape, and variations in cranial capacity. Despite these variations, the *erectus* head can easily be distinguished from that of modern *H. sapiens,* with obvious and predictable points of contrast.

H. sapiens has a nearly vertical cranial vault, the result of a good deal of forebrain development, while the *H. erectus* skull vaults only a little. Additionally, the *erectus* skull is more angular—there is **sagittal keeling** along the top, and the shape of the skull when viewed from the back has been described as a "sagging pentagon" (think barn roof). Most *erectus* skulls have a pronounced **supraorbital torus**, more popularly known as a browridge, and another torus near the nape of its neck. *H. erectus* clearly had neither the sheer amount nor the arrangement of brain matter found in *H. sapiens*, though again, what that might actually mean in terms of its abilities cannot be known securely. However, the fact this head size and shape is typical of both the earliest Javanese finds and the northern Chinese finds, with perhaps as much as a million years between them, is perhaps more telling. And frankly, those populations that some have identified as *georgicus* and *ergaster* are not far different in terms of form. Whatever *H. erectus* (for lack of a better summary designation) was accomplishing over its considerable span of time on the planet was having very little effect on its morphology.

This is all the more strange when we remember that the rise of *Homo erectus* roughly coincides with the start of the geological epoch known as the **Pleistocene** (1.8 mya–12 kya), during which global climate was in great flux. Climate change in and of itself can sort populations into separate niches where adaptation breeds speciation, and *H. erectus* compounded matters by its dispersal into what were likely small, widely scattered populations. That these conditions did not produce a plethora of new and greatly varied species might support the idea that *erectus*, very early on, developed a suite of cultural adaptations that minimized naturally selective pressures in whatever environment it encountered. If this were true, however, you would think we would have more definitive, and more consistent, evidence for it.

On the Way to *Homo sapiens*

Outside of the foray into Georgia (which abuts Asia), did *Homo erectus* (or *Homo ergaster*) reach Europe? While there are some European fossils that have been attributed to *H. erectus* (e.g., Ascenzi et al. 1997), the answer to the question actually depends on whether, in the hominin fossils recovered from the million-year (or so) to 200-thousand-year (or so) range, one sees more than one species or a variable single species. There remain those paleoanthropologists and archaeologists content to refer to all hominin fossils within much of the time period as *H. erectus*, but certainly newer designations have gained a great deal of currency. It should be mentioned that even if, in some parts of the world, more hominin species arose, *H. erectus* lived on in others, and there are even some Javanese fossils, at Ngandong, that have dated quite young, to 53 kya and possibly younger (Swisher et al. 1996). Not all experts agree that the Ngandong fossils are *erectus*, but if they are, the species lifespan approaches two million years, which is a decent amount of time, as species go. We have a tendency to equate "going extinct" with failure, and we search for the reasons a species couldn't "keep up," but we must keep in mind that hominins with modern features appear in the fossil record only about 150 kya, so we are in no position, yet, to judge the "success" or "failure" of a species that lasted for two million years. We also have to keep in mind that *one* population of *H. erectus* (or *ergaster*) evolved into something that became ancestral to us, so the species lives on in this way.

The question before us now, however, is how many intermediate species there might have been, where they may have arisen, and where they subsequently lived. As we approach the point at which *Homo sapiens* emerged, there are changes in the archaeological record that could be interpreted as indicating new species coming into being. At long last there are definitive cultural developments in various parts of the world; for example, hearths more widely accepted as such, dating to around 400 kya, and what appear to be wooden spears dating back equally far (Thieme 1997). While the Acheulean industry remains common, a new, more efficient means of striking off stone tools from a core, the **Levallois technique,** takes hold around 250 kya. These achievements, however, do not correspond to more modern-looking fossils; if anything, the morphological features we associate with *H. erectus* become more exaggerated during this period. Encephalization continues, but we also find robust skulls with pronounced supraorbital tori and more facial **prognathism** than we might expect with the more vertical profile of *H. sapiens* virtually on the horizon. It is hardly any wonder that for years, cautious paleoanthropologists have taken the measure of all the evidence and resigned themselves to a summary label of "archaic *Homo sapiens,*" breathing a sigh of relief when something that could be called *Homo sapiens* actually does emerge from this motley collection.

Nonetheless, brave "splitters" have ventured into the heap to try out a few species designations. One that has become popular is *Homo heidelbergensis,* thought to have originated in Africa (despite the European name) about a million years ago, with some populations filtering into Europe via Gibraltar, while others stayed in Africa. Fossils from this potential species have been recovered in abundance from productive sites in modern-day Spain, supporting the idea of a Gibraltar crossing. The species name *Homo antecessor* was initially proposed for some of the earliest of these finds (circa 800 kya), but as of this writing a number of paleoanthropologists open to the idea of *Homo heidelbergensis* tend to believe this designation can be applied to the alleged *antecessor* finds as well, unless more evidence of a species distinction can be produced (Bower 2008).

These Spanish hominins are not found with anything approaching exceptional stone technology, but there is evidence they applied their technology toward a rather unsavory end. At Atapuerca (the *antecessor* site), hominin bones are found with the same sort of stone tool cut marks we see on the bones of game animals. Charges of cannibalism should not be leveled lightly—they are all too often disproved, both in the present day and in the past—but the conclusion that the Atapuerca hominins were cannibals is not unreasonable from available evidence (Carbonell et al. 2010). At a younger site nearby, Sima de los Huesos, there is another mystery regarding how hominin dead were treated. The remains

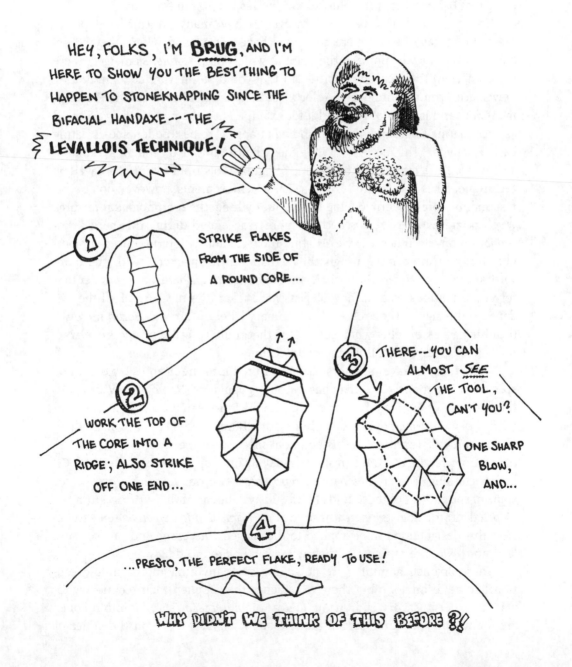

of a number of individuals are gathered at the bottom of a pit, along with animal bones. While at least two **taphonomists** (Fernández-Jalvo and Andrews 2003) assayed the assemblage as having resulted from a mudflow, Eudald Carbonell and Marina Mosquera (2006) believe it is possible the hominins were engaged in some sort of mortuary ritual.

Some supporters of the species designation *H. heidelbergensis* further propose that the species followed a divergent evolutionary course—the African population eventually yielded *Homo sapiens,* possibly through yet more intervening species, while the European population yielded **Neandertals.** Neandertals maintained the robust features of their alleged predecessors, and in fact, in northern Europe, these features were enhanced. European Neandertals are said to have a classic appearance, while those Neandertals who ranged further southward, into what is now Israel, and eastward, into Iraq and Uzbekistan, were more delicate.

While there are hints of Neandertal morphology going back much further, it is currently thought that the classic Neandertal form emerges about 130 kya and persists until about 28 kya. This span encloses much of what is popularly known as the Ice Age, a time of alternating glacial advance and retreat over the northernmost portions of Eurasia and North America (southern glaciation increased as well, but had little effect beyond the land mass of Antarctica). Scholars tend to avoid the term "Ice Age" because glaciation was hardly a unique event in Earth's history—today's global warming notwithstanding, we remain in something of an icy period, though the ice is fast (too fast?) dwindling. It is certainly the case, however, that Europe during the heyday of the Neandertals was icier, and this may have shaped the Neandertal body in several ways.

In these post-Pleistocene times, this glacier has retreated to the high Alps.

Just as Allen's Rule postulates that a long, lean body is suited to hot conditions (recall Turkana Boy), the same rule covers the opposite scenario—a stout body, with short extremities, can serve to conserve heat. European Neandertals tended to be short overall (though by no means runty) and stocky. It was also the case that Neandertal brains were often larger than those of *Homo sapiens*, but Neandertals are assigned no greater mental capacities on this account. Rather, a large brain was part of a suite of traits that were adaptive in the cold—we see similar characteristics in modern Arctic populations.

This is not to say that Neandertals had no other means of coping with extreme temperatures. Hearths have been found at Neandertal sites, and the scrapers and awls in their **toolkits,** as well as their ready access to the hides of prey animals, suggest they made clothing. Neandertals manufactured many other types of tools, as well; taken altogether, these tools constitute the **Mousterian** industry, typical of Neandertals at their apex. Neandertals were also capable of making **composite** tools; that is, tools from two different types of materials. A wooden spear with a stone point pushed into the shaft is one example. Such equipment makes the case that Neandertals were hunters, though doubtless they would not refuse a meal of scavenged meat. Hunting, in fact, likely provided the bulk of subsistence matter in a climate that was resource-poor in vegetable foods. It would not seem as though Neandertal hunters used their spears in a projectile way; rather, they stabbed prey from close range (Berger and Trinkhaus 1995). While this technique was effective in procuring food, it was also likely a factor in the number of fractures Neandertals suffered, even in their stout long bones. However, according to **paleopathologists,** these fractures often healed. Thus, fractures were not an automatic death sentence in the Neandertal world. That individuals survived such traumata has been taken as indirect evidence for the stirrings of human compassion—surely victims must have received convalescent care from their friends and/or relatives. This is not, however, necessarily so, in that the body has been known to heal even from quite serious injury without assistance (Dettwyler 1991).

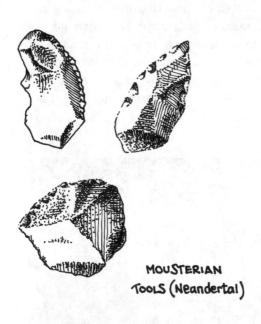

MOUSTERIAN
TOOLS (Neandertal)

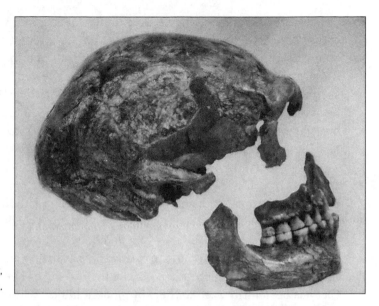

Neandertal from Spy,
Belgium.

There are other ways the Neandertal lifestyle left its mark on the body. Periods of food scarcity had an impact on tooth formation (Ogilvie et al. 1989). And some Neandertals had thicker bones in their right arms than their left, likely reflecting the regular application of tremendous thrust, of the sort that would be needed to penetrate the tough hide of a large mammal (Schmitt and Churchill 2003). The same effect can be seen in, for example, a modern-day tennis player. That it was more often the right arm than the left suggests that right-handedness was prevalent, just as it is in modern humans.

So Neandertals controlled fire, had a complex toolkit with specialized implements, hunted large game animals with proficiency if not elegance, and made clothing—were they, for all intents and purposes, human? With regard to other forms of human behavior, we are not so sure. They do seem to have vocalized—the discovery of a Neandertal **hyoid** bone, resembling the modern human counterpart that keeps the larynx in its unusually low position within the neck, provides convincing evidence for this capacity (Arensburg et al. 1990)—but we have no idea whether the sounds they made constituted anything we would recognize as language. Neandertal sites are generally devoid of any objects we might, even at a stretch, construe as art. Neandertals do appear to have buried their dead, for reasons that go beyond a practical means of disposal. Neatly laid-out skeletons have been found with what might be **grave goods,** objects deliberately placed with corpses in advance of burial. At the Shanidar excavation in what is now Iraq, pollen in the grave site suggests that the body was surrounded by flowers, from plants with medicinal properties (Solecki 1977). But why? Did flowers have the same sort of significance they have at funerals today? Or was it just because the corpse smelled bad? Were the plants used in an attempt to cure the individual before death? Or were they part of the individual's pharmacopeia; that is, was he some sort of healer? Some archaeologists have viewed the entire matter with skepticism—Jeffrey Sommer, for example, suggests that the pollen could have been moved into the grave through the action of a local rodent (Sommer 1999)—but why go to the effort of burying the dead at all? Unfortunately, dead Neandertals tell no tales, at least—to this point—not in the detail we might like.

One observation we *can* make with some security is that Neandertal "culture," such as it is, becomes more differentiated as time goes on. Toolkits, like the Châtelperronian industry generally attributed to late Neandertals (e.g., Bailey and Hublin 2008, though see Higham et al. 2010 for a challenge to this interpretation), include a greater variety of implements, and a few artifacts that could be interpreted as art appear. But are Neandertals changing on their own, as João Zilhão and colleagues (2006) assert? Or are they taking on the trappings of a culture that has been introduced to them by modern humans, our direct ancestors (Harrold 1989)? Whatever the answer(s) to these questions, the following point emerges: whether Neandertals are developing their own cultures and/or whether they are being influenced by outsiders surely grants them in both instances something very similar, if not identical, to a human quality of mind.

However, we have brushed past another important point. Within their time on the planet, the range of Neandertals began to overlap with that of modern humans. This happened relatively early on in Israel, at about 90 kya, and later in Europe, at about 40 kya. While, as mentioned above, Neandertals in Southwest Asia were not so robust as the classic Neandertals of Europe, all are nonetheless distinguishable from modern humans in terms of morphological characteristics. Hence, we can identify Neandertal sites and modern human sites in both regions. To date, we have not found sites where Neandertal and modern human fossils are mixed. We do not really know, then, what the extent of contact might have been. Did the two groups encounter each other? Were these isolated incidents or regular occurrences? To the degree technology transfer may have taken place between the two groups, could it have been accomplished solely via found artifacts and not via direct communication? Again, the archaeological record has yet to yield clear information on such matters.

The astute reader may already have noticed that I seem to be ducking a vital issue: did Neandertals and modern humans interbreed? After all, if sexual contact took place, we could presume the two populations engaged in other forms of contact. Until quite recently, however, majority opinion was swayed toward the conclusion that Neandertals and modern humans were not interfertile; that is, they were two different species, *Homo neanderthalensis* and *Homo sapiens,* and never the twain did meet. Fossils that seemed to be a mix of both populations, like the juvenile unearthed at Lagar Velho in Portugal (Duarte et al. 1999), were dismissed; "simply a chunky . . . [modern human] child," pronounced Ian Tattersall and Jeffrey Schwartz (1999) with finality. But amazingly, as I was writing the first draft of this chapter, the Max Planck Institute for Evolutionary Anthropology, the very same authority whose DNA comparisons of Neandertals and modern humans convinced so many that interbreeding was likely wholly precluded (e.g., Serre and Pääbo 2008), reversed itself on the strength of extensive further research—interbreeding *had* taken place, with at least 1% and possibly as much as 4% of the genome of modern non-African populations donated by Neandertal forebears (Green et al. 2010), though the data are inconclusive regarding whether interbreeding was a matter of a brief, intense flurry, or occasional encounters over a long period of time.

Either way, this was an astonishing assertion, bound to cause both jubilation and dismay as well as a good deal of rethinking among biological anthropologists. Not so long ago, there were two diametrically opposed schools of thought, both with fervent proponents, on the evolution of modern humans. The first school turned on the premise that Neandertals and modern humans were absolutely separate species (indeed, that modern humans were a separate species from all other hominins); a second school was founded on the conviction that Neandertals and modern humans (and for that matter, a good many other hominin groups) were merely subspecies of the same species, *Homo sapiens* (for lack of a better summary term). To open the next chapter, I will briefly recount the histories of these two schools of thought, but while

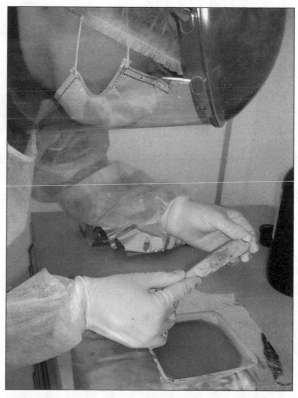

Extracting Neandertal DNA at the Max Planck Institute, Leipzig, Germany.

each is illustrative of recent leading trends in evolutionary studies, ultimately they both return us to a very old question: What is a species?

QUESTIONS FOR DISCUSSION AND REVIEW

- What do stone tools tell us about the beings that made them? What *don't* they tell us?
- Describe a way relative dating techniques work together with chronometric techniques.
- What would we have to find to think in terms of hominin origins lying *outside* Africa?
- Discuss the different ways we might interpret the story of early *Homo*.
- Do research into a hominin industry mentioned in this chapter (Oldowan, Acheulean, Mousterian) and find out how the tools were made and what they were used for.

KEY WORDS

encephalization	half-life	Allen's Rule
archaeological record	igneous (rock)	melanin
artifact	radiogenic	sagittal keeling
feature	radiometric	supraorbital torus
material culture	paleomagnetism	Pleistocene epoch
relative dating	sedimentary (rock)	Levallois technique
chronometric dating	tectonic	prognathism
stratigraphy	competitive exclusion	Neandertal
stratum (*pl.* strata)	Dubois	Mousterian
biostratigraphy	bifacial handaxe	composite
kya	Oldowan	paleopathologist
element	tradition (*or* industry,	hyoid bone
isotope	*or* toolkit)	grave goods
radioactive	Acheulean	

HOMININ NAMES TO KNOW

Australopithecus garhi
Australopithecus sediba
Homo habilis
Homo erectus

Homo ergaster
Homo antecessor
Homo heidelbergensis
Neandertal

7

HOMO SAPIENS AND THE (R)EVOLUTION OF CULTURE

Culture hides much more than it reveals,
and strangely enough what it hides,
it hides most effectively
from its own participants.

—Edward T. Hall, *The Silent Language*

The Mysterious Rise of
Homo sapiens (sapiens?)

So here we have come so much closer to the emergence of modern humans, but we are still plagued with the kinds of questions we had to pose about the rise of genus *Homo* in the first place. What is the species *Homo sapiens*? If it could interbreed with Neandertals, is it a species at all? Should the designation *H. sapiens* be extended to hominins that look different from ourselves? Just what is the "norm" for modern humans, and how different is too different?

Even in the present day, human beings are variable morphologically, from individual to individual, and population to population. While all of today's populations have the same sort of brain, there remain skull features, more common among some populations than others, that we interpret as archaic—a bit of a browridge, for instance, or less of a chin. If the range of variation among humans today is such that it is difficult to piece together a prototype from the mix, how do we pick out our immediate ancestors from the fossil record, especially given that over time they must have changed? And in fact, this has proved to be a difficult task; further, not everyone has been happy with how it has proceeded (e.g., Wolpoff and Caspari 1997).

It should be obvious by now that by "modern human," I have not meant, "up to the minute." "Modern" in this instance refers to a point about 160 kya, according to current thinking, when beings that looked very much like ourselves emerged in Ethiopia. Tim White's paleoanthropological team christened these beings *Homo sapiens idaltu* (White et al. 2003), with the qualifying third term, "*idaltu*" ("elder sibling") indicating that they are different enough from us to be classified as a **subspecies** of *Homo sapiens*; we then would be *Homo sapiens sapiens*, though it is generally unnecessary to include the subspecific term. From what we can tell, *H. s. idaltu*, despite its modern appearance, did not emerge with a full set of modern tools in hand, or even in mind; that is, it was only anatomically and not behaviorally modern. Hence the (sub)species and its descendants have been collectively referred to as **anatomically modern humans (AMH),** and we can use this acronym to avoid, for the moment, committing ourselves to a species designation that may not be appropriate. The emergence of "modern" behaviors—some of which actually occur well before 160 kya, some well after—will occupy us for most of this chapter, but clearly we have business left over from the last chapter regarding the rise of "modern" morphology. Therein lies a tale, not only about the evolution of humankind, but the evolution of science.

Once upon a time (to begin the tale in a classic style), there were two opposing perspectives on the evolution of AMH morphology. The first was known as **multiregional evolution,** and while this was held by many on a "commonsense" basis (recall once again that "commonsense" is not necessarily sensible), it was elevated to the status of hypothesis by Franz Weidenreich, who took over at the Chinese excavations after Davidson Black's premature death. Weidenreich discerned morphological commonalities among *H. erectus* and modern Chinese, and believed that there was likely a direct link of descent between the two populations. From this observation grew the proposition that all of the dispersed populations of *H. erectus* (such terms as *ergaster* were not yet in use), wherever they had settled, eventually evolved into *Homo sapiens*. It came to be understood that this could not have happened without a significant amount of **gene flow;** there had to be interbreeding between the populations so that everyone could be brought up to speed, so to speak, on the latest genetic and cultural developments. In other words, there was no speciation until such time as all the *erectus* populations evolved into *sapiens* (allowing for a few outliers that might not have made it). There remained enough geographical and genetic distance between populations, however, to form pools of particular traits; hence different human "races" came into being. Unsurprisingly, the suggestion that there were distinct, long-standing races of human beings, and the implication that some of these races may have missed out on a few items of cutting-edge human equipment, earned this school of thought the label of "racist," which did not enhance its popularity in academic circles. Fierce present-day proponents, however, have sought to rescue multiregionalism from the charge of racism, in a way that will become clearer once I have presented the opposing school of thought (again, the shortcomings of the race concept will be discussed in chapter 10).

This second school came to be known as **Out-of-Africa (OOA)**, though it should be kept in mind that we are talking about AMH and not genus *Homo*, whose emergence both schools would place in Africa. For the OOA adherents, it was not merely modern features that evolved in Africa, it was an entirely new species—*Homo sapiens*—that, in keeping with the traditional concept of species, could not produce offspring with any other population of *Homo*. Hence, that *Homo erectus* became prevalent in the easternmost reaches of Asia and that Neandertals were successful in the harshest climatic conditions of glaciated Europe meant nothing, genetically speaking, to our immediate ancestors. *Homo sapiens* split from a single African founding population, composed of *H. ergaster* or *H. heidelbergensis* or yet another species, and went its separate way both genetically and geographically. Unable to interbreed with the other *Homo* populations it encountered in its travels, it outcompeted them for resources, and eventually the other populations all succumbed to extinction, defeated by whatever mental and technological advantages *H. sapiens* possessed.

This may seem like an extreme view, but it was supported by evidence from a substance that has great cachet in today's world—DNA. In chapter 3, I mentioned there were two types of DNA in your cells; nuclear DNA, of course, but also **mitochondrial DNA (mtDNA).** Mitochondria are what we call **organelles,** "organs" within the cell that accomplish essential functions. **Mitochondria** process oxygen so that the cell can "breathe." We suspect mitochondria have their own DNA because they were once free-standing living creatures; however, they eventually became fully integrated into cells, retaining their DNA as the only vestige of their former independence.

At the time the OOA model of AMH evolution was proposed, mtDNA was believed to have a number of properties which were thought to be virtually absolute, and which will be represented thus in this paragraph. For one thing, mtDNA passed intact from female parent to offspring—unlike nuclear DNA, it did not undergo meiotic mixing and matching when ova were formed, and during

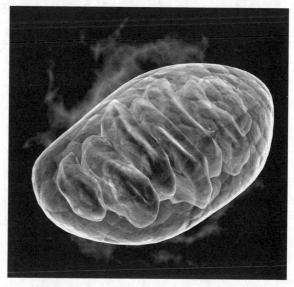

Mitochondrion.

sexual reproduction there was no contribution of male mtDNA to the zygote. You have your mother's mtDNA, and she has her mother's, and so on; if you are male the buck stops here, so to speak, but your sister's children will have it, and so long as a line contains a successfully reproducing female, mtDNA will live on. This does not mean that mtDNA proceeds through the generations unchanged. While it is not altered by gene flow, genetic drift, or natural selection, it *does* mutate. Mutations are random events, but over a long span of time we can expect a certain number of them (just as we can calculate how many ^{40}K atoms will decay to ^{40}Ar in a given period), and from this we can determine the rate of mutation. It was also the case that the origin point of a mutation could be traced back through a female's descendants. In other words, mtDNA seemed to be the perfect "molecular clock."

Hence, based on these premises, Rebecca Cann, Allan Wilson, and Mark Stoneking, in the 1980s, designed a research plan to investigate when and where the first *Homo sapiens* female originated (Cann et al. 1987). The idea was to work our way back through all of the mtDNA mutations that had accrued from the time our species definitively split from its parent line. It turned out that mtDNA samples from African women had the most mutations overall, though a number of these were shared with women from Southwest Asia. Plotting the history of these mutations required a computer, which was programmed to construct possible "family trees" from the available data. Following the principle of Occam's Razor, these trees were the most **parsimonious,** that is, the simplest, that could be assembled. The program yielded many trees, but they were roughly comparable, a matter of substituting one potential descent sequence for another at some point along the line. While some of the trees were rooted in Southwest Asia, the vast majority had their roots in Africa. Applying the rate of mutation to the trees that accounted for the greatest number of mutations yielded the astonishing estimated range of 140,000 to 100,000 years. In other words, if the "molecular clock" was accurate, *Homo sapiens* could have become established as a species as recently as 100 kya.

These results were unexpected, but seemed, at the time, airtight. They created a media storm, centered on the mother of us all, "mitochondrial Eve." Eve and her descendants migrated within Africa, and eventually Out of Africa, to become the sole surviving hominin species in the world today. Ultimately, despite the fact that hominins prior to the birth of Eve had radiated throughout Africa and Eurasia, only one, localized population of hominins—the one in Africa that had yielded *Homo sapiens* such a short time ago—really mattered.

Using Molecules to Measure Time

Allan Wilson, who advised the team of researchers working on the human mtDNA project, was a pioneer in the area of "molecular clock" development. In the 1960s, he and his doctoral student, Vincent Sarich, hypothesized that they could determine the date of the split between hominins and panins by assessing how the rabbit immune system reacted to human and chimpanzee proteins. As you likely know in your own case, the immune system, if it is working properly, works to neutralize foreign matter, be that a bacterium or a donated organ. If your immune system gears up for battle even when dealing with material from a fellow human, you can imagine how active it might get in response to material from outside the species.

On this principle, Sarich and Wilson injected rabbits with albumin from several different primates species. Albumin is a protein essential to regulating the movement of fluids throughout the body. Despite this basic function, the structure of albumin is complex and varies from species to species. Keep in mind that proteins are assembled through the action of genes, and variations in protein structure point to signature genetic distinctions between species. The rabbits, being relatively distantly related to primates, had a strong immunological reaction to primate albumin (yes, this experiment was not rabbit-friendly), but the reaction rate was different depending on the type of primate. The scientists measured these different reaction rates and estimated, via this somewhat crude instrument, that the chimpanzee and human lines split no more than 5 mya (Sarich and Wilson 1967).

This rocked the scientific world—five million years was far too recent a figure for paleoanthropologists of that time to accept. The Sarich and Wilson view came to prevail, however, and most experts narrowed the time frame within which hominin evolution was believed to have occurred. If today we admit such ancient fossils as *Sahelanthropus tchadensis* and *Orrorin tugenensis* into the hominin line, we have to expand the frame just a bit, but the fact that a five-million-year date of divergence, initially shocking, became the standard baseline for this event within modern paleoanthropology indicates just how influential the research of Sarich and Wilson has been.

EXERCiSE

Question: What would "Adam's" paleoanthropological name be?
Look up research.

As is true of just about anything believed to be absolute in science, further research cast doubt on mtDNA as the "perfect" time measurement molecule. It was discovered that the mtDNA from sperm could in fact be incorporated into the zygote, though the extent to which this actually happens under normal conditions remains debatable (e.g., see Cummins 2000 but also D'Aurelio et al. 2004). And certain disorders *do* arise from mtDNA mutations, thus subjecting the bearer of these mutations to the rigors of natural selection; put simply, it would seem as though mtDNA "family trees" can be pruned. None of this fazed OOA proponents unduly—they were willing to admit the mitochondrial clock might run a little slow, but all that needed to be done was account for this in time estimates. The 100,000-year figure had shock value; however, the OOA supporters were not wedded to it. Extending the range for the emergence of *H. sapiens* back to 200,000 years both maintained the integrity of the model and accommodated the *H. s. idaltu* fossils quite nicely.

To add insult to injury, the OOA contingent claimed the moral high ground on the race issue. If *H. sapiens* had come into existence so recently, what we perceive as "racial" differences, such as differences in skin color and eye shape, must have evolved even more recently. Hence, "race" was a superficial matter, genetically speaking; the "basins" within which such variations had collected were quite shallow and entirely subject to spilling over their banks. The multiregionalists counterattacked: the OOA model was actually the more racist, they claimed, in that it held that only one population of genus *Homo* was *sapiens*. Milford Wolpoff, the present-day champion extraordinaire of the multiregional model, even entertained the notion (1996) that genus *Homo* contained merely a single, highly variable species (*Homo sapiens*) from the moment it evolved (the anguished student who at this point thinks, "I memorized all those species names for *nothing*?" should keep in mind that this is a minority view). And certainly, chronic, widespread interbreeding among populations would produce much the same effect as a short species history; that is, one large species within which variations were extended across populations rather than concentrated within them.

While the OOA/multiregional face-off regarding "race" would seem to be a petty squabble, it actually dredges up an unresolved issue: what is a species? More specifically in this instance, how long does it take for species to be established? Does a genetic wall drop down immediately, rendering interbreeding impossible? Or is there a gradual genetic distancing between two taxa, with the possibility of whole or partial reunion lingering for quite some time? While the first event could conceivably happen—say a litter is born that, due to a genetic alteration all the litter mates inherited, can interbreed only within itself—evidence is mounting in support of the second course having taken place rather frequently.

We are accustomed to thinking of **hybrids** as organisms that humans bring about through contrived means, but it would seem nature has tried its hand at the craft as well (see Arnold 1997, 2006). In the case of hominins, if *H. sapiens*, even after millennia of separation, could still produce offspring with Neandertals, then we must certainly revisit the entire concept of species (Arnold 2009; see also Cochran and Harpending 2009). Now, that only 1–4% of the non-African genome is Neandertal may be an indication that such interbreeding did not happen very often. This could be due to the fact that the two populations only rarely encountered each other—that small groups of each type of hominin inhabited the same region over a span of thousands of years does not guarantee contact—but it could also be that genetic distance, of the sort that would interfere with reproduction, had in fact set in, and successful hybridization was difficult to achieve. Thus, there could still be ample justification for establishing a species distinction between, say, *H. sapiens* and *H. neanderthalensis*, but obviously interbreeding cannot be the absolute determinant of whether or not a species has evolved. And if it is not, the question remains, what is? Can, or should, the definition of "species" be a bit fuzzy? Is the idea useful to us in this form?

Clearly those are not questions this textbook will resolve, but once again the thoughtful student should be aware of them. To return, however, to the standoff between OOA adherents and multiregionalists, the situation is no longer so polarized. The former are generally willing to admit they have taken the species concept far too seriously, while the latter concede they may not have taken it seriously enough (e.g., Shea 2010). A variety of compromise models have sprung up that continue to situate the origins of the most "human" developments discussed so far, both morphological and cultural, in Africa, but that additionally allow for some hybridization (both morphological and cultural) between populations as Africans repeatedly broke away from their parent populations to radiate into other land masses already inhabited by prior hominin migrants.

But culture, you will recall, is still something of a shadowy thing 160 kya. The archaeological record tells us with more and more security that prior to 160 kya, there were hominins that hunted, controlled fire, and made specialized implements, but we know that soon—though once again, perhaps not as soon as we might expect—there are even more stunning developments to come.

Human Cultural Behavior

As previously implied, the morphological emergence of AMH was not accompanied by an immediate behavioral revolution, so far as we can tell. There is nothing to indicate that this new species—if that is indeed what it is—possessed new properties of mind. In terms of technology, these hominins persist with the classic forms, continuing to produce handaxes, though with the greater precision of the Levallois technique. One toolmaking specialty, the production of long stone **blades,** has often been read as a sign of modern thinking—manufacturing these blades is tricky, requiring a good deal of skill—but Cara Roure Johnson and Sally McBrearty (2010) claim to have found blades going back 500,000 years. However, while *we* may assess the blade as a significant advance in stoneknapping, our ancestors evidently did not agree—blades turn up only occasionally in material assemblages until about 50 kya. In South Africa, for example, 100,000-year-old blades appear at Klasies River Mouth (Singer and Wymer 1982), but continue to be rare in the area for about 50 ky thereafter.

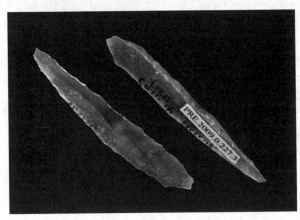

Paleolithic blade technology (Aurignacian).

It should be mentioned that the Blombos Cave site in South Africa has yielded some of the earliest items of bodily adornment as well—shells, dating back to 75 kya, are perforated in a manner to suggest they may have been parts of a necklace (Henshilwood et al. 2004). **Ochre,** a pigment applied both to the body and to objects, was produced at Blombos even earlier, circa 100 kya (Henshilwood et al. 2011); ochre use at Qafzeh Cave in Israel dates back nearly as far (Hovers et al. 2003). Such developments, as leading as they may seem to us today, only dot the archaeological landscape from 100 kya to 50 kya. Future excavations, especially in Africa, may well fill in the gap, but for now, it is prudent to identify 50 kya as a benchmark in human existence. After this point, the production of sculpture, cave painting, exquisitely crafted tools and ornaments—items we associate with "culture" in its modern sense—begins to burgeon.

We tend to assign this sort of material to AMH, even though it is not always found in association with defining fossils, and it *is* often found in regions inhabited by Neandertals. It certainly could be that 40 kya Neandertals, who had not hitherto shown a capacity and/or an inclination to produce such things, became willing and able to do so—recall that even in AMH, such capacities took time to develop. However, that we have recovered blade technology and items of bodily adornment in Africa going back prior to 50 kya suggests that these artifacts—and the thinking required to produce them—originated there among AMH and spread elsewhere (McBrearty and Brooks 2000). In any event, no matter who invented these artifacts and/or proved capable of their manufacture, we know that eventually Neandertals—or at least Neandertal morphological features—die out, leaving AMH sole claim to the species designation *Homo sapiens* (if in fact they did not already have it) and to the things and thinking we recognize as being truly human.

So why did our ancestors' approach to life change so drastically? What was going on, in their minds, in their societies? At this point, the archaeological record is no longer silent on such issues. It speaks via the **symbol,** a device whose operation, if not always its meaning, we understand intimately. To know why the symbol unites us across the millennia, however, we will have to draw on the two anthropological fields that have not, so far, figured obviously in this account: cultural and linguistic anthropology.

You should recall that culture is the central concept of all types of anthropology, but naturally it is of special concern to cultural anthropologists, who have wrangled over its definition for years. Nothing is resolved in this respect—there are even those cultural anthropologists who would just as soon lay the concept aside—but I will admit I have a preference, one that will be indulged here. For me, the symbol is the essence of culture. If we adopt this attitude we can distinguish human behavior from that of all other animals on the planet. We no longer have to argue as to whether we should use the term "culture" to describe why certain behaviors are found in some troops of chimpanzees, and not others. We can acknowledge that the chimpanzee is intelligent without calling it cultural. I do not mean that statement to imply that because of culture, human beings are more intelligent than chimpanzees. In the first place, we do not have a good answer for the question, "what is intelligence?" but whatever it might be overall (if indeed it is something singular), I do not see it as equivalent to the capacity for culture. But I have gotten ahead of myself; I will return to these issues once I have more fully addressed the symbol.

You may be wondering why I assign such importance to the symbol. It's not such a big deal, you say; a symbol is something that stands for something else. A red octagon, for instance, means "stop," and you've known this nearly all of your

Ceci n'est pas une pipe.

"This is not a pipe."
Surrealist painter René
Magritte understood that
a symbol means only
what we say it means
(or not).

life. Anthropologists have a perhaps unfortunate tendency to problematize phenomena that seem quite straightforward; be forewarned that this is what I am
about to do to your stop sign. It is precisely because you are so casual about the
link between a red octagon and the action of stopping that this *is* a big deal. The
point is there is *no necessary connection* between a symbol and its referent.
Symbols have meaning only through cultural consensus. The gap between a symbol and the object for which it stands is filled by the human mind, or more specifically, human *minds* collaborating in creating culture. Ordinarily, however,
you do not even recognize that there *is* such a gap; you have learned, simply as a
person raised in your culture, to make the association between symbol and object automatically.

Symbols are the heart of human language. Every word you speak is a symbol.
The word "dog" in English has a history, and its origins can be traced, but ultimately the connection between "dog" and the designated animal is arbitrary; the
word for "dog" could just as easily be "anjing"—and in fact it is, in Malay. As an
English-language speaker, you only know the meaning of the word "dog" because
everyone around you, unquestioningly, knows it too. You and your fellow language speakers are so comfortable on the level of the symbol that you put spoken
words together effortlessly; this facility is called **syntax.** It certainly involves
mind, but not in its conscious aspect—a good way to disrupt syntax is to think
about your words before you speak them.

You should recognize, too, that every word you write (plus every letter in the
words you write) and a good many of the gestures you use are symbols. Inargu-
ably, writing systems postdate speech, but many linguists believe that meaning-

ful gesture not only preceded it, but led to it (e.g., Armstrong and Wilcox 2007). There is support for this position from a variety of sources. Human children, for instance, pick up gesture before they pick up speech, and this has been interpreted as the linguistic version of "ontogeny recapitulates phylogeny." Additionally, that the great apes have shown a (somewhat controversial) capacity to learn American Sign Language (Ameslan) is taken as an indication that the tendency to synthesize gesture and meaning is common to all species of pongids and hominids, and hominins merely took the logical "next step" in inventing speech.

Personally, however, I would advise caution with respect to this line of thinking. That toddlers can learn meaningful gesture before they learn meaningful sound has a good deal to do with the fact that the human speaking apparatus, as well as the ability to control it, must mature in tandem; once a child *does* come into his own in this respect, he quickly shifts to the vocal channel nearly exclusively, as any parent can tell you. Further, it smacks of teleology to presume that speech would necessarily follow on gesture as a "more advanced" communicative practice. Any person fluent in Ameslan would assert that it is a perfectly adequate and adaptable language in and of itself; there would seem to be no pressing reason to replace gesture with speech. Finally, it should be noted that to the extent great apes have learned symbols when taught, they are as adept with pictograms as Ameslan—there is no necessary favoring of the gestural channel. Perhaps, however, it is that great apes are *truly* adept at training their human trainers—if making a sign or pressing a key or replicating a drawing inspires the trainer to dispense more food or open the door to the play-yard, the ape will learn to do so, once again bearing out my contention that intelligence is not equivalent to culture! The ultimate point here is that speech does not have to follow on gesture; this is a problematic relationship that should be investigated as such. Gesture likely always accompanied speech (it still does), but gesture could have taken on symbolic meaning at the same time or even after hominins started to speak, when, indeed, hominin life generally became subject to the workings of a symbol-making mind.

So we return to the possibility that the control of mouth sound is a key component, if not *the* key component, of the development of the modern human mind. It should be mentioned that we are not the only animal that harnesses an arbitrary sound to a specific, intended meaning, even if our closest relatives show no such proclivity. Animals of various types use sound to give warnings, to convey emotion, to find and retain mates. Vervet monkeys utter one cry when danger soars above them, and a different cry when danger slithers below (Seyfarth et al. 1980). Prairie dogs have an even more elaborate system of calls (Slobodchikoff et al. 2009), and many species of bird deploy sound in a number of strategic contexts. But none of these animals treats the symbolic aspect of these

Prairie dogs are among those animals that have a sophisticated system of communication.

forms of communication as anything more than utilitarian. Much animal behavior is governed by the lock-and-key action of biology, and rightly so, since this gets the job done—most animals are reasonably proficient at eating, mating, and parenting. For human beings, these fundamental activities become encrusted with culture. We eat only what we believe is edible according to our culture; mating at random tends to occasion disapproval if not outright condemnation while socially sanctioned mating is cause for social celebration; and we rear our children in the ways our society recommends. In other words, while certain animals sometimes use symbols, human life is entirely reworked by them.

But how true was this for hominins in the past? Over the millennia we see vocal equipment evolving, allowing hominins to make sounds within a range that would seem needlessly wide if all that had to be accomplished was identifying the whereabouts of a predator. We can guess that over at least part of its time on earth *Homo erectus/ergaster* spoke, at least in a rudimentary way, and, as previously mentioned, the discovery of a Neandertal hyoid bone is a very strong indication that these hominins had language. But had the symbol taken over their lives? In that Neandertals have produced so few artifacts beyond the utilitarian, I would tend to say no. In contrast, the prodigious manufacture of art and artifacts undertaken by AMH in, for instance, **Upper Paleolithic** Europe, suggests these people— and I think we can comfortably use that term, now—were fully linguistic.

Why would that follow? To draw animals on cave walls is ample evidence of a symbol-governed mind. No matter how "realistically" the animal is depicted, it is not the animal itself, though humans barely seem to realize that, since they are so accustomed to conflating representations with reality. I recall, in a 1978 *60 Minutes* report on apes learning sign language, a lesson psychologist Roger Fouts tries to impart to the young chimp Ally (Columbia Broadcasting System 1978). Ally is shown a succession of objects and asked to make the corresponding sign. At one point Fouts pulls out a plastic airplane. Ally duly produces the sign, for which Fouts praises him, but I am always struck by the fact that the object is *not* an airplane. It a plastic model of an airplane (it is, moreover, bright red). Ally learned to make the sign for "airplane," but one has to wonder whether Ally actually understood that the piece of plastic is the "same" as the noisy machine flying overhead. For a human being, however, this is literally a no-brainer.

Symbols are synoptic—they slice continua into segments, separating one designated "thing" from another (Geertz 1957). Thus, in and of themselves they misrepresent reality, but the "error" is compounded when human beings use these building blocks to create grand symbolic structures, like spoken languages and murals on a cave wall, that are at an even further remove from reality. The chaos of everyday experience is thus smoothed over into something seemingly comprehensible in its simplicity. Indistinct phenomena are supplied with artificial edges, inconvenient detail is trimmed, and complexity is reduced to a comforting sense of discrete wholeness. In other words, symbols are the lens through which human beings can see the forest for the trees.

This is in no way how nonhuman animals think. For them it is not survival-minded to see the forest when the trees are thick with menace. According to Temple Grandin ([with Johnson] 2005), the animal mind is consumed by detail—a chain is hitting a gate, something moved that was not previously within view, the ocean has pulled back from its usual bed. These things may be inconsequential, but each one of them could signal danger, and they compel animals to start, veer, withdraw, protect themselves. Grandin believes that animals think in much the same way that an autistic human being thinks—and as she is autistic, this insight is well founded in years of experience. The autistic child becomes upset if a pillow is shifted from one end of the couch to the other. In its new position the pillow is simply not *right*, and if it is not right, it could be very, very wrong.

In their 2009 cultural anthropology textbook, Serena Nanda and Richard Warms, citing Grandin, observe that autistic people do not think culturally—they stand somewhat outside of the process of tacit social consensus that both establishes and maintains culture (Nanda and Warms 2009). Within the process, those of us who do participate fully generate through our thoughts and related behaviors the shared fantasy that our symbols *are* reality. We even believe that we can manipulate reality simply through manipulating our symbolic representations of it. This bizarre conviction is the foundation of such human mainstays as magic and ritual. The conviction is very much with us today, and has been throughout history. In prehistory, it may be in evidence in the Upper Paleolithic caves of, for instance, Lascaux. The images there may not merely tell a story; it is entirely possible they mean to *change* the story.

EXERCiSE

For a fabulous virtual tour of Lascaux Cave, visit
http://www.lascaux.culture.fr/#/en/02_00.xml

Such obviously delusional creatures as ourselves should never have survived. But the irony of our wildly successful tenure on the planet is that cultural thinking led us to an entirely new dimension of **niche construction.** Recall that species have a formative impact on their environments just by following the behavioral patterns they have evolved to pursue. Human beings not only shape their physical environments, but, through culture, they shape their *perception* of their physical environments. In this way, while an animal might receive a negative outcome as a solid indication that whatever caused it should be scrupulously avoided, humans can culturalize such outcomes—an action might have failed because, for example, it was not performed properly, or because the spirits were angry—and fling themselves "once more unto the breach." The irony of human existence is that this expanded form of niche construction has actually worked. We do in fact make the world we imagine, and gloss over any contradictions that might interfere with the stability of this construction, through the same device—culture.

Within this derived environment we can define reality any way we want, but as previously mentioned, I would recommend against identifying cultural thinking as "intelligence." Indeed, cultural thinking can actually impede the ability to determine the best course of action. An experiment was carried out that involved retrieving a piece of candy from an opaque puzzle-box (Horner and Whiten 2005). The researcher showed a group of chimpanzees the steps needed to trigger the opening of a drawer where the candy lay. These steps were elaborate, entailing a number of maneuvers to be executed on top of the box. The chimpanzees duly learned the proper steps and obtained the treat. Human children were equally adept at following these very same steps. When a transparent puzzle-box was substituted for the original, however, it became clear that working the top of the box was entirely unnecessary, and the chimpanzees went straight for the drawer to grab the candy. The children, however, continued to go through the steps they had been taught even when the box was transparent. If intelligence is essentially problem-solving ability, we would have to conclude that the chimp was smarter than the human, or at least the human child. Obviously, however, there is something else going on in the mind of the human. In part, the child is responding to adult authority, but this is not the end of the matter, because later the very same child may upbraid the adult for altering the procedure in some minor way. In short, the child is not only quick to learn the procedure, but just as quickly comes to see it as "the way things are."

Why did this kind of mind evolve? As suggested in chapter 4, the groundwork may have been laid with the primate's enhanced visual equipment, necessitating enhanced mental support. Further brain development was likely encouraged by competitive social systems requiring individuals to commit a good deal to memory—the chimpanzee, for instance, is immersed in political intrigue, and must always be mindful of which of its fellows may be plotting against it and which may be interested in collaborating in a plot. It is also the case that humans and chimps, along with some other primates and even such animals as elephants, have **consciousness**—individuals recognize themselves as distinct beings and can act deliberately according to self-interest. When it comes to hominins, the icing on the cake, it would seem, is a capacity to recognize that *others* have consciousness and that one can extend an understanding of oneself to an understanding of others. Through what psychologists call **socially shared cognition,** hominins could combine mental and emotional resources and greatly exceed an individual's ability to handle her own needs.

But exactly how our ancestors got to this point may always remain a mystery. My sense is that it had something to do with what has been called **cooperative breeding,** though it might be more fitting to call it cooperative child rearing (Hrdy [2009] prefers "alloparenting"). In most social systems, human beings raise their children jointly, pooling parenting resources to provide a safe space for otherwise vulnerable creatures to mature. Far back in the hominin line, this level of cooperation likely took hold slowly, but once it began to reap benefits in terms of infant survival in the capricious conditions of the Pleistocene, it was intensified. Indeed, the space established by collaborative parenting may have become safe enough to mute the cacophony of detail that occupies the animal mind. Young hominins, spared the need for constant vigilance, could experiment and be saved from disastrous results by watchful caretakers. Perhaps, then, there was that much more mind available to apply to innovation—a new tool, a new technique, a new means of relating to others. In other words, security, not necessity, may have been the mother of invention. Later in life, the safe physical space in which hominins had grown up became a space within their minds to which they could return to rest, to devise new solutions to persistent problems, and even to plan how they might rc-create, in the adult world, the blissful obliviousness they had experienced as children.

When our ancestors got to this point is somewhat less problematic, though still tricky to pinpoint. Thomas Wynn and Frederick Coolidge (2004) have suggested that the Neandertal mind (and presumably the minds of prior hominins) was limited in its capacity for socially shared cognition; this could also be said of the modern autistic mind. Whether we subscribe to this view or not, what we *can* say is that first in Africa, then in Europe, and eventually everywhere AMH migrated, there is a veritable explosion of material suggesting the human mind had become cultural in the way we understand the capacity today. These people could represent and likely even transcend reality via art and language. The symbol systems they had created had become their world, a world they preserved in lasting objects, to be apprehended by like minds all these thousands of years later.

Upper Paleolithic (Material) Culture

The term "Upper Paleolithic" does not identify a set span of time so much as it describes the extraordinary expansion of material culture discussed in the previous section. In Europe, this period begins roughly 40 kya, when it is thought AMH first arrived on the continent, although support for this early date of migration has been provided only recently, through a reconsideration of fossils formerly thought to be Neandertal (see Benazzi et al. 2011; Higham et al. 2011). Cultural production in Europe booms shortly thereafter. The same expansion takes place throughout the Old World, but since the archaeological evidence from Europe within this time frame is so prodigious and so well researched, it is this continent that will draw our attention for the next few pages.

The first new tool **tradition** that emerges in Upper Paleolithic Europe is the **Aurignacian,** characterized by the elongated blade whose manufacture did not have staying power, at first, in Africa. The Aurignacian is assigned dates from 40 to 28 kya. AMH fossils found within this range were once dubbed **Cro-Magnon,** after a French site that yielded what was thought to be a prototypical skull, dated to approximately 28 kya. Cro-Magnon, in fact, became a popular means of distinguishing people who looked like us from Neandertals. While paleoanthropologists no longer see the Cro-Magnon skull as prototypical, the name has stuck and will likely continue to be used casually both within and outside of the discipline, though I tend to avoid it.

In addition to blades, another tool that becomes common during the Aurignacian is the **burin,** a chisel-like implement used to engrave stone and bone. Not coincidentally, the Aurignacian also features the earliest known figurines, and possibly the earliest cave art as well, though such art is notoriously difficult to date. It could also be that dogs were domesticated within this time frame; this is, however, a hotly contested issue. Some of the controversy lies in establishing exactly what fossil trace an early dog might leave that is distinguishable from that of a wolf. Certainly the Upper Paleolithic lifestyle might have attracted wolves as camp followers; humans may have quickly dispatched potentially dangerous adults but could have brought orphaned cubs into camp, allowing the gentler ones to live into adulthood. Tame wolves could be of great benefit to Upper Paleolithic peoples—they could help with hunting and provide protection as well as the occasional meal in and of themselves. But that dogs could be eminently useful does not prove they were domesticated this early. There is, how-

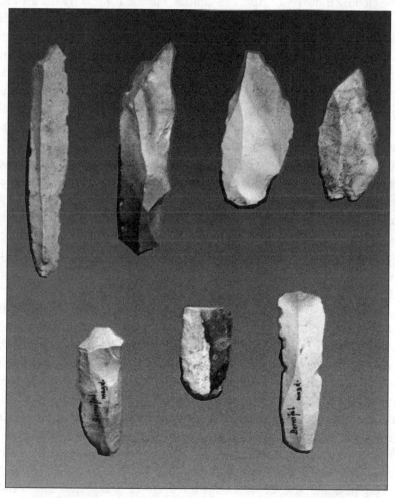

Burins and blades (Magdalenian).

ever, a doglike (as opposed to wolflike) skull, recovered from Belgium, dating back to nearly 32 kya (Germonpré et al. 2009), and at Chauvet Cave in France, there is a canid front paw print, with the shortened middle toe typical of domesticated dogs, believed to be just slightly more recent than the close of the Aurignacian, at 26 kya (Shipman 2009). Outside of Europe, the find of a 33,000-year-old doglike skull from Siberia provides support not only for the ancient existence of dogs but also for the theory that dog domestication happened more than once, in more than one location (Ovodov et al. 2011).

The European Aurignacian was succeeded, in a more limited geographic range, by the **Gravettian** (approximately 28 to 22 kya), which was succeeded, in an even more limited geographic range, by the **Solutrean** (approximately 22 to 17 kya); the closing industry of Upper Paleolithic Europe is known as the **Magdalenian** (be aware of alternate spellings). The identification of tool styles different enough to warrant new designations is as problematic as the identification of new paleospecies, but these terms, and their associated time periods, have become fairly standard. It should be noted, however, that application of the term "Gravettian," for instance, does not necessarily mean that Gravettian-style tools were found at a site; the term may refer only to the time period. There is also an unfortunate tendency to equate tool styles with peoplehood; that is, a society that made Gravettian tools may have seen itself as ethnically "Gravettian," set off from societies manufacturing different tools. While this may be so, it does not have to be so. If there were in fact distinctions being set in place that we would interpret today as "ethnic"—and this is not a foregone conclusion—these distinctions may have been formed within a broad group of people making the same tools; alternatively, peoples who considered themselves to be ethnically distinct might share a toolkit (just because the goods in your household largely come from China does not mean you're Chinese).

It is equally risky to see a succession of toolmaking styles as a matter of intrinsic "improvement." In the first place, it is we who make such judgments as to what is better or worse without living the lives of these prehistoric peoples, but for all that, it is hard to see the stodgy, utilitarian toolkit of the Magdalenian period as any sort of improvement over the elegant Solutrean, during which tools were exquisitely crafted through careful **pressure flaking** and often seem to have been made more for the purpose of exhibition rather than of use. The tendency to read "better" into "subsequent" (or to assign the label of "backward" to any sequence that does not "progress" according to our standards) is the cultural version of the pursuit of Lamarckian perfection. The dangers of this sort of thinking will be more fully explored at the start of chapter 9.

Having said that, the toolkit during the Magdalenian period had its own sort of finesse in the different materials that were effectively combined—composite

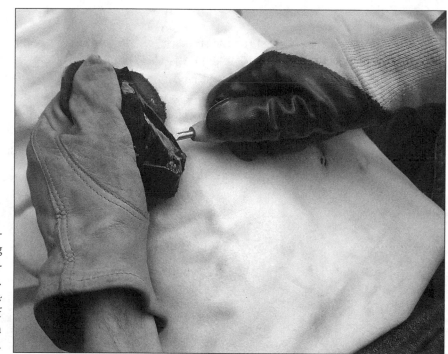

Right: Pressure flaking (using modern tools). *Below:* Collection of Solutrean tools.

tools, involving the successful amalgamation of, say, stone and bone, or stone and wood, became prevalent. The period is also thought to have given birth to the **atlatl**, a spear thrower that would have allowed hunters to kill from a safer distance; the bow and arrow, possibly imported from Africa, may also have been in use at this time, though there is no direct evidence. Overall, though life was still difficult in the Upper Paleolithic, hunters eventually had more efficient killing implements at their disposal and were not so much at risk in pursuing this way of life.

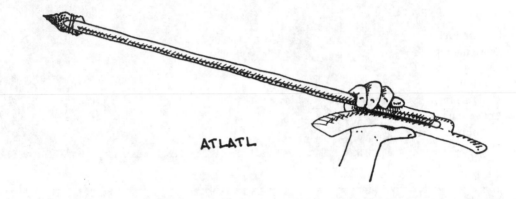

ATLATL

Before we leave Upper Paleolithic Europe, however, there are two well-known products of the period that deserve more exploration. The first is the type of small-scale sculpture that has become known as the **Venus figurine**—popularly, we envision female figures with grossly enlarged breasts and bellies, suggesting pregnancy. Venus figurines begin to appear in the Aurignacian and continue into subsequent periods. It has been suggested that the sculptures may signify the existence of a fertility cult (e.g., Conard 2009) and possibly even rule by females (Gimbutas 1974). However, what we know of historically known hunting peoples is that female fertility is very seldom celebrated among them (Collier and Rosaldo 1981), and while women in such societies often have a good deal of power, we have no real support for the idea that Upper Paleolithic societies were **matriarchal.** In that males are depicted in Magdalenian cave art as solitary while females are shown in groups has intimated to some observers that women and men may have lived separate but equal lives. One alternative explanation proposed for Venus figurines is that they were fantasy dolls for young males, who had too little occasion to engage in activities with flesh-and-blood females (e.g., Mellars 2009). In quite a different vein, it has been mooted that the sculptures were actually made by women and for women, as a means of demonstrating the bodily changes that take place during pregnancy (McCoid and McDermott 1996). However, it could be that our fixation on the figurines with exaggerated maternal features misses the point. Patricia Rice (1981) carried out an extensive survey of such Upper Paleolithic sculptures and concluded that females were depicted not only as pregnant but in all stages of life. Hence, there would seem to be no compulsion on the part of these peoples to think of women primarily as nubile, fecund beings.

The second artistic product for which the Upper Paleolithic is justly famous is cave painting and engraving. Examples of this sort of artwork date back to the Aurignacian but also occur throughout the Upper Paleolithic culture periods. As is true for Venus figurines, there has been much modern speculation as to the thinking behind these extraordinary works, but, of course, no one hypothesis has gathered enough evidence to become

The Venus of Hohle Fels, the oldest figurine known of this kind (circa 35 kya).

a sound theory. There are those experts who believe the artworks have spiritual meaning, and those who, in exasperation at the archaeological tendency to fall back on "deep religious significance" when no other explanation suggests itself, point out that the pictures are pretty, and maybe Upper Paleolithic peoples just liked to look at art. If this was so, however, the artists certainly did not make their works easy to view, since they were often located in a cave's deepest recesses.

In keeping with the idea that Venus figurines were the playthings of restless young men, it has been suggested that cave art was, in essence, the first graffiti (Guthrie 2006). The paintings could tell the story of a great hunt; alternatively, they could depict what the hunters *wished* to happen on the next hunt. **Shamans** could have rendered the figures as a means of demonstrating their power over nature—drawing a game animal wounded with a spear might actually bring about such an event (Clottes and Lewis-Williams 1998; Lewis-Williams 2002). Or perhaps the terms "art" and "power" are too high-flown, and cave "art" is mere doodling. Any or none of these things may be true; importantly, all of them could be true. As in the present day, the meaning of art may have varied from viewer to viewer.

Above: Lions (lionesses?), Chauvet Cave, France.
Below: Reproduction of "Well Scene" image at Lascaux Cave, France.

There is one aspect of cave art worth noting, however, for what it indicates about the development of the cultural mind. It is actually rather difficult to apply pigment to a cave wall. Brushlike implements, though they were in use, are often fairly useless on an uneven sur-face. But any present-day graffiti artist can tell you that spray paint works wonders on any surface, and at least some of the Upper Paleolithic artists under-stood this principle. They may have taken mouthfuls of pig-ment and blown them out to create dots or set a handprint in relief (Lewin 1993). The inges-tion of possibly toxic pigment, along with continuous exhala-tion in the thin air of a cave lit by fire, likely made for artists who were in a seriously altered state of consciousness. It has been observed that abstract de-signs on cave walls resemble **entoptic phenomena,** the sort of patterns one sees just before passing out (Lewis-Williams and Dowson 1988). This altered state could have been actively sought as the catalyst for a shamanic

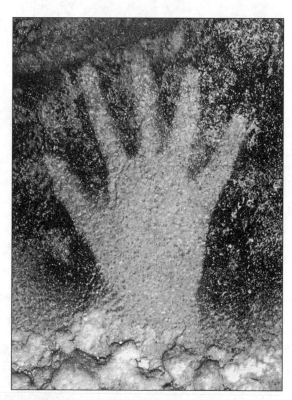

Paleolithic handprint and dots.

trance, and certainly, if the artwork were intended as something more than aes-thetic, it would attain great intensity as the artist progressed from reality into the surreality of hallucination.

I tend, therefore, to favor hypotheses positing that there is something more to this enterprise than art for art's sake, though you are, of course, free to disagree. In closing this section, let me leave you with something that might disturb the mental image you may have developed of the masculine hunting cult working magic deep underground: after having measured the handprint stencils frequently found with cave art, archaeologist Dean Snow believes that many of the artists were women (visit the *National Geographic* website at http://news.nationalgeographic.com/news/2009/06/photogalleries/cave-handprint-actually-women-missions-pictures/index.html).

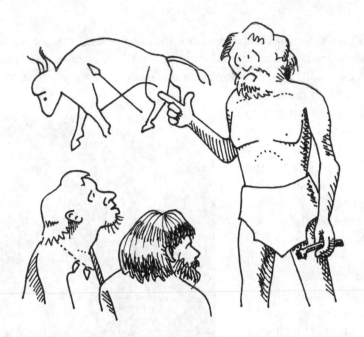

"OK, OOK, YOU'LL HIDE BEHIND THE BUSHES
AND DISTRACT THE BEAST, WHILE MORGH WILL
CIRCLE 'ROUND..."

Cave art—possible explanations?

"KIDS, MOMMY'S GOT A TERRIBLE HEADACHE. JUST DRAW
QUIETLY ON THE CAVE WALLS FOR A LITTLE WHILE, OK?"

Homo sapiens on the Move

According to our current best guess, AMH evolved in Africa around 160 kya, and by 90 kya had migrated at least into what is now Israel, where Neandertals also lived. By 40 kya AMH had moved into another region inhabited by Neandertals—Europe—but Neandertals did not range beyond Europe and Southwest Asia, so far as we know, while AMH continued to hive off new populations into increasingly distant reaches of the globe, some of which had not heretofore had any hominin inhabitants.

One of these places was Australia, which AMH colonized at least as long ago as 45ky, although older dates have been mooted (Gillespie 2002). To reach the continent AMH must have deployed some form of watercraft, possibly a first for hominins (it has been thought that *H. erectus,* circa 800 kya, must have used watercraft to reach the island of Flores in the Indonesian archipelago, but doubts have been raised as to whether a land bridge may have been available, and even whether *erectus* reached Flores at all [Gibbons 1998]). While it could be that hominins other than AMH migrated to Australia—Neandertals were still extant, and recall that *H. erectus* may have held out on Java until 50 kya or so—there is no evidence they did so. Even so, the earliest Australian hominin fossils are puzzling: Lake Mungo 3, a very old fossil, exhibits the more facially gracile features of AMH, but the later Kow Swamp skull is markedly robust. Don Brothwell (1975) offered the hypothesis that at Kow Swamp, human crania were deformed through a cultural practice, but the shape discrepancy might simply illustrate the morphological inconsistency that still stymies us with respect to nailing down what is "modern."

In Australia there is cave art that rivals that of Europe in terms of beauty and complexity, but it may not be as old, as it has yet to be reliably dated. Whether or not the art is ancient, it would seem to be a good indicator that the migrants to Australia had fully modern minds, if not necessarily modern bodies, before they made the trek, as it is unlikely they would develop such similar cultural capacities after the fact of their separation from other AMH populations.

While the issue of human migration into Australia has hardly been free from controversy, it is the human migration into the Americas that has generated the most debate in recent years. This is especially surprising in light of the fact that this was once thought to be a settled matter. The classic view was that *Homo sapiens* moved into the **New World** relatively recently, not long before 12 kya, the means of access being a land bridge, **Beringia,** exposed at what is now the Bering Strait. The cultural evidence for this view lay in the fact that for years artifacts older than 12 ky were not to be found in the New World beyond northern Alaska, where further passage into the continents was blocked by the meeting of two massive ice sheets, the **Cordilleran** to the west and the **Laurentide** to the east. Only after these sheets separated could humans move further south, and they did so swiftly, through the help of a signature tool, the **Clovis** point, which was **fluted** in order to be more securely **hafted** onto a wooden shaft. The Clovis point was thought to be such an effective hunting weapon that it has been accorded some blame for the demise of North America's megafauna (e.g., Martin 1984). But even in Latin America, where the range of many types of mega-fauna did not extend, the Clovis industry became popular. The picture seemed clear—a small group of hunters, armed with Clovis points, bided their time until the ice sheets parted, then streamed down into the New World, successfully establishing themselves in a number of different environments before growing more culturally distinct.

FLUTED CLOVIS POINT

The biological evidence, too, supported the idea that the New World was colonized by a small founding population. There continues to be a good deal of biological commonality among native New World populations, which feature a prevalence of Type O blood (nearly universal prior to significant admixture with foreign groups); a broad face with flaring cheekbones and some prognathism; and the shovel-shaped incisors typical of East Asian peoples. Again interpretation seemed unproblematic—**founder effect** had limited genetic diversity in the initial population in particular aspects, and when the population expanded, diversity remained limited in these aspects.

This view of New World peopling became so well established that evidence to the contrary tended to be dismissed—archaeologists made reference to a "**Clovis barrier**," which seemingly existed in the archaeological record, but most certainly existed in the minds of key experts. Nonetheless, the Clovis barrier has in recent decades been breached in two places. The first is with respect to the timing of New World migration. There are now several sites indicating dates older than 12 kya. For some of these sites—notably, **Topper** in South Carolina and **Pedra Furada** in Brazil—dates for human habitation going back as far as 50 kya have been claimed, but these continue to invite a good deal of skepticism on the part of archaeologists generally. They question whether the material dated at Topper is actually charcoal and whether the alleged artifacts recovered at Pedra Furada may actually be **geofacts**, tool-like stones "manufactured" through natural processes.

Sites that suggest a more "reasonable" timeline relative to the evidence already amassed include **Meadowcroft Rockshelter** in Pennsylvania, whose strata down to 16 ky old have passed the critical muster of a growing number of experts (though archaeologist James Adovasio has asserted there are layers at the site that are older still [Adovasio et al. 1980]), and the site at **Monte Verde** in Chile, which has been widely accepted as a pre-Clovis site, despite some opposition (Fiedel 1999). Monte Verde is now thought to be at least 13,500 years old, though here, too, archaeologist Tom Dillehay sees indications that humans inhabited the site even earlier (Dillehay and Collins 1988). And at Oregon's Paisley Caves, fossilized fecal matter recovered by Dennis Jenkins has been dated to 14.3 kya (see Wayman 2008). Thus, for many New World archaeologists, Meadowcroft and Monte Verde led the way into the millennia prior to the Clovis finds, but other sites have followed, for example, the Buttermilk Creek Complex in Texas that may be as old as 15.5 ky (Waters et al. 2011).

One problem with these claims of early New World colonization is the same problem the colonizers themselves may have encountered—how to get past the northern hemisphere ice sheets? These likely parted more than once within the last 50 ky, creating an **ice-free corridor,** but whether they did so long enough and at the right time for migrants from Asia to pass through remains difficult to ascertain (Clague 2004). It could be, however, that humans could have gained ac-

Meadowcroft Rockshelter, Pennsylvania.

cess to the New World by means other than a Beringia/corridor passage. The possibility has been mooted that Asians may have arrived by boat. An actual trans-Pacific crossing seems highly unlikely, but through canoeing from harbor to harbor—a pattern characterized as **coastal hopping**—migrants could have gradually worked their way down to Chile and beyond. Archaeological evidence of shoreline settlements would literally have been drowned as glaciers receded and the sea level rose. Even so, some post-Clovis coastal excavations (e.g., On Your Knees Cave in Alaska) suggest the existence of such evidence may reasonably be inferred, and hopefully one day recovered (Dalton 2003).

The second breach in the Clovis barrier is a challenge to the notion of one small, genetically uniform founding population. New World archaeology has actually been bedeviled by a distinct paucity of human fossils, even at such sites as Meadowcroft, and it has to be said that the oldest fossils found so far arguably do not move beyond Clovis. However, what is extraordinary about these few very old fossils is that they do not exhibit classic Native American morphological features. The features they *do* exhibit vary—such North American specimens as Spirit Cave and Kennewick are believed to resemble the Ainu people of Japan, while Latin American specimens suggest a relationship to Pacific Island peoples—but they all differ significantly from those of Native Americans, both ancient and modern-day (see Jantz and Owsley 1997; Powell 1999; Powell and Rose 1999).

If in fact evidence mounts that there was more than one Asian population that fed migrants into the New World over a long period of time, it remains debatable as to what that might mean. When news of the Kennewick discovery began to appear in the popular press, some began to imagine that a horde of Clovis-wielding barbarians descended through the ice-free corridor, brutally slaughtering the peaceful peoples already well settled in the lower portion of the Americas. But this certainly does not have to be the case. It could be, rather, that prior migrants interbred with the newcomers, but genetically, the features of the latter came to prevail. And, of course, there could have been both warfare and interbreeding going on, perhaps with one the result of the other.

There is much more to be said regarding this leading development in New World archaeology, but since a good deal of it requires a discussion of the concept of race, further comment will be reserved for chapter 10. In the meantime, I must return to an issue that does not in the least involve bloodthirsty marauders (awwww!) but should nonetheless concern us—how have the archaeological discoveries of the AMH era been dated?

Dating Techniques, Revisited

With our exploration of the Upper Paleolithic, we have entered the range of the best-known of dating techniques—**radiocarbon dating.** Radiocarbon dating has been considered reliable to 40 kya, and given such recent refinements as **accelerator mass spectrometry (AMS),** many experts now trust the technique for dates going back as far as 70 kya (see Taylor 1995). There may be further improvements in the future, but the technique will never yield dates beyond 100 ky, for reasons we will see below.

Like K/Ar dating, radiocarbon dating is premised on the fact that elements may occur in different isotopes, and that some of these isotopes may be unstable and subject to decay. In the case of radiocarbon dating, the element on which we focus is carbon, one of the most common elements on Earth, and the element on which all Earthly life is based. Carbon has multiple isotopes: ^{12}C, which is stable and the most prevalent; ^{13}C, also stable and less common; and ^{14}C, which is unstable and relatively rare. Elements in the upper atmosphere are bombarded by cosmic radiation, which can add to or subtract from subatomic particles in an atom. ^{14}C has two more neutrons than ^{12}C, accounting for both its additional weight and its instability. All forms of carbon, existing in known proportions, are drawn into the **carbon cycle** of life on Earth.

As a living thing, you participate in this cycle. You ingest carbon-based foods, generated from fellow organisms, and you give off carbon, in the form of carbon dioxide, by exhaling. Plants take up this carbon dioxide, you eat the plant, you exhale, and so on. While you are alive, then, you are constantly cycling carbon. When you die—and if this is getting too personal just consider it true of any living thing—the atmospheric ratio of $^{12}C/^{13}C$ to ^{14}C is fixed in your remains; no additional carbon is admitted. The **half-life** of ^{14}C is 5,730 years (more or less); that is, in 5,730 years half the ^{14}C in a sample will have decayed to nitrogen (^{14}N) through the breakdown of one of its extra neutrons into a proton and a beta particle (negatively charged, like an electron). ^{14}N, a stable and abundant isotope in nature, is not trapped in the kind of matrix we assay via radiocarbon dating, so we cannot track its production; we can only track the *depletion* of ^{14}C, relative to ^{12}C and ^{13}C, in a sample. Eventually this depletion becomes measurable (radiocarbon dating cannot determine very recent dates), but when half again of the isotope is lost every 5,730 years, by about 100 ky or so, for all intents and purposes, there is no ^{14}C left to measure.

Recall that one disadvantage of K/Ar dating is that it cannot be carried out on fossils themselves; rather, we must locate volcanic rock thought to be roughly contemporaneous with a fossil. In contrast, radiocarbon dating *has* to be carried out on **organic** matter; that is, the carbon in the sample has to have participated in the carbon cycle of life. While it is good to have a method that can be applied directly to once-living things, there have been drawbacks. One of these has been largely overcome—the advent of AMS has not only increased the accuracy of the ^{14}C count, but it also requires a very small amount of material, so we no longer have to destroy a large portion of a fossil find to obtain an exact date. But clearly another drawback that may never be remedied is contamination—since carbon is the basis for all life on the planet, it is easy for carbon from outside sources to become mixed into a sample, and this, of course, would throw off the count. Even the researcher, of course, sheds carbon, so extreme care must be taken to ensure that a sample to be dated is as devoid of additional carbon as possible.

the CARBON CYCLE

WE CONSUME CARBON WHEN WE EAT PLANTS (or animals that eat plants)...

burp!

WE GIVE IT OFF (plants take it up)...

RIP

... WHEN WE DIE, WE STOP CYCLING CARBON

As onerous as the potential for contamination might be, there is another source of inaccuracy that we have had to take great pains to rectify. When the use of ^{14}C as a dating instrument was first proposed, it was presumed that the atmospheric proportions of $^{12}C/^{13}C$ to ^{14}C were reasonably constant, but we have since found this is not the case. Scientists were alerted to the problem by a dating technique that is the best we have, though unfortunately it is also very limited—**dendrochronology,** or tree-ring dating. You are likely already aware that in temperate climates (or in temperate zones in tropical climates), trees reliably lay down growth rings that mark a year's time; that is, one seasonal cycle. Some years are good for growth, and the ring produced is fat; in other years growth is hampered by, for example, a drought, and the ring betrays this as well. Eventually, in the right kind of tree (e.g., bristlecone pines in the American Southwest, or oaks in Europe), we have a record that not only provides an accurate count of years but a good account of year-to-year climate change. It is possible nowadays to access this record through extracting a pencil-thin core sample from a tree; hence the tree need not die to sate our scientific curiosity. Obviously,

Tree rings.

trees, as long-lived as they are (up to 5,000 years for a bristlecone pine), do not live long enough to date many of the items we want dated. However, by matching tree rings from living samples, through an overlapping succession of samples from preserved wood, scientists have extended the dendrochronological time scale out to nearly 11 kya.

That is still not exceptionally old, but it was enough time for experts to realize that radiocarbon dates were not quite in line with the dates derived from dendrochronology. Since the latter were deemed to be more accurate, it had to be the radiocarbon dates that were wrong, and the fly in the ointment was the atmospheric proportions of carbon isotopes, which were not as constant as had first been thought. The comparison between the timelines was used to work out an idea of how such proportions fluctuate over time, and it is this estimate that has helped us recalibrate the earliest radiocarbon dates calculated. Beyond 11 kya we are on our own again, but what we learn from the period of time when we have an absolute time-measuring device against which to adjust radiocarbon estimates must serve to carry us into the more distant past.

SIDEBAR

Hobbits

The term "hobbit" is the publicity hook attached to a hominin known more formally as *Homo floresiensis*, although there remain those who question this designation. *H. floresiensis* identifies a diminutive species of hominin that lived on the Indonesian island of Flores, where several specimens have been recovered (Brown et al. 2004). The reason they should be discussed before we move on is because they may have existed as recently as 18 kya, well within Upper Paleolithic times. Whether their species lifespan extends long before and/or long after that date, and, for that matter, whether they lived in places other than Flores, is a question only further evidence will answer.

Liang Bua—cave where "Hobbit" was found.

When "hobbits" were first introduced to a wider paleoanthropological audience, there were those who dismissed the small size, and small brains, of the individuals discovered as a mere pathology; "hobbits" were *Homo sapiens,* they asserted, but deformed ones. Others believed that the individuals were healthy, but representative of a group that after years of confinement to one island were subject to a phenomenon known as **island dwarfism**, where species become smaller in response to limited resources;

we have seen this effect in other Southeast Asian species, like the pygmy elephants and rhinoceroses of Borneo. Still others pointed out that the bodily proportions of the "hobbits" were more pre-*Homo* than *Homo*, and began to speculate that there was an OOA radiation of australopithecines that preceded or accompanied that of *Homo erectus*. While not outside the realm of possibility—after all, given current evidence, even the journey of *H. erectus* seems wildly unlikely, and yet it happened—the idea that australopithecines were as peripatetic as early *Homo* is so novel that more supporting material will have to be amassed before it can gain traction.

A recent study of the "hobbit" skulls (Baab and McNulty 2009) concludes that "hobbits" are indeed a different species from *Homo sapiens*, though not a different genus, and that while they might have descended from a population of *Homo erectus*, it is likelier their parent population was either *Homo sapiens* or a yet-to-be-discovered form of *Homo*. For the moment, then, we await further news, while we digest the possibility that even as recently as 18 kya, *Homo sapiens* was not the only version of genus *Homo* on the planet.

The canny student may have caught on to something by this time. In the previous chapter I mentioned that K/Ar dating could be applied toward the determination of dates as young as 100 kya, while this is the upper limit of the radiocarbon technique. You might think we're in the clear, having established a bridge, however slender, between the two methods, but in fact the situation is not so rosy. The extremely long half-life of ^{40}K renders the K/Ar technique progressively less accurate as time approaches the present, while radiocarbon dating, because of the extremely short half-life of ^{14}C, is progressively less accurate as time moves away from the present. Hence, realistically speaking, there is a gap of about 150,000 years, from 200 to 50 kya, that would be better filled by yet another technique, which is, when you stop and think about it, the worst-case scenario when it comes to pinning down AMH prehistory (there are also circumstances under which these techniques cannot be applied whether or not the fossils or artifacts are thought to fall in the correct date range). But of course, we have had to make do. Alternative techniques are plentiful, in fact, but none is as trustworthy as those described thus far. Most of these continue to rely on some radioactive aspect of matter, though they are not necessarily radiometric.

While the various **U-series** techniques would fall into the radiometric category, as they measure the decay of uranium in its various unstable forms (there is no stable form), the related techniques of **thermoluminescence (TL)** and **electron spin resonance (ESR)** are premised on the fact that radioactive elements exist to some extent in all substances, and that their decay pushes electrons out of place. Like K/Ar dating, TL is best carried out on something that was superheated, a description applying to both pottery and hearthstones. Heating disturbs a dense matrix just enough so that dislodged electrons are driven off, leaving a kind of "clean slate," which once again builds up a load of dislodged electrons that cannot escape the matrix under ordinary circumstances. But this new electron load can be discharged by reheating, with the discharge taking the form of light energy measurable against a known rate of electron displacement. In contrast to TL, materials

DATING METHOD	RADIOMETRIC?	WHAT STARTS THE "CLOCK" TICKING?	OPTIMUM DATING RANGE	LIMITATIONS
Potassium-argon (and argon-argon)	Yes Tracks the decay of ^{40}K to ^{40}Ar; half-life of ^{40}K 1.3 billion years	When rock is molten, the original Ar load is driven off; once the rock has hardened, it begins to accrue Ar from the decay of ^{40}K	Millions of years	Can only be used on rock that was once molten
Paleomagnetism	No	When rock is liquid, magnetic particles orient toward the pole and are fixed in this orientation once the rock hardens	Millions of years	Can only be used on rock that was once liquid (igneous or sedimentary)
Radiocarbon	Yes Tracks the decay of ^{14}C to ^{14}N; half-life of ^{14}C 5,730 years	Once an organism dies, it stops cycling carbon, thus fixing its carbon content at that moment	Thousands of years	Can only be used on organic material Reliable to 40 kya; iffy to 70 kya; theoretically possible to 100 kya (but not quite yet?)
Dendro-chronology	No	Birth of the tree	Thousands of years	Can only date out to 11 kya, maximum Best used on long-lived trees from temperate climate zones
Thermo-luminescence	No, but radioactivity is involved	When datable material is heated, loose electrons are driven off; loose electrons, displaced by radioactivity, build up again from that moment	Thousands of years	Used most often on ceramics and hearthstones
Electron spin resonance	No, but radioactivity is involved	The formation of dense bone in an organism. Radioactivity displaces electrons that are trapped in the matrix, producing a magnetic imbalance	Thousands of years	Best used on teeth

Summary of common dating methods.

dated via ESR do not have to be superheated, but the principles behind ESR are much the same. ESR is most effective on teeth, the densest form of bone, in which stray electrons are trapped. Teeth, of course, have a definite starting point—they develop within a fetus during gestation. Electron displacement in a tooth from the time of its formation to the time the tooth is recovered archaeologically produces a magnetic imbalance that can be gauged, once again, against a predetermined rate.

Even very recent dates are contentious, and no paleoanthropologist or archaeologist should base her conclusions on one date alone. To the extent possible, several dating techniques should be applied to any one find, and with any luck the results will intersect within an acceptably narrow range of time. If they do not intersect at all, then the quest to determine which has misfired, and why, is on, and such quests can often turn up new material and new techniques. This is certainly another aspect of the beauty of anthropology—like those earliest culturally minded ancestors, who might persevere with a procedure even after it had seemingly yielded a negative outcome, anthropologists, too, are masters at spinning theoretical gold from practical dross.

QUESTIONS FOR DISCUSSION AND REVIEW

- Summarize the two opposing views of the evolution of *Homo sapiens.*
- How does the human capacity for language shed light on the human capacity for culture?
- Do research on Upper Paleolithic cave art and share the best drawings and most intriguing conclusions with your classmates.
- Discuss the evidence for a people of the New World prior to 12 kya.
- How have dendrochronology and radiocarbon dating been used together to produce more accurate dates?

KEY WORDS

anatomically modern human (AMH)	hybrid	cooperative breeding
	blade	Aurignacian
multiregional evolution	ochre	Cro-Magnon
Out-of-Africa	symbol	burin
mtDNA	syntax	Gravettian
mitochondria	Upper Paleolithic	Solutrean
organelle	consciousness	Magdalenian
parsimonious	socially shared cognition	pressure flaking

atlatl   "Clovis barrier"   radiocarbon dating
Venus figurine   fluted   carbon cycle
matriarchal   haft   organic
shaman   geofact   dendrochronology
entoptic phenomena   Meadowcroft Rockshelter   U-series
Beringia   Monte Verde (Chile)   thermoluminescence
Cordilleran   ice-free corridor   electron spin resonance
Laurentide   coastal hopping   island dwarfism
Clovis

8

Cast Out to Till the Ground

Domestication and Agriculture

It is the agriculturalists, with their commitment to
specific farms and large numbers of children,
who are forced to keep moving, resettling, colonizing
new lands. . . . As a system, over time, it is farming,
not hunting, that generates "nomadism."
Agriculture evokes the curse of Genesis.

—Hugh Brody, *The Other Side of Eden*

When Was the Mesolithic?

Like the Upper Paleolithic, the **Mesolithic** ("Middle Stone [Age]") is more a state of being than a time period. Around 12 kya, as the geologic epoch known as the Pleistocene was coming to a close, the glaciers had once again begun to retreat to the poles, save for those that lingered in high mountain valleys, and the landscape that emerged was changed. In Europe, the megafauna that had sustained Upper Paleolithic populations were becoming rare, but other resources were available—fish and shellfish, small game, a newfound abundance of plant life. In such lush environments human beings—and at this point we can likely say *Homo sapiens* without any qualification—perfected a means of subsistence that we know today as hunting and gathering. Like scavenging, hunting and gathering is a form of **foraging**, but by the Upper Paleolithic, and in fact earlier (though precisely when is a matter for debate), the human subsistence base went well beyond scavenged foods. Thus, the term "foraging," at this point in our exploration of the human story, can be taken to refer only to hunting and gathering.

So, prior to the Mesolithic, human beings had already been hunting and gathering, but within serious environmental constraints over much of the globe. What distinguishes the Mesolithic is the extent to which these constraints were lifted nearly worldwide, allowing for a shift toward the exploitation of a wider variety of foodstuffs, both plant and animal, and a consequent shift in social organization. Present-day and historically known foraging societies typically feature a division of labor that allots most hunting activities to men and plant-gathering activities to women. This division is seldom hard and fast—women

223

may help out on large-scale hunts (Turnbull 1961) and do small-scale collecting and trapping, while men gather more than they might prefer to admit when the hunt has turned up nothing—but there is enough consistency along these lines for human beings to align gender with occupation. That is, such economic roles might be culturalized as in the nature of the sexes—men *are* hunters, women *are* gatherers—with loose ends neatly tucked away into a discrete cultural whole.

Of course, it can be argued there are sound reasons why hunting is generally the province of men. Such methods as spear hunting may require more upper-body strength than women ordinarily have; it is also the case that men are not essential to child care (which is not to say they cannot and/or do not contribute) and thus can go off into the bush unencumbered by a babe in arms or a toddler. On the other hand, gathering vegetable foods would seem to be an ideal activity to couple with child-tending. Gathering can be carried out in a more leisurely fashion, often with a group of women and girls who can share child care, and it does not necessarily take one far from a base camp. Outside of these assessments of the differential capacities and needs of the sexes (with which you may disagree), there is also the ruthlessly pragmatic view, put forth by Ernestine Friedl (1975), that hunting is a more dangerous occupation than gathering and should therefore be allocated to the more expendable sex, seeing as it is far easier to replenish a population with one man and ten women than it is with ten men and one woman. In any event, the overall point is that in contrast to scavenging, thought to be more of a free-for-all in terms of who did what, hunting and gathering involved a greater degree of both economic and social organization, as mere roles came to define different ways of being human. "Different," by the way, does not necessarily mean "unequal." Foragers are notable within the **ethnographic record** for their **egalitarianism,** and this often extends to relations between the sexes.

EXERCiSE

What do you think? Why did sex roles develop?

Given that full-blown hunting and gathering predated the Mesolithic in more temperate parts of the globe, there are those archaeologists who see no need to insert an intervening culture period between the Upper Paleolithic and the **Neolithic** ("New Stone [Age]"), a term that designates the span from the onset of agriculture to the smelting of metals. The point should be taken that we cannot identify "the Mesolithic" as a well-marked band of time enclosing a unique way of life. Importantly, however, what I shall indicate below is that the start of the Neolithic is no less fuzzy. So with, once again, an acknowledgment that our conceptual equipment is faulty, I nonetheless suggest that representing the Mesolithic as a period when hunting and gathering experienced a florescence (a comparable period in the Americas is referred to as **Archaic**) sets up an illuminating comparison between foraging and agriculture.

The Golden Age of Foraging

Foragers may be difficult to detect, archaeologically speaking. They are not prone to building monuments or any sort of lasting structure; they generally live in small groups that range throughout a large territory; their artifacts are simple and often perishable. There are and have been distinct exceptions to these "rules," but to the extent they hold true they complicate the archaeologist's job considerably. However, information the archaeologist cannot extract from the soil may be found in the **ethnographies** cultural anthropologists have written on foraging groups, and reading such works may give the archaeologist clues as to

SIDEBAR

Thinking about Things

Archaeological excavation is not simply a matter of digging down a layer, finding a society, then digging down another layer to find another society. Archaeologist Michael Schiffer (1987) has pointed out that the archaeological record is warped, pulled this way and that in space and time by cultural and environmental formation processes. Fortunately, the archaeologist can often re-create the original context, but first it is necessary to recognize all of the ways it might be distorted.

We humans, Schiffer reminds us, engage in **reuse**—we keep things in cultural circulation, thus delaying their incorporation into the archaeological record. Schiffer identifies four types of reuse:

1. **RECYCLING**—transforming an object into a different kind of object. *Example:* melting down plastic bottles to make a park bench.

2. **SECONDARY USE**—applying the same object to a new function. *Example:* using an old toothbrush to clean tile grout.

(continued)

3. **LATERAL CYCLING**—when the user but not the use changes. *Example:* letting your cousin from out of state have your old prom dress.

4. **CONSERVATION**—keeping an object safe so that it can be given to heirs. *Example:* passing on a set of china from grandmother to mother to daughter. . . .

Though I have cited modern examples above (and you should be able to think of many more), these are quintessential human behaviors that we can locate in the distant past as well as the present. All of them prolong the social life of materials, which themselves attain a history worthy of investigation.

Eventually, however, materials are consigned, deliberately or accidentally, to the archaeological record. Schiffer discusses four types of **deposition:**

1. **DISCARD**—when we intend to dispose of material, or at least don't mind that it's gone. There are three types of discard:

   a. **PRIMARY WASTE**—that is left on the site where it was created. *Example:* fingernail clippings (although it would be *nice* if they were put in the wastebasket, eh?).

   b. **SECONDARY WASTE**—which is gathered up and transported elsewhere, e.g., a landfill.

   c. **DE FACTO WASTE**—which is consciously or unconsciously left behind. *Example:* during the process of moving, you drop a pencil down a floor grate, and you decide it's not worth fishing out.

2. **LOSS**—well, we all know what *that* is. But, the next time you lose something, just tell people, "I contributed it to the archaeological record"—it sounds much more noble.

3. **CACHING**—placing something (other than a human body) in the ground for ritual purposes. *Example:* a time capsule.

4. **BURIAL**—referring specifically to the interment of human corpses plus associated grave goods.

Once the archaeological record is built up, we may have occasion to reclaim objects from it, placing them back in cultural circulation. Forms of **reclamation** include:

1. **ARCHAEOLOGICAL RECOVERY**—e.g., excavated items may be removed from the site and placed in a museum.

2. **SCAVENGING**—when you find something you, or maybe your relatives, lost. *Example:* you dropped a ring on the summit of a mountain, but when you climbed the mountain the following year, miraculously you found the ring.

3. **COLLECTING**—when a stranger finds the ring and keeps it! Collecting can also be more concerted, e.g., pot hunting.

Finally, the archaeological record is regularly disturbed through both human and natural action. Forms of **cultural disturbance** include plowing, digging an irrigation ditch, and laying in a house foundation. But there is also **environmental disturbance:** earthquakes, volcanoes, mud slides, corrosive elements in the air and water. Then there are specific natural agents that act on the archaeological record. We might be able to detect, for example,

1. **FAUNALTURBATION**—the action of animals. *Example:* a dog runs off with a bone and buries it.

2. **FLORALTURBATION**—the action of plants. *Example:* tree roots breaking apart a wall.

3. **CRYOTURBATION**—the action of freezing and thawing. You know how destructive this can be to roads after a long winter.

So the archaeological record is by no means a neat succession of discrete societies, but what fun would that be? The good news is that the record is like a puzzle that, with luck and skill, we may be able to put together, though there will likely always be pieces missing. Schiffer's formation processes also help us to reflect on the human condition, keeping in mind that people in the past were as complex as we are in terms of what they thought and how they behaved. If we can come close to understand-

Floralturbation at Ta Prohm, Cambodia.

ing them through the few messed-up bits and pieces that remain of their lives, we have really accomplished something.

how to interpret the data she does manage to find. In fact, some archaeologists have carried out ethnographic studies on their own; these **ethnoarchaeological** studies differ from standard ethnographies in their emphasis on material use (e.g., Gould 1980; Longacre 1981; Yellen 1977). The archaeologist must understand how materials become involved in human lives, because once the humans are gone, only the materials—and only some of these—will be left.

Unsurprisingly, ethnoarchaeology has often been carried out among foraging peoples. Archaeologists should not think of the few foragers surviving today as mere holdovers from a prior age—like everything else, foraging has changed over time—but as Lewis Binford (1967) once pointed out, ethnoarchaeological and ethnographic studies can serve as sources of reasonable hypotheses to be subjected to testing. What follows, therefore, is a picture of present-day and historically known foragers that we can hold up to the distant past and see how well it accounts for whatever archaeological evidence is available.

The picture is oversimplified because there is and has been a good deal of diversity in foraging lifestyles. Obviously, different environments yield different resources in different proportions. For example, gathering is likely to contribute much more to the diet in temperate climes, while in the Arctic (and, for that matter, in much of North America as well as northern Europe during the colder peri-

Hadza hunter-gatherers.

ods of the Pleistocene), there may be few sources of vegetation available, and women's work might then be directed toward the processing of meats and the production of clothing and blankets from hides. Furthermore, there is an important cultural distinction to be drawn between **immediate-return foragers** (also called **mobile foragers**), who range seasonally within a territory, and **delayed-return foragers,** whose environs are so rich in foodstuffs that they can establish permanent settlements (Woodburn 1982). Clearly, delayed-return foraging might leave a heavier archaeological footprint and thus is less problematic for archaeologists. So for the moment, we will focus on immediate-return foragers to discern what archaeological traces similar peoples of the past might have left behind.

Before I begin, be forewarned I will adhere to the convention of representing ethnographic information in the present tense, since the information was valid at the time it was collected. Certainly, given the great changes that have visited the world within even the relatively short time since the ethnographies were written, the peoples referred to below may no longer live in the manner described.

The expression "immediate-return" refers to the fact that such foragers generally do not hunt or gather more food than is needed in the short term. Gathering is likely done on a daily basis; with respect to hunting, men may take small game every day and collaborate on large-scale hunts when opportunities arise. It would be easy for people like us to conclude that foragers simply cannot master the technology required to store food over long periods, but in fact, they do not betray a sense that this lack of storage facilities is in any way a problem. Early ethnographers, carrying out fieldwork when mobile foraging was more common, were struck by the casual attitude foragers had toward the getting of food (Sahlins 1972). It was as though the world were their refrigerator, with food always available so long as men and women ventured out to obtain it. This belies a popular image of hunters and gatherers living on the brink of starvation, chronically anxious about their next meal. And in fact, studies like that of Richard Lee among the southern African Ju/'hoansi (the suffix "-si" meaning "people"), have indicated that mobile foragers do not simply delude themselves about their capacities to provide sufficiently for themselves and their households (1984). Most foraging diets supply the gamut of nutrients and, generally, sufficient calories.

There are other benefits to be derived from a mobile foraging life. An eclectic diet, with the lean protein of wild game supplemented by nuts, roots, and fruit, lends itself to reasonably good overall health. Since foraged foods contain no processed sugars, mobile foragers seldom suffer from dental caries; their teeth are likelier to be ground to nubs than to rot. Foragers are (or at least were) spared the so-called "diseases of development": diabetes, high blood pressure, coronary artery disease. Given the high-fiber foods they consume, foragers are unlikely to become constipated, and thus escape the circulatory strain long-term bouts of this condition can cause, leading not only to strokes and heart problems but to deafness in old age. The diseases human beings invited or exacerbated with the shift to agriculture, such as influenzas, measles, smallpox, and malaria, were rare or unknown among early foragers. Even had they been exposed to such threats, foraging **settlement patterns**—generally low-density, with small **bands,** each composed of 30 or so individuals, dispersed over a vast expanse of land—inveighed against maintaining them. A virus might wipe out a band completely or would yield survivors with immunity, and either way, the population as a whole would not be exposed.

Obviously none of this means that mobile foragers live forever. Infants may not live long at all, as foraged foods can be hard on their developing digestive systems. As adults, there are a variety of challenges, ranging from the immediately deadly, like snakebite or infection, to the chronic and debilitating, like arthritis and the aftermath of fractures. Foragers might easily see the end of their days at 30 or 40 years of age, but in pre-industrial agricultural societies the lifespan was much the same.

Mobile foragers are often referred to as nomadic, but this is not really an accurate description of the lifestyle. It is true that such peoples seldom establish permanent residences, but they do not wander aimlessly, nor do they simply "follow the herds." Generally, mobile foragers become intimately acquainted with a territory, learning what resources come into season at what time of year, and they relocate within the territory to take the fullest advantage of whatever is abundant (Brody 2000). Such **seasonal scheduling** repeats itself annually, and as foragers move camp they are generally transferring from one familiar place to another throughout the year. In most environments, under most circumstances, foragers can piece together a reasonably ample living year-round, although there may be a gap between seasons and a consequent period of undernutrition that can be manifest on the long bones as **Harris lines,** which mark a slowing of growth.

In contrast, a resource may ripen in quantities that allow for multiple bands to congregate for the full season. The Washo of the American West's Great Basin, for instance, would come together in a huge assembly, called *gumsaba* ("big time"), for the piñon nut harvest (Downs 1966); Tonkinson uses the expression "big meeting" for the same sort of event among Australian aborigines (2002:40n9). Such gatherings among foragers are festive occasions, involving all manner of exchange—the sharing of food, the swapping of valued objects, the forming and renewal of friendships, and the arrangement of marriages. Clearly, a large group of this sort may sustain an infectious disease, but during this time people are sufficiently well-fed to ward off such threats. As the seasonal resource dwindles, however, resistance likely dwindles with it, but by that time—and not coincidentally—the festive atmosphere has dissipated, quarrels arise, and the "big meeting" splits apart, once again, into small, roving bands whose mobility prevents communicable diseases from taking hold.

EXERCISE

What sort of archaeological footprint might seasonal scheduling leave behind?

Ethnographers who have documented mobile foraging cultures have noted that the same casual attitude toward **subsistence** may pervade life in general. The daily round is relaxed and convivial, far from the drudgery we associate with the term "work." In most environments, neither hunting nor gathering constitutes what we would consider to be a day's labor. Adding in such chores as the creation and maintenance of hunting and gathering equipment yields something approaching a 40-hour week, but keep in mind that *we* engage in what could be seen as "household maintenance" over and above time spent on the job (Lee 1984). "Those who work for a living; that's their problem," sang Richard Lee's Ju/'hoan friends merrily as he conveyed them by truck to a lush nut-collecting grove (1984:34). In the early 1900s, well-meaning Christian missionaries distributed steel axes to the Australian Yir Yoront with the idea that the aborigines would dedicate the time saved from stoneknapping toward more "productive" pursuits,

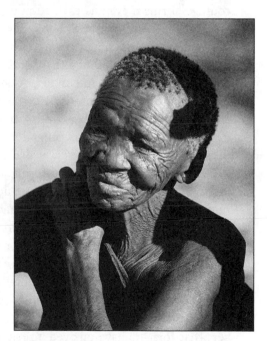

Ju/'hoan woman.

that is, becoming more "Western" in their regard for a hard day's work. In fact the Yir Yoront gratefully received the axes but applied the added leisure toward a pastime the missionaries felt was already too much of a preoccupation: sleeping (Sharp 1952).

As previously mentioned, foragers tend to get by with what people like us consider to be only rudimentary material technology—digging sticks, weapons for hunting, and other simple implements—and we often regard them as "undeveloped" on this account. It should be kept in mind that simple implements are likely portable implements, fitting in well to a mobile lifestyle. But beyond this, as Bicchieri (1990) has noted, what mobile foragers may "lack" (by our lights) in material technology they often make up for in **social technology.** There are all sorts of mechanisms directed at maintaining harmony and cooperation within the group.

Food, especially meat, is shared; items move freely throughout the band and even beyond the band through a form of exchange called **reciprocity,** wherein value is located primarily in the social rather than the economic aspect of the act (Lee 1984). Individuals within mobile foraging society are given credit for their contributions to the band but are actively discouraged, through gossip and ridicule, from becoming too prideful (Boehm 1999; also Lee 1984). The trick is to encourage altruism even as each adult's place as an equal member of the band is acknowledged and honored, but as highly developed as the social technology of foragers can be, the trick does not always work. There *are* slights and perceived slights to equal personhood that touch off disruptive incidents. Band members will actively intervene to curtail episodes of physical violence (Lee 1984; Turnbull 1961). If conflict cannot be contained, the band may have to undergo **fission**—splitting into smaller bands—but even this is a solution more often than a problem, as the groups can generally handle their subsistence needs while tempers cool.

Since a good deal of this information is derived from ethnography and not archaeology, you may well ask how much is really applicable to human lifeways during the Mesolithic. For one thing, modern times have not been kind to foraging peoples. At the hands of farmers and industrialists, foragers have been hunted, persecuted, evicted from their lands, and consigned to the most marginal environments (Brody 2000). Surely the situation was not nearly so harsh when their distant predecessors were "hunters in a world of hunters" (Sahlins 1968). But that in itself might justify projecting at least some of what we have learned recently into the distant past. If in fact cultural anthropologists can assert that foragers have enjoyed a relatively high quality of life, despite years of losing ground, literally and figuratively, to peoples who subsist by different means, conceivably Mesolithic life could have been that much richer.

Having said that, it is entirely possible that some culture traits we associate with foraging today might arise not from the lifestyle itself but from debilitating relations with nonforaging peoples. Edwin Wilmsen, for instance, argues that the Ju/'hoansi are seemingly "classless" because they constitute the "underclass" in a regional class system and that we should not see egalitarianism as the primal political ethos of humankind (1989). When foraging societies could hold their own among other foraging societies, there certainly may have been more leeway to develop systems of internal status differentiation—this would be a boon to archaeologists, in fact, since different statuses are often marked by items of material culture—but ethnography tells us of many egalitarian foraging societies that have not been so hard-pressed by their neighbors, so it is likely that egalitarianism among ancient foragers was at least common, if not exclusive.

The issue that is more germane to our purpose here concerns domestication and agriculture. It was once thought that the reason humans became farmers was obvious—farming was simply a better means of obtaining food, and foragers realized this as soon as a genius among them planted the first seed. But this presumption is teleological, stemming from an inflated sense of ourselves and our subsistence methods. As indicated above, a wealth of data actually indicates that foraging more than satisfies basic human needs of both the physical and emotional varieties. So now, sufficiently enlightened as to the benefits of a foraging lifestyle, we must pose what has become a legitimate question: why *did* foragers, in so many different venues around the globe, become farmers? Before I attempt to answer it, however, it is worth taking a moment to define terms.

Domestication, Agriculture, Sedentism

These three concepts are often associated; that is, we think in terms of formerly nomadic peoples staying put and farming. But while agriculture must involve domestication to at least some extent, domestication does not necessarily lead to agriculture or to sedentism, while sedentism can take place without domestication or agriculture. In short, the relationship between these three endeavors is complex; hence, it is better to treat them separately on the conceptual level, especially since they are not always bundled in reality.

Put very simply, domestication is **artificial selection.** It is not nature, but rather, it is human cultural activities that constitute the "environment" within which some individuals from a species survive and thrive, and some are eliminated. The differences between wild and domesticated wheat are instructive. The seeds of wild wheat are protected by a tough outer coat that remains intact until conditions are optimal for germination. In contrast, the stalk of wild wheat becomes very brittle, in order to release the seeds easily. Neither of these characteristics served human needs in the region where wheat was domesticated—a tough seed coat was indigestible and therefore undesirable, and the method of harvesting tended to dislodge the seeds from many of the stalks. The seeds that made it to the dinner plate were those that were the most tender, retained by stalks that were

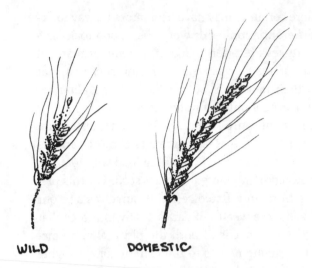

WILD   DOMESTIC

just a bit more flexible. Note that humans were not necessarily making *conscious* selections regarding wheat traits. But the seed they ate was also the seed that was planted to yield the next generation, and over time the tough seed coat and the brittle stalk were bred out of the wheat that humans cultivated (Blumler and Byrne 1991).

The process of domestication is frequently accomplished through human beings, again not necessarily intentionally, commandeering some portion of a species' reproductive cycle. The changes brought about in domesticated wheat were precisely the changes that would have prevented the wheat from returning to a wild state—even if the more flexible stalk could somehow release its seeds, and even if those seeds could remain viable through poor germination conditions, wild wheat, far better equipped to handle these matters, would surely outcompete it. In short, domesticated wheat could no longer reproduce without human aid. This was not a tragedy for the wheat, however, since humans were greatly motivated to ensure its propagation.

Humans inserted themselves, as well, into the reproductive cycles of many animal species. In animals, it is more obvious that one of the means through which domestication is accomplished is by maintaining some form of an infantile state (humans interfere with natural maturity in plants as well, though this is perhaps more difficult to recognize). Recall, from chapter 7, the example of the dog, likely descended from wolf pups taken into human camps. It is often presumed that domestication of this sort would be a lengthy process, but it was achieved by a team working under Russian geneticist Dmitry Belyaev in a mere 40 years (Trut 1999).

In an attempt to understand the effects of domestication, Belyaev began a long-term experiment with foxes. For wild foxes, as for most animals, an important stage of the maturation process is the shift from a trusting newborn to an adult that swiftly reacts to threats by attacking and/or fleeing. The foxes Belyaev selected to produce the next generation of experimental animals were precisely those that were developmentally delayed in taking on these adult behaviors. Obviously the foxes matured in other ways—they were capable of breeding, for example—but eventually Belyaev and his team were able to produce foxes that maintained an infantile temperament all of their lives. This is true of your dog as well. It rolls over to present its belly to you for scratching, but no adult wolf would ever take this risk. Your dog does so because for all of its life you are Momma Dog—a ready source of food, warmth, and grooming—and Momma Dog can (usually) be trusted not to eviscerate her pup.

I should append here (mainly because it's fascinating) that temperament in foxes and wolves would seem to be genetically and/or hormonally linked to an entire suite of disparate traits. Young animals often have mottled or piebald coats, the better to blend in with their surroundings; only later does fur become more uniform in color. The ears of adult animals stand erect, but young animals tend to have floppy ears. Finally, whereas the tail of a mature animal drapes down over the anus, a young animal will carry its tail straight up so that Momma can clean underneath it. Hence, if you have ever wondered why your spotted, floppy-eared dog, tail raised high, looks so much different from a wolf, you now have an inkling. Your dog is essentially a puppy writ big.

FOREVER YOUNG

The retention of immature traits is known as **neoteny,** and clearly it would not be too difficult to effect. Neoteny requires no new genetic material, since every organism goes through a stage of immaturity. The point is to inhibit those genetic actions that then shepherd the organism to maturity. Since individuals vary with respect to the age at which they mature—this is all part of the variation within species that Darwin observed—continually selecting "late bloomers" to parent the next generation may attenuate the transition to maturity until, effectively, it never takes place at all.

There would seem to be something nefarious about humans interfering with such natural and rightful processes as maturity and breeding. But our **domesticates** have taken their revenge, in that human beings have been subject to neoteny as well. One example involves the ability to digest milk, which in most human groups, following a general mammalian pattern, is suspended after infancy. This makes a good deal of sense—milk is for the next baby, not the current one. But in populations that had domesticated such milk-producing animals as cattle and/or goats, an individual whose system could continue to process milk past the point of weaning from the maternal version would be healthier for having access to this wholesome food, thus she would likely have greater reproductive success and the trait would come to proliferate in the population. This and similar specific cases add up to one general trend: most humans became as dependent on their domesticates as domesticates are on them.

The term **agriculture** refers not merely to domestication—recall that wolves likely became dogs in a foraging context—but also to an entire lifestyle centered on planted crops and husbanded animals. In a sense, it is the logical, full-circle result of the development of mutual dependency described above—agriculture is the domestication of the human being. When referring to this lifestyle, cultural anthropologists often distinguish between **horticulture,** cultivation involving the clearing and maintenance of temporary garden plots with relatively simple tools, and agriculture, which is pursued through more complex technologies directed toward opening up larger, more permanent plots of land, and controlling the distribution of water. There are also **pastoralists** who make their living primarily through the keeping of herd animals. These **subsistence strategies** do not necessarily occur in a set sequence—early farmers did not have to pass through horticultural and/or pastoralist stages in order to become agriculturalists. It is fair to say, however, that agriculture as we know it today did not spring full-blown into existence but underwent a period of considerable trial-and-error before reliably yielding sufficient food.

One would think **sedentism**—"settling down" in one place and building reasonably permanent dwellings—would necessarily accompany agriculture, but it is not always the case. There is intriguing evidence from both **Mesoamerica** (Flannery 1968; MacNeish 1964) and the Andes (MacNeish et al. 1983) suggesting that people continued to pursue seasonal scheduling even as some of the stops along their routes were visits to casual gardens they had sown. In Southeast Asia, where even today a deep attachment to ancestral place is culturally important throughout much of the region, it is possible that settlement inspired domestication rather than the other way around (Higham 1989). And of course, as previously mentioned, such delayed-return foragers as the native peoples of the Pacific Northwest were not mobile, like most of the foragers discussed so far, but established stable villages along the coast and on the banks of rivers.

Hence we should not assume that sedentary peoples are by definition agricultural peoples, or that domestication inevitably leads to sedentism. Unquestionably domestication, agriculture, and sedentism often occur together, but if we believe they *must* occur together, we skew the results of archaeological research and miss out on the many and varied ways human beings have organized successful lives.

The Un-Neolithic Non-Revolution

Thus supplied with additional conceptual equipment, we can now return to the question, why did foragers become farmers? Back in the days when the answer to the question was thought to be obvious, archaeologist V. Gordon Childe (1936) coined a phrase to summarize this allegedly golden moment in human prehistory: the **Neolithic Revolution.** "Neolithic," as previously mentioned, refers to a period when humans still relied on wood, stone, and bone implements but applied them to the act of cultivation. This was thought to be revolutionary not only because it changed human lives forever, which it eventually did, but also because it was something radically different from what had happened previously, which it was not.

As you are well aware by now, even scientists are sometimes taken in by their own ideas, coming to see them as such accurate representations of reality that they begin to ignore reality itself. There is a long-standing dichotomy in anthropology—**food procurement** versus **food production.** According to this system of classification, foragers only *procure* food; they do not *produce* it. The expression "food production" is reserved for those groups that apply technology and brain power to manipulate the environment, wresting from it what they wish. The dichotomy harks back to a malignant idea that once infected anthropology, and today has spread outside the discipline: the notion that foragers are the most "primitive" of peoples, technologically—and perhaps mentally?—unable to do anything more than meekly accept what nature has to offer, and starve when it refuses to give up its bounty.

There is a minor problem here in the use of the term "production," to which the anthropologists who devised this scheme intended to impart a specialized meaning; however, the verb "to produce" is far too necessary to everyday communication to be restricted to such a purpose. Of course foragers produce food, even if they only "procure" it from the environment. But far more important is the fact that foragers engage in food production in precisely the sense that the expression was originally designed to describe: they regularly, and knowledgeably, manipulate the environment to gain from it what they want.

We have already discussed some of these activities: hunting technologies, gathering technologies, seasonal scheduling. As effective as these were on a daily and annual basis, there were far more dramatic methods of environmental engineering that were occasionally applied. Both Native Americans (Stewart 2002) and Australian aborigines (Gott 2005) used to "fire" their surroundings, deliberately torching woodlands and grasslands so as to take advantage of secondary growth and the animals that consumed it. While it still might be said that foragers "live lightly on the land" (or at least more lightly than peoples who practice other subsistence strategies), they can certainly leave their mark.

For our purposes here, however, it is most important to note those techniques, for which we have both archaeological and ethnographic evidence, that foragers apply to enhance long-term yields from the resources available to them. At el-Wad Terrace in Israel, a preponderance of bones from male gazelles suggests post-Pleistocene Natufian hunters were being selective with respect to what animals were taken (Bar-Oz et al. 2004); similar attempts at herd management have been identified among other hunting groups. Foragers also try to influence herd movement by, for instance, driving a herd of wild game into a narrow canyon and establishing camp at the mouth of the canyon. Gatherers do what they can to help their favorite plants survive, by, for instance, removing competitive plants from the vicinity and loosening the soil at the base of the plants to allow for more aeration (Tudge 1998). The Batek foragers of Malaysia go further, planting root crops, abandoning them to resume their seasonal rounds, and then returning to harvest what was to them merely a "richer-than-usual stand of wild foods" (Keesing 1976:117; Kirk and Karen Endicott, from whose work Keesing's observation was likely drawn, later wrote that the Batek "treated agricultural efforts as little more than an additional foraging technique" [Endicott and Endicott 2008:89]). Recall that ancient Mesoamericans are believed to have behaved in much the same way.

If the examples above suggest actions you ordinarily associate with agriculture—herding, fencing, weeding, hoeing, planting—that is exactly the point to be made here. Ancient foragers did not have some sort of revelation regarding the potential for herd management to provide more consistent, and more easily obtained, bounties of meat; or the propensity for seed, placed appropriately, to result in new plants—these were things they likely already knew, *as foragers.* And while they exploited this knowledge, they used it, probably for millennia, not to become farmers but to become better foragers. The considerable benefits of a foraging lifestyle, as already described, would hardly be cast aside lightly. There was no Neolithic Revolution, no flash of insight that liberated foragers from their primitive moorings. There was, rather, for most if not all foragers, a suite of well-worn yield-intensification methods that gradually became more important to them, and eventually became indispensable.

So the question before us is not really a matter of why foragers became food producers. The better question is, what conditions had to pertain for foragers to intensify the food-producing techniques they were already practicing? Admittedly, the mental picture called to mind by that question is not quite as thrilling as the one conjured up by a celebration of the first brilliant thinker who planted a seed, releasing his people from the endless, unrewarding slog of hunting and gathering. I confess that like most anthropologists, I actually take pleasure in undermining much-loved "commonsense" notions. But as watered down as our new guiding question has become, I am hoping there may still be some excitement in the answer.

Did They Jump . . . Or Were They Pushed?

For all of its advantages, foraging has one great disadvantage—in most environments, to provide the high quality of life described earlier in this chapter, it requires free access to a good deal of land. Foraging **catchment areas** are so large that they often cannot be defended from encroachment, but in general, foragers are not much prone to engaging in warfare to protect their resources. While one band may lay claim to, say, a waterhole, visitors are welcome to drink so long as they ask permission first. Asking is important—as previously noted, foragers are proud people who need to feel as though they are equal to others in any exchange—but permission is rarely denied. Foragers know that they will also need, one day, to drink at another band's waterhole, so under ordinary circumstances it would make no sense to monopolize such a resource. But even in extraordinary circumstances, when one band might refuse to grant another access to water or foodstuffs, protracted conflict is unlikely. The band that was snubbed would have to choose between fighting and simply moving on to new ground. In the Mesolithic, when population densities were still relatively low, the latter option was probably the better option most of the time.

Given sufficient land, abundant resources, and a dispersed (and dispersible) population, Mesolithic peoples might have carried on as foragers indefinitely. In the first place, since foraging cultures are built around these conditions, foragers perpetuate them simply by living foraging lives. But beyond this, conscious action is often taken. Foragers range widely through territory they hope to exploit. Young men may rove far, mentally mapping every inch of land and learning what it has to offer, then returning with food and knowledge for the women, children, and elderly people who tend to pursue productive activities within and around a base camp. Various means foragers have of coaxing maximum yields out of the resources available to them have already been discussed.

Foragers typically have very low birth rates, for a number of reasons. Children may nurse for several years while being carefully introduced to wild foods, and this on-again-off-again stimulation of the breast suppresses ovulation. As noted above, infant mortality is also high. Over and above these natural checks on population growth, foragers might employ more drastic measures—abortion, infanticide—to reduce the rate of increase still further, ensuring that people would be roughly in balance with the land and resources needed to support a foraging lifestyle.

But the most careful resource management plans can fail, especially when certain factors, like environmental conditions, cannot be controlled. The balance that sustains foraging is easily thrown off. If a situation in which more infants than usual, just by chance, survived into their third year, was coupled with a disaster that destroyed a major food source, foragers would be scrambling for alternatives. The food-producing techniques with which they were already familiar might be pressed into fuller service. The good news is that such techniques could yield a significant amount of food—perhaps not a favored food (Flannery 1973)—relatively quickly. The bad news is that if this food was able to sustain the larger number of infants, the population would remain above the normal level. This state of affairs would be compounded if infants were weaned earlier, given the new availability of "produced" food that could be more readily digestible than wild food. Births might be spaced more narrowly, and population growth would continue. What began as a stopgap measure, meant to tide over the foragers until their preferred resource had recovered, became integrated into a new way of life.

Geographer Carl Sauer (1969) speculated that agriculture had to be the product of leisure, since hungry people would be in no position to experiment with new food-getting strategies that might not work. In contrast, economist Ester Boserup (1965) saw the potential for hunger as the ultimate motivator. Harking back to Malthus (see chapter 2), Boserup believed ancient foragers were chronically subject to **population pressure**—the threat that their numbers would grow larger than the food supply—but rather than meekly submitting to positive checks, humans were inspired by this pressure to devise novel methods of subsistence, one of these eventually evolving into agriculture. In his book *The Food Crisis in Prehistory* (1977), anthropologist Mark Cohen applied Boserup's thinking but reversed the mood; foragers, he said, were not inspired by population pressure, but haunted by it. They did not choose to abandon foraging; rather, they were forced to do so. Cohen's hypothesis suffered criticism because a rise in population *prior* to the onset of agriculture was not evident from the archaeological record. But as indicated above, even a very small increase, especially when accompanied by some form of environmental degradation, could be the undoing of a foraging lifestyle. The situation might not become archaeologically noticeable, however, until a considerable degree of lifestyle change had already taken place.

Despite the dearth of direct support, Cohen's ideas became very influential. Binford (1983) further observed that population pressure was not exerted only from within a society. An especially suitable area for hunting and gathering might become "packed" with groups over time, and eventually the respectful sharing of resources would become impractical. Competition over resources would likely lead to some foraging bands usurping full control, while others were driven to the margins of the territory. Again, food-producing techniques might have to be less casually implemented as the outcast group struggled to maintain itself in a restricted space.

In sum, population pressure, environmental degradation, and competition, either singly or in various combinations, came to be seen the prime "push" factors toward agriculture, and in many respects they may continue to drive agriculture into more elaborate forms, as we will soon see. Having said all of this, however, these general principles may not pertain in specific instances. Bruce Smith and colleagues (2007) see in the southeastern United States, where such plants as sumpweed and goosefoot were domesticated between 4 and 3 kya, the kind of "stress-free" environment Sauer envisioned. Agriculture does not actually "take off" in the region, however, until maize is imported up to 2,000 years later, and it is likely that sumpweed and goosefoot were simply added to the stock of wild foods; no "revolution" was underway. Displaced foragers, intensifying their food-producing practices under duress, would have been far more likely to experience the shift in subsistence strategy as revolutionary, but not in a positive sense, and the change in food-getting activities might have been seen as the least of it.

Whether the road to agriculture was smooth or arduous, eventually more than food-getting began to change. Agriculture generated new cultures, and these eventually left distinctive tracks in the archaeological record. But it is the first signs of these new cultures that we are especially interested in detecting.

Domestication, Agriculture, and the Archaeological Record

Even in the present day, the difference between wild and domesticated is not always clear. Abraham Rosman and Paula Rubel have catalogued the various ways societies on the island of New Guinea dealt with pigs (1989). While in some societies both male and female pigs are husbanded, in others uncastrated males are allowed to roam free and impregnate the females as they choose; in still other societies pigs are only occasionally claimed from the forest as the need arises. Are all of these animals domesticates? The Sami of northern Scandinavia herd reindeer, but in many respects reindeer are no more tame than the same animal we call "caribou" in North America. Anna Lowenhaupt Tsing (2005) writes about the Meratus Dayaks of Indonesian Borneo casually tossing seeds and fruit pits into their front yards—is the resulting accidentally-on-purpose crop wild or domesticated? The point is that these categories, like so many others we have discussed, are fuzzy. It follows that if wild and domesticated are sometimes difficult to identify today, they can be that much harder to pick out within the archaeological record.

With respect to the onset of agriculture, this too can be tricky. As already suggested, people are not farmers just because they have engaged in domestication, the dog being a case in point. Even so, our watchword should be caution, not discouragement. Agriculture eventually emerges in a readily recognizable form from the archaeological record, and the idea is to work our way back to what preceded it, in terms of both biological and cultural change.

Of course, when it comes to animals (and from this point onward we can take that word to mean nonhuman animals), we look to what are generally available—bones. The earliest domesticated animals were often smaller and less sturdy in build than their wild counterparts. While some semblance of herd management can be accomplished before domestication, it can be done much more effectively once a herd is under full human control. Of the animals slaughtered for purposes of consumption, males may greatly outnumber females, indicating that females are being reserved to produce the next generation. Just the fact that bones from the same animal species are aggregated, over a long span of time, might indicate domestication, especially if there is a corresponding aggregation of human bones at the same location. The remains of herds similarly aggregated in life may show signs of diseases that are more easily transmitted when animals are confined to a small space.

I have already mentioned that domestication introduced a number of new diseases to human populations. Diseases were a result of not only direct contact but also indirect contact, if domestication was accompanied by sedentism and thus the establishment of the critical mass needed to sustain diseases **endemically** that might otherwise flare up and die out along with their hosts. While **zoonotic** diseases had always threatened humankind, once humans and animals were living in close proximity on an everyday basis, they could more readily pass diseases to each other and among themselves. Both humans and animals may suffer a great many deaths from acute disease under such circumstances—juveniles likely being especially hard-hit—and the stress of chronic disease might influence mortality rates and have secondary effects that become evident in skeletal remains.

Plants help us out in archaeological detective work by producing not only distinctive pollens but also silicate residues, called **phytoliths.** Since within the process of domestication enough genetic change can build up to produce new species, if plant phytoliths bear more resemblance to those of modern domesticates than of wild varieties, this is an important clue to the wild-or-domesticated status of species. As with animals, sheer amounts of a particular type of plant remains might suggest domestication, although it should be noted that sometimes foragers become equally fixated on a single resource. Then there are instances when our quest to understand domestication is facilitated by a quirk of nature. Grasses, participating in the carbon cycle, take up a stable but relatively rare isotope of carbon, ^{13}C, at a different rate than other plants. Human beings are not prone to eating grasses, but one type of grass in the Americas became maize (i.e., corn), and when humans ingest maize, their remains, as well, take on the same ^{13}C signature typical of grasses.

Apart from biological evidence of domestication and agriculture, there are a variety of cultural clues embedded in the archaeological record. Specialized implements were developed to plant, tend, harvest, and process crops. While some foraging groups worked with clay—Junko Habu (2004) maintains Jōmon pottery of ancient Japan dates back 16.5 ky—agriculturalists were generally more motivated to produce ceramics, especially as long-term storage vessels for preservable plant foods like grain. Cats became important as a means of controlling vermin. Landscapes were organized around cultivation—garden plots, baulks separating plots, irrigation ditches. People grew concerned about when to plant and when to harvest, and observations about the solstice, the equinox, and the phases of the moon were incorporated into architecture and artwork. The fertility of the land was frequently equated

ARE CATS...

...EVER *REALLY* DOMESTICATED?

with the fertility of women and female animals, and significant anxiety, on both practical and existential levels, could be generated by the decline of any form of fertility. These themes were reflected in ritual objects as well as the ceremonies held and the grounds and structures where they were carried out.

With the transition to agriculture, ideas about kinship likely changed in ways that had an impact on how people arranged themselves spatially. Foragers tend to favor **bilateral kinship** systems, in which an individual counts both his mother's and his father's kin equally as his own kin. This builds up a huge stock of kin in and of itself, but foragers do not stop there—they often extend the metaphor of kinship to anyone with whom they plan to engage in an ongoing relationship. Reflecting this expansive sense of kinship, foraging camps may consist of temporary shelters arranged in a ring, with doorways opening onto a central area where food is processed and shared, and people enjoy each other's company on a full-time basis.

Huts arranged in a circle and opening out onto a central plaza

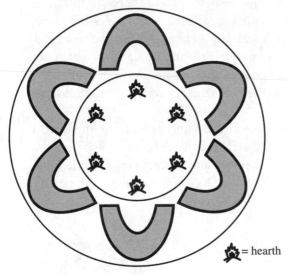

= hearth

Ju/'hoan foraging camp (adapted from Lee 1984).

Cultivators, on the other hand, frequently reckon descent only through one line. Such **unilineal kinship** systems form **descent groups** with a restricted membership and a structure that continues to exist even when individuals who occupy positions in the structure die. At least part of the reason for this version of kinship is a change in attitude toward land. Foragers seldom objectify land—it is not a "thing" to be parceled and distributed, but simply the backdrop for the resources they must exploit. Cultivators, understandably, regard land differently, as itself a resource that a descent group will claim as its own. The more permanent housing of cultivators is less likely to face its neighbors and more likely to face the fields kin work in common. What would be single-family huts in a foraging camp are **extended family** compounds in agricultural villages, as kinsmen cluster around those lands which they are entitled to farm by dint of their membership in the descent group. It is not only living kin that come together in such compounds, however; the dead may be buried or otherwise kept on lineage property, sometimes with **grave goods** marking their occupation and/or their rank within society. Cultivators often have great respect, and even reverence, for their forebears. These are the ancestors who originally cleared the land, and their continued existence, even in the altered state we know as death, deepens a descent group's present-day claim of ownership. While foragers focus on extending kinship through space, cultivators often see kinship as an institution that unites their descent groups through time.

Ideally, the archaeologist trying to determine whether she has unearthed an agricultural community will want data of all types—biological signs of plant and

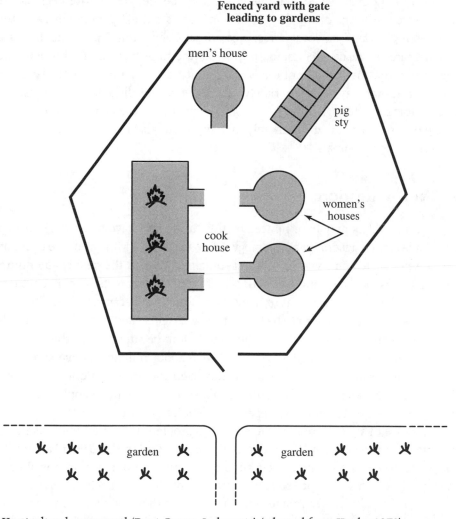

Horticultural compound (Dani, Papua, Indonesia) (adapted from Heider 1979).

animal domestication, artifacts and features that exemplify the kinds of technologies, social arrangements, and ideologies farming peoples are likely to adopt. Any one piece of evidence may be misleading. A dense population may mark a place where foragers gathered regularly for "big meetings"; such implements as **metates** could as easily grind wild as domesticated grain; and a worshipful attitude toward ancestors, and the claim to land a regard for ancestors might support, could be developed in a foraging context, especially one in which productive land was scarce or the object of contention. Archaeologically speaking, delayed-return foragers can look very much like cultivators, the chief distinction lying in the types of foods exploited.

Eventually evidence for cultivation cannot be denied—entire regions are transformed in terms of the density of human and animal populations, and the engineering of land and water resources to suit agricultural purposes leaves a well-demarcated archaeological footprint—but the steps taken up to this point are generally more subtle, and not easily sorted out from other ways of food-getting. And in fact, that may be appropriately descriptive of the allegedly stark transition "from" foraging "to" agriculture—"Neolithic" peoples were simply exercising all of the options they knew, not merely to survive, but also to satisfy their sense of what it was to be human.

The "First" Question

Astute readers may have noticed by this time that I have taken the stuffings out of a favorite question in archaeology, "Who was first?" Mind you, the question is often predicated on a view of cultural "progress" that, as the next chapter more fully explores, is something that both scientists and humanists would be wise to lay aside. All too often we want to know "who was first" because we see whatever milestone that was achieved to be better than what preceded it, and consequently whichever people that passed the milestone first to be superior to other peoples. You are certainly free to believe what you like about human achievements, but when these personal convictions enter into scientific investigations, they prejudice the results, and when they enter into a scheme in which people are sorted into "greater" and "lesser," they engender prejudice against others.

The case of agriculture illustrates another problem with the "who was first?" question: first to do what? If the dog was domesticated in the Upper Paleolithic, thereafter to be incorporated into a suite of hunting equipment that was already reasonably effective, what exactly was accomplished? If ancient foragers deployed food-producing techniques to enhance what they obtained from food procurement, were these people really, in effect, the first farmers? If not, what degree of food production has to be reached before we can account human groups as such? Is this degree detectable from the archaeological record? When we survey prehistory through our teleological goggles, we scan for those elements we expect to find and place a definitional box around them—"domestication of cattle," "cultivation of wheat," "permanent settlement," and so forth. The people actually living through these developments may have had a very different impression of what, if anything, was going on.

Archaeologists sometimes react to the "who was first?" question in ways that simply compound the problems mentioned above. If it is intimated that **Old World** peoples are more "advanced" than those in the **New World** because agriculture came about "first" in the Old World, the New World archaeologist might point out, defensively, the evidence for early domestication on his side of the globe (e.g., Piperno and Pearsall 1998; Smith 1997; Zizumbo-Villareal and Colunga-Garcia Marin 2010). Such a response simply validates the search for "firsts" (not to mention the division of the planet into "old" and "new") and gives credence to the idea that the reputations of those who did not go "first" need to be rehabilitated by an equal or near-equal claim to "firstness." It might be far more productive, however, to put together an ancient archaeological site with an eye toward its total ecological context, not simply one aspect therein, to try and understand what factors seem to have inspired the intensification of food-producing strategies at whatever point. If this point was not in fact reached or was significantly delayed relative to other regions, we could then study how a group was able to manage itself and its resources in such a way that domestication, agriculture, and/or sedentism could be avoided. Given the benefits of a foraging lifestyle, this could certainly be read as success, not failure.

Against that backdrop of attitude adjustment, we can now move on to consider both early and later centers of agriculture. While developments in some centers were exported to others—there is evidence that agriculture in **Mesopotamia** had a direct impact on **Egypt,** either through the movement of seed or the movement of migrants who knew how to farm (or both)—at least some centers developed wholly independently. In the Old World, according to our best guess of the moment, agriculture was taking hold in Southwest Asia, especially in the region we call the **Fertile Crescent,** over 11 kya. "Fertile" Crescent notwithstanding, it would seem as though the region was "pushed" into agriculture precisely by that motivational triumvirate of population pressure, environmental degradation, and competition described earlier (Henry 1989). In fact, agriculture was only a temporary solution to the problem of intensive human settlement there. A long-term buildup of salts in Southwest Asian soils, brought about by millennia of irrigation, has rendered farming difficult if not impossible in many parts of the region today.

Egyptian bas-relief—
peasant with cow.

Agriculture in the **Indus Valley** region of what is now Pakistan may have been instigated, either directly or indirectly, by developments in Mesopotamia, though there are those, like archaeologist Jim Shaffer, who have long argued for independent invention (e.g., Shaffer and Lichtenstein 1999). Either way, Indus Valley agricultural activities appeared relatively early, circa 9 kya, and eventually the region developed its own sphere of influence. Another early agricultural center (circa 11 kya) emerged in what is now **China,** and here we can almost certainly presume independent invention, or independent, at least, from Mesopotamia. While it is occasionally asserted that the region's staple crop, rice, was originally domesticated in Southeast Asia and then taken up in East Asia, at the current moment more observers believe the reverse to be true. Part of the problem in interpreting the evidence may lie in harvesting methods. Southeast Asians used an instrument called a finger-knife (Reid 1988) as a means of cutting rice stalks one at a time—people in the region who continue to favor this equipment say that it is more respectful toward the rice spirit (e.g., Boulanger 2009:108)—and this method of harvest did not bring about the genetic changes that the comparatively brutal harvesting via sickle inspired in Southwest Asian wheat (see, e.g., Unger-Hamilton 1989). So either Southeast Asians domesticated rice early, or they exploited rice in a wild form long after it was domesticated in China. This is yet another example of how the quest to discover "who was first?" is somewhat misguided.

The island of New Guinea is now thought to be an early center of domestication (circa 7 kya) for taro and bananas (Denham et al. 2003). To some extent this has been widely publicized as a means, once again, of "uplifting" what have otherwise been seen as "primitive" peoples to the exalted "status" of "early agriculturalists." You can tell from the number of quotation marks I have included in the previous sentence that I am reiterating such an effort is not only unnecessary but reinforces a false scale of human accomplishment. Yet, since for better or for worse such standards are in place, if conforming to them earns New Guineans a greater measure of respect in the world today, I cannot thoroughly condemn the project.

Interestingly, the reputation of modern Europe has not suffered from the fact that it was not, in ancient times, a center of agricultural invention. Nonetheless, agriculture was exported to the region relatively early, given the proximity of its southeastern quadrant to ancient Anatolia (modern Turkey), and Anatolia's prox-

A taro field in Hawaii.

imity to the Fertile Crescent. Anatolians migrated with their herds and crops into the Greek islands; subsequently both people and crops moved (not always in tandem) onto the mainland and spread westward and eventually northward.

Africa's history as a farming continent is somewhat different. While herding seems to have been practiced in Egypt very early on, the increasing desiccation of the area drew pastoralists inexorably toward the Nile. Thus, population pressure likely drove the onset of agriculture, although, as previously suggested, the "start-up" materials and methods could have come from Mesopotamia. Farming in sub-Saharan Africa was taken up somewhat later. There were likely local experiments with plant domestication, but these were soon superseded by the cultivation of imported cereals.

Unless solid evidence to the contrary turns up, we can reasonably presume that the centers for early domestication and agriculture that arose in the New World were a product of independent invention; in fact, they may have developed independently of each other. Generally we speak of two great centers, one situated in Mesoamerica while the other was in the Andes, though, as mentioned above, some domestication was going on in what is now the southeastern

United States. Maize, however, was the signature agricultural product of the New World, and once it was exported from its point (or points?) of origin, it overwhelmed any other plant domestication efforts. As important as maize became, it has proved difficult to determine just where and when it was domesticated, possibly because, again as indicated above, it was long exploited by foragers as a crop that was only casually sown and harvested while they pursued their seasonal schedule. A recent set of research reports supports an origin site in the Central Balsas River Valley in Mexico, circa 8,700 ya (Piperno et al. 2009; Ranere et al. 2009).

Given the different resources in each hemisphere, and their incorporation into separate streams of agricultural development, it stands to reason that we would find differences between Old World and New World farming; in fact, we find them between Mesoamerican and Andean farming, although in both regions maize became the primary crop. The most striking contrast between the Old World and the New was the lack of animal domesticates in the latter. Dogs had

Herd of llamas.

arrived at the very least with Clovis settlers (Leonard et al. 2002), but in terms of the domestication of New World species, the list is short. The Inuit continued to turn wolves into dogs in the far north. In the Andes, the llama and alpaca were domesticated, as well as the guinea pig. In Mesoamerica, animal domesticates were limited to a few species of fowl, and (if you can really call this domestication) bees.

It has been suggested that animal domestication in the New World was inhibited by a dearth of herd species, but this seems like a strange assertion in light of the legions of bison that roamed the northern plains. Additionally, caribou could have been subject to at least as much taming as the Sami reindeer, and other types of deer, along with pronghorns and rabbits in North America, and peccaries on both New World continents, might have been successfully domesticated. Thus, we should consider an alternative explanation: such species served human needs much more effectively in their wild form, sustaining foraging as an viable subsistence strategy and providing a supplement of meat for horticulturalists who otherwise supported themselves on their garden produce. In other words, there was little impetus to engage in the kinds of costs animal domestication could incur when the value of maintaining wildness was so obvious. Even so, New World peoples would eventually suffer for this "decision," as we will see in the next chapter.

EXERCISE

Draw up lists of Old World and New World domesticates.

So domestication and agriculture took hold in a number of places around the world, at a number of times, in a number of ways. In an important sense, no one was "first," since it is difficult to draw comparisons between such disparate circumstances. But there are elements common to many if not all of these situations—for example, the need to feed a larger population from a smaller amount of land—that help us to understand why cultivation was so often selected as one solution among many for pressing problems. Furthermore, between some areas of early agricultural development there was contact; thus, the chief reason why one society adopted agriculture may have been as simple as a neighboring society having done so. We speak of "centers of domestication" as if these places stood apart from their surroundings, but it is wiser to see the adoption of agriculture as more diffuse, with hundreds of "minicenters," focusing on one or two domesticates, spread out across the globe (Fuller 2010). Over time, some of these places became more agricultural, but many maintained long-standing mixed economies. Archaeologically speaking, none of this looks like a revolution.

The Downside of Agriculture

Eventually, however, agriculture had revolutionary effects. Traditionally, as you know, the onset of agriculture was thought to be a great "moment" for humankind, but theorists like Mark Cohen have encouraged us to see it through a glass darkly. The scientist-of-all-trades (and popular writer) Jared Diamond ran with this suggestion in a short, hard-hitting article that referred to agriculture as "the worst mistake in the history of the human race" (1987). In this article, Diamond draws a picture of prehistoric foraging that is much like the description that heads this chapter. He then discusses how agriculture ruined this Mesolithic idyll. The effect on human stature is perhaps the most dramatic—average human heights crashed with the onset of full-blown agriculture, and, according to Diamond, have yet to recover fully. This decline in stature is associated with the nutritional deficiencies of the agricultural diet, which tends to center on one starchy crop. If the one crop failed, malnutrition was compounded by undernutrition. While it was true that agriculture could support many more people from a smaller amount of land, it did not necessarily support them very well. Nonetheless, agricultural populations continued to procreate, not only because the fertility restrictions that suppress population growth in foraging populations had been lifted, but also because agriculture was more labor-intensive than foraging, requiring more workers.

Human health was affected in other ways. Diamond recites the litany of disease visited upon humans by their animal domesticates (see also Larsen 1995). There was also malaria, a great scourge of humankind. The malarial parasite is carried by mosquitoes, which found fertile breeding grounds in the stagnant pools left on fields that had been cleared of forest.

Additionally, Diamond lists some cultural disadvantages to agriculture. Foraging populations are known for their egalitarianism, he notes, but, in contrast, agricultural societies often develop systems of **social stratification,** in which a privileged few hold dominion over oppressed masses. Oppression is especially visited upon women, who frequently lose their honored status as providers of gathered foods for their households to become virtual beasts of burden in the fields. The difference between hierarchical societies and those of the Mesolithic, Diamond points out, is agriculture, and he indicts the adoption of farming as the beginning of the end for the ideal of human equality.

You might wonder, if foraging life was so good, why so many foragers gave way to agriculturalists, and/or became agriculturalists themselves. As previously mentioned, foragers are inclined to share what they have, not because they are morally superior peoples but because sharing is how they survive. Agriculturalists, on the other hand, are greedy, not because they are morally decrepit but because this is how *they* survive. Agricultural peoples suck out land and water from foraging catchment areas, applying these resources to ensure the survival of domesticates over wild plants and animals, which might further be directly destroyed in order to eliminate competition. Levels of conflict in agricultural societies can be high, as lineages compete with each other over finite parcels of land that must somehow feed their many children; agriculturalists develop weaponry both to defend their own land and to claim the land of others.

Foragers are hardly unacquainted with weaponry and, as noted, have the advantage of better health over their agricultural foes, but they are generally no match for their adversary's greater numbers. As Diamond remarks, "a hundred malnourished farmers can still outfight one healthy hunter" (1987:66). Foragers who were not killed in such an onslaught were shunted to the most marginal lands of a region, where they likely had to intensify their own food-producing techniques in order to survive at all. Competitive exclusion is not really a matter of "may the best man win"—it comes down to what we mean by "best."

Diamond's study in contrasts between foragers and agriculturalists is, of course, far too stark. It was, perhaps, a necessary corrective to the overly rosy depiction of the onset of agriculture that was once standard, and I include Diamond's work here just in case there is a reader who still harbors the conviction that agriculture was an unmitigated good. But it is no more scientifically productive to view agriculture as an unmitigated negative. Clearly there are benefits from agriculture that may outweigh its costs, especially under particular circumstances, and the demands of foraging—the need for mobility, the need for free access to land, the need to keep population numbers low—simply cannot always be satisfied, especially under particular circumstances. And it should be mentioned that foragers and agriculturalists have been known to coexist peaceably in regional systems of mutual economic dependence (Barth 1959), where, for instance, foragers might supply skins and game meat to agriculturalists in exchange for vegetables and dairy products. So antagonism between foragers and agriculturalists is not necessarily a foregone conclusion.

All the same, none of this comes close to overturning Diamond's main point: that agriculture has its dark side, one the average reader may not have anticipated. Brace yourselves, because I am about to dole out the same treatment to another much-cherished icon of human progress—civilization.

QUESTIONS FOR DISCUSSION AND REVIEW

- What are the advantages and disadvantages of foraging as a way of life? What are the advantages and disadvantages of agriculture?

- Illustrate, through plant and animal examples, how domestication is often a matter of encouraging neoteny.

- In what ways was the "Neolithic Revolution" neither Neolithic nor revolutionary?

- Describe the "push" factors that compelled people to take up cultivation.

- Why is the quest for "first person/society to have done _____?" a misguided one?

KEY WORDS

Mesolithic	Harris lines	Neolithic Revolution
Neolithic	subsistence	food procurement
Archaic	social technology	food production
foraging	reciprocity	catchment area
egalitarianism	fission	population pressure
ethnography	artificial selection	endemic
ethnographic record	neoteny	zoonotic
ethnoarchaeology	domesticate (*n.*)	phytolith
immediate-return (*or*	subsistence strategy	bilateral kinship
mobile) foraging	agriculture	unilineal kinship
delayed-return foraging	horticulture	descent group
settlement pattern	pastoralism	extended family
band	sedentism	metate
seasonal scheduling	Mesoamerica	Fertile Crescent

9

THE EVOLUTION OF STATE SOCIETY

Since the emergence of stratification, man's history . . .
has stood opposed to his humanity. The emergence
of power-wielding elites . . . laid the basis for a
new kind of anticollective society whose
vastly accelerated growth was founded not on
the reconciliation of antagonisms between men,
but on their origination and amplification
in slavery, caste, and class.

—Thomas Belmonte, *The Broken Fountain*

All the World's a Stage Theory

In 1877 Lewis Henry **Morgan,** a lawyer and businessman from upstate New York who developed a fascination with the Iroquois League in his youth, published the book *Ancient Society* (1985[1877]), in which he laid out his theory that **cultural evolution** proceeded, in a linear fashion, through three successive stages. The earliest humans, he asserted, began in a state of **Savagery,** progressed through **Barbarism** and thence to **Civilization.** This scheme did not originate with Morgan. We can see its stirrings in classical times, in a fuller treatment by the eighteenth-century philosopher Montesquieu. In fact, only a few years before the appearance of Morgan's book, British scholar Edward Burnett Tylor applied the thinking to the budding field of modern anthropology (Tylor 1871). Morgan, however, incorporated the idea into what would become a well-known depiction of human advancement.

According to Morgan, both Savagery and Barbarism were further subdivided into Lower, Middle, and Upper phases (once again reflecting the archaeological principle, "the deeper the older"), and societies moved from one phase to the next upon devising a key item of technology. Lower Savages "graduated" into Middle Savagery once they had mastered fire; Middle Savages became Upper Savages with the adoption of the bow and arrow; the threshold between Savagery and Barbarism was crossed with the invention of pottery, and so on. The crowning achievement of Civilization was attained through the development of writing. Morgan believed that all **societies,** left to their own devices, would move through these stages in much the same way, although clearly they did not do so

257

"POTTERY, EXCELLENT! YOU'RE NOW A BARBARIAN!"

at the same pace. Human cultural difference could be explained by the fact that some societies had raced through the stages while others lagged behind. By identifying what stage a particular society had reached, students of humanity could therefore understand a good deal more about that society.

Both Morgan and Tylor espoused a view that was considerably more benign than those that had preceded it. Some European scholars of the nineteenth century believed the world's "primitive" peoples were actually the degraded remnants of great civilizations that had run afoul of God and His precepts. Other scholars did not interpret the situation in spiritual terms, but held that "primitive" peoples had "savage minds" that were of a wholly different order than the minds of Europeans. Savages, according to this body of opinion, were unimprovable, incapable of adopting a more sophisticated lifestyle. Morgan and Tylor rejected this contention, and in fact, Morgan's scheme was predicated on the idea that not only *could* primitives improve, they were *driven* to improve by the mere fact of their humanity. This was at the heart of that daunting enterprise that was to become known as anthropology—the notion that whether we are "savage" or "civilized," we are all human, and we can achieve an understanding of each other through humanistic means.

Since our present-day moral sensibilities have by and large continued in this vein, we might see Morgan and Tylor as exceptionally enlightened for their time. But there was a seamy underbelly to Morgan's stage theory, one that the great American anthropologist Franz **Boas** (mentioned in chapter 1) was compelled to point out. If anthropology were simply a matter of determining which rung of the ladder of progress a particular society had reached, then we would learn nothing of other societies outside of the ways they fell short of the benchmark of civilization. In other words, we allegedly "civilized" peoples were using our own standards to judge others, a failing known as **ethnocentrism.** Ethnocentrism in-terferes with precisely the sort of learning to which anthropologists claim to as-pire. We can hardly appreciate the fullness of other lifeways if we see them only as arrested stages of our own history.

Though Morgan's book purported to explain ancient society, it was more in-famously applied to assess the status of contemporary peoples. Even so, archae-ology has also been rife with stage theories. For example, the Stone Age culture periods Paleolithic-Mesolithic-Neolithic have been used to represent a society's transition from hunting to agriculture; beyond the Stone Age, following the scheme of the nineteenth-century Danish museologist Christian Jürgensen Thomsen, came the Bronze Age and the Iron Age. It is not that iron smelting can-not follow on the manufacture of bronze; clearly that did in fact happen, and in more than one part of the globe. What is problematic is the different values placed on these developments, and not merely in terms of smelting technol-ogy—Iron Age peoples are presented as "more advanced" overall and poised to make further "advancements." Societies that did not "progress" in these ways were "backward," somehow "stuck in time" (see Fabian 1983). Again, such pro-nouncements are ethnocentric, but they are not simply innocent expressions of prejudice. They became intertwined with colonial and postcolonial power and formed the basis for "development" programs that, more often than not, stripped "backward" peoples of their beliefs, land, and livelihoods. Archaeolo-gists who continue to espouse stage theories, even if only in the sense of repeat-ing labels that have become entrenched in the discipline, play into the hands of governments and corporations today that can use the image of a degraded past (still haunting those who appear mired in it) to justify the power structure of the present day (Pyburn 2009).

There is more to be said about ethnocentrism, but I will reserve it for chapter 10. In the meantime, we should note that Morgan's scheme was not only ideolog-ically unsavory but scientifically unsound. The observant reader may have no-ticed that the "evolution" in Morgan's version of "cultural evolution" harked back not to Darwin but to Lamarck. Just as Lamarck's model of evolution featured an organism deliberately pursuing a higher form, so, too, would Morgan's Savage so-ciety march inexorably, if sometimes slowly, toward Barbarism and thence to Civ-ilization. There was no need to examine the circumstances around such dramatic leaps forward because the circumstances were immaterial; humans would com-plete this "necessary sequence of progress" (Morgan 1985[1877]:3) simply be-cause it was their nature to do so. Acceptance of this "fact," therefore, precludes a good deal of scientific investigation.

For Morgan, context was so trivial it did not matter that human societies had contact with each other. Morgan deplored colonialism as an unwarranted interference in the natural development of another society (1985[1877]:16). While, once again, we may consider his intentions honorable, the fact is that human beings are and have been mutually involved, in situations of colonization as well as many others. Human societies are not "silos" wherein change takes place irrespective of what is happening in other societies. Very simply put, it is impossible to determine whether each society has within itself the capacity to develop the bow and arrow when the chief reason one society has the bow and arrow is because the society on the other side of the river has it.

In this book, I have encouraged you to think in terms of context. Biological evolution results from the interaction of organisms with their environment. The shift to agriculture involves the intensification of food-producing strategies under a complex of pressing conditions. Thinking contextually demands that we subject such "just-so" stories like that told by Morgan to critical scrutiny. In particular, this chapter explores the portion of the story that addresses humankind's alleged crowning achievement—the rise of civilization.

State Society

Morgan was hardly the only man of his day, or for that matter prior, to write a "just-so" story about the rise of civilization. In fact, such stories remain common today. On this subject, we are bedeviled by many of the same assumptions traditionally made about the rise of agriculture—it was inevitable, it was intrinsically an improvement over what preceded it, and it somehow matters who was "first" insofar as these innovators must have been "more advanced" than other societies. I hope I have inspired you at the very least to question these assumptions regarding agriculture; now it is time to continue the interrogation while we look into the onset of civilization.

What I shall do first, however, is to lay aside the term "civilization." In and of itself it perpetuates the assumptions above. The word "civilized" is often used as a synonym for "genteel," that is, the pinnacle of refined behavior, and people who are not "civilized" bear the burden of abundant negative adjectives—primitive, crude, ignorant, brutal. A more neutral term for "civilization" is **state,** and this is the term I will use from now on.

Although the world today is divided into states (e.g., China, India, the United States of America), they are a relatively recent human invention, appearing in the archaeological record only about 6 kya, according to our current best guess. State society is a complex political form shaped by three organizing principles, acting in concert: centralization, specialization, and social stratification. **Centralization,** the linchpin of the trio, refers to the treatment of **power,** which is differentially distributed throughout society. Power is arranged concentrically, with one person or a small group of rulers having authority over a larger group of lesser rulers, who hold sway over still larger groups of still lesser rulers, and so on. Rulers occupying positions toward the outer fringes of power may be granted some leeway to handle local affairs as they see fit, but with respect to key issues, lesser rulers must all, in one way or another, answer to the center or risk the wrath of the state.

Specialization describes the deconstruction of activities requiring diverse skills to complete, and their reconstitution along occupational lines. To be sure, a foraging society is specialized insofar as men and women generally have separate tasks, but any one man can likely hunt, construct nets, and manufacture spears and arrows; any one woman knows where the best fruit and nut gathering sites are located and can make the carrying implements needed to transport food to camp; both sexes may have some personal command over healing powers upon which they call when the need arises. In a state society some or all of these activities might be allocated to people who develop expertise in only one of them, performing that one to the exclusion of others. In this way, while a foraging household, involving both an adult man and an adult woman, is reasonably self-sufficient, survival in a state society (which usually entails something well beyond mere subsistence) likely implicates many more people acting together to accomplish the stuff of day-to-day living.

Finally, as mentioned in the previous chapter, positions established by centralization and specialization are further organized into systems of **social stratification,** with people occupying positions in the uppermost layer having greater privileges than those immediately below, who have greater privileges than those immediately below, and so on down to the base of the system.

It is not as though these organizing principles are wholly absent in nonstate settings; they may be found singly, in pairs, or even altogether, but they do not rework society in a radical sense. Even in state societies, there are often areas of life and livelihood that are left strategically untouched—it was not until industrial times, for example, that the essential activity known as food production was pushed through the grid of centralization/specialization/social stratification, though an account of that development is a subject for another book. In this book, we need to understand how and why the grid was assembled. To approach this task, the contrast between states and nonstates will prove instructive. Once again, we will call on the corpus of ethnographic data compiled by cultural anthropologists to assemble a set of ideas that may help us better understand the past.

Kin-Based Political Organization

As noted above, the state is a political form, but what does that mean? In cultural anthropology, the term "political" is expanded to its broadest possible meaning, subsuming all aspects of a society's handling of power. All human societies must grapple with the issue of power—who has it? how long does he have it? does she hold it as an individual or as a member of a group? is its use approved by society? and so on. We have already seen that state societies organize power concentrically, but how else might it be organized?

Combing through the ethnographic record (and as in the previous chapter, I will present ethnographic information in the present tense even if the society has greatly changed since the information was gathered), we can draw out three distinct patterns of political organization among nonstate societies. Before we explore these patterns, however, we must stop defining such societies negatively; that is, in terms of what they are not. Indeed they are *non*states, but what they *are* is **kin-based.**

Human beings put together systems of kinship from ideas about mating and ideas about descent. Note the word "ideas"—as is true of anything else human, cultural thought complicates what strikes us today as strictly biological. You already know, from chapter 8, that it is possible to see kinship as proceeding equally through both mother and father (i.e., bilaterally) or through one parental line or the other (i.e., unilineally), and these are only two ways of conceptualizing kin-relatedness; there are many more that we will not explore here. What we can say is that however kinship is defined, in kin-based societies it is, as Lee has asserted, the "central organizing principle" (1984:57). Such vital functions as allocating resources, allocating power, rearing children, and caring for the infirm, which in state societies are often farmed out to specialized institutions, are in kin-based societies managed entirely through kinship. Kinship of this sort is serious stuff; it is a system of rights and obligations, not that "warm and fuzzy" feeling that may overcome you in the company of your parents and/or children. Members of kin-based societies may feel warmly toward each other, but more importantly, common kinship gives them a sense of entitlement within their societies (Rosenberg 1990). Individuals may not be the same in terms of attributes or abilities, but they are all Ju/'hoansi, or Inuit, or Washo, or what have you, and unless they have committed truly foul acts they cannot be disenfranchised from the group.

Entitlement in and of itself is a source of power, but that does not mean that everyone, in all kin-based societies, is empowered in the same way, or even at the same level. An exposition of the three patterns of political organization, mentioned above, will show that even though kin-based societies can be distinguished from state societies with respect to the treatment of power, they can also be distinguished from each other.

NONCOMPETITIVE EGALITARIANISM

Following the Endicotts (2008), who themselves draw upon such precursors as James Woodburn (1982), we can call the first pattern **noncompetitive egalitarianism.** This pattern is especially common among mobile foragers. In such societies, there is in fact an ethos of equality, with each person claiming a rightful measure of power. Richard Lee, while conducting a search for a headman, or leader, among the Ju/'hoansi, was finally advised by a Ju/'hoan friend to stop looking, since, as the friend explained succinctly, "Each one of us is headman over himself" (1984:89).

But that is not the whole story; Ju/'hoansi, like other noncompetitive egalitarians, actively demolish the undue power claims of others. Christopher Boehm (1999) refers to this process as **"reverse hierarchy"**; however, the end result is not an inverted pyramid of power, but a plane. Where we, in our own society, might expend time and effort enhancing our power over others, noncompetitive egalitarians apply the same resources to maintaining equality. In the Ju/'hoan case, this involves ruthless disparagement of the would-be powermonger's accomplishments; for example, a hunter who has taken down a huge beast that will feed the camp for days will have his kill ridiculed and his skill maligned if he merely hints that he deserves more respect, because of this one feat, than his fellows. Lee found, to his chagrin, that even the visiting anthropologist was not spared such punishment. "We cool his heart and make him gentle," said a Ju/'hoan man, explaining the practice (Lee 1969:4).

COMPETITIVE EGALITARIANISM

Given the fiercely enforced equality of noncompetitive egalitarian societies, it might be surprising to learn that the second kin-based political pattern I will discuss is also identified as egalitarian, or, specifically, **competitive egalitarianism.** Competitive egalitarianism is typical of horticultural **tribes** whose gardening and husbandry reliably produce a surplus of storable material that can be thought of as **wealth** (horticulturalists whose productivity is lower tend to adhere to a noncompetitive egalitarian pattern). In stark contrast to noncompetitive egalitarianism, individuals in competitive egalitarian societies can and in fact are encouraged to attain power over others. These societies are still considered to be egalitarian, however, because they are "equal opportunity"; any adult (generally male) who chooses to enter the fray can compete for power. An aspiring leader must have wealth, but he must *spend* that wealth in a way that benefits the group as well as himself. Wealth is only a means to an end; it is not an end in itself. Wealth joined to generosity is a recipe for power; hoarding wealth not only renders hoarders powerless but also subjects them to scorn, accusations of sorcery, and even, in some circumstances, execution.

The archetype of the wealthy, generous leader is the **big man,** a political figure found in many New Guinean societies (in some of these societies there are also "big women," but generally there are constraints on women's pursuit of power in such societies; this is an important subject but one that will not be covered here). Big men compete viciously in the arena of generosity, and each puts together an entourage of young men whose marriages he has financed. For men to be married is a societal good, as is compensatory payment dispersed among the bride's relatives, and a big man is given full credit, as well as great prestige, for his support of such activities. He is not begrudged his power so long as he uses it wisely. This, however, is tricky, especially on a continuous basis, because his fellow tribesmen are always watchful regarding any inkling of selfishness on his part. They, as worthy caretakers of their households in their own right, have enough power among them to limit the individual power a big man might otherwise gain. His ambition is held in check by rightful demands on his wealth, made on behalf of the entire society.

In our society, as well, wealthy individuals may share their wealth, but our attitude toward this act is different. If a billionaire bankrolls a foundation, we ooh and aah at his magnanimity. He certainly *can* do this, but he is not *expected* to do so, and his power as a wealthy man is not threatened if he does not. In a New Guinean tribe, admiration for such behavior would be tempered by a strong sense on the part of tribesmen that a big man is only doing what he must. They would not ooh and aah; their attitude might be better expressed in the surly observation, "It's about time."

This is not the only way a competitive egalitarian society differs from a state society. Leadership among competitive egalitarians is decentralized. New Guinean big men do not act together to form a system of rule. Further, there may be five big men in one village, but if one dies or ceases giving, the village does not feel compelled to replace him. At any one time, there are as many or as few big men as have the resources and desire to compete. The village has no real need of these leaders, insofar as villagers can generally handle their own day-to-day affairs. But if big men can prove their value to society through amassing and redistributing wealth, they are welcome to do so.

CHIEFDOM

Citizens of a state will find the third kin-based political form, a **chiefdom,** far more familiar. Descent groups within chiefdoms are often **ranked,** and individuals are born into higher or lower statuses according to this system of rank. Power is centralized in the person of the **chief,** whose right to rule is acknowledged and approved by his subjects. The position of chief is fixed, and when a chief dies his position must be filled. One service a chief may perform for his society is coordinating specialized productive activities so that a steady food supply is assured. And not only does the chief lead his people, but he and his nearest kin constitute an **elite** that enjoys the twin privileges of freedom from the drudgery of subsistence along with the prerogative to claim a percentage of the subsistence yield produced by others. This **tribute** is generally collected on behalf of the chief himself, who then redistributes it to his elite fellows (and sometimes, strategically, beyond). The elite may still be recognized as

Hawaiian chiefs, 1890.

kin-related to the lower-ranking descent groups, but that its members are exempt from such necessary pursuits as subsistence chores indicates that in a chiefdom, the unifying metaphor of common kinship is being stretched to its limits.

So chiefdoms feature centralization, specialization, and at the least a two-tiered system of social stratification—are they, for all intents and purposes, equivalent to states? There are certainly some anthropologists who have made that argument. But there are others who maintain that chiefdoms remain kin-based societies (e.g., Sahlins 1963), and chiefdoms that become states have crossed a qualitative line. In support of the latter position, we can explore the concept of *mana* in Polynesian society.

With the expansion of peoples from mainland Asia into the Pacific, chiefdoms were founded on many of the islands/island groups of Polynesia—e.g., Fiji, Samoa, Tonga, Hawai'i. The migrants brought with them the idea that all living (and some nonliving) things were united through mana, an inner force that humans might direct toward their own ends. Mana was at once a means through which a chief could claim great power, and a check on that power. Chiefs had more mana than anyone else, which was why they not only *could* rule, they *must* rule—it was the role in society they were born to fulfill. But all Polynesians had mana to some extent, and this belief could reinforce or even replace a sense of common kinship as an emblem of entitlement. In extreme circumstances—a destructive storm, drought or flooding that ruined crops—it was understood that the storehouses of tribute a chief had collected were meant to serve all his people, and at this point he had to behave responsibly with his wealth or suffer the dire consequences of being deposed or killed. In other words, ordinarily a chief could do as he pleased and his subjects would approve and might even revel in his larger-than-life conduct. But in times of crisis, it became obvious that a chief only ruled at the kindly behest of his people, who could, if necessary, apply their combined power toward the removal of his.

So whether chiefdoms are really states may once again be more of an argument over the way we classify things, and not over the things themselves. For our purposes, we will leave the argument there, to address the question at its heart: how did the autonomous, empowered individuals of kin-based society become the dependent, loyal subjects of a state?

SUMMARY OF KIN-BASED POLITICAL FORMS
• Noncompetitive egalitarian society
• Competitive egalitarian society
• Chiefdom

From Kin-Based to State Society

For all that I have been condemning stage theory, I acknowledge that the three kin-based political forms described above certainly *can* form, and in many instances evidently did form, a progression—noncompetitive egalitarian society to competitive egalitarian society to chiefdom. Regarding the first transition, we can hark back to the previous chapter as to why it might come about: political change was likely driven by economic change—a shift from foraging to some form of cultivation—which in turn could have been driven by the triple-whammy of population pressure, environmental degradation, and competition.

The same unholy trio, continuing unabated, might have had a hand in the second transition as well. That chiefdoms developed in Polynesia may not simply have been a matter of the notion of mana having accompanied the migrants from the mainland. Island ecologies are delicate in the first place, and if human beings arrive in droves, transforming natural habitat into garden and farm, there will likely be a buildup of population pressure that cannot easily be released into neighboring territories, as might happen on a continent. At that point, as Patrick Kirch has observed, "sustainability comes at a price" (1997:38). Kirch describes the situation on the island of Tikopia, where, through abortion and infanticide, along with the promotion of heroic but likely suicidal voyages for young men, the price of a stable population was exacted in babies and potent males. In contrast, on the island of Mangaia, population numbers were suppressed across the board by the terroristic activities of strongmen who would stop at nothing to achieve dominance. These are, however, the endpoints of a continuum. On many Pacific islands there was an attempt at middle ground; for example, society might cede sufficient authority to a chief to manage people and resources judiciously but would retain enough overall power to remove a chief should he abuse his position. We can appreciate that this was a difficult balance to maintain, especially as populations continued to grow and/or the environment continued to deteriorate.

Island societies, in short, are constantly contending with natural limits. Since islanders cannot readily take new territory, their societies "expand" inwardly, becoming increasingly more elaborate in terms of political and social order. But it is not only island societies that encounter such limits. Robert Carneiro (1970) once proposed that states develop from nonstates precisely due to similar situations of **circumscription.** Within a region, population pressure puts a strain on resources, possibly already depleted through years of human mismanagement (Dickson 1987). People begin to fight over resources, and eventually full-scale warfare breaks out. War chiefs consolidate forces and earn victories; vanquished populations answer to their conquerors. Eventually the entire region is brought under the control of the most powerful chief—or, at this point, king.

The circumscription hypothesis calls upon those factors we already see as having inspired, at least in some instances, the adoption of agriculture and extends their influence to the development of states. This is a viable line of thinking; none of us knows to what degree everyday human action is shaped by long-term conditions over which, ultimately, we have little control. As previously suggested, it is no accident that forager "big meetings" break up over quarrels that occur just as the resources that brought people together are giving out. Even so, the Tikopia/Mangaia contrast just recounted indicates that environment *constrains* human adaptation, but does not *determine* it. The people of these islands faced, broadly, the same problem but "solved" it in different, and by our standards equally drastic, ways. State formation was yet another way to deal with the problem of population growth. But the state also came "at a price"—the transfer of power from society at large to a ruling elite, one whose ambition was no longer effectively contained by kinship or mana or any genuine appeal to societal unity. It was not, however, the elite that paid the price.

Chiefdoms and states both feature an elite, but the difference between the two political forms is that the balance of power has definitively shifted—**elitism** displaces kinship as the "central organizing principle." In a chiefdom, society maintains a check, however tenuous, on elite actions, but in a state, the elite is free to pursue its own interests. In fact, it can apply some portion of its power toward installing those interests as the common good. This campaign becomes more credible if the **ideological** ground is prepared through a redefinition of the concept of *person*.

In a chiefdom, there is already a separation between elite and nonelite insofar as the elite, spared subsistence duties, lives qualitatively differently from the lower strata. Further, chiefly authority is often supported through spiritual means, with the chief as a sort of conduit between ordinary people and the divine. The earliest state societies greatly elaborated on such ideas. The line between elite and nonelite became so well-marked that kinship could no longer reach across it. Kinship remained important, but only *within* social strata, which were reinforced and reproduced through a prohibition on cross-strata marriage. The ruler in a state society was not just a conduit for the divine; he perhaps *was* divine. He was of a different order of personhood, a superior order, one that may have gone beyond simply being human.

This political transformation was clearly impressed upon the archaeological record, but with the rise of states there were a number of other developments that caught the discerning eye. For some archaeologists, political change seemed less like a leading edge than merely a response to ecological and economic change. The matter of which came first may always be debatable, but in the ensuing section, I will demonstrate the advantages of keeping the political uppermost in our mind when considering the origin of the state.

State Formation—A Model

States leave behind a good deal of material evidence of their existence, but, as always, we must be careful not to project into the past modern-day notions on what makes a state. No one datum is absolutely diagnostic, but taken altogether, the outline of a state may become visible.

PARTIAL MODELS

In his evolutionary scheme, Morgan included the standard view that a writing system made a state. **Writing** is the transfer of spoken language to a visual representation, either of the sounds we use or the ideas we express. It is true that while writing systems are unique to state societies, not all state societies develop them. For example, the Inca empire did not have writing, although knotted strings, called **quipu,** served as a means of record keeping. So writing indicates the presence of a state, but the absence of writing does not preclude its presence. I might add here that the Inca state was also "missing" other elements we associate with a state, such as watercraft and the wheel. Neither was practical within the realm of the Inca, but more to the current point, neither was essential to state formation.

Long-distance trade has been, for some, a dead giveaway of a state—surely centralized leadership was required to ensure goods moved smoothly and securely over vast distances. Yet, humans engaged in long-distance trade for millennia prior to the rise of the earliest states. The building of monuments is also often associated with state societies, in that such structures would seem to have required a large labor force drawn together under a centralized command structure. But then we must remember the earthen mounds that were built by kin-based peoples throughout the eastern United States; further, the massive Monks Mound at Cahokia, as well as the stone circles at Stonehenge and Avebury in England, were the products of chiefdoms, at least according to the stock opinion at present.

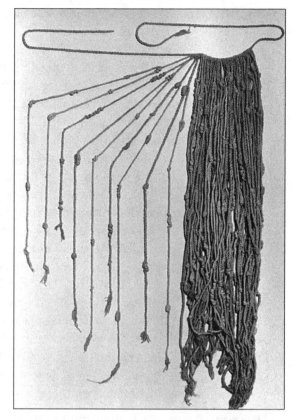

Quipu.

A famous hypothesis regarding the origin of the state, proposed by Karl Wittfogel (1957), identified the construction of irrigation systems as the project that must have instigated the development of political centralization, but ancient Hohokam villages in the American Southwest managed an irrigation system very well without state control (Hunt et al. 2005); such a system has also existed for centuries on the island of Bali, where local groups have struggled to *exempt* irrigation from state interference (Lansing 1987). Even population size and density may not be definitive regarding the emergence of a state. According to archaeologist Kent Flannery (1972), the historically known Chimbu of New Guinea maintained an incredibly dense population through a complex set of rituals that curbed potentially disruptive behavior to the extent that it did not need to *be* curbed by centralized leadership.

So states *probably*, if not without exception, involve large populations concentrated in a relatively small territory, writing or some other means of record keeping, long-distance trade, monument-building, and inventive technologies—

but what brought states together in the first place? Were human beings simply destined, because of their extraordinary intellectual powers, to form state societies? Were they nudged in this direction by environmental conditions that demanded a greater degree of centralization in order to manage them? As you already know, I tend to dismiss the first question, while relegating the second to a kind of background hum whose motivational power may in fact be chronic but not obvious in everyday human affairs. I suggest that if we examine the immediate political motivations of people in the different social strata that emerge in chiefdoms and continue in states, we can discern a context that comfortably accommodates all of the phenomena mentioned above, and then some.

Credit for this line of thought is overdue. Although the model I am about to introduce is my own, it is inspired by such hypotheses as the "action theory" of Joyce Marcus and Kent Flannery (1996) that focuses on the exercise of elite power as a driving force in societal change. Only a few years earlier, Elizabeth Brumfiel had observed that archaeologists were increasingly applying such politically freighted concepts as gender, class, and faction to their research (1992); one example is the work of Christine Hastorf and Sissel Johannessen, who proposed that the shift in the Andes from the consumption of maize to the manufacture of corn beer, used even today by low-status individuals to buy favor from potential benefactors, also marked the transition from kin-based to state society (1993). So I am not quite out on a limb here, but students should be aware that there are certainly other valid opinions on these matters.

POLITICS FIRST—THE BIG PICTURE?

To put together a politics-first model of state formation (refer to the Model of State Formation, on the following page, throughout this section), let's elaborate on the sort of regional set-up I mentioned at the end of chapter 8. I indicated, following Barth, that societies practicing different subsistence strategies can coexist reasonably peaceably in one region while engaging in mutually beneficial trade. "Reasonably peaceably" does not rule out the occasional skirmish, and "societies" does not mean there is no social traffic between groups—people from different societies may intermarry and/or may move back and forth between cultures. Even so, no society is intent on absorbing another, and the fact that they all specialize (as societies, not as individuals) in a particular form of production their neighbors need actually encourages the maintenance of separateness. If foragers become cultivators they may neither produce the wild meat and skins desired by surrounding societies, nor would they be willing to trade for the dairy products of pastoralists or the grain of agriculturalists. There is a complementarity within the regional system that is valuable enough to foster its preservation.

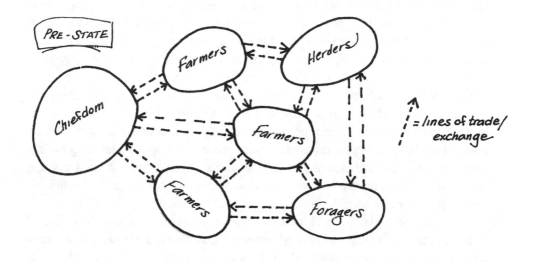

PRE-STATE

Chiefdom · Farmers · Herders · Farmers · Farmers · Foragers

= lines of trade/exchange

Model of State Formation

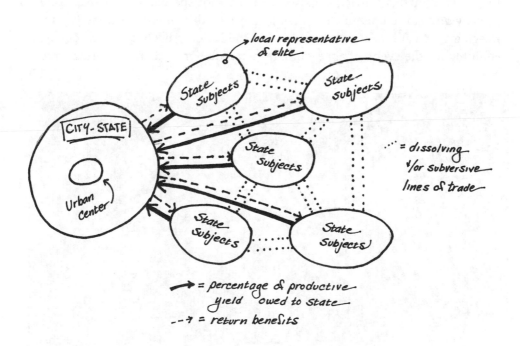

local representative of elite

CITY-STATE

Urban Center

State Subjects

= dissolving ⁺/or subversive lines of trade

= percentage of productive yield owed to state

--→ = return benefits

On occasion there are events that upset this balance—for example, pastoralists may deplete forage in their own lands and begin to range onto the lands held by agriculturalists—but the regional system can likely mitigate small shocks of this sort. Eventually, however, a threat to the system may gather enough momentum to overload any capacity for adjustment. In a crisis situation—a drought, a flood, a plague—the lower strata of a chiefdom may cede that much more power to the chief to handle the crisis. Once it is resolved, the chief may seize on any means to maintain his power. If he was at all effective during the crisis, it was likely because he took control of natural forces in a mundane and/or spiritual sense. That is, an identification with nature proved strategic in elevating his status to something beyond mere personhood, and symbols that continued to stress this relationship reminded his people—and himself—that he could tap into reserves of power inaccessible to ordinary men and women.

The central lands of the chiefdom—now an evolving city-state—are cleared of subsistence activity; they are used instead to build replicas of natural phenomena alleged to have fallen under the ruler's sway. A common feature is the man-made mountain. It is a deeply held conviction among many diverse peoples that gods reside on mountaintops or at the very least can be reached more easily at that level. Why this conviction exists is a matter for speculation—perhaps gods actually *do* reside on mountaintops, or perhaps the thin mountain air helps us to imagine spiritual forces more readily—but the belief is likely quite ancient, accounting for the eventual appearance of **pyramids** (or similarly towering struc-

Maya pyramid at Chichén Itzá.

tures) in societies around the world. Other features often found in the new urban center are lush gardens and zoos, indicating that the ruler controls both flora and fauna. Fountains and canals demonstrate the ruler's command over the precious resource of water, and it is likely that command *does* extend, both practically and ideologically, over actual irrigation systems (Wittfogel was not wrong about the connection between irrigation and centralized power, just in his assumption that irrigation *mandates* centralized power). The miniature "world" at the heart of the city may be uninhabited by any save the ruler himself, though elite housing might be arrayed around the perimeter. The urban center is a showcase of elite power; merely to live there would be like establishing a household inside a church.

The elite may live in or near the urban center, but the rest of the city is populated by what I call the **elite retinue,** consisting of those occupational specialists whose activities support the elite in some way. Of course security is important. The elite must have guards, police to enforce **social control** within the state, and a military to defend the state from outsiders, and/or to seize their lands before they become powerful enough to mount a challenge. The military has to be equipped with weaponry; thus people skilled at arms manufacture are incorporated into the elite retinue. But still more designers/craftspeople are needed: architects; engineers; makers of jewelry, fine cloth, and other sumptuary items that serve as emblems of elite power. If the ruler is not himself a religious specialist, he may require the services of priests. Merchants channel trade in and out of the city, swelling city coffers even as they keep enough of the profit to make the elite uneasy on occasion. Then, of course, there are servants, cooks, groundskeepers, and all of those workers who spare the elite the onerous burden of caring for itself. Since members of the elite retinue generally pursue their occupations on a full-time basis, they cannot pursue subsistence on their own but must be provided for out of elite stores. For this reason, the interests of the elite retinue are clearly aligned with those of the elite.

Because of the growing number of people who need to be fed, the elite must tap new sources of subsistence production. The problem is compounded by the fact that subsistence activities have likely been crowded out of the city. This is of little consequence when neighboring societies might dedicate a percentage of their own subsistence production to supplement the urban food supply. But how to enlist their cooperation? Overtures may involve positive incentives—access to luxury goods and new technologies, protection from enemies—but the potential for the city to use its military might to force compliance is equally if not more persuasive. Whatever arrangement is made, once outlying societies agree to transfer some of their productive yield to the city, this tribute must be monitored by specialists who record the transaction and administer punishment if the correct amount is not delivered. Writing appears to have grown out of these record-keeping systems (Schmandt-Besserat 1992). It should surprise no one in the present day that the earliest written documents of which we know are, for all intents and purposes, tax returns.

As time passes it becomes more likely that the quota of goods moving into the city will be raised, while the quota of return goods and services is diminished. The state often acts, as well, to criminalize the movement of goods between outlying societies so that any production beyond that needed for subsistence is shunted into the city. What had been a thriving network of regional trade is reorganized into productive cells that channel their surplus into the city. Formerly standalone societies swap autonomy for the security a state pledges to provide.

Perhaps needless to say, the city-state eventually leaves a well-defined archaeological footprint. The urban center, with its ring of elite housing, stands out amidst the lesser housing and workshops of the elite retinue. The movement of goods between city and outlying communities can be tracked. Over time there accrues a tremendous buildup of material: human remains, craft objects, structures, waste, and environmental damage.

As life in the zone immediately surrounding the city, overexploited in terms of both its human and natural resources, begins to deteriorate, the state ranges farther to bring new societies into its ambit. State societies, in fact, generally value growth of all kinds. Adding new subsistence producers undercuts any leverage the old producers may have developed, and conquering distant lands yields a wealth of battle captives, disenfranchised from their original kin groups, who can be applied to a number of purposes (e.g., slavery, military service, concubinage) that either enhance the power of the ruler's kin group and/or interrupt the solidarity of rival kin groups. Internal increase is also of value to the state. State societies may have originated, at least in part, as a means to accommodate a growing population, but once established, the state develops its own reasons to promote a high birthrate. The more people, the more workers, the more production; in accord with the principle of supply and demand, life may even become "cheap" enough to be expended on increasingly elaborate and dangerous projects.

To this point I have likely conveyed the impression that states were simply vehicles to aggrandize the elite at the great expense of others. There are, however, benefits associated with states. Of course some of these accrue disproportionately to the elite—archaeologists can tell you that privilege is manifest in its skeletal remains, and not merely because elite corpses are interred with a lavish helping of grave goods. By and large, the elite enjoys better overall health than the rest of the population (see, e.g., Danforth 1999), though ironically, this may not apply to those at the very apex of the social structure, who may compromise their life chances through such ill-advised practices as multigenerational inbreeding. Elite thinking can certainly be carried too far, but outside of a few exceptions, elite status consistently correlates with good health. The elite is thus a kind of reservoir of fit individuals who can best cope with threats to species survival, should they arise.

If that seems of minor value compared to the disadvantages of states, consider the competition that ensues between members of the elite retinue vying to maintain or enhance their privileged positions. Such specialists perfect their crafts and/or develop new ones, yielding what are now seen to be breakthroughs in engineering and in art and architecture. We might also reflect on the material and psychic rewards that can be gained from membership in a competently run state, though Americans, traditionally wary of government, may have little appreciation for the pride even low-status state subjects might legitimately take in their rulers and systems of rule. Monica Smith (2006) suggests that states can and have achieved a genuine consensus of interest between elite and commoners. Mark Lehner and Zahi Hawass believe that the pyramids of Egypt were built not by slaves but by fraternal organizations of laborers who were proud of, and well compensated for, their work for the pharaoh (see Tyldesley 2011, and interview text at Nova Beta, http://www.pbs.org/wgbh/nova/ancient/who-built-the-pyramids.html). Also, as recently observed by Marc Levine (2011), class relations within states have been complex and variable, often more a matter of negotiation between well-matched partners as opposed to one group imposing its will on another. Nominally subordinate populations may retain considerable autonomy regarding local governance, land rights, and, as previously mentioned, irrigation systems. Thus, we cannot assume that the state in all instances is relentlessly oppressive and/or that the masses have no power to act on their own behalf.

Having said all of that, it should be clear by this time that though there are benefits attached to states, at least for some, there are also benefits attached to living in kin-based societies, arguably for many more. It has generally been presumed that states, like agriculture, were an intrinsic good, and that the answer to the question, "Why did states form?" was, quite simply, "because they provided a better life for people." I have tried to sketch out a different answer to that question, and I shall continue to work with the answer by filling in detail from specific cases, but given that kin-based political forms, like foraging economic forms, are not as "savage" as originally thought, it could be that the question we really *should* be asking is: "Why were states *allowed* to form?"

Old World States—The Power of Rivers

It is time to take the model laid out in the previous section and apply it to what we know of the earliest states. Naturally, since it *is* a model, it will not fit every situation perfectly, but I believe it is sufficiently elastic to accommodate variation.

States developed in a number of places in the Old World, at various times. Of course one of these was "first," but again the status of "first" says nothing more than the fact that due to particular circumstances the elite was able to pull away from the rest of society earlier than elsewhere. Some of these states influenced state formation in nearby and possibly distant regions; other states seem to have arisen on their own. I will not be recounting a history of these states; that would require several other books that have frankly already been written—look them up! What I will do is draw on the archaeological record at well-known state sites to illustrate and elaborate upon the ideas offered above.

In the Old World, agricultural populations understandably tended to gather in river basins, to take advantage of the annual flooding that deposited rich soil in the floodplain. As essential as this process was, it was also capricious—some years the floods were weak, and in other years the floods were far too strong. Irrigation helped to "tame" floodwaters so that they could provide a reliable flow of water throughout the growing season. Unsurprisingly, the power of rivers became equated with the power of rulers, who might even be seen as responsible for the river's life-giving bounty. This was especially well-marked in the case of the Egyptian pharaoh and his association with the Nile, but other Old World river systems, and their central place in the systems of state rule that grew around them, emerge from ancient times: the Tigris and Euphrates, the Indus, the Huang He.

MESOPOTAMIA

So far as we know right now, the earliest states arose in the region we call **Mesopotamia,** whose root words refer to being in the middle of rivers—the Tigris and Euphrates. In the name of the first city-state, Uruk, we can discern the name of modern-day Iraq. Uruk emerged from a farming village around 6 kya, and like other city-states of the region, its landscape was dominated by a **ziggurat,** a huge man-made mountain that could be ascended, via stairway, to a ritual space at its "summit." Today we see Uruk as one of the **Sumerian city-states.** Although the city-states were eventually brought together under one ruler, for much of their existence they did not enjoy political unity, and in fact competed ferociously with one another, their numbers waxing and waning over time. Nonetheless, the Sumerian city-states left a legacy that remains in evidence today, every time you count the degrees of a circle or the minutes of an hour.

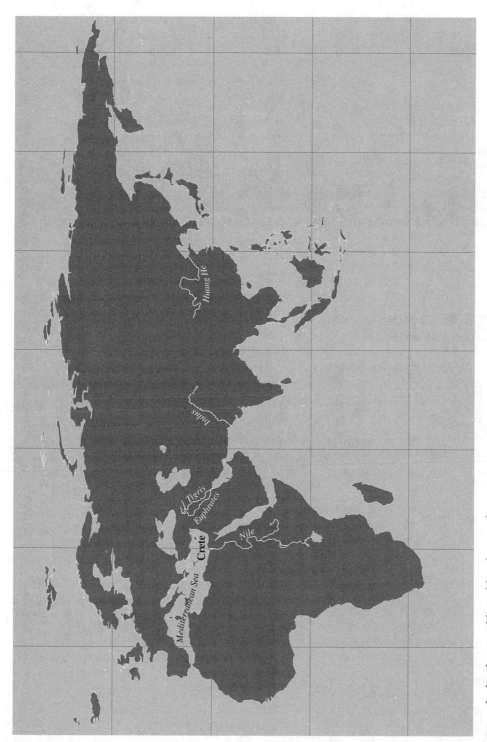

Water bodies key to Old World early state formation.

Ziggurat at Ur.

SIDEBAR

The Sumerian Legacy

It may not have been good for the Sumerians that their city-states were so frequently embattled, but it was good for us. The Sumerian elite perennially needed new means to maintain their position over the masses, and each Sumerian city-state perennially needed new means to defeat its rivals. These driving needs created a frenzy of competition, and developments were encouraged in all of those areas we associate today with "civilization": trade, warfare, engineering, architecture.

Sumerian inventors devised sailboats, wheeled carts, and the plow, an innovation in cultivation that remained standard for thousands of years thereafter. Sumerian builders learned that arches were not only easier to assemble but also stronger than apertures shorn up by post-and-lintel construction (think Stonehenge), since the weight of the keystone, at the top of the arch, is

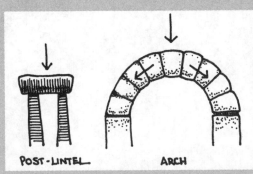

POST-LINTEL   ARCH

evenly distributed throughout the supporting stones. Domes were put together using the same principle.

The Sumerians had a counting system based on the number 60. This enabled them to count to 12 on one hand by ticking off the finger segments with the thumb, and to keep track of the number of 12s on the other hand. Although, of course, we do not use a Base-60 counting system today, the numbers 12 and 60 are key to understanding a good many measurements—the 24-hour day, the 360° circle, even a dozen eggs—and all of these can be traced back, through several intervening societies, to the Sumerians.

One key development in the region of Mesopotamia (though it may have developed independently elsewhere) was the discovery of **bronze** circa 5.5 kya. For millennia prior, human beings had been using copper to make tools, but copper has a drawback—it is soft and cannot hold an edge effectively. Creating an **alloy** of copper and another metal (i.e., bronze), solves this problem. A number of metals stiffen copper, but such options as arsenic and lead tend to wreak havoc on the health of metalsmiths. Eventually tin was found to be the most practical option, and a lively regional trade in tin began. Since the Tigris and Euphrates valleys have few mineral resources, the Sumerians, and subsequent states in the region, were especially motivated to expand trade routes. Bronze was all-purpose, used for statuary, drinking vessels, tools, and weaponry.

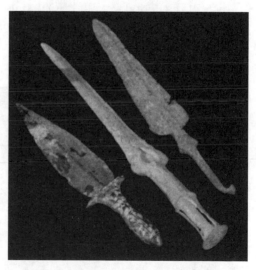

Bronze weaponry in the Sumerian style.

EGYPT

It is difficult to know exactly to what degree change in Mesopotamia had an impact on state formation in **Egypt.** Population began to cluster in the Nile Valley circa 6 kya, with pastoralist peoples relocating their herds from a hinterland that was becoming too dry to sustain them. People in the area soon took advantage of Southwest Asian cereal crops, though, as mentioned in the previous chapter, it is unclear whether these were trade items or whether migrants arrived with them.

City-states emerged from the regions flanking the Nile, and while some of these sites continued to stand out from the landscape, they were united in one polity by a pharaoh circa 5 kya (generally identified as Narmer, though this is in dispute). In essence, Egypt had come together as a **nation-state,** proving early on that a city-state is not the limit of what one ruler might control.

From Egypt we learn of another function of writing that serves elite interests. The Egyptian **hieroglyphic** script was used to document the greatness of the pharaoh. Writing, in addition to being inscribed on monuments, was a kind of monument in and of itself, in that it would preserve the (exalted) memory of the pharaoh for generations. It should be mentioned that the elite was not necessarily any more literate than anyone else in a state. Scribe was yet another specialized position commonly found within the elite retinue.

Egypt can teach us one more lesson about states. Today we think of ancient Egypt as an extraordinarily steady, even stagnant state, mired in tradition. This is not quite true. Those things we see as quintessentially Egyptian—pyramids, mummification, a characteristic way of rendering the human form—are products of the period we call the Old Kingdom (circa 4,600 to 4,100 ya). To the extent they endured thereafter, they did so not because rule was stable but because it was tumultuous. Between 4 and 2 kya, Egypt suffered invasions, but its conquer-

Abu Simbel (Egypt).

ors quickly realized the advantage of being pharaoh. They would set up their own dynasties to rule Egypt much as it had been ruled. In these instances the elite stratum no longer had to deflect attention from their kinship with the rest of the population—the imported dynasties were literally not kin-related to the Egyptians. But preserving the trappings of prior dynasties provided a sense of continuity across the drastic shift in ruling powers. In many respects the new pharaoh would become more Egyptian than the Egyptians themselves.

CHINA

Precisely the same lesson can be learned from **China,** which was also frequently invaded. But the outsiders would be swiftly **Sinicized,** assuming not only the position but the traditions of the emperors they displaced. This was, of course, well after the initial establishment of the Chinese state, which was hard-won. The Huang He river system, from 5 kya onward, was packed with walled villages. We should be careful not to assume that such walls were erected for defensive purposes—it could be, for instance, that the famous walls of Jericho were initially built to protect against mud slides (Bar-Yosef 1986)—but in the Chinese case, defense indeed seemed a paramount concern. There were fierce rivalries between chiefdoms, and almost constant warfare. Chiefs themselves were embattled, facing both external and internal challenges, and were doubtless open to any device that might help set them above others.

One device was **scapulimancy,** along with other methods of **divining;** that is, predicting the future (Keightley 1985). Archaeological evidence indicates a near-obsession with divining in prestate China; it certainly helps that divining literally left its mark on bones and turtle shells. Scapulimancy involved driving a heated poker into the shoulder blade of an animal (e.g., a deer) so that it would crack; the cracks were subsequently "read" to discern their meaning. Skilled scapulimancers could crack the bone in just the right way to produce a desired result. A chief who received a favorable reading might go on to wage a successful military campaign against his enemies— the conviction that one's efforts have earned a divine stamp of approval should not be underestimated as a motivational force—and the scapulimancer would not only be handsomely remunerated but retained for his continued service. Spiritual advisers are thus key

Scapulimancy, China—after the bone was cracked, the prophecy was recorded in writing on the same material.

figures in the elite retinue, in both ancient and modern times (recall that Nancy Reagan had an astrologer, and Bill Clinton consulted with motivational speaker

Great Wall of China.

Tony Robbins). They face none of the risks they compel a ruler to take and yet enjoy all of his glory. And in the state that 2,000 years ago would unite what we now know as modern China, that glory was extreme—the sacred and secular power of the Chinese emperor was on a par with that of the Egyptian pharaoh.

INDUS VALLEY

This may not have been true of the elite in the **Indus Valley city-states,** e.g., Harappa and Mohenjo-Daro, that arose circa 4.5 kya. Both Harappa and Mohenjo-Daro were organized along pragmatic lines, their buildings and thoroughfares laid out according to a grid pattern. There were also working sewers that channeled waste far away from living quarters. While elite housing was sumptuous, very few monuments were built, and it could be that the elite was not that far elevated over commoners. Part of the problem (if you consider it thus) could have lain in the suggestion that kinship remained an important social "glue" not only between the higher and lower levels of society but also between the local people and the lands from which they had migrated; kin ties may have been cultivated to open and maintain lines of long-distance trade. By 3,700 ya, the two cities were abandoned, seemingly peaceably, and rural residents continued subsistence farming without the added burden of tribute. However, there was perhaps enough state machinery (in terms of infrastructure and political attitudes) still in place for Aryan-speaking pastoralists, moving in from the north, to set themselves up as a ruling elite circa 3.5 kya. The political-religious tension generated by this "invasion" (we have yet to determine how warlike it was) gave rise to Hinduism.

CRETE

There is one more Old World state whose experience we will troll for material to enhance our understanding of state formation—the **Minoan** state founded circa 4 kya by migrants from Anatolia (modern-day Turkey). Unlike the other Old World states so far discussed, the water body that dominated Minoan life both practically and ideologically was not a river but the Mediterranean Sea. Like the Indus Valley city-states, the Minoan state, centered on the island of Crete, became a hub of regional trade. As previously implied, an emphasis on trade was tricky for a state to manage—if the elite itself was in charge of trade, its daily exercise of mundane power might limit its spiritual authority, but if trade were the province of a mercantile segment of the elite retinue, merchants might become too powerful for the elite to control. Hence the Minoan state elite, like the Indus Valley state elite, appears to have had difficulty separating itself from the rest of the populace. Compounding this weakness were natural forces that threatened elite and commoner alike.

The Mediterranean basin is a geologically active region, with frequent earthquakes and volcanic eruptions. The Minoans believed these were caused by giant

Minoan palace at Knossos, Crete.

Minoan bull.

bulls coursing under the sea floor, and elaborate spectacles were held to demonstrate control over the beasts. But these efforts were ultimately to no avail, and when the Minoan outpost of Thera literally exploded in an eruption that shook the entire region and produced a destructive tsunami, the days of the Minoan state were numbered (Hadingham 2008). It actually persevered for about 200 years following the disaster, engaging in a desperate florescence, but eventually its trade routes, and its regional dominance, passed to the city-state of Mycenae on the Greek mainland. The Mycenaeans also adopted the spiritual equipment of the Minoans—it is not unusual for the history of prior states to become the myth of succeeding ones—and this sacred corpus was assumed, in turn, by the Greek city-states that were to prove such a great influence on subsequent European thought. This is why Poseidon, the Greek god of the sea, is often represented as a keeper of bulls.

BP, BC, AD, and Other Imperfect Ways of Recording Time

The astute student may have noticed that I avoid the usual ways of representing time. I tend to write about phenomena as having existed *x* number of years ago. Another way of expressing this is to use the abbreviation BP, or "before present." The sticking point of this method is that the present keeps moving into the future. In other words, when we say "before present," just what "present" do we mean? 1950? 2000? 2012? This isn't a problem when we are referring to something that is millions of years old but is increasingly troublesome as we approach the present day, when 50 years begins to matter with reference to such events as the eruption at Thera. I generally work with 2000 as "the present"—this is, of course, a good round number—but of course we are already more than a decade beyond that.

The alternative is to set a fixed point in time and gauge dates in reference to that point. And this is what we *have* traditionally done when we identify dates as BC ("before Christ") and AD (*Anno Domini;* that is, the "year of our Lord" onward). The touchy aspect of this method is in setting the fixed point. There are certainly millions of people in the world who believe that the birth of Jesus Christ is a perfectly appropriate moment on which to fasten all time, but of course there are the millions of non-Christians who may feel as though no one religious figure deserves this honor. Come on, you may say, there has to be a fixed point, and the birth of Christ is as good a point as any, especially when so many dates have already been gauged in this way. And you are right; there are others in the world, Christians and non-Christians alike, who see this matter as a done deal and not worth contesting. Some attempt has been made to draw attention away from Christ's birth through the abbreviation BCE ("before Christian [or Common] Era"), but this would not seem to be all that helpful. We also tacitly acknowledge the BC/AD system every time we mention a year in the Gregorian calendar; "2012" is actually "AD 2012"; that is, 2012 years after the birth of Christ.

(continued)

There are other niggling matters: was Jesus actually born when we believe He was? And do we account for the fact that as the linchpin between eras, His birthday must fall in the Year Zero, since 1 BC would mark the start of the prior year, and AD 1 would mark the start of the following year? These questions may be important from a theological standpoint, but they do not much affect us here, given their relatively minor impact on the measurement of time.

Since I began my account of (pre)history in the millions-of-years range, using "mya" dates, I have stayed with this system even as it has become more cumbersome with respect to more recent times. This choice was a matter of consistency, not of any feeling one way or the other regarding religion.

New World States— The Power of Boundary-Crossing

Whether the first human beings arrived in the New World 50 or 15 kya, they were already well in place by the time Old World states began to form. Despite numerous hypotheses that have been mooted over the years regarding outside influence—the Chinese, the Egyptians, the Greeks, and aliens from outer space have all been suggested as the bearers of statecraft to the New World—there is no cogent reason to believe that New World states resulted from anything other than independent invention. This conclusion is supported by the fact that New World states, which often had the typical features described earlier, were nonetheless significantly different from those in the Old World.

One difference is simply an extension of an aspect of the New World Neolithic—the near-absence of domesticated animals. There were no beasts of burden to pull plows or haul blocks of stone for the building of monuments. The llama can serve as a pack animal, but beyond a 50-pound load the animal tends to balk. The upshot is that the only reliable beasts of burden in the New World were humans themselves. Since in the New World there is no shortage of grand monuments, humans obviously fulfilled this capacity admirably.

The New World also differed in its use of metals. While New World peoples knew how to work metal (Easby 1965), they seldom used it for anything but ornaments. This in itself supported elitism—recall the elite needs visible emblems

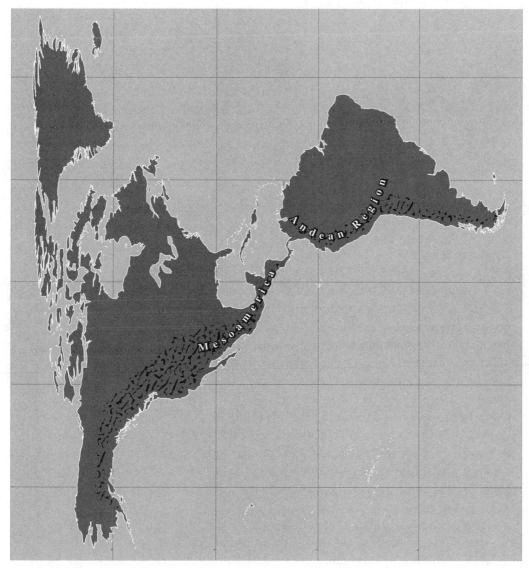

Zones of early state formation in the New World.

of its position over the populace—but the manufacture of metal weaponry, also supportive of elite designs, was not pursued. The material of choice for weaponry was **obsidian,** which was in many respects the "tin" of the New World. People went to extraordinary lengths to obtain it, and great city-states like Teotihuacán initially coalesced around its trade (Spence 1967).

Obsidian.

A good deal of what spurred on state formation in the Old World actually seemed to inhibit it in the New. As previously noted, herd animals like bison, deer, and caribou did not need to be domesticated to be a ready source of subsistence for kin-based peoples. Canoes cinched the kin-based societies of the California coast into one large trading network. The rivers of Oregon, Washington, and British Columbia, teeming with salmon, inspired the growth of delayed-return foraging societies, not agriculture, and in the southern United States, Cahokia—politically complex but perhaps not quite a state—developed at the confluence of the Mississippi and the Missouri.

In New World states, rivers were of course important, but they did not take on the same symbolic significance they had in Old World states. In the regions of the New World where states did form—Mesoamerica and the central Andes—evidently the most striking feature of the landscape to its first human settlers was the fact that stark highlands rose quickly out of jungle lowlands. Recall the hypothesis that people in these regions traveled between ecozones to gain subsistence, hence deferring a shift to agriculture. A mastery of different environments was not only key to survival but also became wound into New World conceptions of power. People who could cross the boundaries between realms—mundane and/or sacred—functioning effectively in all of them, were powerful people. This idea was applied first to shamans (as it is today), to chiefs, and, once states arose, to kings and emperors.

The archetypal symbol of boundary-crossing, prominent in both Mesoamerica and the Andes, was the jaguar, a large cat (genus *Panthera*, shared with lions, tigers, and leopards) whose range once extended from the American Southwest all the way into southern Latin America. While its preferred habitat is tropical forest, it can also live in deserts and highlands. It can climb trees, ford rivers (yes, it can swim), and occasionally get past a boundary humans would just as soon keep in place—it can kill and eat people. Rulers of New World states were often depicted as **were-jaguars,** or humans with jaguar features. To identify with the jaguar was to declare oneself equally at ease in all environments.

MESOAMERICA

In Mesoamerica, while city-states began to emerge circa 2.5 kya, they were presaged in the previous millennium by a society (or set of societies) we call the **Olmec.** Where the Olmec originated, how their culture developed, and whether they ever came together in states (as opposed to chiefdoms) remain unresolved questions. What we do know is that they established traditions and styles that were taken up by subsequent Mesoamerican societies—in this way they can be seen as a **source culture** for the region.

The jaguar was prominent in Olmec art and spiritual thinking, as was a concern for measuring time, which among the Maya became a near-obsession. The Olmec built pyramids as well as earthen platforms, and while some of these supported ceremonial

Olmec were-jaguar.

centers, others became the basis for residential communities. These platforms might be an expansion of an island in a swamp, as at La Venta in the Mexican Gulf region, or a wetland filled in from scratch, as was true at nearby San Lorenzo. In either case, the water displaced into the surrounding area was turned toward agricultural purposes; hence the food supply was not dependent on the capricious annual flooding of a river. The Aztecs borrowed and expanded on the technology needed to convert swampland into farmland and residential space; their accomplishments in this area of expertise greatly impressed the first Europeans to visit the region. Finally, the Olmec set another precedent that was to carry over into subsequent Mesoamerican societies—while warfare was certainly endemic in the region from early on, the sites of La Venta and San Lorenzo were apparently destroyed by their own people (Coe 1968). The Mesoamerican elite often had difficulties recognizing that fine line between driving a population to produce more and inciting rebellion against unreasonable demands.

In popular thought, the **Maya** are seen as an ancient people whose state suffered a tragic collapse. This idea erases the people, or more accurately, peoples, in the present day who call themselves Maya. Today's Maya are subdivided into a number of populations living in different countries, speaking different languages, and practicing different cultures. The Maya of the past were likely no less differentiated, and though they established many city-states over the period when they had the greatest impact on Mesoamerican political life, these city-states were not united. Even so, there were traditions they held in common, and great urban centers like Palenque and Tikal stood out in a Maya sphere of influence that spanned the highlands and lowlands in a classic Mesoamerican display of power.

Olmec stone head.

The Maya had a writing system and also a sophisticated counting system that included a zero. As previously mentioned, the Maya, like most agricultural peoples, were concerned with the measurement of time. It was important to know when to plant and when to harvest, especially given the various ecozones that were exploited. The Maya devised a calendar of 20-day months, but the elite lived by a different, sacred calendar, of 13-day months. This stressed not only the separateness of the elite but also its command over the seemingly natural passage of time itself.

Maya rulers were associated with jaguars, of course, but they were also symbolized by trees. Tree roots dig deep into the underworld, while the branches of trees reach heavenward—trees are, thus, boundary-crossers, knitting together the earth and sky. Maya rituals were carried out both in caves and atop massive pyramids. One act a ruler would perform before his people was to cut himself, letting his royal "sap" flow on behalf of his society. This ritual was reproduced, less grandly, by heads of households seeking divine favor for their families. When the Europeans told the story of Jesus, a great king who was nailed to a tree and shed his blood for his people, the Maya were already well acquainted with the concept.

It was once thought that the Maya brought on their own "demise" through overexploiting the environment, but their methods of food-getting, often entailing man-made imitations of natural ecologies, have been re-evaluated and found to be not only effective but sustainable (e.g., Beach et al. 2002; McNeil et al. 2010; Nations and Nigh 1980). The weakness of Maya city-states likely lay in the overexploitation of human labor, not land; Maya subsistence farmers could withdraw their services fairly readily if they found a ruler to be oppressive. Eventually Maya political influence contracted and the great ceremonial centers were abandoned. When the Europeans came, the Maya had re-established kin-based societies, though some of these were chiefdoms. But as far as the Europeans were concerned, the preeminent Mesoamerican society at the time of their arrival was the awe-inspiring **Aztec** state.

ANDEAN REGION

I will conclude this chapter with some comment on the Euroamerican encounter, but first we must visit the Andes. There were a great many similarities between Mesoamerica and the Andes. Again the idea of traveling from highlands to lowlands, taking advantage of the fruits of each ecozone, was important, as an early religious complex we call El Paraíso, apparently built by subsistence-oriented, kin-based peoples, would seem to bear out. The complex features several levels and staircases by which to reach them, all of this perhaps reflective of the jagged Andean landscape (see Quilter 1985). In the Andes as well as Mesoamerica, the jaguar was a key motif, and the two regions shared a vi-

Chavín stela, drawn by Antonio Raimondi.

tal crop, maize, that was likely domesticated in the north but then moved southward. This may not have happened with respect to statecraft, however. We have
no firm indication at this time that political developments in one region were
communicated to the other, and it is possible that the Mesoamerican and Andean states developed independently.

The Andean society comparable to the Mesoamerican Olmec was **Chavín de
Huántar,** which served as a source culture for ideas taken up by other Andean societies. Though Chavín was a highland society, it evidently had contact with population centers in the lowlands—likely in the Amazon basin, which we are only
now beginning to recognize as home to chiefdoms and possibly states (e.g., Dorfman 2002; Mann 2008)—from which it obtained maize and the jaguar motif.
Over the centuries, the Andes spawned many city-states; notable among them
was Moche, well-known for its unique and sometimes pornographic (by our standards) pottery, and Nazca, whose claim to fame lies in the huge line drawings
whose form can be discerned only through an aerial view. On Lake Titicaca,
which straddles the border between Peru and Bolivia, the kingdom of Huari em-
ployed agricultural methods that were so effective they are being revived and re-
applied today. Eventually Andean states became more ambitious, seizing more
territory, but none grew as large and quickly as the **Inca** state. The Inca were no-
nonsense about conquest—they sent in an army, they made arrangements for a
village to convey its share of tribute to the empire, and then they moved on. As

The Inca empire made use of an extensive network of roads.

was the case in Mesoamerica, the initial European reaction to Native American accomplishments was one of admiration. In the long run, as we all know, this did not stop the Europeans from taking over.

We are well past the traditional dividing line between prehistory and history at this point, and this chapter has gotten very long, but please be patient—a few closing words about the Euroamerican invasion are in order.

East Meets West

It is often presumed that the reason a small number of Europeans was able to subdue the great states of the New World so quickly, relatively speaking, was that European weaponry was "more advanced" than that of the New World. This notion demands qualification.

The most powerful weapon the Europeans brought into the New World was one of which they were initially unaware—germ warfare. For centuries Europeans and other Old World peoples had been living in proximity with domesticated animals, passing disease back and forth. In the 1500s, some of the diseases, like smallpox, remained a scourge in Europe; others, like measles, had largely been reduced to childhood infections from which most children recovered. This phalanx of disease hit the New World full-on. Of course, in the New World there were very few domesticated animals, but even had New Worlders engaged more broadly in animal husbandry, there is no guarantee they would have been any more resistant to the germ load imported from Europe, though they might have been able to give as good as they got. European disease killed even where Europeans were not present—some have suggested that Huayna Capac, who ruled the Inca empire just prior to Pizarro's arrival, died of smallpox that had passed through the isthmus from Mesoamerica. Compared to disease, the European efforts to kill and enslave the native populations of the Americas were feeble, but because of the microbial edge the Europeans enjoyed, these efforts eventually saw success. It should be noted, however, that despite the decimation of the New World population, significant military resistance was mounted against the Europeans, and even after the downfall of the great New World states, kin-based peoples continued to fight against European encroachment, making effective use of the horses Europeans had brought.

It turned out that obsidian-tipped weaponry was in fact no match for European metals, but again this was an accident of history—obsidian weapons work well within the context of other obsidian weapons. There was nothing intrinsically "more advanced" in manufacturing metal weaponry; it was simply that

New World peoples did not apply metals to this purpose, and did not suffer for this "choice" until the encounter with Europeans.

The particulars are also important when we consider the demise of both the Aztec and Inca states. In the early 1500s, the Aztecs were nearing the end of a spectacular killing spree, instigated by the emperor Moctezuma's close adviser Tlacaélel, who claimed the sun god desired more human blood. Hernán Cortés arrived in a year when, according to prophecy, the white-faced god **Quetzalcoatl** was to return from the mythical city of Tula (once the center of the very real Toltec state) to bring peace. Quetzalcoatl was generally represented as a feathered serpent, a boundary-crosser equally at home in the realms of earth and sky, but if Cortés was the embodiment of Quetzalcoatl, these more fantastic features could evidently be suppressed for the purpose of appearing human. Whether the Aztecs truly believed Cortés was Quetzalcoatl, the fact was that their murderous frenzy had run its course. But by this time, neighboring peoples, the victims of Aztec bloodlust, were more than willing to collaborate with Cortés to wreak revenge on their enemy. So Cortés and his forces had help from local allies in tak-

Quetzalcoatl.

ing down the Aztec state; disease and metal weaponry, at this point, were the least of it.

Circumstances were equally fortuitous for Francisco Pizarro in the Andes, though it took several attempts on Pizarro's part to fully press his advantage. The Inca empire was just emerging from a bloody succession struggle. The Inca had borrowed a custom from the preceding Chimú state, that of **split inheritance**, which was based on the premise that even in death, the lands the ruler had conquered and the wealth he had collected continued to belong to him (belying the adage, "you can't take it with you"). Royal sons, therefore, had to engage in their own campaigns of conquest; hence the Inca empire grew very large very quickly, though obviously a sense of overall political solidarity had yet to be set in place. After Huayna Capac died, sons Huascar and Atahualpa competed viciously for his position. Atahualpa was victorious, but the empire was weakened by the protracted warfare. When Pizarro kidnapped Atahualpa in 1532, holding him literally for a king's ransom, the incident likely cemented the impression, on the part of peoples minimally invested in the Inca empire-building project, that Atahualpa had lost divine favor and was therefore unfit to rule. This was further confirmed when Pizarro executed Atahualpa. The Inca empire discorporated, and the Europeans, appointing themselves as ruling elite, took charge of its remains.

The Europeans were no less facile with the concept of divine favor; they could certainly see their takeover of the Americas as having been ordained by God. Later they would enlist science to tell the story of the conquest: the Europeans were "of superior stock" compared to the frail

Machu Picchu.

native Americans who had no resistance against disease any European child could overcome. The native Americans did not have the mental wherewithal to recognize the "benefits" of animal husbandry or metal weaponry. In short, the accidents of history that gave the Europeans an upper hand in the New World were passed through the filter of "race," a concept that continues to skew the popular and even the professional interpretation of the human condition. The exploration of this concept is the subject of our tenth, and final, chapter.

SIDEBAR

The (Pre?)History of Writing

"Prehistory is the period before recorded history," begins the Wikipedia entry on the subject (accessed February 28, 2011). If this is the case, we have far exceeded our mandate, as Sumerian **cuneiform**, generally thought to be the earliest true writing system, emerges over 5 kya. Chinese is also a very early system, possibly predating the development of writing in Mesopotamia. So why have we proceeded past these milestones? Surely, at some point, even the considerable intellectual ambitions of anthropology are exhausted, and the historians must rightly take over.

Cuneiform.

The problem is that this seemingly firm dividing line between prehistory and history is—and you've certainly heard *this* before—fuzzy. Are experts entirely in agreement regarding the definition of writing, and what systems qualify? Do we stop prehistory at cuneiform when the rest of the world remains preliterate? What about state societies, like that of the Inca, that did not develop writing—are they the only state societies we can discuss?

Additionally, there are those writing systems we have yet to translate. The people in the Indus Valley had a writing system, but we have only in the past few decades made some headway in understanding it (e.g., Possehl 1996). We continue to be stymied by Linear A, the Minoan script, although scholars are now reasonably sure that it was yet another means of recording whether subjects had paid the proper amount of tribute to their king. Even so, it would be better to know this than merely to assume it.

The Mycenaeans, who borrowed so much from the Minoans, also borrowed Linear A. In their hands it became Linear B, which they used to represent their own language, an early form of Greek. With the decline of Mycenae, control of sea trade (and written trade language) passed to a collection of eastern Mediterranean city-states known altogether as Phoenicia. The Phoenicians used a simple alphabet, composed of characters that represented sounds, to facilitate commerce. They conveyed this written language throughout the Mediterranean, where in each port it was adapted to suit the vernacular. Since the Phoenician alphabet is directly ancestral to our own, it really *is* time to quit—the rest, as they say, is history.

QUESTIONS FOR DISCUSSION AND REVIEW

- Critique Lewis Henry Morgan's scheme of cultural evolution.
- How are state societies different from those that are kin-based?
- Describe how some of the classic features of state societies serve to establish and maintain elite privilege.
- How did New World states differ from Old World states?
- Discuss the advantages and disadvantages of state societies.

KEY WORDS

Morgan	chiefdom	Egypt
Savagery	rank	nation-state
Barbarism	chief	hieroglyphics
Civilization	elite	China
society	tribute	Sinicize
Boas	circumscription	scapulimancy
ethnocentrism	elitism	Indus Valley city-state
state	ideology	Minoan state
centralization	writing	obsidian
specialization	quipu	were-jaguar
social stratification	pyramid	Olmec
power	elite retinue	source culture
kin-based	social control	Maya
noncompetitive egalitarianism	Mesopotamia	Aztec
reverse hierarchy	Sumerian city-state	Quetzalcoatl
competitive egalitarianism	ziggurat	Chavín de Huántar
tribe	bronze	Inca
wealth	alloy	split inheritance
big man	cuneiform	

10

HUMAN VARIATION, PAST, PRESENT . . . AND FUTURE?

A science without regard
for people's welfares and feelings
is a science that is difficult to justify.

—Jonathan Marks,
What It Means to Be 98% Chimpanzee

The Peopling of the Americas—Reprise

To this point, we have mainly been studying the past, often the far distant past. I would maintain there is an intrinsic value to this study—increasing your personal storehouse of knowledge is never a bad thing (it's why you're in school, after all), and you never know when a fact you have committed to memory may come in handy. But beyond simply exercising your brain, this textbook has been aimed at correcting, or at the very least greatly qualifying, popular impressions. If we are aware that agriculture is not an ecologically sound choice in all circumstances, we may enlarge the spaces available in this modern world to pursue other subsistence strategies; if we see the state as having come about not from an innate drive to progress but from the vested interests of those who benefited most, we may regard similar "progressive" proposals in the future with somewhat more caution. Those aims are, admittedly, idealistic, but there is one area of popular misconception whose correction, via anthropology, can have an immediate, concrete impact on your life: the issue of **race.**

To open our address of this issue, I will return to a subject I let drop in chapter 7. You will recall that in recent decades there has been a good deal of new thinking regarding the peopling of the Americas. We now regularly wander past the "Clovis barrier" to consider the question of how long human beings have lived in the New World; further, the notion that the earliest occupation began with a single small, biologically uniform founding population has suffered intense scrutiny. I should mention, in passing, that there are certain populations broadly referred to as "native American" today whose roots are distinct from those of other native populations, namely, the Inuit and the Hawaiians. Having acknowledged this, the term "Native American" in this chapter will, unless otherwise stipulated, refer to those populations of both the northern and the southern New World continents whose ancestors were mislabeled "Indians."

In 1996, a skeleton emerged from a riverbank in the town of Kennewick, Washington. It was presumed initially to be a relatively recent murder victim, and for this reason it was given over to James Chatters to study. Chatters, who ran an archaeological consulting firm, was also frequently called in on criminal investigations as well, given his familiarity with human skeletal morphology. Like any good coroner nowadays, Chatters made an educated guess with respect to the race of the victim—probably a white man, he thought, given the elongated head, flattened profile, and the bilobed chin that would dimple the flesh if it were present. This assessment of race was neither unusual nor unwarranted, though further investigation might prove it wrong. In this particular case, however, there was no need to continue treating the victim as contemporary once Chatters found a stone spear point lodged in the pelvis. Chatters sent a sample of the remains off to a radiocarbon lab, and the results were astounding. Kennewick Man, as the fossil was to become known, was estimated to be close to 9,500 years old. Once this was discovered, a spokesman from the Umatilla, a Native American tribe resident in the eastern Washington/Oregon border area, declared the tribe's intention to take custody of the bones (see Downey 2000; Thomas 2000).

Since Kennewick Man was indisputably a pre-Columbian fossil, that meant he could be claimed as ancestral by the Native American tribes of the region, and repatriated—that is, reburied—according to their customs. It is not the point of this book to recount the litany of wrongs Native Americans have suffered during and after the colonization of their lands by European invaders, but one particularly sore point has been the desecration of Native American artifacts and remains. Euroamericans had not only unearthed a great deal of these over the centuries but had also justified withholding them from their proper context in the name of science. For many Native American tribes, ancestors are still tribal members, and their remains should not be treated as though they were mere articles of scientific curiosity. Unearthing human remains was like evicting a person from his rightful home, and that was a process all too familiar to Native Americans. For years, however, they did not have the political clout to stop further atrocities, let alone reverse the ones that had already taken place.

This situation changed during the administration of the first President Bush. In 1990, Congress enacted the Native American Graves Protection and Repatriation Act (**NAGPRA**). NAGPRA provided for the repatriation of artifacts and remains kept in federally funded institutions; it also stipulated that with respect to any new finds on federal lands, local tribes could lay claim to them and treat them as they saw fit. While the passage of NAGPRA was seen as a benchmark for Native rights, it was less welcomed by archaeologists and biological anthropologists, who were acutely aware that because of the new law, carrying out their research would become a vastly more complicated enterprise.

SIDEBAR

NAGPRA

NAGPRA, or the Native American Graves Protection and Repatriation Act (Public Law 101-601; 25 USC 3001 et seq.) was passed by Congress in 1990 and amended twice since (visit the government website, http://www.nps.gov/nagpra/). Section 3, pages 169–170, contains the following stipulations (25 USC 3002, Ownership; 25 USC 3002(a), Native American human remains and objects):

(a) The ownership or control of Native American cultural items which are excavated or discovered on Federal or tribal lands after November 16, 1990, shall be (with priority given in the order listed)—

(1) in the case of Native American human remains and associated funerary objects, in the lineal descendants of the Native American; or

(2) in any case in which such lineal descendants cannot be ascertained, and in the case of unassociated funerary objects, sacred objects, and objects of cultural patrimony—

(A) in the Indian tribe or Native Hawaiian organization on whose tribal land such objects or remains were discovered;

(B) in the Indian tribe or Native Hawaiian organization which has the closest cultural affiliation with such remains or objects and which, upon notice, states a claim for such remains or objects; or

(C) if the cultural affiliation of the objects cannot be reasonably ascertained and if the objects were discovered on Federal land that is recognized by a final judgment of the Indian Claims Commission or the United States Court of Claims as the aboriginal land of some Indian tribe—

(continued)

(1) [sic] in the Indian tribe that is recognized as aboriginally occupying the area in which the objects were discovered, if upon notice, such tribe states a claim for such remains or objects, or

(2) [sic] if it can be shown by a preponderance of the evidence that a different tribe has a stronger cultural relationship with the remains or objects than the tribe or organization specified in paragraph (1), in the Indian tribe that has the strongest demonstrated relationship, if upon notice, such tribe states a claim for such remains or objects.

NAGPRA also applies to Alaskan natives and to the natives of the other Pacific islands that fall under the jurisdiction of the United States, e.g., Guam.

Today's archaeologists and biological anthropologists certainly recognize and condemn the cavalier treatment of artifacts and remains that has taken place, even under scientific auspices, and they join with Native Americans in deploring the activities of collectors who traffic in such items for profit. But many archaeologists and biological anthropologists believed a law restricting their access to their objects of study was unnecessary, since they felt perfectly capable of working out arrangements with Native Americans that were satisfactory to the needs of both parties (it helps that "archaeologists/biological anthropologists" and "Native Americans" are not mutually exclusive groups). Whether or not these arrangements were as satisfactory as claimed, after the passage of NAGPRA there were no longer grounds for negotiation unless the Native Americans chose to open them, and Native Americans were not always amenable to persuasion, given the abuses of the past.

Laws are written in stark terms, for the purpose of clarity. What had been a flexible, contingent situation was suddenly frozen in place, with opposing sides drawn up and very little room to maneuver. Some archaeologists and biological anthropologists understandably became resentful. As far as they were concerned, before NAGPRA they were responsible scientists, carrying out studies they saw as having a benefit for humankind in general; after NAGPRA they were deemed cultural imperialists who invoked science to defend the unconscionable capture and imprisonment of Native American ancestors. Resentment, however, does not justify what happened next in the saga of Kennewick Man.

In the press conference that followed the revelation of Kennewick Man's age, Chatters knew it was inappropriate to refer to the fossil as "white." "White" was a modern Euroamerican term referring to modern Euroamerican ideas about human difference, and it would have been imprudent to project these ideas into the distant past. Instead, Chatters said that the features of Kennewick Man were "Caucasoid-like," believing this to be simply descriptive of the head shape and chin. But the term was taken up by the media as Caucasian—that is, "white." Unsurprisingly, there was a flurry of headlines suggesting that the first Americans may have been Europeans; subsequent coverage dismissed the outrage of Native Americans over such suggestions as a fear that science might demolish their claim to indigenous status. In a *60 Minutes* report on the Kennewick dust-up (aired October 25, 1998), a question along the following lines was posed: are Native Americans simply afraid they'll lose their casinos if it's proved their ancestors weren't the first ones here? There were even those who mooted the possibility that the conquest of the Americas by Europeans was merely satisfying the long-standing demand for justice after the "tawny Mongoloids" (Thomas 2000:xix) from Asia descended on the peaceable Caucasian pioneers. Perhaps needless to say, this sort of speculation was at best unhelpful, at worst deliberately provocative. Anthropologists were certainly among the many who objected.

But some archaeologists and biological anthropologists dove below the hype to grab what they saw as a glimmer of truth in all of the muck—Kennewick Man was not an Indian, and therefore the Umatilla had no right to his remains. While NAGPRA makes reference to proving "cultural affiliation" to remains, it is clear that culture is being conflated with biology in that a "lineal" connection must be indicated. In the countersuit scientists filed against the Umatilla claim, it was asserted that Kennewick Man's cranial morphology bore no resemblance to Indians either present or past. In terms of modern populations, the cranium was said to be far more similar to that of the Ainu in Japan, a people believed to be a remnant of a

Ainu in traditional dress.

widespread "Caucasoid" migration that had taken place shortly after *Homo sapiens (sapiens)* evolved. The scientists maintained Kennewick was thus biologically distinct from Indians and should be surrendered to science for unobstructed study. The presiding judge accepted the evidence presented by the scientists and ruled against the Umatilla.

But what exactly did the scientists prove? To explore this question, it is important to lay down those things we know, and/or think we know, about human variation.

Understanding Human Biological Variation—The Bullet Points

- **HUMAN BEINGS TODAY CONSTITUTE ONE AND ONLY ONE SPECIES.** There is no getting around this. It is obvious that there are no biological breeding barriers between human populations. Not only *can* we produce fertile offspring with people from different populations, we regularly *do.* Such factors as geography, religious differences, and ethnic and class prejudices have at various times and/or in various places constrained our choice of mates, but even when and where these constraints have been particularly binding, human beings often manage to breed across population lines successfully.

- **GENETICALLY SPEAKING, HUMAN BEINGS ARE REMARKABLY ALIKE.** Forget, for a moment, what you have been conditioned to see on the surface. This similarity goes well beyond the level introduced in the preceding bullet point. The different populations of chimpanzee today, though constituting one species altogether, are far more genetically variable than the present-day human species (Becquet et al. 2007). You may recall, from chapter 7, that there have been two explanations proposed for this. The first is that *Homo sapiens (sapiens)* is a relatively young species, arising circa 200 kya; hence there has been very little time for variation to accrue. The second is that *Homo sapiens (sapiens)* is the genetically streamlined version of a much older species, arising circa 2 mya, that was considerably more internally variable in the past, with some of these variations (e.g., heavy browridges, pronounced facial prognathism, etc.) having been "ironed out" through interbreeding between populations. Either way, the present-day result would be a species with very little genetic variation. And either way, all human beings today are related, harking back to common human roots at some point in time. To the extent we are "unrelated," this is only a matter of degree.

Keep in mind that there are two types of genetic change we can track. Change in nuclear DNA is tugged hither and thither by mutation, gene flow, genetic drift, and natural selection. All of these processes coming into play within a small population coping with a new environment can bring about changes in nuclear DNA very quickly, although generally change is more measured, since an evolutionary "direction" within a larger population already reasonably well adapted to its surroundings is harder to establish. Change in mtDNA is steadier overall, since it happens only (or at least primarily) through mutation. As described in chapter 7, supporters of the Out-of-Africa scenario for modern human origins (the "young" view, above) took note of mtDNA variation in the world today, took note of those populations in which mtDNA mutations were most numerous, and then worked their way back to the putative ancestress for all of humankind, "mitochondrial Eve." But we cannot really tell whether Eve was actually the beginning of a new species, especially without knowing what her nuclear DNA was like. She may simply have been part of a cell of intense evolutionary activity that for one reason or another had a great impact on what was to come.

In fact, in terms of both explanations for human origins, it may be most useful, once again, to think of hominin populations as chronically spinning off such "laboratories"; that is, small daughter populations within which evolutionary "experiments" were carried out. As these daughter populations migrated, they were subjected to new challenges with respect to predators, disease, and climate conditions that culled out some genetic possibilities even as others proliferated. Nonetheless, no hominin population whose descendants survive today became isolated to the point that its accumulated change in nuclear DNA became the basis for a new species. There was genetic traffic between populations, and whether that has been taking place for 200 ky or 2 my, it has produced the same highly regularized result. Cultural traffic, as well, promoted regularization, not only of the genome but of the environment. The widespread use of fire, for instance, reduced the threat of predators and diminished the threat of certain pathogens through the cooking of food.

- **Each human being is epi/genetically unique.** This is obvious simply from scanning your classroom. You look different from the people sitting next to you, and the people sitting in front and behind you. Although, as human beings, your genotypes are very similar, in the ways they do vary they can produce phenotypes that seem dramatically distinct, especially when we are culturally attuned to noticing specific distinctions. Remember, too, that genes are only the beginning—there are the subsequent knock-on effects that may even introduce difference between identical twins, and when all is said and done, no one can duplicate the genetic, epigenetic, and environmental path you traveled.

- **HUMAN POPULATIONS VARY IN THEIR ALLELES AND ALLELE FREQUENCIES.** The results of our long history of genetic "experimentation" in different environments are still evident. Chronic exposure to the sun's rays can wreak havoc on the human body—we are nowadays aware of the dangers of skin cancer, of course, but there are also essential vitamins that are depleted by such exposure. One way the detrimental effects of sun exposure can be managed is to develop a "sun shield" of **melanin** produced by skin cells called **melanocytes.** All human beings have melanocytes, but they are minimally active in some populations, active only when triggered by sun exposure in other populations, and always active in still other populations. In northerly climates, in which the problem might be too little as opposed to too much sun, dropping the "sun shield" by producing less melanin is adaptive. That way the body can synthesize sufficient quantities of Vitamin D, a substance that contributes to a sound reproductive system. Vitamin D is also needed in childhood to prevent rickets, a crippling disease that will likely take its victim out of the breeding pool (Jablonski 2006).

Recall that we define a population as a group within which one is likeliest to select mates. If an adaptation is favored in a particular environment, it will probably spread within the population where it was developed, and into other populations sharing the same environment, simply through the mechanism of successful breeding. Think of an adaptation as an "accessory" that one population "borrows" from another in order to cope with a similar problem. If the problem disappears, the accessory may remain, so long as it is no detriment to successful breeding in that environment. In fact, it may continue to be favored via sexual as opposed to natural selection, in that members of the population come to see the accessory as attractive, a feature they desire in a prospective mate.

- **IN HUMAN BEINGS, VERY FEW "ACCESSORIES" CO-VARY; THAT IS, THEY DO NOT FORM A COMPLETE "PACKAGE" OF TRAITS THAT MUST BE PASSED ON WHOLE FROM ONE GENERATION TO THE NEXT.** It is possible to have dark skin and blue eyes. It is possible to have light skin and tufty hair. We have never found a genetic connection between skin color and mental acuity, or sexual drive. The "accessory" metaphor in this sense is especially apt—these traits can be "worn" in a number of combinations. Can we call a population in which a set of these accessories shows up consistently a "race"? Biologists have applied this word to nonhuman animals in populations that differ in fur or feather color, size, or beak shape. So with respect to humans, the answer is "yes"—with two important qualifications. The first is that human beings resist the kind of isolation that produces "races" in other species— we move even between islands and interbreed despite the "strangeness" of the others we encounter. The second is that the term can be applied only in a localized way. To apply it, for example, to all dark-skinned people is to cast too wide a net; within the net you would find far more human beings who are more genetically different from each other (within that narrow range in which humans *do* differ) than they are alike (Lewontin 1972). In other words, applying "race" to human beings in the way we typically have tells us very little, and hardly anything of biological significance, about the huge population the term encloses. But having used "race" for so long in this scientifically sloppy way, we really cannot salvage the term for a more specialized purpose.

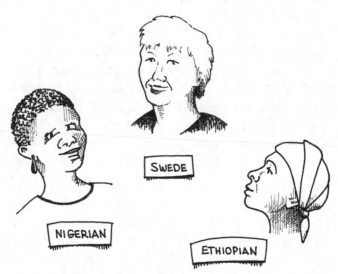

Which two people are genetically more alike?

a. The Nigerian and the Ethiopian

b. The Ethiopian and the Swede

c. The Swede and the Nigerian

d. It cannot be determined from the information given

A student once asked me, "If racial traits don't co-vary, then why does Obama look black?" The fact is, however, that President Obama does not "look black." He "looks" like someone whose skin color is influenced by both of his parents. His complexion is lighter than that of his father. The problem in this instance is particular to American culture—anything that "looks black" to us, to whatever degree, marks a person as "black." We *could* see the matter as the late Haitian dictator "Papa Doc" Duvalier once, allegedly, expressed it: that people who exhibit any "whiteness" at all should be considered white (Kessen 1993). Or we could subdivide the spectrum of skin color into many different categories. In short, Obama does not intrinsically "look black"—Americans *see* him as black because we have been conditioned by our history to do so. Within American "blackness" there is a tremendous number of different genetic combinations, overlapping with "whiteness" to such an extent that it makes no sense to draw a biological line between the "two" populations. Hence it follows that . . .

- **THERE ARE NO "PURE RACES."** Some of you reading this book may consider yourself to be of "mixed race"; others are certainly aware that a growing number of people in the United States are the product of "biracial" pairings. This is not confined to the United States. With globalization, there is more contact between human populations, even those vastly separated by geography and culture, than ever before, and some of that contact includes marriage and family. Given this newly intense level of global exchange, it is understandable that some people think "race-mixing" is a modern phenomenon and, at one time, there were largely "pure races," containing concentrated "racial traits," that are only now being broken out and shared. This is untrue.

"Pure races" do not exist, now or in the past. As noted in the last chapter, human populations are not "silos," either culturally or biologically. It is possible that over the long course of human existence, very small groups were isolated for extended periods (some of them doubtless becoming extinct), but nothing on the scale of a "race," in the outsized sense discussed above, could have been exempt from gene flow. For most of their time on the planet, human beings lived in relatively dispersed populations, moving about, meeting, merging, and undergoing fission. It is not as though alleles were constantly, and in large quantities, being passed back and forth between all populations, but they were transferred often enough to prevent a minute number of differences in a population from snowballing into a large number of differences, eventually leading to speciation. Gene flow, and the flow of cultural material and knowledge, prevented human gene pools from becoming stagnant. This brings me to my last point.

- **EVERYTHING CHANGES.** It stands to reason that if each "race," today, is actually a catch-all of traits in a variety of combinations, responding as needed to environmental conditions, the same sort of mixing-and-matching was taking place in the past. What seems biologically "fixed" today is actually quite mutable. Nina Jablonski, for instance, hazards that light and dark skin in human beings evolved more than once (2006). Even such features as head shape, once thought to be irrefutably indicative of "race," can change over just a few generations, as Franz Boas, in the study cited in chapter 1, tried to show. We can do a statistical analysis of the cranial morphology of American populations today and have a reasonable if not foolproof means of assessing the "race" of a murder victim, but we cannot presume that what has some validity today works at all well when applied to the distant past.

Racing Back to Kennewick

So, given everything I have set down in the previous section, what were the scientists able to "prove" about Kennewick Man to the satisfaction of the court? The Kennewick skull does exhibit morphological differences from other Native American skulls, both present-day and those of the past. It is certainly possible that Kennewick had roots in an Asian population that migrated into the New World separately from the population that gave rise to Clovis hunters. But that having been said, Kennewick could still be ancestral to today's Native Americans. And there is currently no way science can categorically rule this out (Goodman 1997).

Look at it this way—you are the descendant of two parents, who each had two parents, and so on. If we take 25 years as the measure of a generation—and that may be too brief a span with respect to today's late breeders, but too long as we move back in time—there are four generations in a century, and 360 in 9,000 years. So do the math. Fifty years ago (using the 25-year figure), your two parents were born; 25 years earlier their four parents were born; and going back 100 years we find your eight great-grandparents. Two hundred years ago your direct ancestors numbered 128; 500 years ago 524,288 of your ancestors were born. Given the vagaries of meiosis, the majority of these people will not have contributed any alleles to you, though of course those alleles had a far better chance of being distributed into the immediately descendant generations. Go back a generation from 500 years ago and the number of your ancestors tops one million. We are nowhere near 9,000 years ago, but we will stop there, because in another hundred years the numbers would be truly astronomical, and of course that is hardly the end of the matter.

Now, I have to confess something: there's a drag on this progression, because there have never been trillions of people at any one time on the planet. Ancestors are reused when they produce offspring with kin (sure it happens—you're related to far more people than you know), and after a while—more recently than 9,000 years ago, in fact—the number of your ancestors on each generational level actually begins to narrow. Even so, at the 9,000 year mark, you have a huge number of ancestors, most of whom have contributed no DNA to you at all (see Luke Jostin's blog at www.genetic-inference.co.uk/blog/2009/11/how-many-ancestors-share-our-DNA/). So you cannot look like all of your distant ancestors; in fact, especially considering that traits and populations themselves change over the years, it is far more likely you resemble none of them. Kennewick Man, even with his "non-Indian" skull, could nonetheless have held a place in the ancestry of modern Native Americans.

But what about mtDNA? With mtDNA, we do not have to deal with an exponential number of ancestors. You inherit mtDNA from your mother, who inherited it from her mother, who inherited it from her mother, and so on. So in this way we trace a single, unbroken line of descent. If the mtDNA of Kennewick Man features mutations that we do not find in any Native American today, surely he cannot be ancestral to them, right? Well, no. In the first place, Kennewick Man passed on no mtDNA to his descendants—the woman or women with whom he produced offspring would have to do that, and we have no idea what her/their mtDNA was like. If he had a sister who produced offspring, his mtDNA would be passed on, but her line may not have endured to the present day. In the second place, as it happens, we have yet to recover usable mtDNA from Kennewick. Lodged for millennia in a riverbank, his DNA was literally washed away (see Kaestle 2000; Merriwether et al. 2000; Smith et al. 2000).

So Kennewick Man, whether or not his roots were different from those of the Clovis hunters, whether or not his appearance was distinct from theirs, may be directly ancestral to today's Native Americans. He also may not be. Was he Umatilla? Another tricky question, since there may not have been any semblance of a group calling itself Umatilla at the time (though I suspect this is not what the Umatilla believe). While archaeologists can construct sensible culture sequences—what appear to be "lineal" artifacts—and connect them to present-day peoples, there is no guarantee that a progression of artifacts correlates to the descent lines of a modern tribe. Remember, human societies are not silos, plus everything changes. Peoples share culture, adopting new ways of doing things even as they let others lapse. When it comes to a 9,000-year-old fossil, the determination of cultural affiliation is no more assured than the determination of biological affiliation.

In short, NAGPRA all too often sends science on a fool's errand. This is not to say that NAGPRA should be scrapped—it is still important to recognize Native American rights with regard to the culturally appropriate disposal of artifacts and remains—but science simply may not be able to provide the information needed in contested cases. It may be best to accept the authority of the Native American tribe laying the claim, although this does not resolve the disposal of Kennewick Man, since the Umatilla is not the only tribe that has claimed him (see Walker and Jones 2000).

So, given everything I have said above about race, how can reputable scientists state with confidence that Kennewick is not of the same "race" as Native Americans? How can the media have had a field day with the idea that Native American claims to indigenous status were now in jeopardy? Why does NAGPRA presume that biological affiliation automatically confirms cultural affiliation, and vice versa? Where did *these* silly ideas about race come from? Well . . . from, uh, anthropologists.

SIDEBAR

The Solutrean-Clovis Connection?

As if the issue of New World settlement were not already sufficiently complex, a rather old theory has recently been revived. Archaeologists Bruce Bradley and Dennis Stanford believe that we should not be looking toward Asia for the source population(s) of New World migrants, but toward Europe (Bradley and Stanford 2004). There is a striking resemblance between the Clovis industry and the Solutrean industry of western Europe, they claim, and if we consider it possible humans could have engaged in coastal hopping around the northerly Pacific Rim, then a similar voyage may have been undertaken from the east, across the northern Atlantic. The discovery of New World sites that break the Clovis barrier, along with the ancient fossils that are "Caucasoid" in appearance, completes the picture.

However pretty, the picture has its critics, notably Lawrence Straus, who takes note of the many differences between the two tool traditions, not to mention the difficulties in fitting together the timelines (Straus, Meltzer, and Goebel 2005). Archaeologically speaking, the evidence for an early North Atlantic entry into North America is circumstantial, and obviously debatable. Even so, the hypothesis has been mooted and awaits more support. If the arguments in this chapter hold any weight at all, however, this support will not be forthcoming from Kennewick Man and those few scattered, aberrant skeletons whose features lie outside the Native American norm.

Race and the History of Anthropology

When Europeans set sail to discover new routes into the sphere of Asian trade, they discovered much more, by way of "new" lands and "new" peoples (that is, new to Europeans). Their first encounters with these peoples were frequently disastrous, with loss of life on both sides. But there were also productive (in every sense) liaisons—you may already have learned during your schooling that Cortés had a Native mistress, known to us as La Malinche, who played a role in bringing down the Aztecs—and efforts to dehumanize non-Europeans, no matter how "savagely" they had reacted to European contact, were offset by admiration for the accomplishments of, for instance, the Aztec and Inca states; a need for cooperation with local populations in unfamiliar circumstances; and, of course, interbreeding. Hence, the efforts of the monk Sepúlveda to have the Natives of the New World declared "natural slaves" came to nothing, although this hardly meant Natives were treated well (see, e.g., Pagden 1982).

Europeans did regard the peoples they encountered as inferior in one primary aspect—they were not Christian—but this situation was rectified by missionaries who swiftly followed in the footsteps of the first wave of European explorers. Despite this extraordinarily successful missionization campaign, there remained those Europeans who tried to organize the world in terms of a spiritual hierarchy, with non-Europeans having fallen, in some way, from the Lord's graces. Although the Bible had great authority, it was obviously not consistent in identifying the world's populations as qualitatively different in the eyes of God, and passages that suggested the peoples of the earth varied in terms of origin, hence spiritual worth, were contradicted by passages that reaffirmed the oneness of humankind.

In the eighteenth century, the character of European (and Euroamerican) colonialism began to change. Moral objections were mounting against the enslavement of sub-Saharan Africans on tropical and sub-tropical plantations. While the bravery and fortitude of early abolitionists should not be downplayed, it must also be noted that maintaining a force of ornery slaves that had to be fed, in good times and in bad, was increasingly expensive, especially when **peasants,** providing for their own subsistence under the colonial yoke, might be coerced into dedicating some of their labor (or the labor of their children) to the upkeep of plantations. But the salability of foreign wares was already in decline—Europeans could no longer make huge profits simply by moving products from one part of the world to another—and the great trading firms were struggling to survive by century's end (the Dutch East India Company famously went bankrupt on December 31, 1799, at 11:59:59 PM).

For European countries to remain solvent, they needed to add value to the raw materials being extracted from overseas, and this was done through manufacturing, a process through which finished items were mass-produced. This created market saturation quickly, however, and once again the peoples outside Europe were eyed for their potential to supply cheaper labor while at the same time possibly providing a new market for goods. In other words, global economic matters were coming to a head—a decision had to be reached as to whether and how non-Europeans could participate in the new economy. Questions abounded regarding the abilities of these alien beings and the danger involved in granting them any serious role in European enterprise. Europeans continued to look to the Bible for answers to these questions, but they also, increasingly, looked to science, which was beginning to establish itself as a font of knowledge that was not necessarily Biblically supported.

You will recall that the eighteenth century was a time of great developments in the life sciences—the period completely encloses the lifespan of Linnaeus, for instance, and just beyond its end Lamarck is credited with popularizing the term, "biology." Linnaeus made some attempt to classify human beings according to type (with respect to the human populations of his day he saw these different types as "varieties," not "species"), and the effort was furthered by a German doctor named Johann Friedrich **Blumenbach.** In 1775 Blumenbach, after assessing and measuring the skull shapes of a variety of populations, hazarded that there were in essence four "races" of humankind. He later revised this number to five—Caucasian, Mongolian, Ethiopian, American, and Malayan (Bhopal 2007). Although Blumenbach's early work involved statements regarding the varying aptitudes and the relative beauty of these "races," in later life he became convinced that the "races" were the equal of each other and were not, in fact, the distinct entities the labels he had used would imply. Nonetheless,

Johann Friedrich Blumenbach, 1752–1840.

the damage was done. Contemporary and subsequent scientists, seeking to further one form or another of a racist agenda, borrowed both from Blumenbach's terminology and his idea that the comparative study of skulls "proved" the existence of separate human populations to devise their own systems of racial types.

The work of Samuel **Morton** provides an infamous example. Beginning in the 1820s, Morton, a Philadelphia physician, set out to establish that the different "races," which in his opinion numbered four, could be ranked in terms of their intellectual capacities. Morton believed that sheer skull size might directly correlate to intelligence. He amassed a collection of skulls from the various races and measured their volume by filling them with mustard seed—he later switched to lead shot—and then pouring out and weighing the contents. As you might anticipate, Morton found that the skulls of "Caucasian" people, overall, were larger than those of "Negroes," "Mongolians," and (Native) "Americans." Morton's work was thought to bear out **polygenesis,** the idea that God had not created "Man" as a single entity; rather, the different "races" had resulted from separate creation events. Supporters of polygenesis believed their view to be "advanced" because they had not simply accepted the Bible's word on the matter but had undertaken scientific experiments to determine the "truth." Advocates of this view may not have been any more racist than others of their day, but clearly the notion that the "races" had distinct origins was very useful to those who wanted to justify the position of "Caucasians" over other "races." Europeans were *naturally* superior—that explained everything.

Stephen Jay Gould, in his well-known book *The Mismeasure of Man* (1981), demolished Morton's methodology. Morton was highly selective in terms of *which* skulls he would measure—the "Negro" sample, for instance, contained a preponderance of skulls from women, which tended to be smaller that those of men. It was also quite possible to shake a skull in order to fit in more seed or shot, thus arranging for the "appropriate" amount. Gould did not believe Morton was *consciously* skewing the results of his research. The underlying problem was a very strong preconception on Morton's part of what those results would be.

There is more to be criticized here. Within the range of human brain size, a bigger brain is not necessarily a better brain. There is no correlation between brain size and intelligence, at least with respect to what we generally mean by that term. Frankly, the methodology used to form the concept of "intelligence" as a unified, measurable "thing" contained in the brain (more in some than in others) is also highly suspect, but that will not concern us here (though see Hanson 1993, if you would like to follow up on this). What we will examine are Morton's preconceptions. His skull experiment—and the many thereafter modeled on it— was organized *through* the prism of race. Morton already believed races existed, so what remained to be done was to collect a representative sample of skulls from each "race" and measure skull volume within each sample. Some of the skulls were larger than what he expected, some smaller, but within each racial category he was able to establish an average skull size—the point to averaging, after all, is to smooth over discrepancies into one intermediate figure. What we do not know is what would have happened had Morton started with racially unidentified skulls and tried to sort them into "races." Would he have been able to draw the "correct" racial lines through the sample? It seems highly unlikely.

Think of the matter this way. Let's say you were to divide your class into two groups based on height: Group A consists of those students who are over 5'7" tall and Group B consists of those who are exactly 5'7" or under. Height in humans is a genetically governed property that is further influenced by the impact of environment and in these ways is comparable to certain "racial" characteristics like skin color. The first difference you might notice between the

Craniometry.

two student groups is that Group A contains a larger proportion of the males in the class, but there may be other genetic differences between the groups, and genetic similarities within them. It may be that the majority of students in Group B have Type A blood, while the blood type that dominates Group A is Type O. It may be that there are more students in Group A who are left-handed, or have brown eyes.

Wait a second, you may say, whatever differences that exist between the groups and similarities within them have to be accidental, since height is only one of many traits we might have used to divide the class; further, the dividing line of 5'7" is arbitrary. But here's the point: *precisely the same can be said about such traits as skin color.* If you were to divide your class according to skin color, you would first have to decide, for instance, how many skin colors there actually are— dark brown, medium brown, tan, ivory? You might skip over this task simply by accepting the strange American notion that conforming even slightly to the racial stereotype we call "black" means that a student is "black" (since she [or he] has been treated as a "black" person throughout her life, that is likely how she identifies herself as well). But even if you were to believe there were only two skin colors in the class, it could still vary as to where you draw the line between them.

Now, this isn't quite fair, since in all human populations there are taller and shorter people, while such traits as dark skin color are concentrated in certain regions. Human populations are not so intermixed that we have eradicated all the "basins" wherein particular traits have pooled. So if we notice, in the present day, that on the whole "white" people in the United States have very little facial prognathism, there is no harm in a forensic anthropologist observing the same trait in a modern skull and guessing that it may have belonged to a "white" person, especially when there are other methods that can be applied to corroborate this assessment. But there is no necessary link between skin color and prognathism; it just so happens that in the European populations from which Euroamericans descended, these two traits, independent of each other, collected.

In the nineteenth century, however, many European and Euroamerican scientists did not think along these lines. They believed racial traits *were* linked, and that these traits in fact came as a package within racial categories. So scientists took the racial categories as givens, and counted, measured, and weighed within them. Of course the scientists discovered a great many similarities—recall that human beings are remarkably alike—but they also, especially if they were honest with themselves, discovered differences. Nonetheless, they privileged the similarities over the differences because as far as they were concerned races existed, and one would simply expect more similarity within racial categories than between them. As previously mentioned, statistics helped here by resolving extremes into an average. These statistics had the veneer of science—surely numbers were free of cultural bias—and became the foundation for the discipline we know today as anthropology.

Nineteenth-century anthropology was, in fact, dominated by the race concept. "Race" was thought by many to determine everything about a person—what culture he practiced, what language he spoke. As discussed earlier, there *was* a disagreement between those I label "hard racists," who believed that the "lower races" were little better than animals, needing management as opposed to encouragement; and "soft racists" like Tylor and Morgan, who saw the "lower races" as more like children, primitive for the moment but capable of improvement, especially under the tutelage of "civilized" people. The vision of the "soft racists" was more humanitarian, but they were still racists, harboring the belief that biology was in large part destiny, even if there was some leeway for cultural change. While "hard racists" counseled strongly against racial interbreeding, some of the "soft racists" advocated "race mixing" as a means of infusing the inferior gene pools of the "lower races" with the biological stuff they needed to jump-start their march toward civilization.

It took Franz **Boas** to break the bonds between "race," culture, and language. In 1911, in the Introduction to *A Handbook of American Indian Languages*, he made the case explicitly that the three were independent variables, and that one could not presume anything else about a human group simply from knowing "race." In Boas' version of anthropology, culture was to displace "race" as the über-concept of the discipline. Culture was a product of the mind, not the body, and it had to be investigated not through calipers and measuring sticks but through deep, concerted consultation with the people the anthropologist wished to understand. This consultation was to be governed by the philosophy of **cultural relativism,** meaning that the anthropologist was to privilege the view of his native consultants, not his own, in putting together an **ethnography.** According to Boas, each society was unique, with a unique history. Melding these disparate histories together under one derogatory label—e.g., "Savagery"—was **ethnocentrism** masquerading as science.

Franz Boas, 1858–1942.

Boas was a man of his time and did not always live up to the principles he espoused regarding both culture and "race" (e.g., Visweswaran 1998). He doubted that native consultants *really* knew their own history and might need the expertise of the anthropologist, after all, to truly understand it (Ingold 1986). He believed that "race" existed, and never abandoned the calipers and the measuring sticks, though he thought the data they produced could be helpful toward constructing a revised concept of "race" as something that was malleable over the generations. He crusaded throughout his academic life against racism in the United States (e.g., 1962[1928]), but he also disturbed hundreds of Native American graves for the purpose of selling their contents to museums (Thomas 2000).

Contradictions eventually emerged in the Boasian vision of anthropology as well. In promoting cultural relativism, along with a humanistic methodology for both eliciting and recording cultural information, Boas set up a dichotomy between science and the humanities that of late has threatened the integration of the four-field approach he thought necessary to fully grasp the human condition. Most of the cultural anthropologists, and many of the linguists, have allied themselves with the humanistic camp, while the more science-oriented archaeologists and especially biological anthropologists, harking back to their own disciplinary history of experimentation and measurement, scorn the subjectivity and what they saw as methodological laxity on the part of their more culturally oriented colleagues.

While I have tried to present science and humanism as creating a dynamic and potentially constructive tension within anthropology, there is no question my view is idealistic. Some of the brickbats hurled at those archaeologists and biological anthropologists who brought the case of Kennewick Man to court came from cultural anthropologists. More recently, when the American Anthropological Association eliminated the word "science" from the official description of the anthropological mission, this brought forth a storm of protest spearheaded by biological anthropologists and archaeologists who felt betrayed (see, e.g., Wade 2010b, and the statement by Dominguez et al. 2010, justifying the change). In my attempt to write this book from a four-field perspective, I fully expect to invite invective from both sides in this debate. But I also expect that some of my current colleagues will be reminded of the promise of four-field anthropology (whether or not I have come close to fulfilling that promise), and I hope that some of my future colleagues will revitalize this promise through the anthropological work they carry out.

The study of the race concept is one area on which all of the subfields of anthropology can be brought to bear. "Race" in the sense I have just described does not exist as a biological entity, but it certainly exists as a cultural entity. In the United States, where we infer descent from appearance, and any sign of "blackness" consigns you to the "black" category, it makes a difference in your life chances as to whether you are "white" or "black." In Brazil, where "race" is simply a matter of skin color, regardless of parentage, people with darker skin are taunted and belittled (e.g., Sheriff 2000). South Africa may have thrown over its system of racial apartheid, but its legacy lingers still. And for years in Australia, the children of aboriginal mothers and Euroaustralian fathers were whisked away so that their aboriginal traits could be bred out of their descendants (Anderson 2003). The statement, "Race does not exist as a biological entity," is not a magic spell; it cannot change what we have experienced as racialized beings. Culture may be a product of the mind, but in everyday life it is put into practice. Culture has consequences—and some of those consequences are biological.

The Manufacture of Race

From the late 1400s into the 1700s, the point to European activities in foreign lands was to transfer wealth into the coffers of the budding European states. These efforts were not always well managed, the failure of the Spanish galleon trade being one notable example, and a good deal of wealth was subsequently sucked away by China until the British plugged the leak by trafficking in opium (Wolf 1982). Nonetheless, this phase of mercantile capitalism was by and large a boon to Europe but a drag on the resources of the rest of the world. As previously mentioned, the European (and Euroamerican) shift into industrial capitalism demanded even more from the colonies—it required their transformation ecologically, economically, and politically. Kin-based societies were re-moved from their territories, which could then be alienated to capitalist enterprise; the excess population of states could be relocated to serve new enter-prises all over the globe. "Racial" lines hardened, and colonial caste systems emerged. Native peoples no longer had control of their lands or their livelihoods. Their numbers and morale were decimated by disease, enslavement, and reset-tlement at the whim of their colonial masters.

In this context, "race" had a function—it could mark those who were "natu-rally" suited to a particular role in the production process. The Spaniards and Portuguese had committed a grave error in colonial governance by losing control of imported slave populations. Slaves escaped to the countryside, interbred with indigenous tribes, and formed renegade bands resistant to state control. In con-trast, the American South largely contained the ambitions of its African slaves via color—the slaves were readily identifiable if they ran away, and though some managed to make new lives for themselves in Native American enclaves, Native Americans might as readily turn them in for a reward (Wolf 1982). Being African in the American South was to experience segregation across the board. "White"-dominated institutions held the power to define who Africans were in terms of

Slave plantation, South Carolina, 1862.

their economic, social, and legal standing. There were laws against "race-mixing," and even though these were regularly broken, they did serve to limit such relations. "White" Southerners and "black" Southerners were divided into populations as surely as dispersal and geography had divided ancient peoples, and in many ways these "racial" divisions were strengthened in the wake of emancipation, as white Southerners closed ranks around their eroding privileges.

Segregation was not in place long enough to encourage the formation of biological breeding barriers between the populations, but African Americans suffered disproportionately from an environmental condition that generated serious biological effects: poverty. Whether the freed slaves remained in the South or migrated North, they were dogged by poverty. In the late nineteenth century, and in fact up to the present day, poverty in the United States has meant undernutrition and malnutrition, substandard housing, disease and chemical exposures, and the chronic stress of both job insecurity and the violence that springs from, as James Baldwin put it, "the rage of people who cannot find solid ground beneath their feet" (1955:71). These were the man-made features of environmental context in modern times.

Around the world, the process of modernization, known as "progress" to those who reaped its benefits without shouldering its costs, took a similar toll. Colonial governance in the nineteenth century was modeled after the emergent industrial process, with centralization, specialization, and social stratification applied to converting the colonies into factories. Different peoples were identified either by "race" or its companion concept, **ethnicity,** and slotted into "appropriate" productive capacities. Some peoples, indeed, served nonproductive functions, as an underclass whose existence underscored the relative privilege of working for pennies a day, and/or as a cautionary tale illustrating the dire fate of those who refused or were deemed incapable of development. Landlessness frequently forced such populations to migrate to urban areas both within and outside their home countries, forming enclaves hemmed in by discrimination even as their cheap labor was welcomed by employers and resented by those who were also competing for jobs. Again, these enclaves came about because of poverty, and they often remained in its grasp.

It is not as though Europeans never tried to alleviate the suffering they had caused, but they continued to regard the way they were and the way they lived as superior—products of "progress" as opposed to accidents of biocultural prehistory. Europeans did not realize that as a population they were exceptional in key ways that stemmed, as noted in chapter 8, from their long acquaintance with animal husbandry. Not only had they become accustomed to the diseases of their domesticates, but they were also more likely to be lactose-tolerant than other peoples, and, associated with this, more resistant to such disorders as diabetes, in that the ability to digest milk beyond infancy was achieved through a higher tolerance of sugars in general. Other populations not only retained a reasonable biological check on lactose tolerance but also were often genetically and epigenetically designed to make the most of sugars, which tended to be scarce in a number of the world's preindustrial diets (Allen and Cheer 1996). When Europeans introduced milk to their colonies as a means of providing a cheap, nourishing food to impoverished communities, they actually sickened thousands in the short term, and in the long term introduced them to a diet that, if they could overcome the problem of undernutrition, would leave them especially prone to obesity and diabetes. To add insult to injury, Europeans defined lactose intolerance and sugar-maximizing capacities as pathologies.

Poverty has any number of knock-on effects. People in poverty are often forced to reside in areas that are polluted and rife with infectious disease. A person whose childhood is spent battling infection often has few biological reserves to dedicate to anything else, like growth and a healthy adulthood (e.g., Hornberg and Pauli 2007). While this is a worthwhile general point to make, we should be aware that situations of poverty, and thus their effects, vary. Around the world, severe poverty is associated with undernutrition, but in places like the United States, poverty has often lent itself as much to malnutrition. Cheaper foods are often high in calories and especially in fats. They frequently contain an abundance of salt and sugar as well, to reintroduce the flavor that the mass-production process removes. Such foods are filling and convenient, the latter quality especially important to parents who work outside the home to the extent that shopping for and preparing healthy food would take up time they do not have. Obesity is a growing problem for all Americans today, but it has a more devastating impact on the poor. We can then add in the higher risks for other problems that come with obesity—diabetes, heart disease, breathing difficulties.

You might think that poverty provides the perfect environment for producing hardier human beings—people who could survive poverty would have to be genetic supermen, right? But the ugly secret of natural selection is that, in the short term at least, it is less "survival of the fittest" than "failure of the frail" (Weiss 2010); that is, what immediately emerges from the struggle for existence is not the best individuals, but simply not the worst. Having said that, poverty further suppresses the selection and retention of adaptive traits because so many individuals are capriciously eliminated by its effects. A poor child is hardly "frail" if he cannot survive the considerable number of biological and cultural threats that poverty generates, and the child who somehow makes it through this extremely constrictive gantlet—this time around—is scarcely "fit."

In short, it is not "race," but the culturally created conditions of wealth and poverty that stratify the world. To the extent wealth and poverty are aligned with "race," this is a product of history—fairly recent history, at that—and not un-changing, supposedly deep-rooted genetic and biological predispositions. For ex-ample, on occasion we read about cancers that are more apt to afflict African Americans than other populations, or medicines that are more effective in treating African Americans for the same disorders from which other populations suffer. However, we should be very careful before we attribute such phenomena to "race."

Genotypes differ along "racial" lines—skin color *does* vary because alleles vary—and there certainly can be noticeable consequences, also along "racial" lines. It stands to reason, for instance, that dark-skinned people need Vitamin D supplements in sun-deprived environments lest they fall prey to rickets (Jablon-ski 2006). But does a susceptibility to a certain type of cancer lie in that small per-centage of the genome dedicated to skin color, or in the type of poverty that has disproportionately beset African Americans? Does a medication work more effec-tively because it addresses a defect of the genome, or of the environment, or of the intricate interplay between both that has taken place in relatively recent times? Of course, in one important respect it hardly matters why—if a medicine helps you, you take it. But every time we associate "race" with an illness, or "race" with a cure—or, for that matter, "race" with a prehistoric skeleton—we re-inforce the idea that "races" exist as ancient silos, storing a huge number of unique and co-varying alleles. I fear our society may never get past this, no mat-ter how many textbooks students read on the subject.

The Future of Evolution

Circa 160 kya, human beings, in their AMH form, evolved. Like any viable species, they maintained a stock of variations that were put to good use in the new environments encountered through migration and over the years. Dark skin protected human beings from overexposure to the sun; in latitudes where this was less of a danger, light skin helped human beings synthesize sufficient quan-tities of Vitamin D. A long, lean body type was better adapted to hot, dry climates because heat could be released quickly; short, stocky bodies were favored in cold climates because they retained heat. The human form was fundamentally plas-tic, readily adapted to a wide array of environmental circumstances.

When hominin minds became cultural minds, culture was one more factor in environmental change and subsequent adaptation. To review just some of the examples discussed in this textbook (see Cochran and Harpending 2009 for more): animal husbandry exposed humans to a number of diseases that were eventually reduced to chronic rather than acute threats. A relaxation of the genetic ban on milk consumption beyond infancy allowed certain populations to incorporate this food into their diets. Stagnant water on fields cleared for agriculture became prime breeding grounds for mosquitoes; mosquitoes were in turn vectors for disease-causing organisms, notable among them malarial parasites. The sickle-cell allele was one of several genetic devices, all of them partial and imperfect, that emerged to counter the malarial scourge. The rise of states created an elite class better protected from the insults to health that others had to face. Europeans shipped such livestock-borne diseases as measles and smallpox around the world, and these turned out to be more powerful weapons against New World populations than cannon and swords. Native Americans dealt with their losses through fashioning new lifestyles based on the very beasts that had wrought so much havoc. To the extent wealth and poverty, within the Eurocolonial process, became intercorrelated with concepts of race and ethnicity, populations featuring different phenotypes were segregated and those that were poor had to cope with a larger and more profound set of risks. The world today continues to use wealth and poverty to mete out life chances differentially, and to blame "race" when disadvantaged peoples fail to "rise above."

Those ancestors of ours who developed different skin colors and body shapes in response to new environments doubtless had no inkling as to the eventual consequences. In contrast, culture change would seem to be undertaken with intention, but a quotation from Foucault might put the matter best: "People know what they do; frequently they know why they do what they do; but what they don't know is what what they do does" (in Dreyfus and Rabinow 1982:187). Foragers who began to intensify their food-producing strategies under the impetus of population pressure had no idea where such activities might lead. Agriculturalists newly exposed on a grand scale to malaria could not have known how their red blood cells might be altered in response. Human beings *have* engaged in planned culture change, though these plans easily go awry. More often, culture changes despite—or sometimes even because of—our efforts to control the process. The genetic and epigenetic effects of culture change generally slip under the radar.

Evolution along these lines will continue on much as it always has, though we may be more aware of it than we have been—we have recently learned, for example, that the human Y chromosome has been changing rapidly for millennia (Hughes et al. 2010). But nowadays we deliberately alter DNA to produce desired results. We shoot pig genes into corn to enhance its nutritional value. We engineer viruses to deliver medical treatment and bacteria to gobble up the oil from spills. We are experimenting with stem cells and gene therapy. Through genetic manipulation we may be able to build human beings who can resist certain diseases or withstand exposure to radiation. In short, humans today are assuming conscious charge of the evolutionary processes of mutation, gene flow, and natural selection, not to mention the chimerical creation of new organisms from the DNA of separate species. Culture is a part of who we are and has always been enmeshed in human biology, but through our cultural minds we now seek to draw that biology far more fully under our control.

The success of such efforts may be limited only by our moral sensibilities, and even these may change as the potential for growing drought-tolerant crops, mitigating the effects of pollution, eliminating disease, and extending the human lifespan—possibly indefinitely, through cloning—becomes increasingly evident. Yet, the Foucault quotation, above, continues to apply. We humans, especially paid scientists, are often so focused on one immediate result that we cannot recognize contingent results or long-term effects. On occasion we tease ourselves with the deliciously horrifying possibility that a virus will escape the laboratory and devastate the planet, but so far—or so far as we know—this is entertainment, not reality.

The choices before us are not unfettered. They are constrained by economics, politics, and ethics, not to mention biology. All of these things can change, but whether, and how, they should change are questions that all human beings must debate fully, even within constraints. In this textbook I have tried to loosen at least one constraint—that of ignorance—but it is now up to you to work on the others.

QUESTIONS FOR DISCUSSION AND REVIEW

- Discuss the good and bad aspects of NAGPRA.
- Choose a "bullet point" on race and provide further support for it.
- Critique the idea that Kennewick Man cannot be ancestral to modern Native Americans.
- Why must it be true that your ancestors interbred with kin? Discuss reasons why this happened.
- How does the modern context continue to perpetuate the idea of race? How is this idea put into practice?

KEY WORDS

NAGPRA	peasant	polygenesis
race	Blumenbach	cultural relativism
melanocyte	Morton	ethnicity
co-vary		

GLOSSARY

Note: This glossary does not necessarily contain all forms of a word. For instance, "anthropology" is here, but not "anthropological," even though the latter is used frequently in this textbook. If you cannot find a word, try looking for reasonable variations.

accelerator mass spectrometry (AMS)—an enhancement of the technique of **radiocarbon dating** that increases accuracy and allows for testing of only a very small amount of material.

Acheulean—the name given to the tool **industry** featuring the **bifacial handaxe.** Though other hominins manufactured bifaces, the Acheulean is generally represented as the signature industry of *Homo erectus* (*Homo ergaster* for those who support the view that African *H. erectus* was a different species from its Asian cousins).

adaptation—the process of adjusting to environmental change; also, a development that enables this process.

adaptive—said of a trait that helps an organism to survive and reproduce successfully in a particular environment.

adenine (A)—a **nitrogenous base** involved in the makeup of **DNA** and **RNA.**

agriculture—a lifestyle wholly dependent on the cultivation of domesticated crops and the husbandry of domesticated animals. The term is also applied, more specifically, to a **subsistence strategy** involving intensive use of land, labor, and technology to accomplish cultivation over large tracts of land.

allele—a variant of a gene.

Allen's Rule—the proposition that human body type is influenced by climate. Tropical environments might favor lean bodies with long extremities, in order to provide the maximum amount of skin surface from which to radiate heat. Conversely, cold climates might favor thick bodies with short extremities, in order to conserve heat. Clearly, however, there are other ways (physiological, behavioral, and cultural) of handling these two extremes, so Allen's Rule is not hard and fast.

alloy—a melding of two or more metals, e.g., **bronze** is an alloy of copper and tin.

alpha male—in this book, a male gorilla that heads up a band of females whose breeding services he attempts to monopolize.

altruism—selflessness; helping others at some risk to oneself.

amino acid—the smaller molecules that, when strung together, make up **proteins.**

analogy—a similarity between species that came about due to **convergent evolution**, and not because the species share a recent common ancestor.

anatomically modern human (AMH)—hominin populations with features like our own, though there may be minor variations insofar as there is no one definition of "modern." Anatomically modern humans are *Homo sapiens,* but there may be other populations, with nonmodern features (e.g., Neandertals) that also share that species designation.

anthropology—a social science dedicated to the study of human beings past and present, most especially in the aspects of culture-making as a property of the human mind and as a property of human societies.

antisense strand—the "side" of the **DNA** "ladder" on which the genetic code is "written." An antisense strand may become a **sense strand** if the genetic code switches tracks from one side of the "ladder" to the other. Be aware that some sources use different terms for "sense" and "antisense"; I abide by these because they imply complementary opposition. *See* **strand, sense strand.**

ape—a type of primate (**superfamily** *Hominoidea*) distinguishable from (most) monkeys in having a broader torso and no external tail.

ape–human divide—what differentiates ape from human, both in the present and in the past.

arboreal—tree-dwelling.

archaeological record—all of the archaeological data recovered to this point.

archaeology—the field of anthropology whose main focus is understanding the peoples and cultures of the (often far distant) past.

Archaic—the New World counterpart to the culture period **Mesolithic.**

artifact—material evidence of human (cultural) behavior.

artificial selection—generally referring to human interference in the breeding processes of plants and animals; instead of nature setting the conditions within which some individuals thrive and some do not (**natural selection**), these conditions are set by humans.

association—in archaeology, referring to biological or cultural remains that are found so near to each other it might safely be assumed that they existed at the same time; biological remains could belong to the same organism.

atlatl—a spearthrower. Atlatls impart greater force to the flight of a spear.

Aurignacian—a tool **tradition** associated with the earliest appearance of **AMH** in Europe, circa 40 kya.

Aztec—a **Mesoamerican** people whose state, centered at Tenochtitlan (modern-day Mexico City), was dominant in the region at the time of the arrival of the European explorers.

band—the traditional political unit of a **mobile foraging** society, generally consisting of 30 to 100 individuals.

Barbarism—the second stage of **cultural evolution**, according to Morgan.

base pairs—the two **nitrogenous bases** that make up one "rung" of the **DNA** "ladder." **Adenine** can only be joined to **thymine** (via two hydrogen bonds), while **cytosine** can only be joined to **guanine** (via three hydrogen bonds).

Beringia—the land bridge that periodically existed between Russia and Alaska.

bifacial handaxe, often called merely biface, or handaxe—the signature tool of the **Acheulean industry.**

big man—the literal translation of the word for "leader" in many New Guinean societies. The New Guinean "big man" is typical of leaders in **competitive egalitarian** societies.

bilateral kinship—kinship reckoned through both mother's and father's sides equally.

binomial nomenclature—the naming system Linnaeus eventually adopted, identifying organisms by their generic and species names (i.e., [*Genus*] [*species*]).

biological anthropology (also known as **physical anthropology**)—the field of anthropology that focuses on the origins and development of humans as biocultural (inseparably biological and cultural) beings.

biology—the study of living things.

biostratigraphy—using the fossils embedded in **stratigraphy** to work out a corresponding evolutionary sequence.

bipedal—walking on two limbs.

blade—a long, thin stone flake, requiring a great deal of skill to produce. Blade production is often seen as the signature toolmaking activity of the European **Upper Paleolithic,** although they are found earlier in Africa.

Blumenbach, Johann Friedrich (1752–1840)—German doctor whose 1775 effort to classify human "races" inspired all such subsequent efforts.

Boas, Franz (1858–1942)—the American anthropologist who conceived of the discipline as consisting of four essential fields: cultural anthropology, biological (physical) anthropology, archaeology, and anthropological linguistics. Boas removed "race" from the center of the anthropological enterprise, advancing the claim that race, culture, and language varied independently.

brachiation—a form of **locomotion** involving using the limbs to swing from branch to branch.

bronze—an **alloy** of copper and another metal which stiffens it, usually tin.

Buffon (Comte de Buffon; 1707–1788)—naturalist whose ideas had an influence on **Lamarck.**

burin—a tool for chiseling and engraving.

carbon cycle—the circulation of carbon between organisms; e.g., animals exhale it, plants take it up.

catastrophism—the notion that the Earth and life on Earth were formed and transformed quickly through a series of extraordinary events.

catchment area—a zone of resource exploitation.

cathemeral—neither **nocturnal** nor **diurnal,** but having active and quiescent time during the day, along with active and quiescent time during the night.

cell biology—the study of the natural workings of cells.

Cenozoic era—the most recent (in fact, ongoing) **era** of geologic time.

centralization—the concentration of power that is, along with **specialization** and **social stratification,** essential to the organization of **state society.**

centromere—the compact midsection (roughly) of a chromatid where its duplicate is attached, thus creating the X-shaped structure we associate with chromosomes.

Châtelperronian—a European tool **industry** most often attributed to late **Neandertals,** although some have seen *Homo sapiens (sapiens)* as responsible for its manufacture.

Chavín de Huántar—an ancient **source culture** that seems to have inspired a good deal of the art and ideology of subsequent Andean states.

chief—the central leader of a **chiefdom.**

chiefdom—a **kin-based** pattern of political organization involving leadership by a central figure, the **chief.** A chief's authority over his (her) people is generally supported by society, unless he shirks his duty to serve his people in times of crisis.

China—a state that arose in the Huang He river region and grew to unify an area comparable to that of modern China.

chromatid—a length of DNA that constitutes one-half of a **chromosome.**

chromosome—actually two identical lengths of DNA bound together at the center (roughly), though generally the term is applied to the entire X-shaped structure. The genetic material is duplicated because the cell is preparing to divide.

chronometric—referring to the measurement of time. A chronometric dating method seeks to establish the narrowest possible range of years within which a fossil or artifact is located in time. Contrast with **relative** dating techniques, like **stratigraphy.**

circumscription—environmental and/or cultural limitations that gradually intensify, eventually forcing an outcome, e.g., the rise of the state.

Civilization—the third stage of **cultural evolution,** according to Morgan. "Civilization" is often used to mean **state society.**

clade—**taxa** taken altogether with their ancestors, harking back to a common ancestor for the entire grouping. Clades thus express time depth, defining evolutionary lines.

class—the broadest level of taxonomic classification that Linnaeus devised.

Clovis—the earliest regularized **industry** of the New World, dating back to 12 kya.

Clovis barrier—the idea, once prevalent in New World archaeology, that the New World was simply not peopled prior to 12 kya.

coastal hopping—a means of reaching the New World from Asia by sea, hugging the coastline and canoeing from berth to berth.

coding gene—a gene that directs the formation of a **protein.**

codominant—alleles that interact in such a way that both are expressed in the **phenotype.**

codon—a set of three contiguous **nitrogenous bases,** coding for an **amino acid** or for a start or stop to **protein** synthesis, on a **strand** of **DNA.**

comparative osteology—the study of animal bones with an eye toward being able to distinguish the bones of one species from the bones of another.

competitive egalitarianism—a **kin-based** pattern of political organization where individuals can attain and hold positions of power but only if they behave in ways that fill societal needs.

competitive exclusion—in a situation in which two species are competing for the same resources in the same environment, the likelihood that one species will win out over the other, extinction for the "loser" being the probable result.

composite—said of tools manufactured from more than one material, e.g., bone and wood.

consciousness—self-awareness.

context—used most often in this textbook to refer to the temporal/spatial environment (taken broadly) in which a **fossil** or **artifact** is embedded.

convergent evolution—similar traits evolving in two distinct evolutionary lines.

cooperative breeding—the rearing of offspring by the entire group, not just by one parent or a breeding couple.

Copernicus, Nicolaus (1473–1543)—the scholar most often given credit for shifting European thought toward the idea of a **heliocentric** (not **geocentric**) solar system.

Cordilleran—the westernmost ice plate that covered North America. When joined with the easternmost plate (the **Laurentide**), this likely formed an insuperable barrier to land migration southward.

co-vary—always occur together.

cranial—referring to the head; with respect to human bones, cranial means anything above the neck.

Cretaceous—the third and final **period** of geologic time, extending from 135 to 65 mya, within the **Mesozoic era.** The close of the period, and the era, is marked by the notorious K/T extinction, which saw the definitive end of the "Age of Dinosaurs."

Cro-Magnon—the term popularly applied to the earliest **AMH** (and their descendants) in Europe, although the actual Cro-Magnon fossil is neither the oldest nor typical.

crossing over, *see* **recombination.**

cultural anthropology—the field of anthropology whose main focus is understanding the peoples and cultures of the present day (relative to the time of the anthropologist).

cultural disturbance—the disruption of the **archaeological record** through human activities; e.g., plowing, putting in building foundations.

cultural evolution—simply put, culture change, though this expression is generally taken to refer to the idea that human societies move through stages from "primitive" to "advanced." This idea will be challenged in this book.

cultural relativism—the practice of understanding others in their own terms and not the terms of the observer.

culture—the largely unspoken consensus, as to the nature of life and how to behave, achieved by a society of beings who understand their world in terms of **symbols.**

culture-bound—tied to a particular view of the world; ethnocentric.

cuneiform—a term used for the early writing systems of Southwest Asia.

cytosine (C)—a **nitrogenous base** involved in the makeup of **DNA** and **RNA.**

Darwin, Charles (1809-1882)—one of two men in the mid-1800s who advanced the view that new species may come about by way of **natural selection.**

delayed-return foraging—a form of foraging involving **sedentism** and the collection of foodstuffs intended for long-term storage; contrast with **immediate-return foraging.**

deme—a population "basin" within which particular frequencies of alleles are concentrated.

dendrochronology—tree-ring dating.

deposition—consigning objects to the **archaeological record,** either deliberately, through, e.g., discard, or accidentally, through loss.

derived—said of traits that mark a species or a group of species as unique; **shared derived** characteristics are, in fact, the means by which we assign genus and species status.

descent group—a bounded kin structure produced by **unilineal kinship**; a lineage.

digit—a finger or a toe.

directional natural selection, *see* **natural selection.**

display—a show of force. Dominance struggles among gorillas and chimpanzees are as likely to be won via display as actual force.

disruptive natural selection, *see* **natural selection.**

diurnal—primarily active during daylight hours.

divining—foretelling the future.

DNA (deoxyribonucleic acid)—a complex molecule that constitutes the genes of living organisms.

domesticate—to tame, but often used in this book as a noun; that is, something domesticated.

domestication—the process of bringing a wild animal or plant under human control, often through interfering with the normal course of maturation.

dominant—said of the **allele** that is expressed when two alleles of a gene are brought together during the breeding process.

double helix—the "twisted ladder" shape of **DNA.**

double-stranded—descriptive of the **DNA** molecule, which is composed of two strands of nucleotides joined in a ladder formation at the center of the "rungs." *See* **strand.**

Dubois, Eugène (1858–1940)—Dutch anatomist who undertook the first expedition with the intent of finding premodern human fossils. Material he excavated on the island of Java (Indonesia) was later classified as *Homo erectus.*

ectothermy—the ability to survive while body temperature varies according to external conditions; popularly known as "cold-bloodedness."

egalitarianism—a sense that power is shared equally by all adult members of a group.

Egypt—the state that formed in the Nile Valley, Northeast Africa; also the name of the country located there today.

electron spin resonance (ESR)—a dating technique that measures the magnetic imbalance that builds up in a tooth from the displacement of electrons caused by the radioactive decay of trace elements.

element—the atomic types (hydrogen, helium, lithium, beryllium, boron, etc.) that make up all matter in the universe.

elite—a group of people relieved of subsistence duties; the elite is empowered to claim a percentage of the subsistence yield of others.

elite retinue—the religious/administrative/security/craft specialists gathered together by the elite to serve its needs. Like the elite, the elite retinue is frequently excused from subsistence duties and thus must be provided for out of elite supplies.

elitism—the central organizing principle of state society.

encephalization—the gradual enlargement of the hominin head over millions of years of evolution.

endemic—said of a disease that is chronically present within a population but is seldom lethal to its host; contrast with *epidemic.*

endocast—a mold of, for instance, a brain, when over time minerals seep into a skull and harden, taking on the features of the soft matter that was displaced.

endothermy—the ability to maintain a constant body temperature regardless of external conditions; popularly known as "warm-bloodedness."

entoptic phenomena—patterns one sees prior to passing out.

environmental disturbance—the disruption of the archaeological record through natural activities; e.g., earthquakes, floods.

epicycle—a smaller circle traced inside an allegedly circular planetary orbit.

epigenome—the complex of interactions between genetic action and environmental factors. "Environment" here should be taken broadly, referring to the environment within the cell, the environment outside the organisms, and all the ways these are mediated.

epistemology—a way of knowing.

epoch—an interval of geologic time; subdivision of a **period.**

era—the broadest level of geologic time classification with which we will be concerned in this textbook.

estrus—the state of being fertile in female mammals; during this period, the female will solicit the sexual services of at least one male. In such primates as baboons and chimpanzees, the female's condition is indicated by an outsized swelling of the "sexual skin" around the genitalia.

ethnicity—the quality of being ethnic; that is, of having actual and/or perceived bloodlines in common, though ethnicity is often thought of in terms of common cultural traits, e.g., language, religion.

ethnoarchaeology—the study of present-day lifeways, especially with respect to **material use,** in order to better understand the past.

ethnocentrism—using one's own cultural standards to judge others.

ethnographic record—a compilation of all ethnographic data ever recorded. The ethnographic record does not actually exist, although there have been attempts, like the Human Relations Area Files (HRAF), to realize it.

ethnography—the primary research product of the cultural anthropologist. An ethnography is an account of one people, but the word "ethnography" can also refer to all of the data contained in individual ethnographies.

ethology—the study of animal behavior.

evo-devo—short for "evolutionary development," a new school of biological thought premised on the idea that differences between organisms result less from their basic genetic blueprints and more from the knock-on effects of key genetic actions that take place while the organism is developing.

evolution—biologically speaking, changes in lines of descent that bring about change within species or that establish new species.

extended family—a multigenerational unit of kin, living together in one household or housing compound.

faith—a way of knowing that relies on belief in phenomena whose existence cannot be proved (or disproved) by science.

falsification—the act of disproving a hypothesis.

family—a taxonomic rank between **order** and **genus.**

feature—an **artifact** that is not readily portable, like a building or a hearth.

Fertile Crescent—a horseshoe-shaped area extending from the east end of the Mediterranean to the Persian Gulf; believed to be a region of early cultivation.

field—a subdivision of general anthropology. In the United States, anthropology adopted the "four-field approach"; that is, the overall discipline of anthropology ("general anthropology") was seen as divided into archaeology, biological (or physical) anthropology, cultural anthropology, and linguistic anthropology (or anthropological linguistics). Not all countries adhere to this approach, and in fact there are American anthropologists who reject it. This textbook, however, is very much a product of the four-field approach, and (I hope) bears out its value.

filial—pertaining to a descendant generation.

fission—the breakdown of **bands** into even smaller social units, generally as a result of intractable conflict.

fixity of species—the idea that God, at the time of Creation, "fixed" each species into its proper place in the world; hence species could not go extinct or give rise to other species.

fluted—said of spear points that have a groove down the middle; this facilitates the **hafting** of a stone point into a wooden spear shaft.

folivorous—leaf-eating.

food procurement—the getting of food simply by taking advantage of natural processes; contrast with **food production.**

food production—the getting of food through active manipulation of the environment; e.g., agriculture.

foraging—a **subsistence strategy** involving the getting of food through (generally) minimal manipulation of the environment. Both **scavenging** and hunting-and-gathering are forms of foraging; for the most part, in this book, "foraging" refers to the latter.

foramen magnum—the hole at the base of the skull through which the spinal cord passes into the brain.

forensic anthropology—a subfield of biological anthropology that focuses on identifying human remains and determining the time and cause of death of an individual.

fossil—material evidence that something was once alive.

fossil locality—a place where fossils are found, in contrast to a **site,** which has archaeological materials (e.g., artifacts).

founder effect—an extreme form of **genetic drift** that occurs when a very small population is hived off from a large population. A member of the small population (the "founder") may by chance be carrying an allele whose effects are amplified in the more limited gene pool.

fovea centralis—a pit at the back of the eye that helps primates to focus on faraway objects.

frame shift mutation—the change that results when a nitrogenous base or nucleotide is knocked out of a DNA strand but the strands try to knit together again, regardless. Such mutations are usually too drastic in their effects for life to be sustained.

frugivorous—fruit-eating.

gamete—a cell, with only half the normal complement of genetic material, that will combine with a similar cell during sexual reproduction to form a **zygote.** Gametes from males are known as **sperm;** females produce **ova** (eggs).

gene—a sequence of **nitrogenous bases**, on a **strand** of **DNA**, that performs a function; e.g., instigating and directing **protein** synthesis, regulating protein synthesis, inhibiting or accelerating the action of other genes.

gene flow—the movement of alleles from one population into another.

gene pool—all of the alleles available for interbreeding purposes within a **population.**

genetic drift—the tendency for allele frequencies to vary simply as a function of limitations on genetic potential.

genome—the genetic endowment of an organism or a species.

genotype—the alleles an organism has, without regard to how they interact.

genus (*pl.* **genera**)—a subdivision of a Linnaean order.

geocentric—descriptive of a concept of the solar system that places the Earth at its center.

geofact—something that looks like an **artifact** but was actually produced by natural processes.

Geologic Time Scale—a means of classifying time from the moment of Earth's inception to the present. Eons are subdivided into **eras,** which are subdivided into **periods,** which are subdivided into **epochs,** and so on. Momentous geological events mark where one interval ends and the next begins.

geology—the study of the formation and history of Earth.

gibbon—a type of small ape, resident in South and Southeast Asia.

gracile—delicate; not stocky.

grave goods—materials buried with corpses that may indicate the decedent's status in life.

Gravettian—an **Upper Paleolithic** tool **tradition** said to follow in a progressive sequence between the **Aurignacian** and **Solutrean** traditions. The dates of the European Gravettian are generally given as 28 to 22 ky.

Great Chain of Being—the idea that all of God's creations could be organized into a status hierarchy, with "Man" at the top and all other creatures arrayed below him.

Great Rift Valley—a huge trench that cuts through several countries of eastern/southeastern Africa.

grooming—in primates, a form of pleasurable physical contact involving the combing of fur, along with the removal of insects.

guanine (G)—a **nitrogenous base** involved in the makeup of **DNA** and **RNA.**

haft—to fix a stone spear point into a wooden shaft.

half-life—with respect to a particular **radioactive** element or **isotope,** the amount of time needed for half of the element in a sample to decay.

Harris lines—horizontal marks on bones indicating that growth was interrupted by periods of food scarcity. Harris lines are generally smoothed over in adult bones, but if an individual dies in youth the lines are visible.

heliocentric—descriptive of a concept of the solar system that places the Sun at its center.

heterozygous—having two different alleles for a trait; the organism itself is referred to as a **heterozygote.**

hieroglyphics—the Egyptian writing system, dominated by pictographs.

holistic—referring to wholeness; taking interconnections into account. For example, the idea behind the "four-field approach" in anthropology is that an anthropologist specializing in one field must know something about the other anthropological fields to understand fully what it is to be human.

hominid—a member of the taxonomic **family** *Hominidae.* Traditionally, *Hominidae* covered only human beings and their ancestors reaching back to the **LCA,** and there are many paleoanthropologists who continue to abide by this usage. In this textbook, however, I adhere to the view that family *Hominidae* includes the African great apes as well, which are consequently only set off from human beings at the **subfamily** level.

hominin—a member of the **tribe** *Hominini,* which, according to the usage followed in this book, subsumes humans and their ancestors stretching back to the **LCA.** At the tribal level, *Hominini* is set off from *Panini,* which subsumes chimpanzees and bonobos.

homologue—given one chromosome from one parent, the corresponding chromosome from the other parent. Organisms inherit two complete sets of genetic material from each parent; hence each chromosome has its **homologous** counterpart, and each gene on the chromosome has its homologous counterpart, save (in mammals) for the genes on the sex-linked chromosomes (one portion of the "X" chromosome has no counterpart on the "Y").

homology—a similarity between species that derives from the fact that the species share a recent common ancestor.

homozygous—having two of the same alleles for a trait; the organism itself is referred to as a **homozygote.**

horticulture—a **subsistence strategy** involving the cultivation of crops on small plots of land. Horticulture involves minimal use of labor and technology when compared to **agriculture.**

humanities—those disciplines that focus on human expression of facts and/or feelings; e.g., art, literature, music, philosophy. History, since it is drawn from records kept by humans, has traditionally been assigned to the humanities, though nowadays there are those who see it as more of a **social science.**

Hutton, James (1726–1797)—an early supporter of **uniformitarianism.**

hybrid—an organism that is the offspring of two subspecies, or possibly species if the concept is reconsidered in light of the fact that successful interbreeding sometimes takes place.

hyoid—a bone in the throat that supports the larynx.

hypothesis—a guess, derived from observation, as to why something happens. A hypothesis must be subjected to further testing in order to support or disprove it.

ice-free corridor—a passageway that may have periodically opened between the **Cordilleran** and **Laurentide** ice sheets of North America; the idea is that an ice-free corridor must have been available for land passage through to the more southerly reaches of the New World during the time of initial human colonization, if this is in fact how human colonization was carried out.

ideology—a system of ideas that supports a society.

igneous—said of rock that was formed through volcanic action.

immediate-return foraging—a form of **foraging** involving the collection of only enough food to last for a few days at most. Immediate-return foragers are generally **mobile foragers** as well, ranging frequently within a territory. Contrast with **delayed-return foraging.**

Inca—the name applied to an Andean people, the ancient state they established, and the ruler of that state. Different terms could be applied to each, but since Inca is the term with which most people are familiar, I have decided to adhere to this oversimplified usage.

incomplete dominance—an interaction between different **alleles** at a locus that results in the partial expression of both alleles in a **phenotype.**

Indus Valley—an area, in what is now Pakistan, of early agricultural and state development.

Indus Valley city-states—the states, e.g., Harappa, Mohenjo-Daro, that arose in the Indus river region circa 4.5 kya.

industry—a set of tools that exhibits a particular style. Industries are often associated with particular peoples assumed to be responsible for their manufacture. Equivalent terms are **tradition** and **toolkit.**

infraorder—a taxonomic subdivision of a **suborder.**

Inheritance of Acquired Characteristics—the notion that biological changes accrued by an organism can be passed genetically to offspring.

intelligent design (ID)—the idea that the universe and all of its components could not have come together without the guiding force provided by a sentient entity.

island dwarfism—the tendency for small size to be favored in species adapting to island environments with limited resources.

isotope—a variant of an **element.** An isotope is to an element what an **allele** is to a gene.

karst—limestone that has been rendered brittle by years of erosion.

kin-based—said of a society whose central organizing principle is kinship (as culturally defined by that society).

knuckle-walking—the means of locomotion preferred by gorillas, chimpanzees, and bonobos when they are on the ground

kya—abbreviation for "thousands of years ago." "K" is derived from an ancient Greek word for "thousand."

Lamarck, shortened form of Jean-Baptiste Pierre Antoine de Monet, Chevalier de Lamarck (1744–1829)—a scientist who distilled the evolutionary thinking of his day into an influential theory. This theory did not withstand the rigors of further testing.

Laurentide—the easternmost ice plate that covered North America. When joined with the westernmost plate (the **Cordilleran**), this likely formed an insuperable barrier to land migration southward.

Law of Dominance and Recessiveness—Mendelian principle stating that of a pair of "factors" (particles of inheritance), one will suppress the expression of the other.

Law of Independent Assortment—Mendelian principle stating that during the breeding process, with respect to two pairs of "factors" (particles of inheritance) governing different traits, the traits will occur in offspring in a ratio that indicates the pairs do not affect each other.

Law of Segregation—Mendelian principle stating that "factors" (particles of inheritance) remain discrete during the breeding process.

LCA—Last Common Ancestor; in this textbook, a term applied to the parent species at the point of divergence between the line that would eventually yield humans and the line that would eventually yield chimpanzees and bonobos.

lemur—one of several species of strepsirhine confined in their range to the island of Madagascar and a few surrounding islands.

Levallois technique—a means of stone tool manufacture involving a specially prepared core from which tools could be struck with greater precision.

linguistic anthropology (or "anthropological linguistics")—the field of anthropology whose focus is the study of language as a product of human society. Linguistic anthropologists may be interested in the origins of language, linguistic development and change, language acquisition, and/or the ways in which language influences our perception of reality.

Linnaeus, Carolus (Carl Linné; 1707–1778)—Swedish naturalist who designed a system of classification (**taxonomy**) for all life forms.

locomotion—how an organism moves.

locus (*pl.* **loci**)—the place of a particular gene within a **genome.**

logical positivism—the idea that natural phenomena are fully knowable through the scientific examination of evidence.

loris—one of several species of nocturnal strepsirhines maintaining populations in southern Asia.

lumper—a taxonomist who tends toward caution with respect to naming new species, genera, etc.

Lyell, Charles (1797—1875)—an author who wrote powerfully in support of **uniformitarianism.**

Magdalenian—the last **Upper Paleolithic** tool **tradition,** following the **Solutrean.** The dates of the European Magdalenian are generally given as 17 to 12 ky. Magdalenian tools were rugged and efficient, making full use of diverse materials. The Magdalenian period is especially famous for its cave art.

Malthus, Thomas Robert (1766–1834)—cleric who, at the turn of the nineteenth century, wrote an essay regarding the dangers of overpopulation.

mammal—a class of animals characterized by **endothermy,** mammary glands, and at least a partial bodily covering of hair, or modified hair.

mana—in Polynesian societies, a powerful force residing in people and things.

marsupial—a mammal that bears live offspring but expels the offspring relatively early on so that they must mature in an external pouch. Though members of the class *Mammalia* (along with **monotremes** and **placental mammals**), there is currently some disagreement as to what lower-order infraclasses/subclasses must be instituted to express accurately the relationship between these three groups.

material culture—the remains of human culture as expressed in **artifacts** and **features.**

matriarchal—ruled by women.

Maya—a number of linguistically and culturally related **Mesoamerican** peoples whose ancestors built great urban centers that held sway over territory in both uplands and lowlands region.

Meadowcroft Rockshelter—an archaeological site in Pennsylvania, excavated by James Adovasio and a student team, that is now widely accepted as a pre-Clovis site (16 kya).

meiosis—a type of cell division only undertaken by specialized cells located in the male testes and the female ovaries. The end product of meiosis is four sex cells (potential **gametes**) with half the complement of chromosomes normal for a species.

melanin—a pigment which, in a number of forms, is produced by most organisms. In humans, melanin (occurring in two forms) affects skin color, hair color, and eye color.

melanocyte—a skin cell that produces **melanin.**

Mendel, Johann "Gregor" (1822–1884)—Austrian monk whose research with pea plants uncovered the basic principles of genetics.

Mesoamerica—the middle portion of the continents of the New World, extending from Mexico to Panama (the traditional division of the New World into North and South America divides the continents at the southern border of Mexico).

Mesolithic—a term referring to the "golden age of hunting and gathering," prior to the widespread adoption of cultivation as a primary subsistence method.

Mesopotamia—literally, "the land between the [Tigris and Euphrates] rivers," in what is now Iraq.

Mesozoic era—the interval of geologic time, extending from 250 to 65 mya, popularly known as the "Age of Dinosaurs."

messenger RNA (mRNA)—the type of **RNA** that forms itself against the **DNA** code (**transcription**) and transports its "message" to the **ribosomes.**

metate—a grinding stone and tray.

mineralization—the partial or complete substitution of inorganic matter for organic matter in fossils.

Minoan state—the state that arose circa 4 kya on the Mediterranean island of Crete.

mitochondria—the organelles within a cell that process oxygen. Mitochondria carry their own DNA, owing to the likelihood that they were once free-standing organisms.

mitochondrial DNA (mtDNA)—DNA carried in the mitochondria of cells. Since mitochondrial DNA (or mtDNA) are not (or at least minimally) affected by any evolutionary process other than mutation, we can calculate the rate of mutation and estimate the date when two descent lines diverged.

mitosis—simple cell division, producing (ideally) two identical cells.

mobile foraging—another term for **immediate-return foraging,** referring to the likelihood that such peoples range frequently within a territory.

monogenic—governed by the action of a single gene. Monogenic traits are also known as Mendelian traits.

monotreme—a member of the mammalian **order** *Monotremata,* which includes the few species of egg-laying mammals in existence today. The term "monotreme" refers to the "one hole" through which monotremes, like reptiles and birds, pass bodily waste and eggs. Though members of the class *Mammalia* (along with **marsupials** and **placental mammals**), there is currently some disagreement as to what lower-order infraclasses/subclasses must be instituted to express accurately the relationship between these three groups.

Monte Verde—an archaeological site in Chile, excavated by Tom Dillehay and his team, that is now widely accepted as a pre-Clovis site (13.5 kya).

Morgan, Lewis Henry (1818–1881)— nineteenth-century American lawyer and business-man whose avocation was anthropology. Morgan wrote *Ancient Society* (1877), a book that introduced a technologically based scheme of unilineal **cultural evolution.**

morphology—form; can be applied to specific types of form, such as skeletal morphology.

Morton, Samuel (1799–1851)—Philadelphia doctor who set out to prove the different "races" of humankind had different mental capacities, literally and in terms of intel-lect. Morton's experiments involved filling skulls with a substance (e.g., lead shot), and then pouring out and measuring the amount.

Mousterian—the tool **industry** seen as characteristic of **Neandertals** for most of their time on Earth.

multiregional evolution—the theory that modern humans evolved from prior popula-tions that had dispersed throughout Africa and Eurasia; most of these populations re-tained the ability to interbreed (hence were not separate species) and through this mechanism eventually produced uniform "modern" features in all surviving popula-tions, though retaining minor regional variations.

mutation—genetic change brought about through the disarrangement of genes, and/or the disarrangement of chromosomes.

mya—abbreviation for "millions of years ago."

NAGPRA—acronym for Native American Graves Protection and Repatriation Act, a law that entitles Native Americans (and other native groups) to claim artifacts and human remains found on federal lands so long as an acceptable case for biological and/or cul-tural affiliation to a modern tribe can be made.

nation-state—a state whose population spans a region as opposed to being clustered in urban centers.

natural sciences—those disciplines that focus on the workings of the natural world; e.g., biology, geology, physics.

natural selection—the emergence of traits in a species that provide survival advantages under prevailing environmental conditions. Natural selection can operate in a **stabiliz-ing** way, reinforcing a standard range of traits within a species. However, it can also be **directional,** when one end of the standard range becomes favored, or **disruptive,** when both ends of the standard range are favored at the expense of what was formerly the norm.

Neandertal—a hominin whose (sub)species lifespan extended from, roughly, 120 to 30 kya. For part of their time on earth, Neandertals overlapped in both space and time with *Homo sapiens*. Recently there has been renewed support for the idea Neandertals and *H. sapiens* could have interbred, although it is too early to say whether the species designation *H. neanderthalensis* will be discarded in favor of setting Neandertals off in a **subspecies,** *Homo sapiens neanderthalensis*. Neandertals were named after the Neander Valley, in Germany; in the German word for valley, *thal*, the "h" is silent, and so it has recently been left out of the word Neandertal, though it is retained in the Lin-naean designation *neanderthalensis*.

Neolithic—a term referring to ancient societies that adopted agriculture but had not (yet) smelted metals.

Neolithic Revolution—an expression referring to the allegedly "revolutionary" onset of agriculture.

neoteny—the retention of immature characteristics in adult organisms.

New World—that portion of the inhabited world that includes North and South America.

niche—where a species fits into an environmental context.

niche construction—the mutually transformative interaction between a species and its environmental **niche.**

nitrogenous base—a fundamental component of **DNA** and **RNA.** Nitrogenous bases, in **base pairs,** make up the "rungs" of the DNA "ladder."

nocturnal—primarily active during nighttime hours.

noncoding genes—genes that perform functions other than directing protein manufacture.

noncompetitive egalitarianism—a **kin-based** pattern of political organization involving very little status differentiation.

nucleotide—A "building block" of **DNA,** composed of a sugar, a phosphate group, and a **nitrogenous base.**

nucleus—the part of the cell where the **DNA** that directs **protein** manufacture is stored. The nucleus is located roughly centrally and is walled off from the rest of the cell by a semipermeable membrane.

obsidian—a glasslike volcanic rock that can yield a sharper, cleaner cutting edge than steel.

Occam's Razor (or **Ockham's Razor**)—the principle of parsimony. Following Occam's Razor in science is to disprove the simplest (i.e., most **parsimonious**) answer to a problem before moving on to more elaborate explanations. The "razor" refers to the need to "slice through" the theoretical buildup that may interfere with our ability to see matters clearly.

Old World—that portion of the inhabited world that includes Eurasia, Africa, and Oceania.

Oldowan—the name given to the first hominin tool **industry.** The Oldowan featured very simple tools, stone cobbles with a few flakes nicked off.

Olmec—an ancient **source culture** that seems to have inspired a good deal of the art and ideology of subsequent **Mesoamerican** states (e.g., **Maya, Aztec**).

omnivorous—having an eclectic diet.

opposability—the ability to oppose, for instance, the thumb against the other **digits.** Most primates have at least some degree of this type of opposability.

order—a subdivision of a Linnaean **class.**

organelles—literally, "little organs," referring to the structures inside the cell that perform specialized cellular functions.

organic—carbon-based.

organism—a living thing.

Out-of-Africa (OOA)—the theory that **anatomically modern humans** arose in Africa 100–200 kya, as a separate species (*Homo sapiens*); this new species went on to outcompete hominin populations all over the globe, eventually becoming the one and only surviving hominin species. The theory is sometimes referred to as OOA-2, to distinguish it from the much older African emergence, and subsequent dispersal, of *Homo erectus* (i.e., OOA-1).

ova (*sing.* **ovum**)—eggs, in the sense of the gametes that females contribute to the breeding process.

paleoanthropological window—the span of time from the existence of the **LCA** to the first manufactured stone tools; approximately 7 to 2.5 mya according to current information.

paleoanthropology—the subfield of **biological anthropology** focusing on the origins and biocultural development of human beings.

paleomagnetism—a dating technique that has developed from the fact that the Earth's magnetic pole has shifted 180° several times within the history of the planet. Magnetic particles floating in a liquid rock matrix preserve a record of the direction of the magnetic pole when the matrix hardens.

paleontology—the study of ancient life.

paleopathology—the study of ancient disorders, diseases, and injuries, made manifest through their impact on bones. Think prehistoric *CSI.*

paleoprimatology—the study of ancient primates.

palynology—the study of plant pollen. Fossilized pollen can tell us a good deal about ancient environments.

panin—a member of the taxonomic **tribe** *Panini;* that is, modern-day chimpanzees and bonobos, and their ancestors going back to the split with the human line.

parsimonious—referring to a working solution to a research problem that involves the least elaboration.

particulate—composed of particles.

parvorder—a taxonomic subdivision of an **infraorder.**

pastoralism—a **subsistence strategy** centered on the keeping of herd animals.

peasant—a subsistence cultivator who must also set aside a percentage of what he produces to support the state society of which he is a part.

Pedra Furada—a set of archaeological sites in Brazil for which excavators claim a 50 ky occupation date.

period—an interval of geologic time; subdivision of an **era.**

Permian—a geologic **period** extending from 295 to 250 mya; the end of the Permian is marked by a mass extinction involving the estimated loss of 90–95% of the Earth's species.

phenotype—the end result of an interaction between alleles.

phylogeny—how different species are related in terms of ancestry and descent; a "family tree."

physical anthropology, *see* **biological anthropology.**

phytolith—silicate residues produced by plants.

Piltdown Man—an early twentieth-century fossil find thought to be the "missing link" insofar as it exhibited both human and ape traits in the combination expected at the time. The find was actually a hoax; it consisted of a modern (though old) human skull and a relatively recent orangutan jaw treated to appear ancient.

placenta—a mass of tissue that regulates the traffic of nutrients and waste products between female parent and her developing offspring.

placental mammal—a mammal that can retain its young internally, with the help of a placenta, for a long time; the young are subsequently born at a later stage of maturity.

Though members of the class *Mammalia* (along with **marsupials** and **monotremes**), there is currently some disagreement as to what lower-order infraclasses/subclasses must be instituted to express accurately the relationship between these three groups.

plasticity—adaptability.

Pleistocene—a geologic **epoch** spanning (roughly) 1.8 mya to 12 kya. The Pleistocene was a time of great climatic flux, with glaciers advancing from and retreating to the poles.

plesiadapiforms—potentially the earliest primates, though many paleontologists reject this view. Plesiadapiforms appear in the fossil record nearly 65 mya.

point mutation—in DNA, the swapping-out of one nitrogenous base for another.

polygenesis—the idea, popular in the 1800s, that the various "races" of humankind were the product of separate Creation events.

polygenic—referring to a trait whose expression is governed by the action of more than one gene.

population—a group within which an organism is likeliest to find mates. A population may be identical to a **species,** but it is more often the case that a species occurs in several populations. For instance, if you are an American, you *can* interbreed with someone from Papua New Guinea (the two of you are of the same species) but you very likely won't (each of you lives in a different population).

population pressure—an uptick in population that puts a strain on a people's traditional methods of getting food.

postcranial—with respect to human bones, referring to anything from the neck down.

potassium-argon dating—a (radiometric) dating method based on the fact that when rock is molten, its original argon load is driven off; hence, any argon that has built up from the time the rock has cooled must be the product of the decay of ^{40}K to ^{40}Ar. Determining the ratio of ^{40}K to ^{40}Ar yields a date. (Note: K is the chemical symbol for potassium, thus "potassium-argon dating" is often abbreviated as K/Ar dating.)

power—the ability to command the will of others.

prehensile—able to grasp.

pressure flaking—fine-tuned stoneknapping work effected by the use of bone to force off small bits of stone from the edges of tools.

primate—a member of the Linnaean **order** *Primates;* the order includes such **organisms** as monkeys, apes, and human beings.

primatologist—a person who studies present-day primates.

primitive—referring to a trait that has been preserved (with some modification) in an evolutionary line even as it diverges into new species. Primitive traits are successful traits, remaining relatively constant over time, because they continue to confer an advantage.

prognathism—a jutting-out of the lower part of the face.

protein—one of many types of compound molecules, consisting of long chains of **amino acids,** that are the "building blocks" of life. Both the structural components (e.g., collagen) and function components (e.g., hormones) of your body are proteins. We do not consider proteins to be life forms in and of themselves, but they have "lively" properties. When they become corrupted they can cause disease, e.g., bovine spongiform encephalopathy, commonly known as "mad cow disease."

punctuated equilibrium—the idea that evolution has a kind of herky-jerky pace, with long periods of species stability interrupted by bursts of **speciation** in response to drastic environmental change.

Punnett square—a diagram indicating the probability of particular results from the breeding process.

pyramid—a man-made mountain, found in a number of early states.

quadrupedal—walking on four limbs.

Quetzalcoatl—an **Aztec** mythical figure, both birdlike and snakelike, whose appearance was said to presage a period of peace.

quipu—the knotted strings used in the **Inca** state to keep records.

race—**subspecies;** a word meant to identify localized, somewhat isolated populations in which a number of traits have begun to **co-vary.**

radioactive—referring to a property of certain **elements** and forms of elements that are unstable, decomposing, over time, into other elements and/or forms of elements by giving up atomic particles.

radiocarbon dating—a **chronometric** dating technique that relies on the decay of Carbon-14 (^{14}C). At this time, radiocarbon dates are reliable out to 70 kya.

radiogenic—generated by radioactive action.

radiometric—pertaining to methods of measuring time that rely on the radioactive properties of certain elements and **isotopes.**

rank—differences in status that apply not only to individuals but to, for instance, kinship groups.

recessive—said of the allele that is not (obviously) expressed when two alleles of a gene are brought together during the breeding process.

reciprocity—a form of exchange that fosters social equality between participants. Reciprocity is often the primary form of exchange in **mobile foraging** societies.

reclamation—retrieving objects from the archaeological record and placing them back in cultural circulation.

recombination (or **crossing over**)—during **meiosis,** a "gene swap" that may take place between **homologous** chromosomes when they are in proximity in advance of the first meiotic division.

relative—used in this textbook to characterize dating techniques, like **stratigraphy,** that establish a **temporal** sequence but not **chronometric** dates.

replication—the process in which **DNA** "unzips" itself down the middle and re-forms into two identical molecules.

reuse—prolonging the cultural life of objects, hence distorting the **archaeological record.**

reverse hierarchy—in a **noncompetitive egalitarian** society, effort expended toward keeping everyone on the same social level.

ribosomes—cell structures where **proteins** are manufactured.

RNA (ribonucleic acid)—a complex molecule that constitutes the genes of viruses, and in other organisms assists DNA in operationalizing its blueprint.

robust—generously proportioned; in paleoanthropology, used most commonly to describe the paranthropines, although it is only their facial features that are heavy.

sagittal crest—a prominent ridge on the top of the skull (e.g., that of a gorilla or of *Paranthropus boisei*), to which jaw muscles are attached.

sagittal keeling—an angle, as opposed to rounding, at the top of the skull, typical of *Homo erectus.* Sagittal keeling is not as pronounced as a **sagittal crest.**

Savagery—the first stage of **cultural evolution,** according to Morgan.

savanna chimpanzee—chimpanzees, resident in the West African country of Senegal, that have adopted a terrestrial lifestyle.

Savanna Hypothesis—the idea that many **shared derived** traits in humans, e.g., **bipedalism** and **encephalization,** are rooted in the fact that our ancestors adopted a **terrestrial** lifestyle. This hypothesis has suffered serious challenge in recent decades due to the possibility that such hominins as *Ardipithecus ramidus* were woodland bipeds.

scapulimancy—the practice of foretelling the future by heating and cracking animal bones and turtle shells.

scavenger—an organism whose primary food is carrion.

science—the search for laws that govern the behavior of elements, biological beings, and heavenly bodies. These laws emerge from processes of observation and experimentation.

seasonal scheduling—the habit of **mobile foragers** not to range at random, but to learn all the resources of a territory and to relocate to exploit them as they come into season.

sedentism—settling in one place.

sedimentary—pertaining to rock formed from materials gathered within a moist (though not volcanic) matrix, e.g., a riverbed, that subsequently hardens.

segregated—separate.

sense strand—the "side" of the **DNA** "ladder" that is the "mirror image" (in DNA terms) of the side on which the genetic code is "written." A sense strand may become a **antisense strand** if the genetic code switches tracks from one side of the "ladder" to the other. Be aware that some sources use different terms for "sense" and "antisense"; I abide by these because they imply complementary opposition. *See* **strand, antisense strand.**

settlement pattern—how a society is organized spatially; e.g., in dispersed, mobile **bands,** or concentrated in permanent villages.

sexual dimorphism—a difference in form between the males and females of a species. Most often, with respect to primates, the expression refers to the fact that males are larger than females in a particular species.

sexual selection—mate preference.

shaman—a person who has access to the spirit world, giving him the power to heal, to offer petitions on behalf of human beings, and potentially to take life.

shared derived—said of traits that characterize a species or group of species. Shared derived characteristics provide evidence of relatedness.

sickle-cell allele—an allele that compromises the ability of red blood cells to carry oxygen to bodily tissues. People who receive two sickle-cell alleles (from each parent) will suffer from a disease known as sickle-cell anemia, which is generally fatal when untreated.

Sinicization—the act of becoming Chinese; many of the conquerors of China, seeking to settle into the throne quickly, adopted many of the trappings of their predecessors.

social control—the reinforcement of right behavior and the punishment of wrong behavior.

social science—a discipline (e.g., anthropology, economics, sociology, political science, psychology) that focuses on the realities humans create as a function of living in societies. At some institutions history may be included in the social sciences, while psychology, which tends nowadays to locate human emotion and behavior in biology, may not be.

social stratification—the development of a fixed hierarchical structure that is, along with **centralization** and **specialization,** essential to the organization of **state society.**

social technology—a set of techniques designed to maintain harmony within a group.

socially shared cognition—the human (likely pan-hominin) ability to collaborate on such mental projects as making language and devising common cultural understandings.

society—a group of people who, due to similarities of situation and experience, create a common **culture.**

sociobiology—an **ethological** approach that reads behavior as stemming primarily from the drive to transfer one's genome into the next generation.

socioecology—an **ethological** approach that stresses ecological context; an organism is not a standalone entity but is the product of a complex of interactions with its environment.

Solutrean—an **Upper Paleolithic** tool **tradition** said to follow in a progressive sequence between the **Gravettian** and **Magdalenian** traditions. The dates of the European Solutrean are generally given as 22 to 17 ky. The Solutrean tradition was distinguished by elegant and sometimes outsized spear points, possibly crafted for ritual purposes or simply for the sake of showing off a stoneknapper's skill.

somatic cell—an ordinary cell of the body, as opposed to sex cells. Somatic cells have a full complement of chromosomes, while sex cells (potential gametes) are **haploid,** with half the usual complement.

source culture—a society whose art, architecture, ideology, etc. are adopted by subsequent societies.

specialization—the subdivision of whole tasks along occupational lines that is, along with **centralization** and **social stratification,** essential to the organization of **state society.**

speciation—the making of new species.

species (*pl.* **species**)—a subdivision of a Linnaean **genus.** Generally the term refers to a group of organisms that can breed successfully only within the group.

sperm—the gamete that males contribute to the breeding process.

split inheritance—the Andean practice of disenfranchising royal offspring, so that they would have to win their own lands and resources.

splitter—a taxonomist who has a tendency to name new species, genera, etc., on the strength of evidence more conservative taxonomists would consider insufficient.

stabilizing natural selection, *see* **natural selection.**

state—a politically complex human society involving a permanent leadership structure and members sorted into socioeconomic classes.

stem—a word that designates the first representatives of an evolutionary line; e.g., stem primates.

stereoscopy—an attribute of the primate brain that feeds visual images into both hemispheres simultaneously so that the images can be interpreted as one image (though with depth).

strand—one "side" of the DNA "ladder," consisting of **nucleotides** joined together "vertically." Be forewarned that in some sources the word "strand" is used to refer to the DNA molecule as a whole. In common parlance, "strand" means any sort of stringlike object, but I am narrowing its usage here for purposes (I hope) of clarity. *See* **double-stranded.**

stratigraphy—the horizontal layering of earth. Layers, or **strata**, can often be distinguished from each other given varying environmental conditions over time; thus, the sequence of strata can tell us not only about the passage of time but the history of environmental change. Fossils and artifacts embedded in a **stratum** are likely as old as the stratum.

stratum (*pl.* **strata**)—a layer, in this textbook generally referring to a layer of earth that can be distinguished from the strata below and above it.

subfamily—a taxonomic subdivision of a **family.**

suborder—a taxonomic subdivision of an **order.**

subsistence—life's "bare necessities"; what one needs to survive in a given physical/cultural environment.

subsistence strategy—the primary means of food-getting for human groups. Examples of subsistence strategies are foraging, horticulture, and pastoralism.

subspecies—a taxonomic term applied to a population "basin" in which unique allele frequencies have collected, though not sufficiently and/or of the right type to prohibit successful interbreeding between that population and other populations of the species. "Subspecies" is essentially equivalent to Linnaeus' "variety" and to the term "race" as applied to nonhuman animals. Subspecific designations are generally not indicated unless there is a need to call attention to these minor variants.

Sumerian city-states—state societies that developed in the region of the rivers Tigris and Euphrates; the city-state of Uruk is thought to have been the first state ever founded.

superfamily—a taxonomic rank that links together related **families.**

superorder—a taxonomic rank that links together related **orders.**

supraorbital torus—a bony protrusion above the eyes, commonly known as a browridge.

symbol—an element of communication to which meaning is assigned via social consensus.

syntax—the ability to utter sentences from words placed in the order appropriate to a particular language; human syntax is a seemingly effortless, subconscious process.

taphonomy—the study of **fossil** formation and deposition.

tarsier—a small Asian primate that is the sticking point with respect to whether we divide the **order** *Primates* into two **suborders** called *Prosimii* and *Anthropoidea*, or *Strepsirhini* and *Haplorhini*. If we consider the tarsier to be more closely related to monkeys than to lemurs, the latter set of designations prevails, and the tarsier is considered to be a haplorhine. This is the position adopted in this textbook.

taxon (*pl.* **taxa**)—a group of organisms considered to be related; taxa are potentially species, or genera, etc., within the Linnaean classification system.

taxonomy—a system of classification, most often used in reference to the classification of life forms.

tectonic—referring to the large plates that make up the crust of the Earth.

teleology—the tendency to read history as a logical progression toward an obvious result; interpreting the past in terms of the present.

temporal—referring to time; compare to spatial.

terrestrial—ground-dwelling.

theory—a **hypothesis** that, having been subjected to a number of different tests, has not been disproved. Theories are the best scientific explanations for phenomena we can devise from available evidence.

thermoluminescence (TL)—a dating technique that measures the light energy emitted by electrons trapped in such matrices as hearthstones and ceramics. That these things were heated when in use drove off the original electron load; what builds up in the meantime is the product of radioactive decay.

thymine (T)—a **nitrogenous base** involved in the makeup of **DNA.**

toolkit, *see* **industry.**

toolmaker—a being that actually fashions a tool from materials that cannot be applied to the purpose intended without modification.

tool user—a being that applies naturally occurring materials toward a specific purpose.

Topper—an archaeological site in South Carolina for which its chief excavator, Albert Goodyear, claims a 50 ky occupation date.

tradition, *see* **industry.**

transcription—the process of "reversing" the DNA code, performed by **messenger RNA.**

transfer RNA (tRNA)—the type of **RNA** that forms itself (in **translation**) against the **transcribed** DNA code carried to the **ribosomes** by **messenger RNA,** and fetches the amino acid called for.

translation—the process of "un-reversing" the **transcribed** DNA code carried by **messenger RNA** to the **ribosomes.** Translation is performed by **transfer RNA.**

Triassic—a geologic **period** extending from 250 to 203 mya. The transition from the prior **Permian** epoch was marked by a mass extinction of Earth's species; the close of the Triassic was marked by a smaller extinction event.

tribe (as applied in the Linnaean classification system)—a taxonomic level that falls between **family** (and related terms) and **genus.** *Also* **tribe** (as applied to human groups)—frequently, the most relevant political unit in horticultural and pastoralist societies. As opposed to foraging **bands,** tribes often encompass more than one village or encampment.

tribute—payment due a chief for his services to society, generally in the form of subsistence yield or an agreed-upon currency into which such value could be converted.

troop—a group of chimpanzees, comparable to, e.g., a flock of sheep or a pride of lions.

uniformitarianism—the notion that the Earth and life on Earth were formed and transformed gradually through a succession of ordinary processes.

unilineal kinship—kinship reckoned through only one line (mother's or father's).

Upper Paleolithic—generally denoting the culture period in Europe when modern cultural behavior appears to come into full flower (roughly from 40 to 12 kya).

uracil (U)—a **nitrogenous base** involved in the makeup of **RNA.** Uracil substitutes for what would be **thymine** in **DNA.**

U-series—dating techniques based on the decay of the various **isotopes** of uranium.

variety—a subdivision of a Linnaean **species,** since referred to, taxonomically, as **subspecies.**

Venus figurine—the term used to label a variety of female figures carved during the **Upper Paleolithic.**

vertebrate—an animal with a backbone, classified altogether as subphylum *Vertebrata.*

Wallace, Alfred Russel (1823–1913)—one of two men in the mid-1800s who advanced the view that new species may come about by way of **natural selection.**

wealth—surplus production (generally storable) that enhances the status of the producer and/or owner.

were-jaguar—a being with both human and jaguar features (along the same lines, a were-wolf is half-man, half-wolf).

writing—the rendering of spoken language in visual form, through symbols that stand for sounds and/or symbols that stand for ideas.

ziggurat—the massive, mountain-like temple dominating **Sumerian city-states.**

zoonotic—referring to nonhuman animals.

zygote—the cell that results from the synthesis of ovum and spermatozoon during sexual reproduction. A zygote develops into an embryo, which develops into a fetus.

REFERENCES

Aczel, Amir D. 2007. *The Jesuit and the Skull: Teilhard de Chardin, Evolution, and the Search for Peking Man.* New York: Riverhead Books (Penguin Group).

Adovasio, J. M., J. D. Gunn, J. Donahue, R. Stuckenrath, J. E. Guilday, and K. Volman. 1980. Yes, Virginia, it really is that old: A reply to Haynes and Mead. *American Antiquity* 45, 3: 588–595.

Agnew, Neville, and Martha Demas. 1995. The Laetoli trackway. *Getty Conservation Institute Newsletter* 10.3. http://www.getty.edu/conservation/publications/newsletters/10_3/feature2_1.html@laetoli. Accessed 16 September 2010.

Alemseged, Z., F. Spoor, W. H. Kimbel et al. 2006. A juvenile early hominin skeleton from Dikika, Ethiopia. *Nature* 443: 296–301.

Allen, John S., and Susan M. Cheer. 1996. The non-thrifty genotype. *Current Anthropology* 37, 5: 831–842.

Amundson, Ron. 2005. *The Changing Role of Development in Evolutionary Thought: Roots of Evo-Devo.* Cambridge: Cambridge University Press.

Anderson, Warwick. 2003. *The Cultivation of Whiteness: Science, Health, and Racial Destiny in Australia.* New York: Basic Books.

Ardrey, Robert. 1961. *African Genesis.* New York: Dell.

———. *The Territorial Imperative: A Personal Inquiry into the Animal Origins of Property and Nations.* New York: Atheneum.

Arensburg, B., L. A. Schepartz, A. M. Tiller, B. Vandermeersch, and Y. Rak. 1990. A reappraisal of the anatomical basis for speech in Middle Paleolithic hominids. *American Journal of Physical Anthropology* 83: 137–146.

Armelagos, George J., and Dennis P. Van Gerven. 2003. A century of skeletal biology and paleopathology: Contrasts, contradictions, and conflicts. *American Anthropologist* 105, 1: 53–64.

Armstrong, David F., and Sherman Wilcox. 2007. *The Gestural Origin of Language.* Oxford: Oxford University Press.

Arnold, Michael L. 1997. *Natural Hybridization and Evolution.* New York: Oxford University Press.

———. 2006. *Evolution through Genetic Exchange.* Oxford: Oxford University Press.

———. 2009. *Reticulate Evolution and Humans: Origins and Ecology.* Oxford: Oxford University Press.

Ascenzi, A., A. Benvenuti, and A. G. Segre. 1997. On the paleopathologic findings exhibited by the late *Homo erectus* of Ceprano, Italy. *Human Evolution* 12, 3: 189–196.

Baab, Karen L., and Kieran P. McNulty. 2009. Size, shape, and asymmetry in fossil hominins: The status of the LB1 cranium based on 3D morphometric analyses. *Journal of Human Evolution* 57, 5: 608–622.

Bailey, S. E., and J.-J. Hublin. 2008. Did Neanderthals make the Châtelperronian assemblage from La Grotte du Renne (Arcy-sur-Cure, France)? 191–209. In Katerina Harvati and Terry Harrison, eds., *Neanderthals Revisited: New Approaches and Perspectives.* Dordrecht, The Netherlands: Springer.

Baldwin, James. 1955. *Notes of a Native Son.* Boston: Beacon Press.

Balter, Nicholas. 2011. Profile: Lee Berger, Paleoanthropologist now rides high on a new fossil tide. *Science* 333: 1373–1375.

Bar-Oz, Guy, Tamar Dayn, Daniel Kaufman, and Mina Weinstein-Evron. 2004. The Natufian economy at el-Wad Terrace with special reference to gazelle exploitation patterns. *Journal of Archaeological Science* 31: 217–231.

Barras, Colin. 2009. Richard Leakey: Passionate, prickly and principled. *New Scientist* 204, 2730: 32–33.

Barth, Fredrik. 1959. *Political Leadership Among Swat Pathans.* London: University of London, Athlone Press.

Bar-Yosef, Ofer. 1986. The walls of Jericho: An alternative interpretation. *Current Anthropology* 27, 2: 157–162.

Beach, Timothy, Sheryl Luzzadder-Beach, Nicholas Dunning, Jon Hageman, and Jon Lohse. 2002. Upland agriculture in the Maya lowlands: Ancient Maya soil conservation in Northwestern Belize. *Geographical Review* 92, 3: 372–397.

Becquet, Celine, Nick Patterson, Anne C. Stone, Molly Przeworski, and David Reich. 2007. Genetic structure of chimpanzee populations. *Public Library of Science: Genetics* 3, 4: 617–262.

Belmonte, Thomas. 1979. *The Broken Fountain.* New York: Columbia University Press.

Belshaw, Robert, Vini Pereira, Aris Katsourakis, Gillian Talbot, Jan Pačes, Austin Burt, and Michael Tristem. 2004. Long-term reinfection of the human genome by endogenous retroviruses. *Proceedings of the National Academy of Sciences of the USA* 101, 14: 4894–4899.

Benazzi, Stefano, Katerina Douka, Cinzie Fornai, Catherine C. Bauer, Ottmar Kullmer, Jiří Svoboda, Ildikó Pap, Francesco Mallegni, Priscilla Bayle, Michael Coquerelle, Silvana Condemi, Annamaria Ronchitelli, Katerina Harvati, and Gerhard W. Weber. 2011. Early dispersal of modern humans in Europe and implications for Neanderthal behaviour. *Nature* online, doi:10.1038/nature 10617.

Bennett, Matthew R., John W. K. Harris, Brian G. Richmond, David R. Brown, Emma Mbwa, Purity Kiura, Daniel Olago, Mzalendo Kibunja, Christine Omuombo, Anna K. Behrensmeyer, David Huddart, and Silvia Gonzalez. 2009. Early hominin foot morphology based on 1.5-million-year-old footprints from Ileret, Kenya. *Science* 323: 1197–1201.

Berger, Lee R., Darryl J. De Ruiter, Steven E. Churchill, Peter Scmid, Kristian J. Carlson, Paul H. G. M. Dirks, and Job M. Kibii. 2010. *Australopithecus sediba*: A new species of *Homo*-like australopith from South Africa. *Science* 328: 195–204.

Berger, T. D., and E. Trinkhaus. 1995. Patterns of trauma among Neandertals. *Journal of Archaeological Science* 22: 841–852.

Bhopal, Raj. 2007. The beautiful skull and Blumenbach's errors. *British Medical Journal* 335: 1308–1309.

Bicchieri, M. G. 1990. Comment, 123, on Solway, Jacqueline S., and Richard B. Lee, Foragers, genuine or spurious? Situating the Kalahari San in history. *Current Anthropology* 31, 2: 109–146.

Binford, Lewis R. 1967. Smudge pits and hide smoking: The use of analogy in archaeological reasoning. *American Antiquity* 32, 1: 1–12.

———. 1981. *Bones: Ancient Men and Modern Myths.* New York: Academic Press.

———. 1983. *In Pursuit of the Past.* New York: Thames & Hudson.

Blinderman, Charles. 1986. *The Piltdown Inquest.* Buffalo, NY: Prometheus.

Blumler, Mark A., and Roger Byrne. 1991. The ecological genetics of domestication and the origins of agriculture. *Current Anthropology* 32, 1: 23–54.

Boas, Franz. 1911. Introduction, 5–83. In Franz Boas, ed., *Handbook of American Indian Languages*, Part I. Washington, DC: Government Printing Office.

———. 1962[1928]. *Anthropology and Modern Life.* New York: W. W. Norton.

———. 1970[1911]. Changes in bodily form of descendants of immigrants. *Reports of the Immigration Commission*, volume 38. New York: Arno and the New York Times.

Boaz, Noel T., Russell L. Ciochon, Xu Qinqi, and Liu Jinyi. 2000. Large mammalian carnivores as a taphonomic factor in the bone accumulation at Zhoukoudian. *Acta Anthropologica Sinica* Supplement to Vol. 19: 224–234.

Boehm, Christopher. 1999. *Hierarchy in the Forest: The Evolution of Egalitarian Behavior.* Cambridge: Harvard University Press.

Boserup, Ester. 1965. *The Conditions of Agricultural Growth: The Economics of Agrarian Change Under Population Pressure.* Chicago: Aldine.

Bosveld, Jane. 2009. Huge population of lowland gorillas found. *Discover* 30, 1: 46–47.

Boulanger, Clare L. 2009. *A Sleeping Tiger: Ethnicity, Class, and New Dayak Dreams in Urban Sarawak.* Lanham, MD: University Press of America.

Bower, Bruce. 2001. Earliest ancestor emerges in Africa. *Science News* 160, 2: 20.

———. 2008. European roots. *Science News* 173, 13: 196–197.

Bradley, Bruce, and Dennis Stanford. 2004. The North Atlantic ice-edge corridor: A possible Palaeolithic route to the New World. *World Archaeology* 36, 4: 459–478.

Brain, C. K. 1981. *The Hunter or the Hunted? Introduction to African Cave Taphonomy.* Chicago: University of Chicago Press.

Breuer, Thomas, Mireille Ndoundou-Hockemba, and Vicki Fishlock. 2005. First observation of tool use in wild gorillas. *Public Library of Science: Biology* 10: 1371.

Broberg, Gunnar. 1994. *Homo sapiens*: Linnaeus's classification of Man, 156–194. In Tore Frängsmyr, ed., *Linnaeus: The Man and His Work*, revised edition. Canton, MA: Science History.

Brody, Hugh. 2000. *The Other Side of Eden: Hunters, Farmers, and the Shaping of the World.* New York: North Point Press (Farrar, Straus & Giroux).

Brothwell, D. 1975. Possible evidence of a cultural practise affecting head growth in some late Pleistocene East Asian and Australian populations. *Journal of Archaeological Science* 2: 75–77.

Brown, P., T. Sutikna, M. J. Morwood, R. P. Jatmiko, E. Wayhu Saptomo, and Rokus Awe Due. 2004. A new small-bodied hominin from the Late Pleistocene of Flores, Indonesia. *Nature* 431: 1055–1061.

Browne, Janet. 1995a. *Charles Darwin: Voyaging* (volume I of a two-volume biography). New York: Alfred A. Knopf.

———. 1995b. *Charles Darwin: The Power of Place* (volume II of a two-volume biography). New York: Alfred A. Knopf.

Brumfiel, Elizabeth M. 1992. Distinguished Lecture in Archaeology: Breaking and entering the ecosystem—gender, class, and faction steal the show. *American Anthropologist* 94, 3: 551–567.

Brunet, Michel, Alain Beauvilain, Yves Coppens, Emile Heintz, Aladji H. E. Moutaye, and David Pilbeam. 1995. The first australopithecine 2,500 kilometres west of the Rift Valley (Chad). *Nature* 378: 273–275.

Brunet, Michel, et al. (37 co-authors). 2002. A new hominid from the Upper Miocene of Chad, Central Africa. *Nature* 418: 145–151.

Burkhardt, Richard W., Jr. 1977. *The Spirit of System: Lamarck and Evolutionary Biology.* Cambridge, MA: Harvard University Press.

Butler, Declan. 2001. The battle of Tugen Hills. *Nature* 410: 508–509.

Cann, Rebecca L., Allan C. Wilson, and Mark Stoneking. 1987. Mitochondrial DNA and human evolution. *Nature* 325: 31–36.

Carbonell, Eudald, Isabel Cáceres, Marina Lozano, Palmira Saladié, Jordi Rosell, Carlos Lorenzo, Josep Vallverdú, Rosa Huguet, Antoni Canals, and José Maria Bermüdez de Castro. 2010. Cultural cannibalism as a paleoeconomic system in the European Lower Pleistocene. *Current Anthropology* 51, 4: 539–549.

Carbonell, Eudald, and Marina Mosquera. 2006. The emergence of a symbolic behaviour: The sepulchral pit of Sima de los Huesos, Sierra de Atapuerca, Burgos, Spain. *Comptes Rendus Palevol* 5, 1/2: 155–160.

Carneiro, Robert L. 1970. A theory of the origin of the state. *Science* 169: 733–738.

Carroll, Sean B. 2005. *Endless Forms Most Beautiful: The New Science of Evo-Devo and the Making of the Animal Kingdom.* New York: W. W. Norton.

Carroll, Sean B., Benjamin Prud'homme, and Nicholas Gompel. 2008. Regulating evolution. *Scientific American* 298, 5: 60–67.

Cavallo, John A. 1990. Cat in the human cradle. *Natural History* 99, 2: 54–60.

Childe, V. Gordon. 1936. *Man Makes Himself.* London: Watts & Co.

Chomsky, Noam. 1995. Interview for Gene Searchinger, *The Human Language Series, Part I: Discovering the Human Language.* New York: Ways of Knowing Library. Available on DVD.

Ciochon, Russell L., and A. Brunetto Chiarelli. 1980. Paleobiogeographic perspectives on the origin of the *Platyrrhini,* 459–493. In Russell L. Ciochon and A. Brunetto Chiarelli, eds., *Evolutionary Biology of the New World Monkeys and Continental Drift.* New York: Plenum Press.

Clague, John J. 2004. Environments of northwestern North America before the last glacial maximum, 63–94. In David B. Madsen, ed., *Entering America: Northeast Asia and Beringia Before the Last Glacial Maximum.* Salt Lake City: University of Utah Press.

Clamp, M., B. Fry, M. Kamal, X. H. Xie, J. Cuff, M. F. Lin, M. Kellis, K. Lindblad-Toh, and E. S. Lander. 2007. Distinguishing protein-coding and noncoding genes in the human genome. *Proceedings of the National Academy of Sciences of the USA* 104, 49: 19428–19433.

Clarke, C. A., G. S. Mani, and G. Wynne. 1985. Evolution in reverse: Clean air and the peppered moth. *Biological Journal of the Linnean Society* 26, 2: 189–199.

Clottes, J., and D. Lewis-Williams. 1998. *The Shamans of Prehistory: Trance and Magic in the Painted Caves.* New York: Abrams.

Cochran, Gregory, and Henry Harpending. 2009. *The 10,000 Year Explosion: How Civilization Accelerated Human Evolution.* New York: Basic Books.

Coe, Michael D. 1968. San Lorenzo and the Olmec civilization, 41–72. In Elizabeth P. Benson, ed., *Dumbarton Oaks Conference on the Olmec.* Washington, DC: Dumbarton Oaks Research Library and Collection Trustees for Harvard University.

Cohen, Mark N. 1977. *The Food Crisis in Prehistory: Overpopulation and the Origins of Agriculture.* New Haven: Yale University Press.

Collier, Jane F., and Michelle Z. Rosaldo. 1981. Politics and gender in simple societies, 275–329. In Sherry B. Ortner and Harriet Whitehead, eds., *Sexual Meanings: The Cultural Construction of Gender and Sexuality.* Cambridge: Cambridge University Press.

Columbia Broadcasting System. 1978. *Talk to the Animals.* New York: McGraw-Hill Films.

Conard, Nicholas J. 2009. A female figurine from the basal Aurignacian of Hohle Fels Cave in southwestern Germany. *Nature* 459: 248–252.

Cook, Laurence M. 2003. The rise and fall of the *Carbonaria* form of the peppered moth. *The Quarterly Review of Biology* 78, 4: 399–417.

Cook, Laurence M., S. L. Sutton, and T. J. Crawford. 2005. Melanic moth frequencies in Yorkshire, an old English hot spot. *Journal of Heredity* 96, 5: 522–528.

Cooper, Dai. "The Anthropology Song: A Little Bit Anthropologist," www.youtube.com/watch?v=LHv6rw6wxJY. Uploaded October 3, 2009.

Coppens, Yves. 1994. East Side Story: The origin of humankind. *Scientific American* 270, 5: 88–95.

Cummins, J. M. 2000. Fertilization and elimination of the paternal mitochondrial genome. *Human Reproduction* 15 (Suppl. 2): 92–101.

Cuvier, Georges. 1836. Elegy of Lamarck. *Edinburgh New Philosophical Journal* 20: 1–22.

D'Aurelio, Marilena, Carl D. Gajewski, Michael T. Lin, William M. Mauck, Leon Z. Shao, Giorgio Lenaz, Carlos T. Moraes, and Giovanni Manfredi. 2004. Heterologous mitochondrial DNA recombination in human cells. *Human Molecular Genetics* 13, 24: 3171–3179.

Dalton, Rex. 2003. Archaeology: The coast road. *Nature* 422: 10–12.

Danforth, Marie Elaine. 1999. Nutrition and politics in prehistory. *Annual Review of Anthropology* 28: 1–25.

Dart, Raymond. 1925. *Australopithecus africanus:* The man-ape of South Africa. *Nature* 115: 195–199.

Darwin, Charles. 1901[1874]. *The Descent of Man and Selection in Relation to Sex*, 2nd edition. London: John Murray.

———. 2006[1859]. *On the Origin of Species by Means of Natural Selection*. Mineola, NY: Dover.

de Heinzelin, Jean, J. Desmond Clark, Tim White, William Hart, Paul Renne, Giday Wolde-Gabriel, Yonas Beyene, and Elisabeth Vrba. 1999. Environment and behavior of 2.5-million-year-old Bouri hominids. *Science* 284: 625–629.

de Waal, Frans. 1997. *Bonobo: The Forgotten Ape*. Berkeley: University of California Press.

———. 2007. *Chimpanzee Politics: Power and Sex among Apes*, 25th anniversary edition. Baltimore: Johns Hopkins University Press.

Denham, T. P., S. G. Haberle, C. Lentfer, R. Fullagar, J. Field, M. Therin, N. Porch, and B. Winsborough. 2003. Origins of agriculture at Kuk Swamp in the Highlands of New Guinea. *Science* 301: 189–194.

Dettwyler, K. A. 1991. Can paleopathology provide evidence for compassion? *American Journal of Physical Anthropology* 84: 375–384.

DeVore, Irven. 1965. Male dominance and mating behavior in baboons, 266–289. In Frank A. Beach, ed., *Sex and Behavior*. New York: John Wiley & Sons.

Diamond, Jared. 1987. The worst mistake in the history of the human race. *Discover* 8, 5: 64–66.

———. 1992. *The Third Chimpanzee: The Evolution and Future of the Human Animal*. New York: HarperCollins.

Dickson, D. Bruce. 1987. Circumscription by anthropogenic environmental destruction: An expansion of Carneiro's (1970) theory of the origin of the state. *American Antiquity* 52, 4: 709–716.

Dillehay, Tom D., and Michael B. Collins. 1988. Early cultural evidence from Monte Verde in Chile. *Nature* 332: 150–152.

Dominguez, Virginia R., Leith Mullings, Debra L. Martin, and Edward Liebow. 2010. Long range plan. www.aaanet.org/about/Governance/Long_range_plan.cfm. Accessed 06 February 2011.

Dorfman, John. 2002. The Amazon Trail. *Discover* 23, 5: 54–60.

Downey, Roger. 2000. *Riddle of the Bones: Politics, Science, Race, and the Story of Kennewick Man*. New York: Copernicus.

Downs, James F. 1966. *The Two Worlds of the Washo: An Indian Tribe of California and Nevada*. New York: Holt, Rinehart & Winston.

Dreyfus, Hubert L., and Paul Rabinow. 1982. *Michel Foucault: Beyond Structuralism and Hermeneutics*. Chicago: University of Chicago Press.

Duarte, C., J. Mauricio, P. B. Pettitt, P. Souto, E. Trinkhaus, H. Van Der Plicht, and J. Zilhão. 1999. The early Upper Paleolithic human skeleton from the Abrigo do Lagar Velho (Portugal) and modern human emergence in the Iberian Peninsula. *Proceedings of the National Academy of Sciences of the USA* 96, 13: 7604–7609.

Easby, Dudley T. 1965. Pre-Hispanic metallurgy and metalworking in the New World. *Proceedings of the American Philosophical Society* 109, 2: 89–98.

Eldredge, Niles, and Stephen Jay Gould. 1972. Punctuated equilibria: An alternative to phyletic gradualism, 82–115. In Thomas J. M. Schopf, ed., *Models in Paleobiology*. San Francisco: Freeman, Cooper.

Emerson, Ralph Waldo. 1948[1836]. *Nature*. New York: The Liberal Arts Press.

Endicott, Kirk M., and Karen L. Endicott. 2008. *The Headman Was a Woman: The Gender Egalitarian Batek of Malaysia*. Long Grove, IL: Waveland Press.

Etler, D. A., T. L. Crummett, and M. H. Wolpoff. 2001. Longgupo: Early *Homo* colonizer or late Pliocene *Lufengpithecus* survivor in South China? *Human Evolution* 16, 1: 1–12.

Fabian, Johannes. 1983. *Time and the Other: How Anthropology Makes Its Object*. New York: Columbia University Press.

Fellows, Otis E., and Stephen F. Milliken. 1972. *Buffon*. New York: Twayne.

Fernández-Jalvo, Yolanda, and Peter Andrews. 2003. Experimental effects of water abrasion on bone fragments. *Journal of Taphonomy* 1, 3: 147–163.

Fiedel, S. J. 1999. Artifact provenience at Monte Verde: Confusion and contradictions. *Discovering Archaeology* 1, 6: 1–12.

Finn, J. K., T. Tregenza, and M. D. Norman. 2009. Defensive tool use in a coconut-carrying octopus. *Current Biology* 19, 23: R1069–R1070.

Flannery, Kent V. 1968. Archeological systems theory and early Mesoamerica, 67–87. In Betty J. Meggers, ed., *Anthropological Archaeology in the Americas*. Washington, DC: Anthropological Society of Washington.

Flannery, Kent V. 1972. The cultural evolution of civilizations. *Annual Review of Ecology and Systematics* 3: 399–426.

Flannery, Kent V. 1973. The origins of agriculture. *Annual Review of Anthropology* 2: 271–310.

Friedl, Ernestine. 1975. *Women and Men: An Anthropologist's View*. New York: Holt, Rinehart & Winston.

Fuentes, A. 2000. Hylobatid communities: Changing views on pair bonding and social organization in hominoids. *Yearbook of Physical Anthropology* 43: 33–60.

Fuller, Dorian Q. 2010. An emerging paradigm shift in the origins of agriculture. *General Anthropology* 17, 2: 1, 8–12.

Geertz, Clifford. 1957. Ethos, world view, and the analysis of sacred symbols. *Antioch Review* 17, 4: 421–437.

Germonpré, Mietje G., Mikhail V. Sablin, Rhiannon E. Stevens, Robert E. M. Hedges, Michael Hofreiter, Matthias Stiller, and Viviane R. Després. 2009. Fossil dogs and wolves from Paleolithic sites in Belgium, the Ukraine and Russia: Osteometry, ancient DNA and stable isotopes. *Journal of Archaeological Science* 36: 473–490.

Gibbons, Ann. 1998. Ancient island tools suggest *Homo erectus* was a seafarer. *Science* 279: 1635–1637.

———. 2005. Facelift supports skull's status as oldest member of the human family. *Science* 308: 179–180.

———. 2011. Skeletons present an exquisite paleo-puzzle. *Science* 333: 1370–1372.

Gilbert, Clément, Sarah Schaack, John K. Pace II, Paul J. Brindley, and Cédric Feschotte. 2010. A role for host-parasite interactions in the horizontal transfer of transposons across phyla. *Nature* 464: 1347–1350.

Gillespie, R. 2002. Dating the first Australians. *Radiocarbon* 44: 455–472.

Gimbutas, Marija. 1974. *The Gods and Goddesses of Old Europe.* London: Thames & Hudson.

Goodall, Jane. 1971. *In the Shadow of Man.* Boston: Houghton Mifflin.

———. 1986. *The Chimpanzees of Gombe: Patterns of Behavior.* Cambridge, MA: Belknap Press of Harvard University Press.

Goodman, Alan. 1997. Racializing Kennewick Man. *Anthropology Newsletter* 38, 7: 3, 5.

Gott, Beth. 2005. Aboriginal fire management in south-eastern Australia: Aims and frequency. *Journal of Biogeography* 32, 7: 1203–1208.

Gould, R. A. 1980. *Living Archaeology.* Cambridge: Cambridge University Press.

Gould, Stephen Jay. 1981. *The Mismeasure of Man.* New York: W. W. Norton.

Grandin, Temple, with Catherine Johnson. 2005. *Animals in Translation: Using the Mysteries of Autism to Decode Animal Behavior.* New York: Scribner.

Graves, Ronda R., Amy C. Lupo, Robert C. McCarthy, Daniel J. Wescott, and Deborah L. Cunningham. 2010. Just how strapping was KNM-WT 15000? *Journal of Human Evolution* 59, 5: 542–554.

Green, Richard E. et al. (54 co-authors). 2010. A draft sequence of the Neandertal genome. *Science* 328: 710–722.

Gribbin, John, and Michael White. 1995. *Darwin: A Life in Science.* London: Simon & Schuster UK.

Grisanzio, James. 1993. The monkey's medicine chest. *Technology Review* 96, 6: 13–14.

Groves, Colin. 1997. Species concept in paleoanthropology, 13–20. In Charles Oxnard and L. Freedman, eds., *Perspectives in Human Biology, Volume 3: Human Adaptability and Lessons from the Past.* Singapore: World Scientific.

Groves, Colin. 2008. *Extended Family: Long-Lost Cousins: A Personal Look at the History of Primatology.* Arlington, VA: Conservation International.

Guthrie, R. Dale. 2006. *The Nature of Paleolithic Art.* Chicago: University of Chicago Press.

Habu, Junko. 2004. *Ancient Jomon of Japan.* Cambridge: Cambridge University Press.

Hadingham, Evan. 2008. Minoan tsunami. *Discover* 29, 1: 8–14.

Hall, Edward T. 1959. *The Silent Language.* Garden City, New York: Doubleday.

Hanson, F. Allen. 1993. *Testing Testing: Social Consequences of the Examined Life.* Berkeley: University of California Press.

Haraway, Donna. 1989. *Primate Visions: Gender, Race, and Nature in the World of Modern Science.* New York: Routledge.

Harrold, F. B. 1989. Mousterian, Châtelperronian and early Aurignacian in Western Europe: Continuity or discontinuity? 677–713. In P. Mellars and C. Stringer, eds., *The Human Revolution: Behavioural and Biological Perspectives in the Origin of Modern Humans.* Princeton: Princeton University Press.

Hastorf, Christine A., and Sissel Johannessen. 1993. Pre-Hispanic political change and the role of maize in the Central Andes of Peru. *American Anthropologist* 95, 1: 115–138.

Heider, Karl G. 1979. *Grand Valley Dani: Peaceful Warriors.* New York: Holt, Rinehart and Winston.

Henry, Donald O. 1989. *From Foraging to Agriculture: The Levant at the End of the Ice Age.* Philadelphia: University of Pennsylvania Press.

Henshilwood, Christopher S., Francesco d'Errico, Karen L. van Niekerk, Yvan Coquinot, Ze-nobia Jacobs, Stein-Erik Lauritzen, Michel Menu, and Renata García-Moreno. 2011. A 100,000-year-old ochre-processing workshop at Blombos Cave. *Science* 334: 219–222.

Henshilwood, Christopher S, Francesco d'Errico, Marian Vanhaeren, Karen van Niekerk, and Zenobia Jacobs. 2004. Middle Stone Age shell beads from South Africa. *Science* 304: 404.

Higham, Charles. 1989. *The Archaeology of Mainland Southeast Asia: From 10,000 BC to the Fall of Angkor.* Cambridge: Cambridge University Press.

Higham, Thomas, Roger Jacobi, Michèle Julien, Francine David, Laura Basell, Rachel Wood, William Davies, and Christopher Bronk Ramsey. 2010. Chronology of the Grotte du Renne (France) and implications for the context of ornaments and human remains within the Châtelperronian. *Proceedings of the National Academy of Sciences of the United States of America* 107, 47: 20234–20239.

Higham, Tom, Tim Compton, Chris Stringer, Roger Jacobi, Beth Shapiro, Erik Trinkhaus, Barry Chandler, Flora Gröning, Chis Collins, Simon Hillson, Paul O'Higgins, Charles FitzGerald, and Michael Fagan. 2011. Earliest evidence for anatomically modern humans in northwestern Europe. *Nature* online, doi:10.1038/nature 10484.

Himmelfarb, Gertrude, ed. 1960[1798]. *On Population: Thomas Robert Malthus.* New York: Modern Library.

Holloway, Ralph L., Ronald J. Clarke, and Phillip V. Tobias. 2004. Posterior lunate sulcus in *Austraolopithecus africanus:* Was Dart right? *Comptes Rendus Palevol* 3, 4: 287–293.

Hood, Dora. 1964. *Davidson Black: A Biography.* Toronto: University of Toronto Press.

Hornberg, Claudia, and Andrea Pauli. 2007. Child poverty and environmental justice. *International Journal of Hygiene and Environmental Health* 210, 5: 571–580.

Horner, Victoria, and Andrew Whiten. 2005. Causal knowledge and imitation/emulation switching in chimpanzees (*Pan troglodytes*) and children (*Homo sapiens*). *Animal Cognition* 8: 164–181.

Hovers, E., S. Ilani, O. Bar-Yosef, and B. Vandermeersch. 2003. An early case of color symbolism: Ochre use by early modern humans in Qafzeh Cave. *Current Anthropology* 44: 491–522.

Howard, Jonathan C. 2009. Why didn't Darwin discover Mendel's laws? *Journal of Biology* 8, 2: 15.1–15.8. http://jbiol.com/content/8/2/15. Accessed 20 August 2010.

Hrdy, Sarah Blaffer. 1977. *The Langurs of Abu: Female and Male Strategies of Reproduction.* Cambridge, MA: Harvard University Press.

———. 1984. When the bough breaks. *Sciences* 24, 2: 45–50.

———. 2009. *Mothers and Others: The Evolutionary Origins of Mutual Understanding.* Cambridge: Belknap Press of Harvard University Press.

Hughes, Jennifer F., Helen Skaletsky, Tatyana Pyntikova, Tina A. Graves, Saskia K. M. van Daalen, Patrick J. Minx, Robert S. Fulton, Sean D. McGrath, Devin P. Locke, Cynthia Friedman, Barbara J. Trask, Elaine R. Mardis, Wesley C. Warren, Sjoerd Repping, Steve Rozen, Richard K. Wilson, and David C. Page. 2010. Chimpanzee and human Y chromosomes are remarkably divergent in structure and gene content. *Nature* 463: 536–539.

Hunt, Robert C., David Guillet, David R. Abbott, James Bayman, Paul Fish, Suzanne Fish, Keith Kintigh, and James A. Neely. 2005. Plausible ethnographic analogies for the social organization of Hohokam canal irrigation. *American Antiquity* 70, 3: 433–456.

Hutton, James. 1959[1795]. *Theory of the Earth*, Volumes I and II. New York: Hafner.

Ingold, Tim. 1986. *Evolution and Social Life*. Cambridge: Cambridge University Press.

Isler, Karin, and Carel van Schaik. 2006. Costs of encephalization: The energy trade-off hypothesis tested on birds. *Journal of Human Evolution* 51: 228–243.

Jablonski, Nina G. 2006. *Skin: A Natural History*. Berkeley: University of California Press.

Jakubowski, Moshe, and Joseph Terkel. 1982. Infanticide and caretaking in non-lactating *Mus musculus*—influence of genotype, family group and sex. *Animal Behavior* 30: 1029–1035.

James, Steven R. 1989. Hominid use of fire in the Lower to Middle Pleistocene: A review of the evidence. *Current Anthropology* 30, 1: 1–26.

Janson, Charles H. 2000. Primate socio-ecology: The end of a Golden Age. *Evolutionary Anthropology* 9, 2: 73–86.

Jantz, R. L., and D. W. Owsley. 1997. Pathology, taphonomy, and cranial morphometries of the Spirit Cave mummy. *Nevada Historical Society Quarterly* 40: 57–61.

Johanson, Donald C. 1999. The Leakey family. *Time* 153, 12: 180–184.

Johanson, Donald C., and Kevin O'Farrell. 1990. *Journey from the Dawn: Life with the World's First Family*. New York: Villard Books.

Johanson, Donald C., and Maitland A. Edey. 1981. *Lucy: The Beginnings of Humankind*. New York: Simon & Schuster.

Johnson, Cara Roure, and Sally McBrearty. 2010. 500,000 year old blades from the Kapthurin Formation, Kenya. *Journal of Human Evolution* 58, 2: 193–200.

Jolly, Alison. 1999. *Lucy's Legacy: Sex and Intelligence in Human Evolution*. Cambridge, MA: Harvard University Press.

Jolly, Clifford J. 1993. Species, subspecies, and baboon systematics, 67–107. In William H. Kimbel and Lawrence B. Martin, eds., *Species, species concepts, and primate evolution*. New York: Plenum Press.

Jostin, Luke. How many ancestors share our DNA? www.genetic-inference.co.uk/blog/2009/11/how-many-ancestors-share-our-DNA/. Accessed 05 February 2011.

Kaestle, Frederika. 2000. Report on DNA analysis of the remains of "Kennewick Man" from Columbia Park, WA. www.nps.gov/archeology/Kennewick/Kaestle.htm. Accessed 06 February 2011.

Kappeler, Peter M. 2000. Lemur origins: Rafting by groups of hibernators? *Folia Primatologica* 71, 6: 422–425.

Kay, R. F., C. Ross, and C. A. Williams. 1997. Anthropoid origins. *Science* 275: 797–804.

Keesing, Roger M. 1976. *Cultural Anthropology: A Contemporary Perspective*, 2nd edition. New York: Holt, Rinehart & Winston.

Keightley, David N. 1985. *Sources of Shang History: The Oracle-Bone Inscriptions of Bronze-Age China*. Berkeley: University of California Press.

Kemp, T. S. 2005. *The Origin and Evolution of Mammals*. Oxford: Oxford University Press.

Kessen, William. 1993. A developmentalist's reflections, 226–229. In Glen H. Elder, Jr., John Modell, and Ross D. Parke, eds., *Children in Time and Place: Developmental and Historical Insights.* Cambridge: Cambridge University Press.

Kesten, Hermann. 1945. *Copernicus and His World.* New York: Roy.

Kettlewell, Bernard. 1973. *The Evolution of Melanism: The Study of a Recurring Necessity.* Oxford: Clarendon Press.

Keynes, Randal. 2001. *Annie's Box: Charles Darwin, His Daughter, and Human Evolution.* London: Fourth Estate (HarperCollins).

Kimbel, W. H. et al. (16 co-authors). 1996. Late Pliocene *Homo* and Oldowan tools from the Hadar Formation (Kada Hadar Member), Ethiopia. *Journal of Human Evolution* 31: 549–561.

Kirch, Patrick V. 1997. Microcosmic histories: Island perspectives on "global" change. *American Anthropologist* 99, 1: 30–42.

Kitzmiller v. Dover Area School District, Case No. O4CV2688, United States District Court for the Middle District of Pennsylvania. 2005 U.S. Dist. (court opinion available as PDF document at http://www.pamd.uscourts.gov/Kitzmiller/Kitzmiller-342.pdf).

Kluckhohn, Clyde. 1949. *Mirror for Man.* New York: McGraw-Hill.

Koerner, Lisbet. 1999. *Linnaeus: Nature and Nation.* Cambridge: Harvard University Press.

Kortlaandt, Adriaan. 1972. *New Perspectives on Ape and Human Evolution.* Amsterdam: Stichting Voor Psychobiologie.

Lander, Eric S. et al. 2001. Initial sequencing and analysis of the human genome. *Nature* 409: 860–921.

Lansing, J. Stephen. 1987. Balinese "water temples" and the management of irrigation. *American Anthropologist* 89, 2: 326–341.

Larsen, Clark Spencer. 1995. Biological changes in human populations with agriculture. *Annual Review of Anthropology* 24: 185–213.

Leakey, Meave G., C. S. Feibel, I. McDougall, and A. Walker. 1995. New four-million-year-old hominid species from Kanapoi and Allia Bay, Kenya. *Nature* 393: 62–66.

Leakey, Meave G., Fred Spoor, Frank H. Brown, Patrick N. Gathogo, et al. 2001. New hominin genus from eastern Africa shows diverse Middle Pliocene lineages. *Nature* 410: 433–440.

Leakey, Richard E., and Roger Lewin. 1978. *People of the Lake: Mankind & Its Beginnings.* New York: Avon.

Lee, Richard B. 1969. Eating Christmas in the Kalahari. *Natural History:* 1–4.

———. 1984. *The Dobe !Kung.* Fort Worth, TX: Holt, Rinehart & Winston.

Leonard, Jennifer A., Robert K. Wayne, Jane Wheeler, Raúl Valadez, Sonia Guillén, and Carles Vilà. 2002. Ancient DNA evidence for Old World origin of New World dogs. *Science* 298: 1613–1616.

Lepre, Christopher L., Hélène Roche, Dennis V. Kent, Socia Harmand, Rhonda L. Quinn, Jean-Philippe Brugal, Pierre Jean Texier, Arnaud Lenoble, and Craig S. Feibel. 2011. An earlier origin for the Acheulian. *Nature* 477: 82–85.

Levine, Marc N. 2011. Negotiating political economy at Late Postclassic Tututepec (Yucu Dzaa), Oaxaca, Mexico. *American Anthropologist* 113, 1: 22–39.

Lewin, Roger. 1993. Paleolithic paint job. *Discover* 14, 7: 67–69.

Lewis-Williams, David. 2002. *The Mind in the Cave: Consciousness and the Origins of Art*. London: Thames & Hudson.

Lewis-Williams, David, and T. A. Dowson. 1988. The signs of all times. *Current Anthropology* 29, 2: 201–217.

Lewontin, Richard C. 1972. The apportionment of human diversity. *Evolutionary Biology* 6: 381–398.

Lillegraven, Jason A. 1975. Biological considerations of the marsupial-placental dichotomy. *Evolution* 29, 4: 707–722.

Lindroth, Sten. 1994. The two faces of Linnaeus, 1–62. In Tore Frängsmyr, ed., *Linnaeus: The Man and His Work*, revised edition. Canton, MA: Science History.

Liu, T., and Ding M. 1984. A tentative chronological correlation of early fossil horizons in China with loess-deep sea records. *Acta Anthropologica Sinica* 3: 93–101.

Longacre, William. 1981. Kalinga pottery: An ethnoarchaeological study, 49–66. In Ian Hodder, Glynn Isaac, and Norman Hammond, eds., *Pattern of the Past: Studies in Honour of David Clarke*. Cambridge: Cambridge University Press.

Lovejoy, Arthur O. 1936. *The Great Chain of Being: A Study of the History of an Idea*. Harvard: Harvard University Press.

Ludwig, Kenneth R., and Paul R. Renne. 2000. Geochronology on the paleoanthropological time scale. *Evolutionary Anthropology* 9, 2: 110–118.

Lyell, Charles. 1990[1830–1833]. *Principles of Geology*, 1st edition, volumes I–III. Chicago: University of Chicago Press.

MacNeish, Richard S. 1964. Ancient Mesoamerican civilization. *Science* 143: 531–537.

MacNeish, Richard S., R. K. Vierra, A. Nelkin-Turner, R. Lurie, and A. García Cook. 1983. *Prehistory of the Ayacucho Basin, Peru. Volume IV: The Preceramic Way of Life*. Ann Arbor: Robert S. Peabody Foundation for Archaeology and the University of Michigan Press.

Maddox, Brenda. 2002. *Rosalind Franklin: The Dark Lady of DNA*. New York: HarperCollins.

Majerus, Michael E. N. 1998. *Melanism: Evolution in Action*. Oxford: Oxford University Press.

Mann, Charles C. 2008. Ancient earthmovers of the Amazon. *Science* 321: 1148–1152.

Marcus, George E. 1991. A broad(er)side to the canon: Being a partial account of a year of travel among textual communities in the realm of humanities centers and including a collection of artificial curiosities. *Cultural Anthropology* 6, 3: 385–405.

Marcus, Joyce, and Kent V. Flannery. 1996. *Zapotec Civilization: How Urban Society Evolved in Mexico's Oaxaca Valley*. New York: Thames & Hudson.

Marks, Jonathan. 2002. *What It Means to Be 98% Chimpanzee: Apes, People, and Their Genes*. Berkeley: University of California Press.

Martin, Paul. 1984. Prehistoric overkill: The global model, 354–403. In Paul Martin and Richard Klein, eds., *Quaternary Extinctions: A Prehistoric Revolution*. Tucson: University of Arizona Press.

Martin, R. D. 1993. Primate origins: Plugging the gaps. *Nature* 363: 223–234.

McBrearty, Sally, and Alison S. Brooks. 2000. The revolution that wasn't: A new interpretation of modern human behavior. *Journal of Human Evolution* 39: 453–563.

McBrearty, Sally, and Nina G. Jablonski. 2005. First fossil chimpanzee. *Nature* 437: 105–108.

McCoid, Catherine Hodge, and Leroy D. McDermott. 1996. Toward decolonizing gender: Female vision in the Upper Paleolithic. *American Anthropologist* 98, 2: 319–326.

McCombie, Susan. 2009. Genetic adaptation to malaria: Revisiting an evolutionary "just so story." Paper presented at the American Anthropological Association Meetings, Philadelphia, PA.

McKusick, Victor A. 2000. Ellis-van Creveld syndrome and the Amish. *Nature genetics* 24: 203–204.

McNeil, Cameron L., David M. Burney, and Lida Pigott Burney. 2010. Evidence disputing deforestation as the cause for the collapse of the ancient Maya polity of Copan, Honduras. *Proceedings of the National Academy of Sciences* 107, 3: 1017–1022.

McPherron, Shannon P., Zeresenay Alemseged, Curtis W. Marean, Jonathan G. Wynn, Denné Reed, Denis Geraads, René Bobe, and Hamdallah A. Béreat. 2010. Evidence for stone-tool-assisted consumption of animal tissues before 3.39 million years ago at Dikika, Ethiopia. *Nature* 466: 857–860.

Mellars, Paul. 2009. Origins of the female image. *Nature* 459: 176–177.

Mercader, Julia, Huw Barton, Jason Gillespie, Jack Harris, Steven Kuhn, Robert Tyler, and Christoph Boesche. 2007. 4300-year old chimpanzee sites and the origins of percussive stone technology. *Proceedings of the National Academy of Sciences of the USA* 104, 9: 3043.

Merriwether, D. Andrew, Graciela S. Cabana, and David M. Reed. 2000. Kennewick Man ancient DNA analysis: Final report submitted to the Department of the Interior, National Park Service. www.nps.gov/archeology/Kennewick/Merriwether_Cabana.htm. Accessed 06 February 2011.

Miller, Steven. 2009 (Feb 28). Christopher Janus 1911–2009: Colorful Chicagoan's biggest stunt, detective mission to find Peking Man, led to fraud plea. *Wall Street Journal.* http://online.wsj.com/article/SB123579056359499267.html. Accessed 27 February 2011.

Milton, Katharine. 1999. A hypothesis to explain the role of meat-eating in human evolution. *Evolutionary Anthropology* 8, 1: 11–21.

Mitani, John C. 1987. Territoriality and monogamy among Agile Gibbons. *Behavioral Ecology and Sociobiology* 20, 4: 265–269.

Moran, Nancy A., and Tyler Jarvik. 2010. Lateral transfer of genes from fungi underlies carotenoid production in aphids. *Science* 328, 5978: 624–627.

Morgan, Lewis Henry. 1985[1877]. *Ancient Society.* Tucson: University of Arizona Press.

Movius, Hallam L., Jr. 1944. *Early man and Pleistocene stratigraphy in southern and eastern Asia* (Papers of the Peabody Museum of American archaeology and ethnology, Harvard University, Vol. XIX, No. 3). Cambridge, MA: Peabody Museum.

Mowat, Farley. 1987. *Woman in the Mists: The Story of Dian Fossey and the Mountain Gorillas of Africa.* New York: Warner Books.

Nanda, Serena, and Richard L. Warms. 2009. *Culture Counts: A Concise Introduction to Cultural Anthropology.* Belmont, CA: Wadsworth.

National Geographic. 2009. PICTURES: Prehistoric European cave artists were female. http://news.nationalgeographic.com/news/2009/06/photogalleries/cave-handprint-actually-women-missions-pictures/index.html. Accessed 21 October 2010.

Nations, James D., and Ronald B. Nigh. 1980. The evolutionary potential of Lacandon Maya sustained-yield tropical forest agriculture. *Journal of Anthropological Research* 36, 1: 1–30.

Newport, Frank. 2010. Four in 10 Americans believe in strict creationism. http://www.gallup.com/poll/145286/Four-Americans-Believe-Strict-Creationism.aspx?utm_source=email%2Ba%2Bfriend&utm_medium=email&utm_campaign=sharing&utm_term=Four-Americans-Believe-Strict-Creationism&utm_content=morelink. Accessed 23 February 2011.

Odling-Smee, F. John, Kevin N. Laland, and Marcus W. Feldman. 2003. *Niche Construction: The Neglected Process in Evolution.* Princeton: Princeton University Press.

Ogilvie, M. D., B. K. Curran, and E. Trinkhaus. 1989. Incidence and patterning of dental enamel hypoplasia among the Neandertals. *American Journal of Physical Anthropology* 82, 2: 231–233.

Olshansky, S. Jay, Bruce A. Carnes, and Robert H. Butler. 2001. If humans were built to last. *Scientific American* 284, 3: 50–55.

Orel, Vítězslav. 1984. *Mendel,* trans. Stephen Finn. Oxford: Oxford University Press.

Ovodov, Nikolai D., Susan J. Crockford, Yaroslav V. Kuzmin, Thomas F. G. Higham, Gregory W. L. Hodgins, and Johannes van der Plicht. 2011. A 33,000-year-old incipient dog from the Altai Mountains of Siberia: Evidence of the earliest domestication disrupted by the Last Glacial Maximum. *PloS ONE* 6, 7: e22821. doi:10.1371/journal.pone.0022821.

Packard, Alpheus S. 1901. *Lamarck: The Founder of Evolution.* London: Longmans, Green.

Pagden, Anthony. 1982. *The Fall of Natural Man: The American Indian and the Origins of Comparative Ethnology.* Cambridge: Cambridge University Press.

Panger, Melissa A., Alison S. Brooks, Brian G. Richmond, and Bernard Wood. 2002. Older than the Oldowan? Rethinking the emergence of hominin tool use. *Evolutionary Anthropology* 11, 6: 235–245.

Pembrey, Marcus E., Lars Olav Bygren, Gunnar Kaati, Sören Edvinsson, Kate Northstone, Michael Sjöström, Jean Golding, ALSPAC Study Team. 2006. Sex-specific, male-line transgenerational responses in humans. *European Journal of Human Genetics* 14: 159–166.

Perrigo, G., L. Belvin, P. Quindry, T. Kadir, J. Becker, C. Vanlook, J. Niewoehner, and F. S. V. Saal. 1993. Genetic mediation of infanticide and parental behavior in male and female domestic and wild stock house mice. *Behavior Genetics* 23, 6: 525–531.

Pickering, Robyn, Paul H. G. M. Dirks, Zubair Jinnah, Darryl J. de Ruiter, Steven E. Churchill, Andy I. R. Herries, Jon D. Woodhead, John C. Hellstrom, and Lee R. Berger. 2011. *Australopithecus sediba* at 1.977 Ma and implications for the origins of the genus *Homo. Science* 333: 1421–1423.

Pickford, Martin, Brigitte Senut, Dominique Gommery, and Jacques Treil. 2002. Bipedalism in *Orrorin tugenensis* revealed by its femora. *Comptes Rendus Palevol* 1, 4: 191–203.

Piperno, Dolores R., and Deborah M. Pearsall. 1998. *The Origins of Agriculture in the Lowland Neotropics.* San Diego, CA: Academic Press.

Piperno, Dolores R., Anthony Ranere, Irene Holst, José Iriarte, and Ruth Dickau. 2009. Starch grain and phytolith evidence for early ninth millennium BP maize from the Central Balsas River Valley, Mexico. *Proceedings of the National Academy of Sciences of the USA* 106, 31: 5014–5018.

Pope, Geoffrey C. 1989. Bamboo and human evolution. *Natural History* 10: 49–56.

Popper, Karl R. 1965. *Conjectures and Refutations: The Growth of Scientific Knowledge.* New York: Harper & Row.

Possehl, Gregory L. 1996. *Indus Age: The Writing System.* Philadelphia: University of Pennsylvania Press.

Powell, Joseph F. 1999. New craniofacial and dental perspectives on Native American origins. *American Journal of Physical Anthropology* (supplement) 28: 224–224.

Powell, Joseph F., and Jerome C. Rose. 1999. Report on the osteological assessment of the "Kennewick Man" skeleton (CEN WW.97.Kennewick). National Park Service Archaeology Program. www.nps.gov/archaeology/Kennewick/powell_rose.htm. Accessed 11 October 2010.

pRiYaAnNo. "The Song of *Homo habilis*," www.youtube.com/watch?v=U0zrGzxjEAY. Uploaded May 12, 2011.

Pruetz, Jill D., and Paco Bertolani. 2007. Savanna chimpanzees, *Pan troglodytes verus*, hunt with tools. *Current Biology* 17, 5: 412–217.

Pyburn, K. Anne. 2009. The future of archaeology as anthropology. *Anthropology News* 50, 9: 9–10.

Quilter, Jeffrey. 1985. Architecture and chronology at El Paraíso, Peru. *Journal of Field Archaeology* 12, 3: 279–297.

Raby, Peter. 2001. *Alfred Russel Wallace: A Life.* Princeton: Princeton University Press.

Ranere, Anthony, Dolores Piperno, Irene Holst, Ruth Dickau, and José Iriarte. 2009. The cultural and chronological context of early Holocene maize and squash domestication in the Central Balsas River Valley, Mexico. *Proceedings of the National Academy of Sciences of the USA* 106, 31: 5014–5018.

Ray, John. 1977[1717]. *The Wisdom of God Manifested in the Works of the Creation.* New York: Arno Press.

Reid, Anthony. 1988. *Southeast Asia in the Age of Commerce 1450–1680. Volume I: The Lands Below the Winds.* New Haven, CT: Yale University Press.

Rice, Patricia C. 1981. Prehistoric Venuses: Symbols of motherhood or womanhood? *Journal of Anthropological Research* 37, 4: 402–404.

Rodman, Peter S., and Henry M. McHenry. 1980. Bioenergetics and the origin of hominid bipedalism. *American Journal of Physical Anthropology* 52: 103–106.

Rosen, Edward. 1984. *Copernicus and the Scientific Revolution.* Malabar, FL: Robert E. Krieger.

Rosenberg, Harriet G. 1990. Complaint discourse, aging, and caregiving among the !Kung San of Botswana, 19–41. In Jay Sokolofsky, ed., *The Cultural Context of Aging.* New York: Bergin & Garvey.

Rosman, Abraham, and Paula G. Rubel. 1989. Stalking the wild pig: Hunting and horticulture in Papua New Guinea, 27–36. In Susan Kent, ed., *Farmers as Hunters: The Implications of Sedentism.* Cambridge: Cambridge University Press.

Russell, Miles. 2003. *Piltdown Man: The Secret Life of Charles Dawson and the World's Greatest Archaeological Hoax.* Stroud, Gloucestershire: Tempus.

Sahlins, Marshall D. 1963. Poor man, rich man, big-man, chief: Political types in Melanesia and Polynesia. *Comparative Studies in Society and History* 5, 3: 285–303

———. 1968. Notes on the original affluent society, 85–89. In Richard B. Lee and Irvin DeVore, eds., *Man the Hunter.* Chicago: Aldine.

———. 1972. *Stone Age Economics.* Chicago: Aldine-Atherton.

———. 1976. *The Use and Abuse of Biology: An Anthropological Critique of Sociobiology.* Ann Arbor: University of Michigan Press.

Sarich, Vincent M., and Allan C. Wilson. 1967. Immunological time scale for hominid evolution. *Science* 158: 1200–1203.

Sauer, Carl. 1969. *Seeds, Spades, Hearths, and Herds: The Domestication of Animals and Foodstuffs.* Cambridge: MIT Press.

Sawada, Yoshihiro, Martin Pickford, Brigitte Senut, Tetsumara Itaya, Masayuki Hyodo, Tamaki Myura, Chicako Kashine, Tadahiro Chujo, and Hirokazu Fujii. 2002. The age of *Orrorin tugenensis*, an early hominid from the Tugen Hills, Kenya. *Comptes Rendus Palevol* 1, 5: 293–303.

Sayre, Anne. 1975. *Rosalind Franklin and DNA.* New York: W. W. Norton.

Schaller, George B. 1963. *The Mountain Gorilla: Ecology and Behavior.* Chicago: University of Chicago Press.

Schiffer, Michael B. 1987. *Formation Processes of the Archaeological Record.* Albuquerque: University of New Mexico Press.

Schmandt-Besserat, Denise. 1992. *Before Writing*, Vols. I & II. Austin: University of Texas Press.

Schmitt, D., and S. Churchill. 2003. Experimental evidence concerning spear use in Neandertals and early modern humans. *Journal of Archaeological Science* 30: 103–114.

Schwartz, Jeffrey H. 1987. *The Red Ape: Orang-Utans and Human Origins.* Boston: Houghton Mifflin.

———. 2005. *The Red Ape: Orangutans and Human Origins*, revised and updated edition. Boulder, CO: Westview.

Sclater, Andrew. 2000. Did Darwin have a copy of Mendel's paper? (response to Robert McFetridge). http://members.shaw.ca/mcfetridge/darwin.html. Accessed 20 August 2010.

Semaw, S., P. Renne, J. W. K. Harris, C. S. Feibel, R. L. Bernor, N. Fesseha, and K. Mowbray. 1997. 2.5-million-year-old stone tools from Gona, Ethiopia. *Nature* 385: 333–336.

Serre, D., and S. Pääbo. 2008. The fate of European Neanderthals: Results and perspectives from ancient DNA analysis, 211–219. In Katerina Harvati and Terry Harrison, eds., *Neanderthals Revisited: New Approaches and Perspectives.* Dordrecht, The Netherlands: Springer.

Seyfarth, R. M., D. L. Cheney, and P. Marler. 1980. Monkey responses to three different alarm calls: Evidence of predator classification and semantic communication. *Science* 210: 801–803.

Shaffer, Jim G., and Diana A. Lichtenstein. 1999. Migration, philology, and South Asian archaeology, 239–260. In Johannes Bronkhorst and Madhav M. Deshpande, eds., *Aryan and Non-Aryan in South Asia: Evidence, Interpretation, and Ideology.* Cambridge: Harvard University Department of Sanskrit and Indian Studies.

Shapiro, H. L. 1939. *Migration and Environment: A Study of the Physical Characteristics of the Japanese Immigrants to Hawaii and the Effects of Environment on Their Descendants.* London: Oxford University Press.

Sharp, Lauriston. 1952. Steel axes for stone-age Australians. *Human Organization* 11, 2: 17–22.

Shea, John J. 2010. Gibraltar rocks: Calpe 2009: Human evolution 150 years after Darwin. *Evolutionary Anthropology* 19, 1: 2–3.

Shea, William R., and Mariano Artigas. 2003. *Galileo in Rome: The Rise and Fall of a Troublesome Genius.* Oxford: Oxford University Press.

Sheriff, Robin E. 2000. Exposing silence as cultural censorship: A Brazilian case. *American Anthropologist* 102, 1: 114–132.

Shipman, Pat. 2001. *The Man Who Found the Missing Link: Eugène Dubois and His Lifelong Quest to Prove Darwin Right.* New York: Simon & Schuster.

———. 2009. The woof at the door. *American Scientist* 97, 4: 286.

Shreeve, James. 1995. Research news. *Science* 270: 1297–1298.

Singer, R., and J. Wymer. 1982. *The Middle Stone Age at Klasies River Mouth in South Africa.* Chicago: University of Chicago Press.

Slobodchikoff, Con N., B. Perla, and J. L. Verdelin. 2009. *Prairie Dogs: Communication and Community in an Animal Society.* Cambridge: Harvard University Press.

Slotten, Ross A. 2004. *The Heretic in Darwin's Court.* New York: Columbia University Press.

Smith, Bruce D. 1997. The initial domestication of *Cucurbita pepo* in the Americas 10,000 years ago. *Science* 276: 932–934.

Smith, Bruce D., with contributions from C. Wesley Cowan and Michael P. Hoffman. 2007. *Rivers of Change: Essays on Early Agriculture in Easter North America.* Tuscaloosa: University of Alabama Press.

Smith, David Glenn, Ripban S. Malhi, Jason A. Eshleman, and Frederika A. Kaestle. 2000. Report on DNA analysis of the remains of "Kennewick Man" from Columbia Park, WA. www.nps.gov/archeology/Kennewick/Smith.htm. Accessed 06 February 2011.

Smith, Monica L. 2006. The archaeology of food preference. *American Anthropologist* 108, 3: 480–493.

Solecki, R. S. 1977. The implications of the Shanidar Cave Neanderthal flower burial. *Annals of the New York Academy of Sciences* 293: 114–124.

Sommer, Jeffrey D. 1999. The Shanidar IV "Flower Burial": A reevaluation of Neanderthal burial rituals. *Cambridge Archaeology Journal* 9, 1: 127–129.

Soulsby, B. H. 1833. Addenda and Corrigenda, 1–65. In B. H. Soulsby, *A Catalogue of the Works of Linnaeus (and Publications More Immediately Relating Thereto) Preserved in the Libraries of the British Museum (Bloomsbury) and the British Museum (Natural History) (So. Kensington).* London: University Press Oxford (John Johnson).

Spence, Michael W. 1967. The obsidian industry of Teotihuacan. *American Antiquity* 32, 4: 507–514.

Stachiewicz, Wanda. 1973. *Copernicus and the Changing World,* 2nd edition. Montréal: Polish Institute of Arts and Sciences in America, Canadian Branch.

Stewart, Omer C. (eds. Henry T. Lewis and M. Kat Anderson). 2002. *Forgotten Fires: Native Americans and the Transient Wilderness.* Norman: University of Oklahoma Press.

Stilwell, Jeffrey D. 2006. Trilobites and Linnaeus: The first fossil reconstruction from 1759. *Archives of Natural History* 33, 1: 101–108

Straus, Lawrence Guy, David J. Meltzer, and Ted Goebel. 2005. Ice Age Atlantis? Exploring the Solutrean-Clovis "connection." *World Archaeology* 37, 4: 507–532.

Strum, Shirley C. 2001[1987]. *Almost Human: A Journey into the World of Baboons.* Chicago: University of Chicago Press.

Sugiyama, Y. 1995. Drinking tools of wild chimpanzees at Bossou. *American Journal of Primatology* 37, 3: 263–269.

Swisher, Carl C., III, G. H. Curtis, T. Jacob, A. G. Getty, A. Suprijo, and Widiasmoro. 1994. Age of the earliest known hominids in Java, Indonesia. *Science* 263: 1118–1121.

Swisher, Carl C., III, W. J. Rink, S. C. Antón, H. P. Schwarcz, G. H. Curtis, A. Suprijo, and Widiasmoro. 1996. Latest *Homo erectus* of Java: Potential contemporaneity with *Homo sapiens* in Southeast Asia. *Science* 274: 1870–1874.

Tatarkiewicz, Wladyslaw, trans. Christopher Kasparek. 1979. Perfection: The term and the concept. *Dialectics and Humanism: The Polish Philosophical Quarterly*, 6, 4: 5–10.

Tattersall, Ian, and Jeffrey H. Schwartz. 1999. Hominids and hybrids: The place of Neanderthals in human evolution. *Proceedings of the National Academy of Sciences of the USA* 96, 13: 7117–7119.

Taylor, R. E. 1995. Radiocarbon dating: The continuing revolution. *Evolutionary Anthropology* 4, 5: 169–181.

Thieme, Hartmut. 1997. Lower Palaeolithic hunting spears from Germany. *Nature* 385: 807–810.

Thomas, David Hurst. 2000. *Skull Wars: Kennewick Man, Archaeology, and the Battle for Native American Identity.* New York: Basic Books.

Thomas, Hedley. 2010. Fossil warriors won't call a truce for Sediba. *The Australian.* http://www.theaustralian.com.au/news/features/fossil-warriors-wont-call-a-truce-for-sediba/story-e6frg6z6-1225852020068. Accessed 26 February 2011.

Tonkinson, Robert. 2002. *The Mardu Aborigines: Living the Dream in Australia's Desert*, 2nd edition. Belmont, CA: Wadsworth.

Trut, Lyudmila N. 1999. Early canid domestication: The farm-fox experiment. *American Scientist* 87: 160–169.

Tsing, Anna Lowenhaupt. 2005. *Friction: An Ethnography of Global Connection.* Princeton: Princeton University Press.

Tudge, Colin. 1998. *Neanderthals, Bandits, and Farmers: How Agriculture Really Began.* London: Weidenfeld & Nicholson.

Turnbull, Colin M. 1961. *The Forest People: A Study of the Pygmies of the Congo.* New York: Touchstone (Simon & Schuster).

Tyldesley, Joyce. 2011. The private lives of the pyramid-builders. BBC Online. http://www.bbc.co.uk/history/ancient/egyptians/pyramid_builders_01.shtml. Accessed 17 June 2011.

Tylor, Edward B. 1871. *Primitive Culture: Research into the Development of Mythology, Philosophy, Religion, Art, and Custom.* London: John Murray.

Unger-Hamilton, Ramona. 1989. The Epi-Palaeolithic Southern Levant and the origins of cultivation. *Current Anthropology* 30, 1: 88–103.

van Schaik, Carel. 2004. *Among Orangutans: Red Apes and the Rise of Human Culture.* Cambridge, MA: Belknap Press of Harvard University Press.

Videan, Elaine N., and William C. McGrew. 2000. Bipedality in chimps and bonobos: Testing hypothesized selection pressures. Paper delivered at the 69th Annual Meeting of the American Association of Physical Anthropologists, San Antonio, TX.

Visweswaran, Kamala. 1998. Race and the culture of anthropology. *American Anthropologist* 100, 1: 70–83.

Vogel, Gretchen. 2007. Scientists say Ebola has pushed Western Gorillas to the brink. *Science* 317: 1484.

Wade, Nicholas. 2010a. A decade later, genetic map yields few new cures. *New York Times* 13 June: A1.

———. 2010b. Anthropology a science? Statement deepens a rift. *New York Times* 09 December: A16.

Walker, Alan, and Pat Shipman. 1996. *The Wisdom of the Bones: In Search of Human Origins.* New York: Alfred A. Knopf.

———. 2005. *The Ape in the Tree: An Intellectual and Natural History of* Proconsul. Cambridge, MA: Belknap Press of Harvard University Press.

Walker, Deward E., Jr., and Peter N. Jones. 2000. Review [of Downey and Thomas]: Other perspectives on the Kennewick Man controversy. *American Anthropologist* 102, 4: 907–910.

Waters, Michael R., Steven L. Forman, Thomas A. Jennings, Lee C. Nordt, Steven G. Driese, Joshua M. Feinberg, Joshua L. Keene, Jessi Halligan, Anna Lindquist, James Pierson, Charles T. Hallmark, Michael B. Collins, and James E. Wiederhold. 2011. The Buttermilk Creek Complex and the origins of Clovis at the Debra L. Friedkin Site, Texas. *Science* 331: 1599–1603.

Watson, James D. 1969. *The Double Helix: A Personal Account of the Discovery of the Structure of DNA.* New York: Atheneum.

Wayman, Erin. 2008. Fossilized feces tell an old tale. *Geotimes* 53, 6: 15.

Weiss, Ken. 2010. The song of the jubjub. *Evolutionary Anthropology* 19: 125–129.

Wheeler, P. E. 1991a. The thermoregulatory advantages of hominid bipedalism in open equatorial environments: The contribution of increased convective heat loss and cutaneous evaporative cooling. *Journal of Human Evolution* 21, 2: 107–115.

———. 1991b. The influence of bipedalism on the energy and water budgets of early hominids. *Journal of Human Evolution* 21, 2: 117–136.

White, Tim D. 2003. Early hominids—diversity or distortion? *Science* 299: 1994–1997.

White, Tim D., Berhane Asfaw, David deGusta, Henry Gilbert, Gary D. Richards, Gen Suwa, and F. Clark Howell. 2003. Pleistocene *Homo sapiens* from Middle Awash, Ethiopia. *Nature* 423: 742–747.

White, Tim D., Berhane Asfaw, Yonas Beyene, Yohannes Haile-Selassie, C. Owen Lovejoy, Gen Suwa, and Giday WoldeGabriel. 2009. *Ardipithecus ramidus* and the paleobiology of early hominids. *Science* 326: 75–86.

Whiten, A., J. Goodall, W. C. McGrew, T. Nishida, V. Reynolds, Y. Sugiyama, C. E. G. Tutin, R. W. Wrangham, and C. Boesch. 1999. Cultures in chimpanzees. *Nature* 399: 682–685.

Whorf, Benjamin Lee. 1941. The relation of habitual thought and behavior to language, 75–93. In Leslie Spier, A. Irving Hallowell, and Stanley S. Newman, eds., *Language, Cultural, and Personality; Essays in Memory of Edward Sapir.* Menasha, WI: Sapir Memorial Publication Fund.

Wilde, H. 1972. Anaphylactic shock following bite by a "slow loris," *Nycticebus coucang. American Journal of Tropical Medicine and Hygiene* 21: 592–594.

Wilmsen, Edwin N. 1989. *Land Filled with Flies: A Political Economy of the Kalahari.* Chicago: University of Chicago Press.

Wilson, Edward O. 1975. *Sociobiology: The New Synthesis.* Cambridge, MA: Belknap Press of Harvard University Press.

Wittfogel, Karl A. 1957. *Oriental Despotism: A Comparative Study of Total Power.* New Haven, CT: Yale University Press.

Wolf, Eric R. 1982. *Europe and the People without History.* Berkeley: University of California Press.

Wolpoff, Milford H. 1996. *Human Evolution.* New York: McGraw-Hill.

Wolpoff, Milford H., and Rachel Caspari. 1997. *Race and Human Evolution: A Fatal Attraction.* New York: Simon & Schuster.

Wolpoff, Milford H., Brigitte Senut, Martin Pickford, and John Hawks. 2002. *Sahelanthropus* or *Sahelpithecus? Nature* 419: 581–582.

Wong, Kate. 2010. Discoverer of "Lucy" raises questions about *Australopithecus sediba,* the new human species from South Africa. *Scientific American* blog, at http://blogs.scientificamerican.com/observations/2010/04/09/discoverer-of-lucy-raises-questions-about-australopithecus-sediba-the-new-human-species-from-south-africa/

Woodburn, James. 1982. Egalitarian societies. *Man* N.S. 17, 3: 431–451.

Wrangham, Richard, and Dale Peterson. 1996. *Demonic Males: Apes and the Origins of Human Violence.* Boston: Houghton Mifflin.

Wynn, Thomas, and Frederick L. Coolidge. 2004. The expert Neandertal mind. *Journal of Human Evolution* 46, 4: 467–487.

Yellen, John E. 1977. Cultural patterning in faunal remains: Evidence from the !Kung Bushmen, 271–331. In Daniel Ingersoll, John E. Yellen, and William Macdonald, eds., *Experimental Archeology.* New York: Columbia University Press.

Zilhão, João, Francesco d'Errico, Jean-Guillaume Bordes, Arnaud Lenoble, Jean-Pierre Texier, and Jean-Philippe Rigaud. 2006. Analysis of Aurignacian interstratification at the Châtelperronian-type site and implications for the behavioral modernity of Neandertals. *Proceedings of the National Academy of Sciences of the USA* 103, 33: 12643–12648.

Zizumbo-Villareal, D., and P. Colunga-Garcia Marin. 2010. Origin of agriculture and plant domestication in West Mesoamerica. *Genetic Resources and Crop Evolution* 57, 6: 813–825.

INDEX

PHOTO CREDITS